The Emergence of
SOCIOLOGICAL THEORY

SEVENTH EDITION

The Emergence of
SOCIOLOGICAL
THEORY

Jonathan H. Turner
University of California, Riverside

Leonard Beeghley
University of Florida

Charles H. Powers
Santa Clara University

Los Angeles | London | New Delhi
Singapore | Washington DC

Los Angeles | London | New Delhi
Singapore | Washington DC

FOR INFORMATION

SAGE Publications, Inc.
2455 Teller Road
Thousand Oaks, California 91320
E-mail: order@sagepub.com

SAGE Publications Ltd.
1 Oliver's Yard
55 City Road
London, EC1Y 1SP
United Kingdom

SAGE Publications India Pvt. Ltd.
B 1/I 1 Mohan Cooperative Industrial Area
Mathura Road, New Delhi 110 044
India

SAGE Publications Asia-Pacific Pte. Ltd.
33 Pekin Street #02-01
Far East Square
Singapore 048763

Acquisitions Editor: David Repetto
Editorial Assistant: Lydia Balian
Production Editor: Astrid Virding
Copy Editor: QuADS Prepress (P) Ltd.
Typesetter: Hurix Systems Pvt. Ltd.
Proofreader: Ellen Brink
Indexer: Ellen Slavitz
Cover Designer: Gail Buschman
Marketing Manager: Erica DeLuca
Permissions Editor: Adele Hutchinson/
                    Karen Ehrmann

Printed in the United States of America

Library of Congress Cataloging-in-Publication Data

Turner, Jonathan H.
The emergence of sociological theory / Jonathan H. Turner, Leonard Beeghley, Charles H. Powers. — 7th ed.
v. cm.
Rev. ed. of: The emergence of sociological theory. 6th ed. c2007.
Includes bibliographical references and index.
ISBN 978-1-4522-0623-3 (cloth) — ISBN 978-1-4522-0624-0 (pbk.)
1. Sociology—History. 2. Sociology—United States—History. 3. Social theory. I. Beeghley, Leonard. II. Powers, Charles H. III. Turner, Jonathan H. Emergence of sociological theory. IV. Title.
HM445.T97 2012
301.0973—dc23   2011031071

This book is printed on acid-free paper.

11 12 13 14 15   10 9 8 7 6 5 4 3 2 1

Contents

About the Authors

Jonathan H. Turner (PhD, Cornell University) is Distinguished Professor of sociology at the University of California at Riverside and University Professor for the University of California. He is the author of 35 books, which have been published in 12 different languages, and many research articles in journals and books.

Leonard Beeghley (PhD, University of California at Riverside) is a professor of sociology, emeritus, at the University of Florida. He is the author of a number of books, primarily in the area of stratification and social policy issues. He has written many articles in research journals and has served in editorial positions for several publishers. He has served on committees within the American Sociological Association.

Charles H. Powers (PhD, University of California at Riverside) is a professor of sociology at Santa Clara University. Under his leadership, the sociology program at Santa Clara won the American Sociological Association's Distinguished Contributions to Teaching Award in 1998. He is the author of several books and research articles focusing on sociological theory and on change management in organizations.

Preface

The first edition of *The Emergence of Sociological Theory* was published in early 1981. At that time, our goal was to examine the first 100 years of sociological theorizing—roughly the period between 1830 and 1930. Over the years, the goals of the book have remained unchanged: to summarize the basic works of each theorist. This book has always summarized each theorist's ideas in great detail. We have never "watered down" the reviews of a theorist's basic works; rather, we have tried to present ideas in their full complexity, although we have also sought to do so in simple language.

There is a temptation in the revisions of books, especially ones that have gone through several editions, to keep adding new materials. In the last edition, we did just the opposite and took away text to make the book more accessible and usable in a wider variety of teaching contexts. In this seventh edition, we have added a few new materials. First, there is a new and longer introductory chapter, and there is a new last chapter (Chapter 16) that reviews the works of the early masters in a more contemporary perspective. The last chapter summarizes nine contemporary theoretical perspectives and variants within these with an eye to documenting how the theorists of sociology's first 100 years continue to inform contemporary theorizing. We also tried to retain the modular structure of the two chapters on each theorist. These two chapters on each theorist can stand alone, the main chapter on each theorist can also stand alone, and all chapters can be read in a different order from that in the book. In the end then, the book is still relatively short, lean, and focused. It can be used in both a quarter and a semester system. In this way, instructors can use the book in a short, focused course where they will examine only the key works, or they can use it in a longer course where they want students to understand the ideas in a historical context.

Jonathan H. Turner

Leonard Beeghley

Charles H. Powers

CHAPTER 1

The Rise of Theoretical Sociology

He became the toast of Europe in 1830. Twenty years later, this once famous Frenchman was ridiculed and regarded as a fool. He had always been a difficult person; he had been arrogant, rude, and unpleasant. He announced that he would now engage in "cerebral hygiene" and no longer read the works of those whom he felt were his intellectual inferiors. He proclaimed himself to be "the Great Priest of Humanity" and the founder of the new "Universal Religion." His followers were a rather odd and ragtag assortment of workers, third-rate intellectuals, and other hangers-on. He would send messages, like the Pope, to his followers; and in fact, he even sent missives to the Pope himself that, in all likelihood, were ignored. The final volume of his great multivolume work—the same work that had made him famous in Europe in 1830—did not receive a single review in the French press in 1842.

Who was this pathetic figure? He was the titular founder of sociology, Auguste Comte, whose life and works will be examined in Chapters 2 and 3. Perhaps it is somewhat embarrassing to have the founder of sociology be a person who clearly went a bit insane. Yet the early Comte had been brilliant and did much to carve out a niche for a new discipline. He wanted to call this new discipline "social physics" because the term *physics* in his time meant to "study the fundamental nature of phenomena"; and so the new discipline would study the fundamental nature of social phenomena. To Comte's dismay, the label "social physics" had been previously used by a Belgian statistician, with the result that he constructed the Latin and Greek hybrid: *sociology*. He did not like this name, but he felt that he did not have a choice. Still, the first volume of his *Course of Positive Philosophy* (1830)—the volume that made him famous—was a brilliant analysis of how science had advanced to the point where the social universe could be systematically studied. Sociology could not emerge, he argued, until the other sciences had advanced and until science in general had become widely accepted as a legitimate mode of inquiry. With the pervasiveness of science today, it is perhaps hard to recognize that science had to fight its way into the intellectual arena because it represented a challenge to the dominance of religion. Indeed, early in the growth of science in Europe, even Galileo had to renounce his views and suffer legal persecution for the insight that the earth was not the center of the universe, nor was the earth the center of our solar system. And, even after several hundred years of success—indeed, thousands of years of success if we count the accomplishments of Arab, Persian, Egyptian, and Greek scholarship—science was still not on a secure footing at the beginning of the nineteenth century; and as the controversy over Charles Darwin's theory of biotic evolution documented, science still had to fight for its place as the final arbiter of knowledge about the natural world. In fact, the current controversy in the United States over teaching evolution in schools attests to the simple fact that, when science contradicts intensely felt religious beliefs, the conflict often becomes political—just as it was in the times of Galileo or Darwin.

Thus, what Comte tried to accomplish in the first volume of *Course of Positive Philosophy* was monumental, and perhaps even risky. The great irony is that Comte began to see himself a few decades later as a quasi-religious prophet rather than as a hard-nosed scientist, although a prophet of a more secular religion (perhaps like Scientology or Unitarianism today). In giving the systematic study of social phenomenon a name—albeit a second-choice name—and then it legitimating a science of the social realm, Comte accomplished a great deal. Few read Comte today, but as we will see shortly, his arguments were hugely legitimating for a new discipline that had to fight its way into academia and science more generally.

In one of those cruel ironies of history, Comte became an important figure again in France and the United States at the turn of the twentieth century. Alas, he could not enjoy his new fame from the grave, but his advocacy for theoretical sociology recaptured the imagination of emerging departments in his native country and in the United States, with the result that his work was once again in vogue. In fact, almost all of the sociology textbooks in the United States published in the early years of the twentieth century had prominent sections devoted to Comte. And so, the "great priest of humanity" thus had one more brush with fame because, and as we will see in the following chapters, his advocacy carried a powerful message of what the new science of sociology could become.

Long before Comte, of course, humans had thought about the universe around them, even the social universe built up from the activities of people adapting to their environments. Indeed, people have always been "folk sociologists," just as most people are today when they make a pronouncement on the causes of some social event, or when they assert what should be done to resolve some problematic social condition. Also, very early on in human history, but accelerating dramatically with the invention of writing, scholars began developing schools and systems of philosophical thought that had many of the elements of sociological analysis. So sociology has existed in one form or another for as long as we have been human, but Comte gave this activity a name and tried—with only partial success—to make it a science like any other natural science. This idea of "a natural science of society"[1] is still controversial in sociology, and we can see the lines of contention in the thinking of the first sociological theorists examined in this book. Some were hard-core scientists—or at least committed to this epistemology. Others were skeptical and, yet, they wanted to study the social world systematically. Thus, the status of sociology as a science was not only questioned in the classical period of theorizing; it is still a contentious issue today.

The emergence of sociology and, hence, sociological theory was inevitable. If Comte had not been born, someone else would have articulated a name for the systematic and even scientific study of the social universe. Herbert Spencer's *The Study of Sociology*[2] might

---

[1]This phrase was borrowed from A. R. Radcliffe-Brown's 1937 series of lectures at the University of Chicago that were published after his death the book, *A Natural Science of Society* (Chicago: University of Chicago Press).

[2]Herbert Spencer, *The Study of Sociology* (London: Kegan Paul, Trench, 1873) made a strong case for viewing sociology as an explanatory science that could overcome human biases and develop laws explaining the dynamics of human social organization.

have become the new manifesto for the discipline, but sociology's official arrival might have been delayed for decades. The emergence of sociology was the culmination of not only a very long history of humans thinking about their creations—the social world—but of broader social and intellectual movements that began to bring Europe out of its "Dark Ages" after the collapse of the Roman Empire. This Renaissance also included new ways of thinking, which collectively are sometimes termed *the Enlightenment*. Once these new ways of thinking began to gain traction, it was inevitable that someone like Comte would come along to give a name to new ways of thinking about the social world. We should, therefore, briefly pause to see what the Enlightenment accomplished and why it set the stage for sociology to make its grand entrance before an often skeptical audience.

The Enlightenment and New Ways of Thinking

The Intellectual Revolution

When the Roman Empire finally collapsed, there followed a period often termed *the Dark Ages*. Much of the learning of Romans and, more important, of Greeks, Arabs, Persians, and Egyptians was lost; and only the faithful scribes of medieval monasteries kept the Eastern and Western intellectual traditions alive. The label, the Enlightenment, is obviously meant to connote a lighting of the dark, but in fact, the Dark Ages were not stagnant[3]; after the initial decline in Western civilization when the Roman Empire finally collapsed, living conditions for most people were miserable; and yet new inventions and new ideas were slowly accumulating, despite the oppressive poverty of the masses, the constant warfare among feudal lords, and the rigid dogma of religion. New forms and experiments in commerce, politics, economics, religion, art, music, crafts, *and* thinking were slowly emerging. As these elements of "the great awakening" were accumulating between the fifth and thirteenth centuries, a critical threshold was finally reached. Change came more rapidly as these innovations

---

[3]There is often a tendency to think that the Dark Ages were stagnant, but societies were slowly being rebuilt after the collapse of the Roman Empire. See Patrick Nolan and Gerhard Lenski, *Human Societies* (Boulder, CO: Paradigm Press, 2009) for a review of the changes that were occurring; these would eventually drive societies toward modernity.

fed off each other. As social structure and culture changed, so did human thinking about the world. Much of what had been lost from the Greeks and Romans, as well as from the early civilizations of the Middle East, was found (in dusty church libraries), rediscovered, and often improved on. Nowhere is this more evident than in how scholars viewed science as a way of understanding the universe.

Francis Bacon (1561–1626) was the first to articulate clearly the new mode of inquiry: Conceptualizations of the nature of the universe should always be viewed with skepticism and tested against observable facts. This sounds like scientific common sense today, but it was a radical idea at the time. This mode of inquiry stimulated great achievements in sixteenth- and seventeenth-century astronomy, including Isaac Newton's famous law of gravity. Thinking about the universe was now becoming systematic, but equally important, it was becoming abstract and yet empirical. The goal was to articulate fundamental relationships in the universe that could explain the many varied ways that these relationships can be expressed in the empirical world. To explain events thus required systematic and abstract thinking—in a word, it required theory. And this way of thinking literally transformed the world.

The Enlightenment was thus an intellectual revolution because it changed how we are to explain the universe, and increasingly, it held out the vision that knowledge about how the universe operates can also be used to better the human condition. In fact, progress was not only possible but inevitable once science and rational thinking dominate how to explain the world, including the social world of our own creation. In England and Scotland, the Enlightenment was dominated by a group of thinkers who sought to justify the industrial capitalism that first appeared in the British Isles. Scholars like Adam Smith believed that individuals should be free of external constraint and should be free to compete, thereby creating a better society. While this might be considered a conservative philosophy today, it was liberal if not radical in its time. In France, the Enlightenment was dominated by a group of scholars known as the *philosophes*. Despite the fact that Adam Smith formulated one of the essential questions of sociology—how are increasingly specialized people working and living in different worlds to become integrated into a complex but coherent society?—it is the philosophes who had more influence on the emergence of sociology, although we should always remember that one of the most important thinkers of the nineteenth century—Karl Marx—saw himself as trying to improve on Adam Smith's economic theory. Sociology thus has it major roots in the intellectual ferment generated by French philosophers, but we must always remember that thinkers in the Anglo world also influenced the development of the new science of sociology.

The new thinking that drove the Enlightenment derived considerable inspiration from the scientific revolution of the sixteenth and seventeenth centuries. Newtonian physics is perhaps the symbolic peak of the Enlightenment because it broke what had been a philosophical dualism between the senses and reason. Reason and the world of phenomena *are not separate* but all part of a new way of knowing. Through concepts, speculation, and logic, the facts of the empirical world can be understood; and by accumulating facts, reason could sort through them and provide explanations for their existence and operation that were more than flights of intellectual fancy or impositions of religious dogma.

The world was no longer the province of the supernatural; it was the domain of the natural, and its complexity could now be understood by the combination of reason and facts. Newton's law of gravity was hailed as the exemplar of how scientific inquiry should be conducted. And gradually, the social universe was included in domains that science should explain. This gradual inclusion was a radical break from the past where the social had been considered the domain of morals, ethics, and religion. The goal of the French philosophes, then, was to emancipate social thought from religious speculation; and while the philosophes were hardly very scientific, they performed the essential function of placing thought about the human condition in the realm of reason. As can be seen in the philosophes statements about universal human rights, law, and natural order (ideas that are at the core of the U.S. Constitution), their work was seen as a radical attack on established authority in both the state and church. From notions of natural laws, it is but a short step to thinking about the fundamental laws not only of human rights but also of human social organization. As will be evident in the next chapter, many of the less shrill and polemical philosophes—first Charles Montesquieu, then Jacques Turgot, and finally Jean Condorcet—actually made this short step and sought to understand the social realm through principles or laws that they felt were the equivalent to those developed by Newton for the physical realm.

Social conditions almost always affect how scholars think about the world, and such was the case for the philosophes who were opposed to the Old Regime (monarchy) in France and who were supportive of the bourgeoisie in emphasizing free trade, free labor, free commerce, free industry, and free opinion. The growing and literate bourgeoisie formed the reading public that bought the books, papers, and pamphlets of the philosophes. These works are filled with seeming "laws" of the human condition but these were ideological statements derived from moral, political, and social philosophies; they were not reasoned laws of the social universe. Yet they contained support and indeed heralded the view that a science of society molded in the image of physics or biology was not only possible but an inevitable outcome of human progress.

The basic thesis of all the philosophes—whether Voltaire, Rousseau, Condorcet, Diderot, or others—was that humans had certain "natural rights," which were violated by the institutional arrangements of the time. It was, therefore, necessary to dismantle the existing social order and substitute a new order that would be more compatible with the rights and needs of humans. This transformation was to occur through reasoned and progressive legislation. And again, one of the cruel ironies of history forced the philosophes to watch in horror as their names and ideas were used to justify the violent aftermath of the French Revolution of 1789—hardly the "reconstruction" of the social order that they had in mind.

In almost all of the philosophes' formulations was a vision of human progress. Humanity was seen to be marching in a direction governed by the law of progress that was as fundamental as the law of gravitation in the physical world. Thus, the philosophes were clearly unscientific in their moral advocacy, but they offered at least the rhetoric of post-Newtonian science in their search for the natural laws of the human order and in their formulation of the law of progress. These somewhat contradictory intellectual tendencies were to be merged together in Comte's advocacy for scientific sociology.

Comte did not have to reconcile these tendencies alone because the most talented of the philosophes, scholars such as Montesquieu, Turgot, and Condorcet, provided the broad contours of reconciliation to Comte: The laws of human organization, particularly the law of progressive development, can be used as tools to create a better social world. With this mixture of concerns—morality, progress, and scientific laws—this new view of possibilities was carried into the nineteenth century. From this intellectual legacy, the young Comte was to pull diverse and often contradictory elements to forge a forceful statement about the nature of a science of society, as is explored in the next two chapters.

New systems of thought do not appear only from heady intellectual debates; new ideas almost always reflect more fundamental transformations in the organization of polity and production. Yet, once created, ideas have the capacity to stimulate new forms of politics and new modes of production. The Enlightenment was thus more than an intellectual revolution; its emergence was a response to changes in patterns of social organization generated by new political and economic formations.

The Political and Economic Revolutions

For most of the eighteenth century, the last remnants of the old economic order were crumbling under the impact of the commercial and industrial revolutions. The expansion of free markets and trade eliminated much of the feudal order during the seventeenth century, but during the eighteenth century new restrictions were imposed by guilds controlling labors' access to skilled occupations and by chartered (by the nobility) corporations controlling vast sectors of economic production. The cotton industry was the first to break the hold of the guilds and chartered corporations, and with each subsequent decade, other industries were subject to the liberating effects of free labor, free trade, and free production. By the time that larger scale industrial production emerged—first in England, then in France, and later in Germany—the underlying economic reorganization had already been achieved. The new industrial base of manufacturing simply accelerated in the nineteenth century the transformations that had been at work for decades in the eighteenth century.

These transformations were profound: labor was liberated from the land; wealth and capital existed independently of the large noble estates; urbanization of the population was depopulating rural areas; competitive industries generated ever-new technologies to stay a step ahead of competitors; markets expanded to distribute finished goods produced by industry and to provide basic resources needed for manufacturing; services increasingly became an important part of the economy; law became concerned with regularizing new economic processes, trade, and privilege for new and often old elites; polity could no longer legitimate its leaders by "divine rights"; and religion was losing much of its influence in general but particularly in its capacity to legitimate polity. As these transformations methodically destroyed the old feudal order as well as the transitional mercantile order of guilds and chartered corporations, the daily lives of people also changed. Family structures began to shrink; new classes such as the urban proletariat and bourgeoisie expanded; people increasingly sold their labor as a commodity in markets; and many other former routines were changed. These changes coupled with memories of the disorder caused by revolution provided the first French sociologists with their basic intellectual problem: How to use the laws of social organization to create a new, less volatile, and more humane social order?

By the time of the French Revolution, the old feudal system was a mere skeleton of its former self. Peasants had become landowners, although tenant farming was still practiced but subject to high rates of taxation. The landed aristocracy had lost much of its wealth through indolence, incompetence, and unwillingness to pursue occupations in the emerging capitalist order. In fact, many of the nobility lived in genteel poverty within the walls of their disintegrating estates, only to have their land purchased by the bourgeoisie or to seek out the bourgeoisie for loans and marital partners for noble but poor children. The monarchy was "diluted" or "polluted" by the selling of titles to the bourgeoisie and by the need to seek loans from those who had money. And so, by the time of the revolution, the monarchy was weak and in fiscal crisis, increasingly depending on the bourgeoisie for support.

The structure of the state perhaps best reflects these changes. By the end of the eighteenth century, the French monarchy had become almost functionless. It had a centralized governmental system but the monarchs were now lazy, indolent, and incompetent. The real power resided in the professional administrators in the state bureaucracy, most of whom had been recruited from the bourgeoisie. The various magistrates were also recruited from the bourgeoisie, and the independent financiers, particularly the Farmers General, had assumed many of the tax-collecting functions of government. In exchange for a fixed sum of money, the monarch had contracted to the financiers the right to collect taxes, with the result that financiers collected all that they could and, in the process, generated enormous resentment and hostility in the population. With their excessive profits, the financiers became the major bankers of the monarchy: the king, nobility, church, guild masters, merchants, and monopolistic corporate manufacturers often went to them for loans—thus increasing the abuse of their power. Thus, when the revolution came, it confronted a governmental system that had been in severe decline for a century, and yet, the violence of the revolution and the decades of instability in France that followed document that bourgeoisie's assumption of power had been incomplete. True, the bureaucracies of the state filled with bourgeoisie functionaries kept the body of the state functioning but often without a head. The ferment of ideas before and after the revolution only underscores a basic truth: Change and especially dramatic change leads individuals to search for answers about "what to do."

In England, the changes were more evolutionary, with the result that sociology did not first emerge in the British Isles. The equivalent of the philosophes in the British Isles also thought about the nature of humans and their basic needs and rights, but they did so in a rather understated, almost passionless manner. The fire was in France because the abuses were greater and the transformation more revolutionary, leading people to think about how to reconstruct society. France was ready for sociology, and once it appeared, thinkers in the British Isles and Germany would find it an appealing way of dealing with the more evolutionary changes in their societies. Sociology was now ready to begin its long climb toward respectability, a journey that took 100 years to achieve at even a modest level of success.

Early Sociological Theory, 1830–1930

In the pages to follow, we will examine the most important theories developed in sociology's first 100 years. This is, of course, a rather arbitrary framing of the "classical" canon in sociology because, as we will see when examining the thinking of those who influenced the classical thinkers, we could easily push the date back for sociology's emergence by another 100 years, but Comte's naming of the discipline and advocacy give us a clear starting point, even if it is somewhat arbitrary. The end point is also a bit arbitrary, but the third decade into the twentieth century is an appropriate end point for the "classical period." First, all of the key figures in this classical period had died. Second, the next 20 years produced surprisingly few new general theoretical approaches like those of the early masters. It was, rather, a period of developing methodologies for studying social life more than an effort to explain the dynamics of social life with theories. It was not until the 1950s that theories revealing the same level of explanatory power of the first masters began to reappear. We could consider the 1950s as the beginning of contemporary theory, although at some point in the very near future, we may need to find a new label for ideas that are now many decades old.

The early masters struggled with the problem of what theory is, and in fact, sociologists still struggle with this issue—as noted earlier. In science, theory is a particular way of explaining how and why events occur, and many thinkers in scientific sociological theory try to produce explanations that are consistent with the epistemology of science. Still others are not so sure about whether or not sociology can be, or even should be, a science; and their doubts are also reflected in the works of the early masters. Thus, theory has meant something different to sociologists from the very beginnings of the discipline labeled sociology. So we can ask, "What makes all of their early masters' work *theoretical*, even if many of its central figures were not dedicated to the epistemology of science?"

One element of the answer to this question is that all of the classical theorists sought to develop *abstract concepts* to denote critical properties of the social universe. Even when describing empirical events during the development of modern societies, they did more than describe. They abstracted above the flow of empirical events and sought to understand the underlying forces driving these empirical events. For example, the forces of capitalism were to be explained by more generic forces of production and distribution. Or, in politics, concepts would be developed about power in general and how power operates in the social world. Even scholars like Max Weber, who did not believe that there are universal properties of the social world like those in the biophysical universe, still developed very general concepts to denote the dynamics of power in many different types of societies.

Another element of what makes the early masters' work theoretical is that their *analysis is systematic.* It seeks to explain the connections among social forces, and how these connections generate, reproduce, or change the social world. Power, production, distribution, sacredness and piety, communities, classes, and other social phenomena are *all connected to each other.* And, it is important to understand these effects in explanations of events in the social world. For example, political actors are influenced by economic actors, and vice versa; politics is greatly influenced by the structure of the class system or by religion; classes are generated by the distribution of resources by organizational units in economy, polity, community, and other social structures; or, all social structures are constrained by culture, and vice versa. Thus, regardless of where one of the classical figures stood on the prospects for scientific theory, they all were dedicated to discovering the most fundamental and important interconnections among social phenomena. Without this kind of knowledge, understanding how the social operates is not possible.

Still another common element in the theories of the early masters was the *concern with modernity* or the transformations of social life that came with industrialization, urbanization, nation-state formation, alternations in the class system, spread of bureaucracies, changes in values and beliefs, science and technology, and many other features of the modern world. Indeed, as we emphasized earlier, it is these kinds of transformative events acting in concert and having causal effects on each other that makes people in general, and scholars interested in explaining these events in particular, seek to develop concepts that can denote the key properties and their causal interconnections and that can explain the dramatic changes that come with modernity. Why did modernity emerge in the first place? What events led to the decline of feudal social forms and the rise of capitalistic forms? What are the underlying properties of modernity—for example, markets, rationality, new cultural beliefs, science, democratic polities, and so on? Answers to these questions would, in turn, allow for understanding of not only why the modern world emerged but also how it operates. And, in trying to understand modernity, early sociologists were often led to early societal formations in an effort to understand what properties of premodern social formations would be conductive to modernization.

Another element is not so obvious, but all of the early theorists in sociology had some implicit notion of *societal evolution* even if, like Max Weber, they explicitly rejected this notion. Comte, Spencer, Marx, Weber, Émile Durkheim, Georg Simmel, and even the philosopher George Herbert Mead all had a view of the world as successively transforming. Some emphasized growth and social differentiation (Comte, Spencer, Durkheim, Mead, and perhaps even Simmel); others emphasized conflicts (Spencer, Marx, and Weber); still others the process of what Weber termed *rationalization* (or the emphasis on rational calculations in ever more social spheres). Some saw evolution as a series of discrete stages (Comte, Spencer, Marx, and Durkheim) or cycles (Spencer) operating inside the increasing differentiation of the social universe. Evolution was an important mode of thinking in the nineteenth century, especially in biology, and many sociologists borrowed this idea explicitly from biology (especially Comte, Spencer, and Durkheim), but they used it to analyze the directional nature of evolution toward more complexity because they could see this trend in their own immediate worlds.

Yet one more element is evident among the early theorists: *debate and dialogue.* For the most part, they responded to each other, sometimes openly but equally often obliquely. For example, Spencer responded to Comte, as did Durkheim; Durkheim was critical of Spencer even as he adopted many of his ideas; Weber was quietly proposing an alternative to Marx's scheme of class and social change; Simmel was critical of Marx without ever really mentioning him by name in his analysis of money; Durkheim implicitly criticized Marx in his analysis of the "forced division of labor." Thus, to varying degrees most of the early theorists were responding to each other, often borrowing but more often criticizing other theorists' key concepts and explanations. One feature of science, and all forms of intellectual competition, is to provide the best explanation of events; and all of the early masters were trying to do so, even with their varying interests and modes of explanation. They all sought attention space[4] by emphasizing the power of their ideas and, at the same time, the weaknesses in their competitors' ideas.

Thus, even though some of the early theorists did not consider themselves to be "hard scientists," they were all theoretical. They were more interested in explaining than describing social reality. And their concepts were abstract and general. Their analyses were systematic and sought to sort out causal connections among phenomena. They all focused on the changes associated with modernity, even the philosopher George Herbert Mead. They all had at least an implicit and, in most cases, an explicit model of social evolution, albeit being

---

[4]Randall Collins, *The Sociology of Philosophies: A Global Theory of Intellectual Change* (Cambridge, MA: Harvard University Press, 1998).

driven by somewhat different dynamics. And they were often in a quiet debate and dialogue with each other (even if the other had died) to develop the better explanation.

The First Masters

Not all of the early masters considered themselves to be sociologists. Karl Marx did not see himself as a sociologist, and in his mind, he was trying to improve on Adam Smith's analysis of capitalism, while being a revolutionary critic of capitalism and what it had wrought on people. It is sociology that adopted Marx rather than the reverse. George Herbert Mead was a philosopher but he too was adopted by students of sociology at his university and, later, by the whole field. And, while Mead is still mentioned in the history of philosophy, he is still very much "alive" in sociology. Comte was, of course, a sociologist, if only by definition. Spencer was a general philosopher, and he subsumed his work in sociology under the general label *Synthetic Philosophy*, but his sociological works written as part of this general philosophy are nonetheless labeled as sociology. Max Weber and Georg Simmel were both self-conscious sociologists and, together, founded the German Sociological Association. Durkheim was, like Comte 60 years before him, an advocate of sociology and held the first sociology chair in France.

There has been a trend in recent decades to include other figures in the pantheon of "early masters" or "classical theorists." Most of these figures were not sociologists but prominent scholars, intellectuals, social activists, and journalists of their time; they were *not* theorists, and their work has had relatively little influence on much of contemporary sociological theory. Their works had sociological implications, and in the case of some, these works were very good sociology. This effort to rewrite sociology's history is understandable because of general efforts today to be inclusive, but the reality is that women and most minorities were excluded from academia by formal and informal discrimination. Without an academic base, it is particularly difficult to do academic work—although some like Simmel managed to build an academic career without being employed in a university, until near end of his life. Or, Spencer was sufficiently wealthy to be able to pursue his interests outside academia, or Marx who was not wealthy but he had a wealthy patron who supported his work outside of academia. Comte soon lost his academic anchorage and indeed all anchorage as his life digressed into delusional ramblings. Yet we cannot remake, except by fiat, these talented persons into theorists—despite the understandable desire to do so by many commentators. Some were more sociological than others but none were theorists in the same mold as the early masters.

We have not included a few scholars who did make theoretical contributions—scholars like Vilfredo Pareto, whose work is one of the cornerstones of modern neoclassical economics; William Graham Sumner who brought Comte and the concern for science well into the twentieth century; Robert Park, Ernest Burgess, and other thinkers who became known as The Chicago School (in the first department of sociology in the world at the University of Chicago); W. E. B. Dubois who was an excellent sociologist and who made some contributions to theories of racial and ethnic dynamics but not to general theories of larger domains of social phenomena; Lester Frank Ward who was the only trained scientist among the first generation of American sociologists; and a number of others. They are not included because we want to stick with the core of the classical tradition that *still informs and guides* sociological theorizing. Some like Pareto should be consulted more; others like Comte and Spencer are not read much anymore are still included because Comte is a key historical figure and Spencer's ideas still inform sociology, although most sociologists remain unaware of Spencer's influence because it is mediated through other prominent figures, beginning with Durkheim but extending through Talcott Parsons and many others in the modern era of sociological theorizing. There is, perhaps, a certain arbitrariness as to who and what we have included and excluded, but there are still implicit objective criteria that we have used. First, were these scholars theorists? Second, did they have an impact on the development of sociology and, especially, sociological theorizing? And, do they still inform sociological theorizing to a high degree? If the answer is "yes" to these questions, then they have been included; and by these criteria, the list of sociology of the first great theoretical masters is short, as might be expected in a new discipline having to legitimate itself and find intellectual niches in conservative academia where discrimination and exclusion by gender, ethnicity, and religion were common.

Conclusion

The theorists explored in the next chapters still have a large impact on contemporary theorizing in sociology, as we will briefly outline in the last chapter on the continuing legacy of the first masters in various theoretical perspectives. These first masters discovered some of the fundamental properties and dynamics of the social universe, and so it should not be surprising that such fundamental insights are part of the modern-day canon in sociology. In some ways, however, their influence may even be too strong. Sociologists often stand in the shadows[5] of these masters rather on their shoulders, with the result that they cannot see the horizon beyond the masters. Whether as science or any body of accumulating knowledge, it is critical to add to the knowledge base; and there is often a fine line between respect of the first masters of a discipline and idolatry, where old texts are read again and again in a highly ritualized manner. These readers do not seek new knowledge, but instead, they seek to express their reverence for now deified scholars—in a manner reminiscent of religious study of the sacred texts. In intellectual activity, and especially science, it is important to expand on insights of the early masters, whether scholars like Newton, Darwin, or Durkheim, then move on and develop ever more powerful explanations of how the universe works. The early theorists of sociology's first 100 years provided a solid beginning and base of insights, which have been expanded considerably over the past 80-plus years. But has sociology reached far enough beyond the masters?

A strong case can be made for opposite answers to this question. At times, it seems that sociology is stuck with repeating the insights of the first theorists; and yet, since 1950 in particular, sociology has dramatically expanded its knowledge base, although this expansion is difficult to see because of overspecialization in the discipline. Not only is research highly specialized, but so are theories that deal

---

[5]Sir Isaac Newton famously remarked in a letter to his rival Robert Hooke dated February 5, 1676 that "*What Descartes did was a good step. You have added much several ways, and especially in taking the colours of thin plates into philosophical consideration. If I have seen a little further it is by standing on the shoulders of Giants.*" The basic metaphor is that by building on the theoretical and empirical base created by others, a theorist sees farther and expands the base of knowledge. To "stand in the shadows" emphasizes that one worships the masters rather than stand on their base of knowledge and expand this base.

with one or two processes in the social universe but never the whole universe or even large portions of this universe. Disciplines often accumulate knowledge as specialists dig deep but never very wide, but at some point, these bodies of specialized knowledge must be integrated.

We suspect that much of the continued fascination with the first masters stems from the fact that they thought "big" and tried to explain large portions of the social universe. They were concerned with how and why the social world was changing in such dramatic ways, and to address this issue, they thought big by searching for the basic social processes driving the social universe. Reading and rereading of their texts meets a need among contemporary sociologists to visualize the social universe as a whole and to expand theorizing beyond the narrow confines of specific research traditions. Yet, ironically, the result is that contemporary theories that try to be more general often stand too close to the masters, secure in their shadow but not seeing as far as they could, or should.

Yet let us hold final judgment to the end when we examine how the theorists of the first 100 years continue to influence theorizing in the second 100 years. What motivates contemporary general theorists is the same impulse that motivated the masters: How do we understand the rapid transformations of society? Their insights are still relevant because they discovered many of the forces that are fundamental to all patterns of social organization. That is why sociologists continue to write and students continue to read textbooks on their achievements.

CHAPTER 2

The Origin and Context of Auguste Comte's Sociology

Since Auguste Comte gave sociology its name, he is generally credited with being the founder of sociology. Yet new ideas are often extensions and codifications of ideas developed by a scholar's predecessors and contemporaries. This is certainly the case for Comte, for he was working within a long French tradition of thinking that gave him the critical elements for his pronouncement that the era of sociology had arrived. Comte was an odd man, and indeed, he went rather insane in his later years, but he was young and well-situated at the time he began to visualize a "system of positive philosophy," with sociology being its culminating science. Before exploring the intellectual influences on Comte, let us briefly review how Comte's biography influenced his thinking.

The Strange Biography of Auguste Comte[1]

Auguste Comte was born in 1798 in Montpellier, a city in the south of France. The period from Comte's birth to his formative years as a student in Paris was socially and politically tumultuous, punctuated by revolution and revolt. At his birth, the Directory ruled France after the Reign of Terror imposed by Robespierre, but within a couple of

---

[1]This brief review borrows heavily from Lewis A. Coser's *Masters of Sociological Thought* (New York: Harcourt Brace Jovanovich, 1978), 13–40, as well as from Frank E. Manuel's *The Prophets of Paris* (Cambridge, MA: Harvard University Press, 1962).

years, Napoleon had led a coup and become first among equals in the council. Before Comte entered school 5 years later, Napoleon had been crowned emperor of France. After Napoleon's defeat in 1814, the throne was restored to the brother of the former king, retaken briefly by Napoleon on his escape from the island of Elba, and restored again to Louis XVIII in 1815 after Napoleon's defeat at Waterloo. For the next 15 years, Louis XVIII, and later his brother, Charles X, ruled France. Yet another revolution established Louis Philippe I, Duke of Orléans, as king in 1830, the publication date for the first installment of Comte's *The Course of Positive Philosophy*. Between 1848 and 1852, a series of popular revolts and military coups reestablished the Empire with Napoleon III as emperor.

The rapid industrialization of France accompanied this constantly changing political landscape. Industrialization brought new classes of individuals, including urban wage earners and expanded numbers of bourgeoisie, as well as new structural systems such as the factory, bureaucracy, and open markets. During these transformations, Comte's career began, enjoyed a promising beginning, and then faded to embarrassment and ridicule. He had been an impressive student in the *lycée* of his hometown, but he had also been a somewhat rebellious and difficult person—traits that, in the end, caused his ruin. On the basis of competitive examinations, in 1814 he secured a place in the École Polytechnique, the elite technical school of France. He soon established himself as a brilliant, though difficult, student. His generation of Parisian students and intellectuals had lost much of their religiosity; yet they retained the desire to construct a new, more stable order in terms of some faith. Many believed that science was this new faith and could be used to make a better society. Moreover, there was a growing feeling that the sciences—both natural and social—could be unified to reconstruct the world. The authority of scientific laws, and their engineering applications, were to be the substitute for religion. These ideas captured Comte, especially because during his years in the *lycée* he had lost his religious faith and abandoned Catholicism.

But the École Polytechnique of Comte's time closed temporarily in a dispute between its students and faculty, on one side, and its financial benefactor, the government, on the other. The dispute was over the mission of the school: Was it to be devoted to pure science, to engineering, or to military training? During the university's closure, Comte briefly returned home but was soon back in Paris, giving private lessons. He even sought to move to America, but his hopes went unrealized when the U.S. government did not create an equivalent technical university. When the École Polytechnique reopened, he did not seek readmission, perhaps because he had made too many enemies.

At this time, in 1817, Comte began his association with Claude-Henri de Saint-Simon, at first as secretary and later as a collaborator. They worked closely together, and most of Comte's major ideas were developed during this period. But he also began to resent Saint-Simon's dominance, especially because Comte had become the intellectual force behind the work that was making Saint-Simon a leading thinker and reformer. Moreover, because Comte was interested in developing theory before ameliorative action, he constantly came into conflict with the activist Saint-Simon and his followers, the Saint-Simonians. By 1824, these tensions had built to the point where Comte acrimoniously broke from Saint-Simon, a move that destroyed Comte's career.

In 1825, Comte married, but the marriage was problematic; hence, instability in his personal and intellectual lives was about to overwhelm him. Yet he began to write the ideas for his most famous work, *The Course of Positive Philosophy*, in which he explicitly created the discipline that became sociology. During this period of creativity, however, he still needed to earn a living, and he was forced to tutor and perform marginal academic tasks that were beneath his abilities and aspirations. In a bold move to recapture some of his fading esteem, he proposed a series of public lectures to communicate his ideas. Forty eminent scientists and intellectuals subscribed to the lectures, but he gave only three before the pressure and tension of the enterprise made him too ill to continue. Three years later, he was sufficiently well to restart the lectures, with many notables still in attendance.

Yet his support was fragile, and his difficult personality drove people away. His grand goal, to incorporate the development of all the sciences in one scheme, was attacked by specialists in each science, so that, as is often the case in academia, a pretentious and ambitious nonacademic soon became an object of derision and ridicule.

Thus, by the time that the first installment of *Positive Philosophy* was published, Comte was becoming more isolated. Yet the first volume received critical acclaim, and his ideas did attract considerable attention. But this acclaim was short-lived. Within a few years, he had fully antagonized the last of his important scientific admirers; he had lost his academic colleagues; he was the confirmed enemy of the Saint-Simonians; he began to lose his old personal friends;

he continued to have marital problems; and he was reduced to ever-more menial and marginal academic work as a reader, tutor, and examiner. When the six volumes of *Positive Philosophy* were completed in 1842, not a single review appeared in the French press. At this point, moreover, his wife left him. Many of Comte's problems were of his own making: He was obnoxious to friends and critics, he was defensive and dogmatic, and he was so arrogant as to cease reading others' works in an act of defiance to his critics (what he termed *cerebral hygiene*).

The titular founder of sociology had gone from promising brilliance to intellectual isolation, at least in France. In England, Comte did exert some influence on both John Stuart Mill and Herbert Spencer, and he influenced subsequent generations of French thinkers, most particularly Émile Durkheim.

In a desperate search for an audience, Comte was reduced to lecturing to a ragtag collection of workers and other interested parties. He had lost, forever in his lifetime, the respect of the scientific, academic, and intellectual community. He began to see himself as the "High Priest of Humanity," making pronouncements to his followers. In his *System of Positive Polity*, his science had taken a backseat to his advocacy—ironically, the very point that had led to his break with Saint-Simon decades earlier. He was a pathetic figure, lecturing to his intellectual inferiors and seeking to create a semi-religious cult of followers. The founder of sociology, the person with the first clear and still relevant vision of what sociology could be, died as a demented fool. The promise and power of his early vision for sociology had been lost—only to be picked up again after his death in 1857.

The Intellectual Origins of Comte's Thought

Comte's sociology emerged from the economic, political, and social conditions of post-revolutionary France. No social thinker could ignore the oscillating political situation in France during the first half of the nineteenth century or the profound changes in social organization that accompanied the growth of large-scale industry. Yet despite the influence of these forces, the content of Comte's sociology represents a selective borrowing of ideas from the Enlightenment of the eighteenth century. Comte absorbed, no doubt, the general thrust of the philosophes' advocacy, but he appears to have borrowed and then synthesized concepts from four major figures: Charles Montesquieu (1689–1755), Jacques

Turgot (1727–1781), Jean Condorcet (1743–1794), and Claude-Henri de Saint-Simon (1760–1825). In addition, Comte seems to have been influenced by the liberal tradition of Adam Smith (1723–1790) as well as by the reactionary traditionalism of scholars such as Joseph-Marie de Maistre and Louis de Bonald.[2] In reviewing the origins of Comte's thought, we will focus primarily on the influence of Montesquieu, Turgot, Condorcet, and Saint-Simon, with a brief mention of the traditional and liberal elements in Comte's thinking.

Montesquieu and Comte

In Chapter 12, when we examine the culmination of French sociology in the work of Émile Durkheim, Montesquieu's ideas will be explored in more detail. For the present, we will stress those key concepts that Comte borrowed from Montesquieu. Written in the first half of the eighteenth century, Montesquieu's *The Spirit of Laws* can be considered one of the first sociological works in both style and tone.[3] Indeed, if we wanted to push back by 75 years the founding of sociology, we could view *The Spirit* as the first distinctly sociological work. However, Montesquieu's great work had too many problems for it to represent a founding effort. Its significance resides more in the influence it had on scholars of the next century, particularly Comte and Durkheim.

In *The Spirit*, Montesquieu argued that society must be considered a "thing." As a thing, its properties could be discovered by observation and analysis. Thus, for Montesquieu, morals, manners, and customs, as well as social structures, are amenable to investigation in the same way as are things or phenomena in physics and chemistry. Comte's concern with "social facts" and Durkheim's later proclamation that sociology is the study of social facts can both be traced to Montesquieu's particular emphasis on society as a thing.

As a thing, Montesquieu argued, society can be understood by discovering the "laws" of human organization. Montesquieu was not completely clear on this point, but the thrust of his argument appears to have been that the laws of society are discoverable in the same way that Newton had, in Montesquieu's mind, uncovered the laws of

---

[2]Coser's *Masters of Sociological Thought* (25–27) is the first work to bring this line of influence to our attention.

[3]Charles Montesquieu, *The Spirit of Laws*, Vols. 1 and 2 (London: Colonial, 1900; originally published in 1748).

physical matter. This point became extremely important in Comte's sociology. Indeed, Comte preferred the label *social physics* to *sociology*. In this way he could stress that social science, like the physical sciences, must involve a search for the laws of social structure and change.

Montesquieu also viewed scientific laws as a hierarchy—a notion that, along with Saint-Simon's emphasis, intrigued Comte. Sciences low in the hierarchy, such as physics, will reveal deterministic laws, as did Newton's principle of gravitation. Sciences higher in the hierarchy will, Montesquieu argued, be typified by less determinative laws. The laws of society, therefore, will be more probabilistic. In this way, Montesquieu was able to retain a vision of human freedom and initiative within the context of a scientific inquiry. Comte appears to have accepted much of this argument, for he stressed that the complexity of social phenomena renders strictly determinative laws difficult to discover. For Comte, sociological laws would capture the basic tendencies and directions of social phenomena.

Montesquieu's *The Spirit* also developed a typology of governmental forms. Much of this work is devoted to analyzing the structure and "spirit" (cultural ideas) of three basic governmental forms: republic, monarchy, and despotism. The details of this analysis are less important than is the general thrust of Montesquieu's argument. First, his analysis implies a developmental sequence, although not to the degree evident in the next generation of social thinkers, such as Turgot and Condorcet. Second, Montesquieu's abstract typology was constructed to capture the diversity of empirical systems in the world and throughout history. Thus, by developing a typology with an implicit developmental sequence, he believed he was achieving a better sense of the operation of phenomena, a point central to Comte's scheme. And third, Montesquieu's separate analysis of the "spirit of a nation" and its relation to structural variables, especially political structures, was adopted by Comte in his analysis of societal stages that reveal both "spiritual" (ideas) and "temporal" (structural) components.

In sum, then, Montesquieu laid much of the intellectual foundation on which Comte built his scheme. The emphasis on society as a thing, the concern for laws, the stress on hierarchies of laws, the implicit developmental view of political structures, the belief that empirical diversity can be simplified through analytical typologies, and the recognition that the social world is composed of interdependent cultural and structural forces all found their way into Comtean sociology, as well as into the sociology of Comte's intellectual successors, such as Durkheim. Montesquieu's ideas were transformed, however, in Comte's mind under the influence of other eighteenth-century scholars, particularly Turgot, Condorcet, and Adam Smith.

Turgot and Comte

Jacques Turgot was one of the more influential thinkers of the eighteenth-century Enlightenment. As a scholar, and for a short time as the finance minister of France, Turgot exerted considerable influence within and outside intellectual circles. His work, like that of many scholars of his time, was not published in the conventional sense but initially appeared as a series of lectures or discourses that were, no doubt, informally distributed. Only later, in the early nineteenth century, were many of his works edited and published.[4] Yet his ideas were well-known to his contemporaries and his successors, particularly Condorcet, Saint-Simon, and Comte.

In 1750, Turgot presented two discourses at the Sorbonne and established himself as a major social thinker. The first discourse was delivered in July and was titled "The Advantages Which the Establishment of Christianity Has Procured for the Human Race."[5] The second discourse was given on December 11, and was titled "Philosophical Review of the Successive Advances of the Human Mind."[6] Although the first discourse is often discounted in sociological circles, it presented a line of reasoning that would be reflected in Comte's writings. Basically, Turgot argued that religion performed some valuable services for human progress; and although Christianity was no longer an important ingredient in human development, it had made subsequent progress possible. Had Christianity not existed, basic and fundamental events such as the preservation of classical literature, the abolishment of cruel treatment of children, the eradication of extreme and punitive laws, and other necessary conditions for further progress would not have been achieved. Comte took this idea and emphasized that each stage of human evolution, particularly the

---

[4]Du Pont de Nemours, for example, published *Collected Works of Baron A. R. J. Turgot*, 9 vols. (Paris, 1808–1811), which, though deficient in many respects, brought Turgot's diverse pamphlets, discourses, letters, anonymously published articles, private memoranda, and so on together for the first time. Comte certainly must have read this work, although it is likely that he also read many of the original articles and discourses in their unedited form. See also W. Walker Stephens, ed., *The Life and Writings of Turgot* (London: Green, 1895).

[5]See Du Pont, *Collected Works*.

[6]Reprinted in English in Ronald L. Meek, ed. and trans., *Turgot on Progress, Sociology, and Economics* (Cambridge, UK: Cambridge University Press, 1973).

religious or theological, must reach its zenith, thereby laying down the conditions necessary for the next stage of human development.

The second discourse of 1750 influenced Comte and other sociologically inclined thinkers more directly. In this discourse, Turgot argued that because humans are basically alike, their perceptions of, and responses to, situations will be similar, and hence, they will all evolve along the same evolutionary path. Humanity, he argued, is like an individual in that it grows and develops in a similar way. Thus, the "human race" will be typified by a slow advancement from a less developed to a more developed state. Naturally, many conditions will influence the rate of growth, or progress, for a particular people. Hence progress will be uneven, with some peoples at one stage of growth and others at a more advanced stage. But in the end, all humanity will reach a "stage of perfection." Comte saw much in this argument because it implicitly accounted for variations and diversity among the populations of the world. Populations differ because their societies are at different stages in a single and unified developmental process.

In this second discourse, Turgot also presented a rather sophisticated economic analysis in which parts are seen as connected in a system or structure. Change occurs as a result of economic forces that inevitably produce alterations in various parts and, hence, in society as a whole. For example, the emergence of agriculture produces an economic surplus, which, in turn, allows for the expansion of the division of labor. Part of this expansion involves commercial activity, which encourages innovations in shipbuilding, and the extensive use of ships causes advances in navigation, astronomy, and geography. The expansion of trade creates towns and cities, which preserve the arts and sciences, thereby encouraging the advance of technologies. Thus, Turgot saw progress in more than a moralistic or metaphorical sense; he recognized that structural changes in one area of a social system, especially in economic activity, create pressures for other changes, with these pressures causing further changes, and so on. This mode of analysis anticipated Marx's economic determinism by 100 years, and it influenced evolutionary theorizing in France for 150 years.

Turgot's next works made more explicit the themes developed in these two early discourses. *On Universal History*[7] and *On Political Geography*[8] were apparently written near the end of Turgot's stay at

---

[7]Meek, *Turgot on Progress.*
[8]Du Pont, *Collected Works.*

the Sorbonne, perhaps around 1755. *On Political Geography* is most noteworthy for its formulation of the three stages of human progress, an idea that became a central part of Comte's view of human evolution. Moreover, Turgot used the notion of universal stages to not only explain human development but also account for the diversity of human societies, an analytical tactic similar to the one used by Montesquieu. All societies of the world are, Turgot argued, at one of three stages, "hunters, shepherds, or husbandmen." In *On Universal History*, he developed the notion of three stages even further, presenting several ideas that became central to Comte's sociology. First, Turgot divided evolution into "mental" and "structural" progression so that development involves change in economic and social structures as well as in idea systems. Second, the progress of society is explicitly viewed as the result of internal structural and cultural forces rather than as a result of intervention by a deity. Third, change and progress can be understood as abstract laws that depict the nature of stasis and change in social systems. And fourth, Turgot's empirical descriptions of what we would now call hunting, horticultural, and agrarian societies are highly detailed and filled with discussion of how structural and cultural conditions at one point create pressures for new structures and ideas at the next point.

Later in his career, probably during the 1760s, Turgot turned his analytical attention increasingly to economic matters. Around 1766, he formulated *Reflections on the Formation and Distribution of Wealth*,[9] which parallels and, to some extent, anticipates the ideas developed by the classical economists in England. Turgot's advocacy of free trade, his analysis of how supply and demand influence prices, and his recognition of the importance of entrepreneurs to economic development are extremely sophisticated for his time. From this analysis, an implicit fourth stage of development is introduced: As capital increasingly becomes concentrated in the hands of entrepreneurs in advanced agricultural societies, a commercial type of society is created. Much of Turgot's description of the transition to, and the arrangements in, this commercial stage were restated by Marx, Spencer, and Comte in the nineteenth century, although only Comte would be directly influenced by Turgot's economic analyses. Yet Comte never expanded Turgot's great insights into the importance of economic variables on the organization and change of society.

---

[9]See Meek, *Turgot on Progress*, for an English translation.

Only the emphasis on entrepreneurial activity in industrial societies was retained, which, in the end, made Comte's analysis of structural change superficial compared with that of Turgot, Spencer, and Marx.

In sum, then, Turgot dramatically altered the course of social thought in the eighteenth century. Extending Montesquieu's ideas in subtle but nevertheless important ways, Turgot developed a mode of analysis that influenced Comte both directly and indirectly. The idea of three stages of progress, the notion that structures at one stage create the necessary conditions for the next, and the stress on the law-like nature of progress became integral parts of Comte's sociology. Much of Turgot's influence on Comte, however, could have been indirect, working its way through Condorcet, whose work was greatly affected by Turgot.[10]

Condorcet and Comte

Jean Condorcet was a student, friend, and great admirer of Turgot; so it is not surprising that his work represents an elaboration of ideas developed by Turgot. Throughout Condorcet's career, which flowered during the French Revolution and then foundered, Condorcet concerned himself with the relation of ideas to social action. In particular, he emphasized the importance of science as a means to achieve the "infinite perfectability" of the "human race." The culmination of his intellectual career was the short and powerful *Sketch for a Historical Picture of the Progress of the Human Mind*,[11] which was written while he was in hiding from an unfavorable political climate.

Written in haste by a man who knew he would soon die, *Progress of the Human Mind* was yet by far his best work. In its hurried passages, Condorcet traced 10 stages of human development, stressing the progression of ideas from the emergence of language and simple customs to the development and elaboration of science. Condorcet felt that with the development of science and its extension to the understanding of society, humans could now direct their future toward infinite perfectibility. Human progress, Condorcet argued, "is subject to the same

---

[10]Indeed, Condorcet wrote *Life of Turgot* in 1786, which Comte, no doubt, read with interest.

[11]Marquis de Condorcet, *Sketch for a Historical Picture of the Progress of the Human Mind* (London: Weidenfeld & Nicolson, 1955; originally published in 1794; translated into English in 1795).

general laws that can be observed in the development of the faculties of the individual," and once these faculties are fully developed,

> the perfectability of man is truly indefinite; and . . . the progress of this perfectability, from now onwards independent of any power that might wish to halt it, has no other limit than the duration of the glove upon which nature has cast us?[12]

The historical details of Condorcet's account are little better than Turgot's, but several important changes in emphasis influenced Comte's thinking. First, Comte's view of progress retained Condorcet's stress on the movement of ideas. Second, Comte reaffirmed the emphasis on science as representing a kind of intellectual takeoff point for human progress. And third, Condorcet's almost religious faith in science as the tool for constructing the "good society" became central to Comte's advocacy. Thus, Comte's great synthesis took elements from Turgot's and Condorcet's related schemes. Comte used Turgot's law of the three stages of progress instead of Condorcet's 10 stages, but preserved Condorcet's emphasis on ideas and on the use of science to realize the laws of progress.

Yet Comte's synthesis was, in some respects, merely an extension of ideas that his master, Saint-Simon, had developed in rough form. And to understand fully the origins of Comte's thought, and hence the emergence of sociology, we must explore the volatile relationship between Saint-Simon and Comte. Sociology was born as a self-conscious field of inquiry from their interaction.

Saint-Simon and Comte

In many ways, Claude-Henri de Saint-Simon represented a bridge between the eighteenth century and the early nineteenth century. Born into an aristocratic family, Saint-Simon initially pursued a nonacademic career. He fought with the French in the American Revolution; traveled the world; proposed a number of engineering projects, including the Panama Canal; was politically active during the French Revolution; became a land speculator in the aftermath of the

---

[12]Condorcet, *Sketch for a Historical Picture* (4). The term *glove* here is ambiguous. It appears to refer to the constraints that the natural world imposes, although these constraints are but minimal—a gloved and gentle hand as opposed to a heavy hand.

1789 Revolution; and amassed and then lost a large fortune. Only late in life, at the turn of the century, did he become a dedicated scholar.[13]

The relationship between Saint-Simon's and Comte's ideas has been debated ever since their violent quarrel and separation in 1824. Just what part of Saint-Simon's work is Comte's, and vice versa, will never be completely determined. But it is clear that between 1800 and 1817, Saint-Simon's ideas were not influenced by Comte because the young Comte did not join the aging Saint-Simon as a secretary, student, and collaborator until 1817. In the 7 years between 1817 and 1824, Comte's and Saint-Simon's ideas were intermingled, but we can see in the pre-1817 works of Saint-Simon many of the ideas that became a part of Comte's sociology.[14] The most reasonable interpretation of their collaboration is that Comte took many of the crude and unsystematic ideas of Saint-Simon, refined and polished them in accordance with his greater grasp of history and science, and extended them in small but critical ways as a result of his exposure to Montesquieu, Turgot, Condorcet, Adam Smith, and the traditionalists. To appreciate Saint-Simon's unique contribution to the emergence of sociology, then, we must examine first the period between 1800 and 1817 and then the post-1817 work, with speculation on the contribution by Comte to this later work.

Saint-Simon's Early Work

Saint-Simon read Condorcet carefully and concluded that the scientific revolution had set the stage for a science of social organization.[15] Saint-Simon argued in his first works that the study of humankind and society must be a "positive" science, based on empirical observation. Like many others of this period, Saint-Simon saw the

---

[13]See Keith Taylor, *Henri Saint-Simon* (London: Croom Helm, 1975), 13–29, for a concise biographical sketch of Saint-Simon.

[14]The most important of these works are *Letters From an Inhabitant of Geneva* (1803), *Introduction to the Scientific Studies of the Nineteenth Century* (1807–1808), *Essays on the Science of Man* (1813), and *The Reorganization of the European Community* (1814). Unfortunately, much of Saint-Simon is unavailable in English translations. For convenient secondary works where portions of these appear, see F. M. H. Markham, *Henri Comte de Saint-Simon* (New York: Macmillan, 1952); and Taylor, *Henri Saint-Simon.* For interesting commentaries, see G. G. Iggers, *The Political Philosophy of Saint-Simon* (The Hague, Netherlands: Mouton, 1958); F. E. Manuel, *The New World of Henri de Saint-Simon* (Cambridge, UK: Cambridge University Press, 1956); and Alvin Gouldner, *Socialism and Saint-Simon* (Yellow Springs, OH: Collier, 1962).

[15]Saint-Simon gave Condorcet explicit credit for many of his ideas.

study of society as a branch of physiology because society is a type of organic phenomenon. Like any organic body, society is governed by natural laws of development, which are to be revealed by scientific observation. As an *organism*, then, society would be studied by investigating social organization, with particular emphasis on the nature of growth, order, stability, and abnormal pathologies.[16]

Saint-Simon saw that such a viewoint argued for a three-part program: (1) "a series of observations on the course of civilization" must be the starting point of the new science; (2) from these observations, the laws of social organization would be revealed; and (3) on the basis of these laws, humans could construct the best form of social organization. From a rather naive and ignorant view of history,[17] Saint-Simon developed a law of history in which ideas move from a polytheistic stage to a Christian theism and then to a positivistic stage. In his eye, each set of ideas in human history had been essential in maintaining social order, and with each transition came a period of crisis. The transition to positivism, therefore, revolved around the collapse of the feudal order and its religious underpinnings. Yet the establishment of an industrial order in European societies, with its positivistic culture of science, was still incomplete.

In analyzing this crisis in European society, Saint-Simon noted that scientific observations had first penetrated astronomy, then physics and chemistry, and finally physiology, including both biological and social organs.[18] With the application of the scientific method to social organization, the traditional order must give way to a new system of ideas. Transitional attempts to restore order, such as the "legal–metaphysical" ideas of the eighteenth century, must yield to a "terrestrial morality" based on the ideas of positivism—that is, the use of observations to formulate, test, and implement the laws of social organization.[19]

Founded on a terrestrial morality, this new order resulted from a collaboration of scientists and industrialists. In Saint-Simon's early thought, scientists were to be the theoreticians, and industrialists were to be the engineers who performed many of the practical tasks

---

[16]The French word *organization* means both "organization" and "organic structure." Saint-Simon initially used the term to refer to the organic structure of humans and animals and then extended it to apply to the structure of society.

[17]For an interesting commentary, see Walter M. Simon, "Ignorance Is Bliss: Saint-Simon and the Writing of History," *International Review of Philosophy*, 14, nos. 3 and 4 (1960), 357–383.

[18]See Peyton V. Lyon, "Saint-Simon and the Origins of Scientism and Historicism," *Canadian Journal of Economics and Political Science* 27 (February 1961), 55–63.

[19]These ideas begin to overlap with Saint-Simon's collaboration with Comte.

of reconstructing society. Indeed, scientists and industrialists were to be the new priests for the secular religion of positivism. Saint-Simon's thought on social reorganization, however, underwent considerable change between 1814 and 1825, when he fell ill. The increasingly political and religious tone of his writings alienated the young Comte, who saw the more detailed study of history and the movement of ideas as necessary for the formulation of the scientific laws of social organization. Ironically, Comte's own work, later in his career, took on the same religious fervor and extremes as Saint-Simon's last efforts.

Comte's early sociological work owed much to Saint-Simon's initial period of intellectual activity. The law of the three stages became even more prominent; the recognition of the successive penetration of positivism into astronomy, physics, chemistry, and biology was translated into a hierarchy of sciences, with physics at the bottom and sociology at the top; and the belief that sociology could be used to reconstruct industrial society became part of Comte's program. Comte, however, rejected much of Saint-Simon's argument. In particular, Comte did not accept the study of social organization as a part of physiology; rather, he argued that sociology was a distinct science with its own unique principles. In this vein, he also rejected Saint-Simon's belief that one law of the entire universe could be discovered; instead, Comte recognized that each science had its own unique subject matter, which could be fully understood only through its own laws and principles. These objections aside, much of Comte's early work represented the elaboration of ideas developed and then abandoned by Saint-Simon as the aging scholar became increasingly absorbed in the task of reconstructing society.

Saint-Simon's Later Work

After 1814, Saint-Simon turned increasingly to political and economic commentary. He established and edited a series of periodicals to propagate his ideas on the use of scientists and industrialists to reconstruct society.[20] His terrestrial morality thus became elaborated into a plan for political, economic, and social reform.

---

[20]All these journals were short-lived, but they eventually gave Saint-Simon some degree of recognition as a publicist. These journals included *The Industry* (1816–1818); *The Political* (1819); *The Organizer* (1819–1820); *On the Industrial System* (1821–1822), actually a series of brochures; *Disasters of Industry* (1823–1824); and *Literary, Philosophic, and Industrial Opinions* (1825). From the latter, a portion on religion was published separately in book form as *New Christianity*, Saint-Simon's last major statement on science and the social order. Another important work of this last period was *On Social Organization.* In all these works, there is a clear change in tone and mood; Saint-Simon is now the activist rather than the detached scholar.

The emphasis was on *terrestrial* because Saint-Simon argued that the old supernatural basis for achieving order could no longer prevail in the positivistic age. Yet by his death, he recognized that a "religious sense" and "feeling" are essential to the social order. People must have faith and must believe in a common set of ideas, a theme that marked all French sociology in the nineteenth century. The goal of terrestrial morality, therefore, is to create the functional equivalent of religion with positivism. Scientists and artists are to be the priests and the "spiritual" leaders,[21] and industrialists are to be the "temporal" leaders and are to implement the spiritual program by applying scientific methods to production and the organization of labor.

For Saint-Simon, terrestrial morality had both spiritual and temporal components. Spiritual leaders give a sense of direction and a new religious sense to societal activity. Temporal leaders ensure the organization of industry in ways that destroy hereditary privilege and give people an equal chance to realize their full potential. The key to Saint-Simon's program, then, was to use science as the functional equivalent of religion and to destroy the idle classes so that each person worked to his or her full potential. Although he visualized considerable control of economic and social activity by government (to prevent exploitation of workers by the "idle"), Saint-Simon also believed that people should be free to realize their potential. Thus, his doctrine is a mixture of free enterprise economics and a tempered but heavy dose of governmental control (an emphasis that has often led commentators to place him in the socialist camp).

Saint-Simon's specific political, educational, and social programs were, even for his time, naive and utopian, but they nevertheless set into motion an entire intellectual movement after his death. Comte, however, was highly critical of Saint-Simon's later writings, and Comte waged intellectual war with the Saint-Simonians after 1825. Although Comte wrote much of Saint-Simon's work between 1817 and 1824, Comte's contribution is recognizable because it is more academic and reasoned than is Saint-Simon's advocacy.[22] Later, Comte's own work took on the same religious extremes as Saint-Simon's. Thus, Comte clearly accepted in delayed and subliminal form much of Saint-Simon's advocacy of science as a functional substitute for religion.

---

[21]Saint-Simon was initially anti-Christian, but with New Christianity, he changed his position so that the new spiritual heads of society were "true Christians" in that they captured and advocated the implementation of the "Christian spirit."

[22]For example, Comte wrote much of *The Organizer* (1819–1820), especially the historical and scientific sections.

Comte's real contribution comes not from Saint-Simon's political commentary but, rather, from his systematization of Saint-Simon's early historical and scientific work because from this effort sociology as a self-conscious discipline emerged.

Conclusion

We can see that Saint-Simon's work encompassed both liberal and conservative elements. He advocated change and individual freedom; yet he desired that change produce a new social order and that individual freedom be subordinated to the collective interests of society. Comte's work also revealed this mixture of liberal and conservative elements, in that the ideas of economic liberals, such as Adam Smith, and conservatives or traditionalists, like de Maistre and de Bonald, all played a part in his intellectual scheme.

Liberal Elements in Comte's Thought

In England, Adam Smith (1723–1790) had the most decisive effect on social thought in his advocacy of an economic system consisting of free and competitive markets. His *Wealth of Nations* (1776), however, is more than a simple model of early capitalism; the fifth book reveals a theory of moral sentiments and raises a question that concerned Comte and, later, Durkheim: How can society be held together at the same time that the division of labor compartmentalizes individuals? For Smith, this dilemma was not insurmountable, whereas for French sociologists who had experienced the disintegrative effects of the revolution and its aftermath, splitting society into diverse occupations posed a real intellectual problem. For French sociologists, the solution to this liberal dilemma involved creating a strong state that coordinated activities, preserved individual liberties, and fostered a set of unifying values and beliefs.

Comte also absorbed liberal ideas from the French followers of Smith, particularly Jean-Baptiste Say, who had seen the creative role played by entrepreneurs in the organization of major economic elements (land, labor, capital). Saint-Simon appears to have had a notion of entrepreneurship in his proposal that the details of societal reconstruction be left to "industrialists," but Say's explicit formulation of the creative coordination of labor and capital by those with "industry" explicitly influenced Comte's vision of how entrepreneurs could create a better society.[23]

Traditional Elements in Comte's Thought

Saint-Simon had attacked those who, in the turmoil of the revolution, wanted to return to the Old Regime. Writing from outside France, Catholic scholars such as de Maistre and de Bonald argued that the revolution had destroyed the structural and moral fiber of society.[24] Religious authority had not been replaced by an alternative, the order achieved from the old social hierarchies had not been reestablished, and the cohesiveness provided by local communities and groups had been allowed to disintegrate. Both Saint-Simon and Comte, as well as an entire generation of French thinkers, agreed with the traditionalists' diagnosis of the problem but disagreed with the proposed solution. The traditionalists believed that the solution was the reinstatement of religion, hierarchy, and traditional local groupings (on the feudal model).

Although Comte became an atheist in his early teens, he had been reared as a Catholic; hence, he shared with many of the traditionalists a concern about order and spiritual unity. The Enlightenment and liberal economic doctrines had also influenced him, and thus, he saw that a return to the old order was not possible. Rather, it was necessary to create the functional equivalent of religious authority and to reestablish non-ascriptive hierarchies and communities that would give people an equal chance to realize their full potential. For Comte, then, the religious element is to be secular and positivistic; hierarchies are to be based on ability and achievement rather than on ascriptive privilege; and community is to be re-created through the solidarity of industrial groups. He thus gave the traditionalists' concerns a liberal slant, although his last works were decidedly authoritarian in tone, perhaps revealing the extent to which the traditionalists' ideas had remained with him.

In reviewing the specific thinkers who preceded Comte, we can see that the emergence of sociology was probably inevitable. Science had become too widespread to be suppressed by a return to religious orthodoxy, and the economic and political transformations of society

---

[23]Naturally, Say and Saint-Simon did not explicitly use the concept of *entrepreneurs*, but they clearly grasped the essence of this economic function.

[24]See Robert A. Nisbet, *Tradition and Revolt* (New York: Random House, 1968).

that industrialization and urbanization caused needed explanation. All that was necessary was for one scholar to take that final step and seek to create a science of society. Drawing from the leads his predecessors provided, Auguste Comte took this final step. In so doing, he gave the science of society a name and a vision of how it should construct theory. Now, let us turn to the substance of Comte's vision.

CHAPTER 3

The Sociology of Auguste Comte

As we outlined in Chapter 1, it is perhaps embarrassing to sociology that its founder was, by the end of his life, a rather pathetic man, calling himself the High Priest of Humanity and preaching to a ragtag group of disciples. In essence, Comte's career had two phases: (1) the early scientific stage where he argued persuasively for a science of society and was the toast of continental Europe for a brief time and (2) a later phase when he tried to make science a new religion for the reconstruction of society. The first phase culminated in his famous, *Course of Positive Philosphy*,[1] a monumental five-volume work that was published serially between 1830 and 1842. The second phase was marked by Comte's personal frustrations and tragedy that found expression in *System of Positive Polity*,[2] published between 1851 and 1854. Even as Comte went over the deep end, he retained a firm belief that discovery of the laws governing the operation of human societies should be used to reconstruct society. For Comte, science did not oppose efforts to

---

[1]We will use and reference Harriet Martineau's condensation of the original manuscript. This condensation received Comte's approval and is the most readily available translation. Martineau changed the title and added useful margin notes. Our references will be to the 1896 edition of Martineau's original 1854 edition: Auguste Comte, *The Positive Philosophy of Auguste Comte*, Vols. 1, 2, and 3, trans. and cond. H. Martineau (London: George Bell & Sons, 1896).

[2]Auguste Comte, *System of Positive Polity*, Vols. 1, 2, 3, and 4 (New York: Burt Franklin, 1875; originally published 1851–1854).

make a better world, but it was first necessary to develop the science half of this equation. For, without deep scientific understanding of how society operates, it is difficult to know how to go about constructing a better society. This theme in Comte's work was simply an extension of the French philosophes' Enlightenment view that human society was progressing to ever-better states of organization.

In our review of Comte's work, we will focus on the early phase where Comte developed a vision for sociology. Indeed, he argued that sociology was to be the "queen science" that would stand at the top of a hierarchy of all sciences—an outrageous prediction but one that gathered a considerable amount of attention in his early writings. Comte's abrasive personality was, eventually, to be his undoing; by the time the last installment of *Course of Positive Philosophy* was published, he was a forgotten intellect. Indeed, not one single review of this last installment appeared in French intellectual circles, but Comte's stamp on the discipline had already been achieved early in his career. Moreover, scholars in England were reading Comte, and subsequent generations of French thinkers all had to come to grips with Comte's advocacy.

Comte's first essays signaled the beginning of sociology; his great *Course of Positive Philosophy* made a convincing case for the discipline. And his later descent can be ignored for what it was—the mental pathology of a once-great mind. Let us begin with the early essays and then move to the argument in *Course of Positive Philosophy*.

Comte's Early Essays

It is sometimes difficult to separate Comte's early essays from those of Saint-Simon, because the aging master often put his name on works written by the young Comte. Yet the 1822 essay, "Plan of the Scientific Operations Necessary for Reorganizing Society,"[3] is clearly Comte's and represents the culmination of his thinking while working under Saint-Simon. This essay also anticipates, and presents an outline of, the entire Comtean scheme as it was to unfold over the succeeding decades.

In this essay, Comte argued that it was necessary to create a "positive science" based on the model of other sciences. This science

---

[3]Auguste Comte, "Plan of the Scientific Operations Necessary for Reorganizing Society," reprinted in Gertrud Lenzer, ed., *Auguste Comte and Positivism: The Essential Writings* (New York: Harper Torchbooks, 1975), 9–69.

would ultimately rest on empirical observations, but, like all science, it would formulate the laws governing the organization and movement of society, an idea implicit in Montesquieu's *The Spirit of Laws*. Comte initially called this new science *social physics*. Once the laws of human organization have been discovered and formulated, Comte believed that these laws could be used to direct society. Scientists of society are thus to be social prophets, indicating the course and direction of human organization.

Comte felt that one of the most basic laws of human organization was the "law of the three stages," a notion clearly borrowed from Turgot, Condorcet, and Saint-Simon. He termed these stages the *theological–military*, *metaphysical–judicial*, and *scientific–industrial* or "positivistic." Each stage is typified by a particular "spirit"—a notion that first appeared with Montesquieu and was expanded by Condorcet—and by temporal or structural conditions. Thus, the theological–military stage is dominated by ideas that refer to the supernatural while being structured around slavery and the military. The metaphysical–judicial stage, which follows from the theological and represents a transition to the scientific, is typified by ideas that refer to the fundamental essences of phenomena and by elaborate political and legal forms. The scientific–industrial stage is dominated by the "positive philosophy of science" and industrial patterns of social organization.

Several points in this law were given greater emphasis in Comte's later work. First, the social world reveals both cultural and structural dimensions, with the nature of culture or idea systems being dominant—an idea probably taken from Condorcet. Second, idea systems, and the corresponding structural arrangements that they produce, must reach their full development before the next stage of human evolution can occur. Thus, one stage of development creates the necessary conditions for the next. Third, there is always a period of crisis and conflict as systems move from one stage to the next because elements of the previous stage conflict with the emerging elements of the next stage. Fourth, movement is always a kind of oscillation, for society "does not, properly speaking, advance in a straight line."

These aspects of the law of three stages convinced Comte that cultural ideas about the world were subject to the dictates of this law. All ideas about the nature of the universe must move from a theological to a scientific, or positivistic, stage. Yet some ideas about different aspects of the universe move more rapidly through the three stages than others do. Indeed, only when all the other sciences—first astronomy, then physics, later chemistry, and finally physiology—have successively reached the positive stage will the conditions necessary for social physics have been met. With the development of this last great science, it will become possible to reorganize society by scientific principles rather than by theological or metaphysical speculations.

Comte thus felt that the age of sociology had arrived. It was to be like Newton's physics, formulating the laws of the social universe. With the development of these laws, the stage was set for the rational and scientific reorganization of society. Much of Saint-Simon is in this advocacy, but Comte felt that Saint-Simon was too impatient in his desire to reorganize society without the proper scientific foundation. The result was Comte's *Course of Positive Philosophy*, which sought to lay the necessary intellectual foundation for the science of society.

Comte's *Course of Positive Philosophy*

Comte's *Course of Positive Philosophy* is more noteworthy for its advocacy of a science of society than for its substantive contribution to understanding how patterns of social organization are created, maintained, and changed. *Positive Philosophy* more nearly represents a vision of what sociology can become than a well-focused set of theoretical principles. In reviewing this great work, then, we will devote most of our attention to how Comte defined sociology and how he thought it should be developed. Accordingly, we will divide our discussion into the following sections: (1) Comte's view of sociological theory, (2) his formulation of sociological methods, (3) his organization of sociology, and (4) his advocacy of sociology.

Comte's View of Sociological Theory

As a descendant of the French Enlightenment, Comte was impressed, as were many of the philosophes, with the Newtonian revolution. Thus, he argued for a particular view of sociological theory: All phenomena are subject to invariable natural laws, and sociologists must use their observations to uncover the laws governing the social universe, in much the same way as Newton had formulated the law of gravity. Comte emphasized in the opening pages of *Positive Philosophy*,

The first characteristic of Positive Philosophy is that it regards all phenomena as subject to invariable natural *Laws*. Our business is—seeing how vain is any research into what are called *Causes* whether first or final—to pursue an accurate discovery of these Laws, with a view to reducing them to the smallest possible number. By speculating upon causes, we could solve no difficulty about origin and purpose. Our real business is to analyse accurately the circumstances of phenomena, and to connect them by the natural relations of succession and resemblance. The best illustration of this is in the case of the doctrine of Gravitation.[4]

Several points are important in this view of sociological theory. First, sociological theory is not to be concerned with causes per se but, rather, with the laws that describe the basic and fundamental relations of properties in the social world. Second, sociological theory must reject arguments by "final causes"—that is, analysis of the results of a particular phenomenon for the social whole. This disavowal is ironic because Comte's more substantive work helped found sociological functionalism, a mode of analysis that often examines the functions or final causes of phenomena. Third, clearly the goal of sociological activity is to reduce the number of theoretical principles by seeking only the most abstract and only those that pertain to understanding fundamental properties of the social world. Comte thus held a vision of sociological theory as based on the model of the natural sciences, particularly the physics of his time. For this reason, he preferred the term *social physics* to *sociology*.[5]

The laws of social organization and change, Comte felt, will be discovered, refined, and verified through a constant interplay between theory and empirical observation. For, as he emphasized in the opening pages of *Positive Philosophy*, "if it is true that every

---

[4]Comte, *Positive Philosophy*, 1:5–6 (emphasis in original).

[5]In Comte's time, the term *physics* meant to study the "nature of" phenomena; it was not merely the term for a particular branch of natural science. Hence, Comte's use of the label *social physics* had a double meaning: to study the "nature of" social phenomena and to do so along the lines of the natural sciences. He abandoned the term *social physics* when he realized that the Belgian statistician Adolphe Quételet was using the same term. Comte was outraged that his original label for sociology had been used in ways that ran decidedly counter to his vision of theory. Ironically, sociology has become more like Quételet's vision of social physics, with its emphasis on the normal curve and statistical manipulations, than like Comte's notion of social physics as the search for the abstract laws of human organization—an unfortunate turn of events.

theory must be based upon observed facts, it is equally true that facts cannot be observed without the guidance of some theory."[6] In later pages, Comte became even more assertive and argued against what we might now term *raw empiricism*. The collection of data for its own sake runs counter to the goals of science:

> The next great hindrance to the use of observation is the empiricism which is introduced into it by those who, in the name of impartiality, would interdict the use of any theory whatever. No other dogma could be more thoroughly irreconcilable with the spirit of the positive philosophy. . . . No real observation of any kind of phenomena is possible, except in as far as it is first directed, and finally interpreted, by some theory.[7]

And he concluded,

> Hence it is clear that, scientifically speaking, all isolated, empirical observation is idle, and even radically uncertain; that science can use only those observations which are connected, at least hypothetically, with some law.[8]

For Comte, then, sociology's goal was to seek to develop abstract theoretical principles. Observations of the empirical world must be guided by such principles, and abstract principles must be tested against the empirical facts. Empirical observations that are conducted without this goal in mind are not useful in science. Theoretical explanation of empirical events thus involves seeing how they are connected in lawlike ways. For social science "endeavors to discover . . . the general relations which connect all social phenomena; and each of them is *explained*, in the scientific sense of the word, when it has been connected with the whole of the existing situation."[9]

Comte held a somewhat ambiguous view of how such an abstract science should be "used" in the practical world of everyday affairs. He clearly intended that sociology must initially establish a firm theoretical foundation before making efforts to use the laws of sociology for social engineering. In *Positive Philosophy*, he stressed,

---

[6]Comte, *Positive Philosophy*, 1:4.
[7]Comte, *Positive Philosophy*, 2:242.
[8]Ibid., 243.
[9]Ibid., 240 (emphasis in original).

> We must distinguish between the two classes of Natural science—the abstract or general, which have for their object the discovery of the laws which regulate phenomena in all conceivable cases, and the concrete, particular, or descriptive, which are sometimes called Natural sciences in a restricted sense, whose function it is to apply these laws to the actual history of existing beings. The first are fundamental, and our business is with them alone; as the second are derived, and however important, they do not rise to the rank of our subjects of contemplation.[10]

Comte believed that sociology must not allow its scientific mission to be confounded by empirical descriptions or by an excessive concern with a desire to manipulate events. Once sociology is well established as a theoretical science, its laws can be used to "modify" events in the empirical world. Indeed, such was to be the historic mission of social physics. As Comte's later works testify, he took this mission seriously, and at times to extremes. But his early work is filled with more reasoned arguments for using laws of social organization and change as tools for creating new social arrangements. He stressed that the complexity of social phenomena gives them more variation than either physical or biological phenomena have, and hence it would be possible to use the laws of social organization and change to modify empirical events in a variety of directions.[11]

In sum, then, Comte believed that sociology could be modeled after the natural sciences. Sociology could seek and discover the fundamental properties and relations of the social universe, and like the other sciences, it could express these in a small number of abstract principles. Observations of empirical events could be used to generate, confirm, and modify sociology's laws. Once well-developed laws had been formulated, they could be used as tools or instruments to modify the social world.

Comte's Formulation of Sociological Methods

Comte was the first social thinker to take methodological questions seriously—that is, how are facts about the social world to be gathered and used to develop, as well as to test, theoretical principles?

---

[10]Comte, *Positive Philosophy*, 1:23.

[11]See, for example, the following passages in *Positive Philosophy*, 2:217, 226, 234, 235, and 238.

He advocated four methods in the new science of social physics: (1) observation, (2) experimentation, (3) comparison, and (4) historical analysis.[12]

Observation

For Comte, positivism was based on use of the senses to observe *social facts*—a term that the next great French theorist, Émile Durkheim, made the center of his sociology. Much of Comte's discussion of observation involves arguments for the "subordination of Observation to the statical and dynamical laws of phenomena"[13] rather than a statement on the procedures by which unbiased observations should be conducted. He argued that observation of empirical facts, when unguided by theory, will prove useless in the development of science. He must be given credit, however, for firmly establishing sociology as a science of social facts, thereby liberating thought from the debilitating realm of morals and metaphysical speculation.

Experimentation

Comte recognized that artificial experimentation with whole societies, and other social phenomena, was impractical and often impossible. But, he noted, natural experimentation frequently "takes place whenever the regular course of the phenomenon is interfered with in any determinate manner."[14] In particular, he thought that, much as is the case in biology, pathological events allowed "the true equivalent of pure experimentation" in that they introduced an artificial condition and allowed investigators to see normal processes reassert themselves in the face of the pathological condition. Much as the biologist can learn about normal bodily functioning from the study of disease, so also social physicists can learn about the normal processes of society from the study of pathological cases. Thus, although Comte's view of "natural experimentation" was certainly deficient in the logic of the experimental method, it nonetheless fascinated subsequent generations of scholars.

---

[12]Comte, *Positive Philosophy*, 2:241–257.
[13]Ibid., 245.
[14]Ibid., 246.

Comparison

Just as comparative analysis had been useful in biology, comparison of social forms with those of lower animals, with coexisting states, and with past systems could also generate considerable insight into the operation of the social universe. By comparing elements that are present and absent, and similar or dissimilar, knowledge about the fundamental properties of the social world can be achieved.

Historical Analysis

Comte originally classified historical analysis as a variation of the comparative method (i.e., comparing the present with the past). But his "law of the three stages" emphasized that the laws of social dynamics could ultimately be developed only with careful observations of the historical movement of societies.

In sum, then, Comte saw these four basic methods as appropriate to sociological analysis. His formulation of the methods is quite deficient by modern standards, but we should recognize that before Comte, little attention had been paid to how social facts were to be collected. Thus, although the specifics of Comte's methodological proposals are not always useful, their spirit and intent are important. Social physics was, in his vision, to be a theoretical science capable of formulating and testing the laws of social organization and change. His formulation of sociology's methods added increased credibility to this claim.

Comte's Organization of Sociology

Much as Saint-Simon had emphasized, Comte saw sociology as an extension of biology, which studies the "organs" in "organisms." Hence, sociology was to be the study of social *organ*ization. This emphasis forces the recognition that society is an "organic whole" whose component "organs" stand in relation to one another. To study these parts in isolation is to violate the essence of social organization and to compartmentalize inquiry artificially. As Comte emphasized, "there can be no scientific study of society, either in its conditions or its movements, if it is separated into portions, and its divisions are studied apart."[15]

---

[15]Ibid., 225.

Implicit in this mode of analysis is a theoretical approach that later became known as *functionalism*. As biology's prestige grew during the nineteenth century, attempts at linking sociological analysis to the respected biological sciences increased. Eventually, scholars began asking the following questions: What is the function of a structure for the body social? That is, what does a structure "do for" the social whole? Comte implicitly asked such questions and even offered explicit analogies to encourage subsequent organismic analogizing. For example, his concern with social pathology revealing the normal operation of society is only one illustration of a biological mode of reasoning. In his later work, Comte viewed various structures as analogous to "elements, tissues, and organs" of biological organisms.[16] In his early works, however, this organismic analogizing is limited to dividing social physics into statical and dynamical analysis.

This division, we suspect, represents a merger of Comte's efforts to build sociology on biology and to retain his heritage from the French Enlightenment. As a scholar who was writing in the tumultuous aftermath of the French Revolution, he was concerned with order and stability. The order of biological organisms, with their interdependent parts and processes of self-maintenance, offered him a vision of how social order should be constructed. Yet the Enlightenment had emphasized "progress" and movement of social systems, holding out the vision of better things to come. For this reason, Comte was led to emphasize that the "ideas of Order and Progress are, in Social Physics, as rigorously inseparable as the ideas of Organization and Life in Biology: from whence indeed they are, in a scientific view, evidently derived."[17] And thus he divided sociology into (1) social statics (the study of social order) and (2) social dynamics (the study of social progress and change).

Social Statics

Comte defined social statics as the study of social structure, its elements, and their relations. He first analyzed "individuals" as the elements of social structure. Generally, he viewed the individual as a series of capacities and needs, some innate and others acquired through participation in society.[18] He did not view the individual as a

---

[16]See, in particular, his *System of Positive Polity*, 2:221–276, on "The Social Organism."

[17]Comte, *Positive Philosophy*, 2:141.

[18]Ibid., 275–281.

"true social unit"; indeed, he relegated the study of the individual to biology—an unfortunate oversight because it denied the legitimacy of psychology as a distinct social science. The most basic social unit, he argued, is "the family." It is the most elementary unit, from which all other social units ultimately evolved:

> As every system must be composed of elements of the same nature with itself, the scientific spirit forbids us to regard society as composed of individuals. The true social unit is certainly the family—reduced, if necessary, to the elementary couple which forms its basis. This consideration implies more than the physiological truth that families become tribes, and tribes become nations: so that the whole human race might be conceived of as the gradual development of a single family. . . . There is a political point of view from which also we must consider this elementary idea, inasmuch as the family presents the true germ of the various characteristics of the social organism.[19]

Comte believed that social structures could not be reduced to the properties of individuals. Rather, social structures are composed of other structures and can be understood only as the properties of, and relations among, these other structures. Comte's analysis of the family then moves to descriptions of its structure—first the sexual division of labor and then the parental relation. The specifics of his analysis are not important because they are flawed and inaccurate. Far more important is the view of structure that he implied: social structures are composed of substructures and develop from the elaboration of simpler structures.

After establishing this basic point, Comte moved to the analysis of societal structures. His opening remarks reveal his debt to biological analysis and the functional orientation it inspired:

> The main cause of the superiority of the social to the individual organism is according to an established law; the more marked is the specialization of the various functions fulfilled by organs more and more distinct, but interconnected; so that unity of aim is more and more combined with diversity of means.[20]

---

[19]Ibid., 280–281.
[20]Ibid., 289.

Thus, as social systems develop, they become increasingly differentiated, and yet like all organisms, they maintain their integration. This view of social structure led Comte to the problem that Adam Smith had originally suggested with such force: How is integration among parts maintained despite increasing differentiation of functions? This question occupied French sociology in the nineteenth century, culminating in Durkheim's theoretical formulations. Comte emphasized,

> If the separation of social functions develops a useful spirit of detail, on the one hand, it tends on the other, to extinguish or to restrict what we may call the aggregate or general spirit. In the same way, in moral relations, while each is in close dependence on the mass, he is drawn away from it by the expansion of his special activity, constantly recalling him to his private interest, which he but very dimly perceives to be related to the public.[21]

Comte's proposed solution to this problem reveals much about how he viewed the maintenance of social structure. First, the centralization of power in government counters the potentially disintegrating impact of social differentiation, which will then maintain fluid coordination among system parts. Second, the actions of government must be more than "material"; they must also be "intellectual and moral."[22] Hence, human social organization is maintained by (1) mutual dependence of system parts on one another, (2) centralization of authority to coordinate exchanges among parts, and (3) development of a common morality or spirit among members of a population. To the extent that differentiating systems cannot meet these conditions, pathological states are likely to occur. Figure 3.1 shows Comte's implicit model of social statics.

In presenting this analysis, Comte felt that he had uncovered several laws of social statics because he believed that differentiation, centralization of power, and development of a common morality were fundamentally related to the maintenance of the social order. Although he did not carry his analysis far, he presented both Herbert Spencer and Durkheim with one of the basic theoretical questions in sociology and the broad contours of the answer.

---

[21]Ibid., 293.
[22]Ibid., 294.

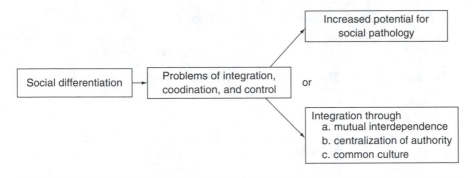

Figure 3.1   Comte's Implicit Model of Social Statics

Social Dynamics

Comte appeared far more interested in social dynamics than in statics, for

> the dynamical view is not only the more interesting . . . , but the more marked in its philosophical character, from its being more distinguished from biology by the master-thought of continuous progress, or rather of the gradual development of humanity.[23]

Social dynamics studies the "laws of succession," or the patterns of change in social systems over time. In this context, Comte formulated the details of his law of the three stages, in which idea systems, and their corresponding social structural arrangements, pass through three phases: (1) the theological, (2) the metaphysical, and (3) the positivistic. The basic cultural and structural features of these stages are summarized in Table 3.1.

Table 3.1 ignores many details that have little relevance to theory,[24] but the table communicates, in a rough fashion, Comte's view of the laws of succession. Several points should be noted: First, each stage sets the conditions for the next. For example, without efforts to explain references to the supernatural, subsequent efforts at more refined explanations would not have been possible; or without kinship systems, subsequent political, legal, and military development would not have occurred, and the modern division of labor would not have been possible. Second, the course of

---

[23]Ibid., 227.

[24]Most of *Positive Philosophy*, Vol. 3, is devoted to the analysis of the three stages. For an abbreviated overview, see Vol. 2:304–333.

Table 3.1   Comte's "Law of the Three Stages"

System	Stages		
	Theological	**Metaphysical**	**Positivistic**
1. Cultural (moral) system			
a. Nature of ideas	Ideas are focused on nonempirical forces, spirits, and beings in the supernatural realm	Ideas are focused on the essences of phenomena and rejection of appeals to supernatural	Ideas are developed from observation and constrained by the scientific method; speculation not based on observation of empirical facts is rejected
b. Spiritual leaders	Priests	Philosophers	Scientists
2. Structural (temporal) system			
a. Most prominent units	Kinship	State	Industry
b. Basis of integration	Attachment to small groups and religious spirit; use of coercive force to sustain commitment to religion	Control by state, military, and law	Mutual dependence; coordination of functions by state and general spirit

evolution is additive: New ideas and structural arrangements are added to, and build on, the old. For instance, kinship does not disappear, nor do references to the supernatural. They are first supplemented, and then dominated, by new social and cultural arrangements. Third, during the transition from one stage to the next, elements of the preceding stage conflict with elements of the emerging stage, creating a period of anarchy and turmoil. Fourth, the metaphysical stage is a transitional stage, operating as a bridge between theological speculation and positivistic philosophy. Fifth, the nature of cultural ideas determines the nature of social structural (temporal) arrangements and circumscribe what social arrangements are possible. And sixth, with the advent of the positivistic stage, true understanding of how society operates is possible, allowing the manipulation of society in accordance with the laws of statics and dynamics.

Although societies must eventually pass through these three stages, they do so at different rates. Probably the most important of the variable empirical conditions influencing the rate of societal succession is population size and density, an idea taken from Montesquieu and later refined by Durkheim. Thus, Comte felt that he had discovered the basic law of social dynamics in his analysis of the three stages, and coupled with the laws of statics, a positivistic science of society—that is, social physics or sociology—would allow for the reorganization of the tumultuous, transitional, and conflictual world of the early nineteenth century.

Comte's Advocacy of Sociology

Comte's *Positive Philosophy* can be viewed as a long and elaborate advocacy for a science of society. Most of the five volumes review the development of other sciences, showing how sociology represents the culmination of positivism. As the title, *Positive Philosophy*, underscores, Comte was laying a philosophical foundation and justification for all science and then using this foundation as a means for supporting sociology as a true science. His advocacy took two related forms: (1) to view sociology as the inevitable product of the law of the three stages and (2) to view sociology as the "queen science," standing at the top of a hierarchy of sciences. These two interrelated forms of advocacy helped legitimate sociology in the intellectual world and should, therefore, be examined briefly.

Comte saw all idea systems as passing through the theological and metaphysical stages and then moving into the final, positivistic, stage. Ideas about all phenomena must pass through these phases, with each stage setting the conditions for the next and with considerable intellectual turmoil occurring during the transition from one stage to the next. Ideas about various phenomena, however, do not pass through these stages at the same rate, and, in fact, a positivistic stage in thought about one realm of the universe must often be reached before ideas about other realms can progress to the positivistic stage. The opening pages of *Positive Philosophy* emphasize,

We must bear in mind that the different kinds of our knowledge have passed through the three stages of progress at different rates, and have not therefore arrived at the same time. The rate of advance depends upon the nature of knowledge in question, so distinctly that, as we shall see hereafter, this consideration constitutes an accessory to the fundamental law of progress. Any kind of knowledge reaches the positive stage in proportion to its generality, simplicity, and independence of other departments.[25]

Thus, thought about the physical universe reaches the positive stage before conceptions of the organic world do because the inorganic world is simpler and organic phenomena are built from inorganic phenomena. In Comte's view, then, astronomy was the first science to reach the positivistic stage, then came physics, next came chemistry, and after these three had reached the positivistic (scientific) stage, thought about organic phenomena could become more positivistic. The first organic science to move from the metaphysical to the positivistic stage was biology, or physiology. Once biology became a positivistic doctrine, sociology could move away from the metaphysical speculations of the seventeenth and eighteenth centuries (and the residues of earlier theological thought) toward a positivistic mode of thought.

Sociology has been the last to emerge, Comte argued, because it is the most complex and because it has had to wait for the other basic sciences to reach the positivistic stage. For the time, this argument represented a brilliant advocacy for a separate science of society, while it justified the lack of scientific rigor in social thought when compared with the other sciences. Moreover, though dependent on, and derivative of, evolutionary advances in the other sciences, sociology will study phenomena that distinguish it from the lower inorganic phenomena as well as from the higher organic science of biology. Although it is an organic science, sociology will be independent and study phenomena that "exhibit, in even a higher degree, the complexity, specialization, and personality which distinguish the higher phenomena of the individual life."[26]

This notion of hierarchy[27] represented yet another way to legitimate sociological inquiry: It explained why sociology was not as developed

---

[25]Comte, *Positive Philosophy*, 1:6–7.

[26]Comte, *Positive Philosophy*, 2:258.

[27]The hierarchy, in descending order, is sociology, biology, chemistry, physics, and astronomy. Comte added mathematics at the bottom because all sciences are ultimately built from mathematical reasoning.

as the other highly respected sciences, and it placed sociology in a highly favorable spot (at the top of a hierarchy) in relation to the other "positive sciences." If sociology could be viewed as the culmination of a long evolutionary process and as the culmination of the positive sciences, its legitimacy could not be questioned. Such was Comte's goal, and although he was only marginally successful in his efforts, he was the first to see clearly that sociology could be like the other sciences and that it would be only a matter of time until the old theological and metaphysical residues of earlier social thought were cast aside in favor of a true science of society. This advocacy, which takes up the majority of pages in *Positive Philosophy*, rightly ensures Comte's claim to being the founder of sociological theory.

Critical Conclusions

Comte gave sociology its name, however reluctantly, because he preferred the label *social physics*, but he did much more: He gave the discipline a vision of what it could be. Few have argued so forcefully about the kind of science sociology should be, and he provided an interesting if somewhat quirky explanation for why this discipline should emerge and become increasingly important in the realm of science. Not all who followed Comte during the past two centuries would accept his positivism—that of a theoretically driven social science that could be used in the reconstruction of society—but he made several important points. First, theories must be abstract, seeking to isolate and explain the nature of the fundamental forces guiding the operation of society. Second, theories must be explicitly and systematically tested against the empirical world, using a variety of methods. Third, collecting data without the guidance of theory will not contribute greatly to the accumulation of knowledge about how the social universe operates. Finally, sociology should be used to rebuild social structures, but these applications of sociology must be guided by theory rather than by ideologies and personal biases.

Comte also anticipated the substantive thrust of much early sociology, especially that of Herbert Spencer and Émile Durkheim. Comte recognized that as societies grow, they become more differentiated, and the differentiation requires new bases of integration revolving around the concentration of power and around mutual interdependence. He did not develop these ideas very far, but he set an agenda. Comte also reintroduced the organismic analogy to social thinking, although many would not see this as a blessing. At the very least, however, he alerted subsequent sociologists that society is a system whose parts are interconnected in ways having consequences for the maintenance of the social whole. This basic analogy to organisms evolved into the functionalism of Spencer and Durkheim.

Still, there is much to criticize in Comte. He never really developed any substantive theory, apart from the relationship between social differentiation and new modes of integration. Most of Comtean sociology is a justification for sociology, and a very good one at that, but he did not explain how the social universe operates. He thought that his "law of the three stages" was the equivalent of Newton's law of gravity, but Comte's law is not so much a law as a rather simplistic view of the history of ideas. It made for an interesting way to justify the emergence of positivism and its queen science, sociology, but it did not advance sociology's understanding of the dynamics of the social universe.

Add Comte's personal pathologies, which made him a truly bizarre and pathetic figure by the time of his death, and we are perhaps justified in ignoring Comte as a theorist who contributed to our understanding of the social universe. We should remember him for his forceful advocacy for scientific sociology. No one has done better since Comte first began to publish his positive philosophy.

CHAPTER 4

The Origin and Context of Herbert Spencer's Thought

Biographical Influences on Spencerian Sociology

Herbert Spencer was born in Derby, England, in 1820. Until the age of 13, he was tutored by his father at home. He subsequently moved to his uncle's home in Bath, where his private education continued.[1] Except for a few months of formal education, Spencer never really attended school outside his family. Still, he received a very solid education in mathematics and science from his father and uncle. In the end, this technical education encouraged him to view himself as a philosopher and to propose a grand project for uniting ethics, natural science, and social science. This great project was termed *Synthetic Philosophy*, an indication that Spencer's work moved far beyond the disciplinary borders of sociology. Only rather late in his career (between 1873 and 1896) did he turn his attention to sociology. He thought big in a time when the intellectual world in general, and academia in particular, was specializing and compartmentalizing.

This breadth and scope of inquiry probably accounts for the popularity of Spencer's work in the second half of the nineteenth century. He raised questions that intrigued both the lay public and scholars in particular specialties. Many of his works first appeared in serial form as installments in popular science magazines, and only later were they

[1] Jonathan H. Turner, *Herbert Spencer: A Renewed Appreciation* (Beverly Hills, CA: Sage, 1985), chap. 1; and *Herbert Spencer, an Autobiography* (London: Watts, 1926).

bound together in book volumes. His ideas remained popular; indeed, 100,000 copies of his books were sold before the turn of the century, an astoundingly high figure for that time and place. Even more amazing, however, is that they are not mere popularizations of ideas but, rather, academic works. Spencer's books could hardly be considered light reading but, apparently, their vision and scope captured readers' imaginations. Anyone who reads Spencer today cannot help but be impressed by the power of his ideas and perhaps even their arrogance, for who would now proclaim it possible to unite all the sciences and questions of ethics under one set of general principles?

If Spencer had received a formal education and advanced degrees from established universities, as his father had, his thinking would probably have been more focused and restrained. By today's standards, elite universities of the past century offered very broad training in letters and science, but even by that yardstick, tradition and established genres would have compelled Spencer to recognize that, after all, one does not undertake to explain the entire universe with a few general principles. Formal education has a tendency to limit horizons and force concentration on narrow topics, but because Spencer avoided the halls of academia in his youth and throughout his career, he was not bound by their rules of scholarship.

In a quiet way, Spencer's work flouts the rules of academia. He never read very much; rather, he picked the brains of distinguished scholars. Instead of burying himself in the library, he frequented London clubs and was friends with the most eminent scientific and literary figures of his time. From them, no doubt, he learned much by listening carefully and asking probing questions.[2] One suspects that Spencer was a kind of intellectual sponge, absorbing ideas on contact. How else could a man write detailed works on ethics, physics, biology, psychology, sociology, and anthropology while maintaining a constant flow of pointed and popular social commentary? Moreover, unlike academics who used students to do much of their legwork, Spencer employed professional academics. His research assistants tended to be PhDs who either needed the money or found the assigned tasks interesting. It seems

---

[2]For example, see Hugh Elliot, *Herbert Spencer* (New York: Holt, Rinehart & Winston, 1917); and David Duncan, *Life and Letters of Herbert Spencer* (London: Methuen, 1908). In his *Masters of Sociological Thought* (New York: Harcourt Brace Jovanovich, 1977), Lewis Coser best summarizes Spencer's relationship with his contemporaries by noting that from informal conversations, Spencer was supplied "with scientific facts he used so greedily as building blocks for his theories. Spencer absorbed his science to a large extent as if through osmosis, through critical discussions and interchanges with his scientific friends and associates" (110).

likely that an uncredentialed private scholar employing credentialed academics represented somewhat of an affront to the academic establishment, although Spencer managed to maintain cordial relations with many important academics.

Despite Spencer's enormous popularity with the literate lay public, however, he was an inordinately private individual. Indeed, he was rather neurotic and odd. He hardly ever gave public lectures; he spent a good part of the day in bed, either writing or complaining about real and imagined ailments; he remained a lifetime bachelor who, at best, had only one great love affair (and even here the nature of the relationship is not clear); he lived in rather sparse and puritan circumstances despite his inherited wealth and substantial royalties; and when he got older, his somewhat dour disposition became punctuated with considerable bitterness as his ideas came under increasing attack and then passed into obscurity. Yet many of those who knew him, and even the nurses who cared for him during his last years of failing health, emphasized that he was still a thoughtful and engaging individual.

It is perhaps not so surprising, then, that Spencer is an enigma to us. He was a lone and private scholar in a time when scholarship was becoming an increasing monopoly of academia, and despite his popularity, he never revealed a public presence and persona. Finally, he was a global thinker in a time of increasing specialization. The result was that as his scholarly ideas were criticized by specialized academics and as his political commentary became less fashionable, he had few students and adherents to carry his case. He was too neurotic to defend himself publicly, although he did make a celebrated and trumpeted tour of the United States in the early 1900s to espouse his moral philosophy (which became an embarrassment to those who recognized the importance of his scholarly ideas). As a consequence, Spencerian philosophy and sociology disappeared very rapidly after he died. No students and academic colleagues carried forward his grand synthesis.

Because Spencer had not received a formal education, he felt himself unqualified to attend college. In 1837, therefore, he sought to use his mathematical and scientific training as an engineer during the construction of the London and Birmingham Railway. The practical application of Spencer's training in mathematics had an enormous effect on his later thinking. He became attuned to the consequences of structural stress on the dynamics of the physical and social universe, and he expressed these consequences as equations (although the relationships were usually stated verbally). The impact of these 4 years as an engineer could not be initially foreseen in the turns that his intellectual life took.

In 1841, when the railroad was completed, Spencer returned to his birthplace in Derby. Over the next few years, he wrote several articles for the radical (for his time) press and numerous letters to the editor of a dissenting newspaper, *The Nonconformist*. In these works, he argued for limiting the power of government, and although these ideas are often defined as "conservative" today, they were seen as "liberal" and "radical" in the nineteenth century. After several years as a kind of fringe figure in radical politics and journalism, he secured a permanent position as a subeditor for the London *Economist* in 1848. The appointment marked a turning point in his life, and from that time on, his intellectual career accelerated. In 1851, he published *Social Statics*,[3] a work that has hurt Spencer's reputation and has been largely responsible for our present-day view of him as a social Darwinist, a libertarian, and perhaps a right-wing ideologue. In this work, he championed the cause of laissez-faire—free trade, open markets, and nonintervention by government. He asserted that individuals had the right to do as they pleased, as long as they allowed others to do the same. Despite its negative impact on our retrospective view of Spencer, however, the book was well received and opened doors into the broader intellectual community, although it remained a burden as he began to write less ideological and more scholarly works.

In 1853, the uncle who had tutored Spencer in science and mathematics died and left Spencer a substantial inheritance. This inheritance allowed him to quit his job as an editor and assume the life of a private full-time scholar. Despite his emotional problems—depression, insomnia, and reclusiveness—he was enormously productive as a private scholar. His collected works span volumes and run into thousands of pages. Moreover, with his more ideological tract out of his system, at least until the end of his life, he used the hard-nosed skills of an engineer and scientist to write a series of brilliant works. In 1854, he published *Principles of Psychology*, which was used as a text at Harvard and Cambridge. In 1862, he published *First Principles*, which marked the beginnings of his grand Synthetic Philosophy. In this book, he sought to unify ethics and science under one set of elementary principles. Between 1864 and 1867, he published the several volumes of his *Principles of Biology*, in which he sought to apply the abstract "first principles" of the universe to the dynamics of the organic realm. In 1873, he began to think about the superorganic—that is, the social

---

[3]For complete references to this and other works by Spencer, see footnotes later in this chapter and in the next chapter, where these works are discussed.

organization of organic forms. In particular, he initiated an analysis of how human organization, as the most obvious type of superorganic organization, could illustrate the plausibility of his first principles. He opened this movement into the domain of sociology with a methodological treatise on the problems of humans studying themselves; in so doing, he emphasized that laws of human organization could be discovered and used in the same way as in the physical and biological sciences. In 1874, the first serialized installments of his *The Principles of Sociology* appeared, and for the next 20 years, he devoted himself to sociology and to articulating the basic laws of human organization. The last portions of *The Principles of Sociology* were published in 1896. At the same time that he was preparing these last parts of his sociology, Spencer was publishing *The Principles of Ethics*, which restated the then-liberal, but now-conservative, social philosophy of laissez-faire. Because this philosophy was published in separate volumes from Spencer's scholarly work in sociology, it intrudes less than might otherwise have been the case.

Thus, although Spencer's work in sociology spans only a 21-year period in a much longer and comprehensive intellectual career, his work in sociology reflects other scholarly and political concerns. In turn, these other concerns are the product of the general intellectual milieu of nineteenth-century England as well as of specific scholars in this milieu. To understand Spencerian sociology, then, we should take note of some of the other forces influencing his thinking.

The Political Economy of Nineteenth-Century England

In contrast with France, where decades of political turmoil had created an overconcern for collective unity, England remained comparatively tranquil. As the first society to industrialize, England enjoyed considerable prosperity under early capitalism. Open markets and competition appeared to be an avenue for increased productivity and prosperity. It is not surprising, therefore, that social thought in England was dominated by ideological beliefs in the efficiency and moral correctness of free and unbridled competition not only in the marketplace but in other realms as well.[4]

---

[4]The major legitimating work in this context was Adam Smith's *An Inquiry Into the Nature and Causes of the Wealth of Nations* (London: Cadell & Davies, 1805; originally published in 1776).

Spencer advocated a laissez-faire doctrine in his philosophic works. Individuals should be allowed to pursue their interests and to seek happiness as long as they do not infringe on others' rights to do so. Government should be restrained and should not regulate the pursuits of individuals. Much like Adam Smith, Spencer assumed a kind of "invisible hand of order" as emerging to maintain a society of self-seeking individuals. Most of Spencer's early essays and his first book, *Social Statics*, represent adaptations of laissez-faire economics. But later, the more scientific analyses contained in his biological works supplemented his social and economic philosophy.

The Scientific Milieu of Spencer's England

Spencer's early training with his father and uncle was primarily in mathematics and science. More important, his informal contacts as a freelance intellectual were with eminent scientists like Thomas Henry Huxley, Joseph Dalton Hooker, John Tyndall, and even Darwin. Indeed, Spencer read less than he listened, for he clearly acquired an enormous breadth of knowledge by talking with the foremost scientists of his time. Biographers have frequently commented on the lack of books in his library, especially for a scholar who wrote with such insight in several different disciplines. Despite his reliance on informal contacts with fellow scientists, however, several key works in biology and physics appear to have had considerable impact on his thought.

Influences From Biology

In 1864, Spencer wrote the first volume of his *Principles of Biology*, which at the time represented one of the most advanced treatises on biological knowledge.[5] Later, as we will see, he sought to apply the laws of biology to "super-organic bodies,"[6] revealing the extent to which biological knowledge influenced his more purely sociological formulations. He credited three sources for some of the critical

---

[5]In *Principles of Biology* (New York: Appleton-Century-Crofts, 1864–1867), Spencer formulated some original laws of biology that still stand today. For example, his formulation of the relationship among growth, size, and structure are still axiomatic in biology. Yet few biologists are aware that Spencer, the engineer turned scientist, formulated the law that, among regularly shaped bodies, surface area increases as the square of the linear dimensions and volume increases as the cube of these dimensions—hence requiring new structural arrangements to support and nourish larger bodies.

[6]This was Spencer's phrase for describing patterns of social organization.

insights that he later applied to social phenomena: the works of Thomas Malthus (1766–1834), Karl Ernst Von Baer (1792–1876), and Charles Darwin (1809–1882).

Malthus

Spencer was profoundly influenced by Malthus's *Essay on Population*. (Malthus, of course, was not a biologist, but his work had an influence in this sphere and hence is discussed in this section.) In this work, Malthus emphasized that the geometric growth of population would create conditions favorable for conflict, starvation, pestilence, disease, and death. Indeed, he argued that populations grew until "checked" by the "four horsemen": war, pestilence, famine, and disease.

Spencer reached a much less pessimistic conclusion than Malthus, for the competition and struggle that ensues from population growth would, Spencer believed, lead to the "survival of the fittest" and, hence, to the elevation of society and "the races." Such a vision corresponded, of course, to Spencer's laissez-faire bias and allowed him to view free and open competition not just as good economic policy but also as a fundamental "law of the organic universe."[7] In addition to these ideological uses of Malthus's ideas, the notion of competition and struggle became central to Spencer's more formal sociology. Spencer saw evolution of societies as the result of territorial and political conflicts, and he was one of the first sociologists to understand fully the significance of war and conflict on the internal patterns of social organization in a society.

Von Baer

Spencer was also influenced by William Harvey's embryological studies as well as by Henri Milne-Edward's work, which had borrowed the phrase "the physiological division of labor" from social thought. Indeed, as Spencer so ably emphasized, biologists had often borrowed from social discourse terms that he was merely borrowing back and applying in a more refined manner to the "super-organic realm." Yet he gave a German, Von Baer, the credit for recognizing that biological forms develop from undifferentiated, embryologic forms to highly differentiated structures revealing a physiological division of labor.

---

[7]See, for example, his *Autobiography;* also see the long footnote in *First Principles* (New York: A. L. Burt, 1880; originally published in 1860).

Von Baer's principles allowed Spencer to organize his ideas on biological, psychological, and social evolution. Spencer came to emphasize that evolution is a process of development from an incoherent, undifferentiated, and homogeneous mass to a differentiated and coherent pattern in which the functions of structures are well coordinated.[8] Conversely, dissolution involves movement from a coherent and differentiated state to a more homogeneous and incoherent mass. Thus, Spencer came to view the major focus of sociology as the study of the conditions under which social differentiation and dedifferentiation occur.

Darwin

The relationship between Darwin and Spencer is reciprocal in that Spencer's early ideas about development exerted considerable influence on Darwin's formulation of the theory of evolution,[9] although Darwin's notion of "natural selection" was apparently formulated independently of Spencer's emphasis on competition and struggle. Only after *On the Origin of Species* was in press did Darwin recognize the affinity between the concepts of *survival of the fittest* and *natural selection*. Conversely, his explicit formulation of the theory of evolution was to reinforce, and give legitimacy to, Spencer's view of social evolution as the result of competition among populations, with the most organizationally "fit" conquering the less fit and, hence, increasing the level and complexity of social organization. Moreover, Darwin's ideas encouraged Spencer to view differences among the "races" and societies of the world as the result of "speciation" of isolated populations, each of which adapted to varying environmental conditions. Spencer's continuous emphasis on environmental conditions, both ecological and societal, as shaping the structure of society, is the result, no doubt, of Darwin's formulations.

The theory of evolution also offered Spencer a respected intellectual tool for justifying his laissez-faire political beliefs. For both organic and superorganic bodies, he argued, it is necessary to let

---

[8]This idea can be found in its early form in one of Spencer's early essays, "Progress: Its Law and Cause," first published in 1857 (*Westminster Review*, April 1857). Also, see Spencer's article "The Developmental Hypothesis," in *The New Leader* (1852).

[9]Indeed, as noted earlier, Darwin explicitly acknowledges Spencer's work in the introduction to *On the Origin of Species* (London: Murry, 1890; originally published in 1859). Moreover, at one point in his life, Darwin was moved to remark that Spencer was "a dozen times his intellectual superior." For more lines of influence, see *Life and Letters of Charles Darwin* (New York: Appleton-Century-Crofts, 1896).

competition and struggle operate free of governmental regulation. To protect some segments of a population is to preserve the "less fit" and thus reduce the overall "quality of civilization."[10]

From biology, then, Spencer took three essential elements: (1) the notion that many critical attributes of both individuals and society emerge from competition among individuals or collective populations, (2) the view that social evolution involves movement from undifferentiated to differentiated structures marked by interrelated functions, and (3) the recognition that differences among both individuals and social systems are the result of their adapting to varying environmental conditions. He supplemented these broad biological insights with several discoveries in the physical sciences to forge the "first principles" of his general Synthetic Philosophy.

Influences From the Physical Sciences

From informal education within his family and from contacts with the most eminent scientists of his time, Spencer acquired considerable training in astronomy, geology, physics, and chemistry. In reading his many works, it is impossible not to be impressed by his knowledge of wide varieties of physical phenomena and their laws of operation. His Synthetic Philosophy thus reflected his debt to the physical sciences, particularly for (1) the general mode of his analysis and (2) the specific principles of his philosophy:

1. All of Spencer's work is indebted to the post-Newtonian view of science— that is, the emphasis on universal laws that could explain the operation of phenomena in the world. Indeed, Spencer went beyond Newton and argued that there were laws transcending all phenomena, both physical and organic. In other words, laws of the universe or cosmos can be discovered and used to explain, at least in general terms, physical, organic, and superorganic (social) events. Spencer emphasized that each domain of reality—astronomical, geological, physical, chemical, biological, psychological, and sociological—revealed its own unique laws that pertained to the properties and forces of its delimited domain. He also believed that at the most abstract level, however, a few fundamental or first principles cut across all domains of reality.

2. In seeking these first principles, Spencer relied heavily on the physics of his time. He incorporated into his Synthetic Philosophy notions of force,

---

[10]It is not hard to see how these ideas were to be transformed into what became known as social Darwinism in America. A more accurate term would have been *social Spencerianism.* See Richard Hofstadter, *Social Darwinism in American Thought* (Boston: Beacon, 1955).

the indestructibility of matter, the persistence of motion, and other principles that were emerging in physics. We will discuss these later when examining his scheme in depth, but we should emphasize that much of the inspiration for his grand scheme came from the promise of Newtonian physics.

Thus, Spencer's Synthetic Philosophy emerged from a synthesis of ideas and principles being developed in physics and biology. Yet the precise way in which he used these ideas in his sociological work was greatly influenced by his exposure to Auguste Comte's vision of a positive philosophy (see the previous chapter). Before we can fully appreciate Spencer's philosophy, therefore, we need to review his somewhat ambivalent and defensive reaction to Comte's work.

Spencer's Synthetic Philosophy and the Sociology of Comte

In 1864, Spencer published an article titled "Reasons for Dissenting From the Philosophy of M. Comte," in which he sought to list the points of agreement and disagreement with the great French thinker.[11] Spencer emphasized that he disagreed with Comte over the following issues: (1) that societies pass through three stages, (2) that causality is less important than relations of affinity in building social theory, (3) that government can use the laws of sociology to reconstruct society, (4) that the sciences have developed in a particular order, and (5) that psychology is merely a subdiscipline of biology.

Spencer also noted a number of points in which he was in agreement with Comte, but he stressed that many other scholars besides Comte had similarly advocated (1) that knowledge comes from experiences or observed facts and (2) that there are invariable laws in the universe. Most revealing are the few passages where Spencer explicitly acknowledged an intellectual debt to Comte. Spencer accepted Comte's term, *sociology*, for the science of superorganic bodies, and, most importantly, he gave Comte begrudging credit for reintroducing the organismic analogy back into social thought.

---

[11]The article is conveniently reprinted in Herbert Spencer, *Reasons for Dissenting From the Philosophy of M. Comte and Other Essays* (Berkeley, CA: Glendessary, 1968). The article was written in a somewhat defensive manner in an effort to distinguish Spencer's first book, *Social Statics* (New York: Appleton-Century-Crofts, 1888; originally published in 1850), from Comte's use of these terms. Spencer appears to have "protested too much," perhaps seeking to hide some of his debt to the positive philosophy of Comte.

Spencer stressed, however, that Plato and Thomas Hobbes had made similar analogies and that Von Baer had influenced much of his organismic thinking.

Yet one gets the impression that Spencer was working too hard at dissociating his ideas from Comte's. That his most intimate intellectual companions, George Elliot and George Lewes, were well versed in Comte's philosophy argues for the considerable intellectual influence of Comte's work on Spencer's initial sociological inquiries. True, Spencer would never accept Comte's collectivism, but he extended two critical ideas clearly evident in Comte's work: (1) social systems reveal many properties of organization in common with biological organisms, and thus, some principles of social organization can be initially borrowed (and altered somewhat) from biology and (2) when viewed as a "body social," a social system can be analyzed by the contribution of its various organs to the maintenance of the social whole. There can be little doubt, then, that Spencer was stimulated by Comte's analogizing and implicit functionalism. But as Spencer incorporated these ideas, they were altered by his absorption of key insights from the physical and biological sciences.

Why Read Spencer?

When compared with the intellectual influences on other scholars whom we will analyze in later chapters, those on Spencer are less clear. He did not attend a university, and so his mentors cannot be traced there. Nor did he ever hold an academic position, thereby avoiding compartmentalization in a department or particular school of thought. As a freelance intellectual, he borrowed at will and was never constrained by the intellectual fads and foibles that sweep through academia. The unrestrained scope of his scheme makes it fascinating, and perhaps this same feature makes his work less appealing to present-day scholars, who tend to work within narrow intellectual traditions.

Yet, as we will explore in depth in the next chapter, Spencer offered many important insights into the structure and dynamics of social systems. Although he presented these insights in the vocabulary of the physics and biology of his time, they still have considerable relevance for sociological theorizing. As we approach the analysis of Spencer's basic works, therefore, we should be prepared to appreciate not only the scope of his ideas but also the profound insights that he achieved into the nature of social systems.

CHAPTER 5

The Sociology of Herbert Spencer

Herbert Spencer saw himself as a philosopher rather than as a sociologist. His grand scheme was termed *Synthetic Philosophy*, and it was to encompass all realms of the universe: physical, psychological, biological, sociological, and ethical. The inclusion of the ethical component makes this philosophy problematic because ideological statements do occasionally slip into Spencer's sociology. Spencer's philosophy was a grand, cosmic scheme, but when he turned to sociology, he made many precise statements and introduced a copious amount of empirical data to illustrate his theoretical ideas. Spencer was, at best, a mediocre philosopher, but he was a very accomplished sociologist, even though he took up sociology rather late in his career. We will begin with the moral philosophy, just to get it out of the way, and then we will turn to his important sociological contributions.[1]

---

[1]Spencer's complete works, except for his *Descriptive Sociology* (see later analysis), are conveniently pulled together in the following collection: *The Works of Herbert Spencer*, 21 vols. (Osnabruck, Germany: Otto Zeller, 1966). However, our references will be to the separate editions of each of his individual works. Moreover, many of the dates for the works discussed span several years because Spencer sometimes published his works serially in several volumes (frequently after they had appeared in periodicals). Full citations will be given when discussing particular works. For a recent review of primary and secondary sources on Spencer, see Robert G. Perrin, *Herbert Spencer: A Primary and Secondary Bibliography* (New York: Garland, 1993).

Spencer's Moral Philosophy: Social Statics and Principles of Ethics

In his later years, Spencer often complained that his first major work, *Social Statics*,[2] had received too much attention. He saw this book as an early and flawed attempt to delineate his moral philosophy and, hence, as not representative of his more mature thought. Yet the basic premise of the work is repeated in one of his last books, *Principles of Ethics*.[3] Despite his protests, his moral arguments have considerable continuity, although we should emphasize again that his more scientific statements can and should be separated from these ethical arguments.

Because Spencer's moral arguments did not change dramatically, we will concentrate on *Social Statics*. The basic argument of *Social Statics* can be stated as follows: Human happiness can be achieved only when individuals can satisfy their needs and desires without infringing on the rights of others to do the same. As Spencer emphasized,

> each member of the race . . . must not only be endowed with faculties enabling him to receive the highest enjoyment in the act of living, but must be so constituted that he may obtain full satisfaction for every desire, without diminishing the power of others to obtain like satisfaction: nay, to fulfill the purpose perfectly, must derive pleasure from seeing pleasure in others.[4]

In this early work, as well as in *Principles of Ethics*, Spencer saw this view as the basic law of ethics and morality. He felt that this law was an extension of laws in the natural world, and much of his search for scientific laws represented an effort to develop a scientific justification for his moral position. Indeed, he emphasized that the social universe, like the physical and biological realms, revealed invariant laws. But he turned this insight into an interesting moral dictum: Once these laws are discovered, humans should obey them and cease trying to construct, through political legislation, social forms that violate these

---

[2]Herbert Spencer, *Social Statics: Or, the Conditions Essential to Human Happiness Specified, and the First of Them Developed* (New York: Appleton-Century-Crofts, 1888). This was originally published in 1851; the edition cited here is an offset print of the original.

[3]Herbert Spencer, *Principles of Ethics* (New York: Appleton-Century-Crofts, 1892–1898). A very high-quality and inexpensive edition of this work is published by Liberty Press, Indianapolis.

[4]Spencer, *Social Statics*, 448.

laws. In this way, he was able to base his laissez-faire political ideas on what he saw as a sound scientific position: The laws of social organization can no more be violated than can those of the physical universe, and to seek to do so will simply create, in the long run, more severe problems.[5] In contrast with Comte, then, who saw the discovery of laws as the tools for social engineering, Spencer took the opposite tack and argued that once the laws are ascertained, people should "implicitly obey them!"[6] For Spencer, the great ethical axiom, "derived" from the laws of nature, is that humans should be as free from external regulation as is possible. Indeed the bulk of *Social Statics* seeks to show how his moral law and the laws of laissez-faire capitalism converge and, implicitly, how they reflect biological laws of unfettered competition and struggle among species. The titles of some of the chapters best communicate Spencer's argument: "The Rights of Life and Personal Liberty," "The Right to the Use of the Earth," "The Right of Property," "The Rights of Exchange," "The Rights of Women,"[7] "The Right to Ignore the State," "The Limit of State-Duty," and so forth.

In seeking to join the laws of ethics, political economy, and biology, Spencer initiated modes of analysis that became prominent parts of his sociology. First, he sought to discover invariant laws and principles of social organization. Second, he began to engage in organismic analogizing, drawing comparisons between the structure of individual organisms and that of societies:

> Thus do we find, not only that the analogy between a society and a living creature is borne out to a degree quite unsuspected by those who commonly draw it, but also, that the same definition of life applies to both. This union of many men into one community—this increasingly mutual dependence of units which were originally independent—this gradual segregation of citizens into separate bodies, with reciprocally subservient functions—this formation of a whole, consisting of numerous essential parts—this growth of an organism, of which one portion cannot be injured without the rest feeling it—may all be generalized under the law of individuation. The development of society, as well as the development of man and the development

---

[5] Ibid., 54–57.

[6] Ibid., 56.

[7] Spencer's arguments here are highly modern and, when compared with Marx's, Weber's, or Durkheim's, are quite radical. Spencer was a feminist long before there was "feminism."

of life generally, may be described as a tendency to individuate—
to become a thing. And rightly interpreted, the manifold forms
of progress going on around us, are uniformly significant of this
tendency.[8]

Spencer's organismic analogizing often goes to extremes in *Social
Statics*—extremes that he avoided in his later works. For example,
he at one point argued that "so completely . . . is a society organized
upon the same system as an individual being, that we may almost say
that there is something more than an analogy between them."[9]

Third, *Social Statics* also reveals the beginnings of Spencer's functionalism. He viewed societies, like individuals, as having survival
needs with specialized organs emerging and persisting to meet these
needs. And he defined "social health" by how well various specialized
"social organs" met these needs.

Fourth, Spencer's later emphasis on war and conflict among societies as a critical force in their development can also be observed.
Although decrying war as destructive, he argued that it allows the
more organized "races" to conquer the "less organized and inferior
races"—thereby increasing the level and complexity of social organization. This argument was dramatically tempered in his later scientific
works, with the result that he was one of the first social thinkers to see
the importance of conflict in the evolution of human societies.[10]

In sum, then, *Social Statics* and *Principles of Ethics* are greatly
flawed works, representing Spencer's moral ramblings. We have
examined these works first because they are often used to condemn
his more scholarly efforts. Although some of the major scientific
points can be seen in these moral works, and although his scientific
works are sprinkled with his extreme moral position, his ethical and
scientific efforts nonetheless have a distinct difference in style, tone,
and insight. Thus, we would conclude that the worth of Spencer's
thought is to be found in the more scientific treatises, relegating his
ethics to deserved obscurity. We will therefore devote the balance of
this chapter to understanding his sociological perspective.[11]

---

[8]Spencer, *Social Statics*, 497.

[9]Ibid., 490.

[10]Ibid., 498.

[11]It should be remembered that this perspective was developed between 1873 and 1896. For
a more complete and detailed review of Spencer's sociology during this period, see Jonathan H.
Turner, *Herbert Spencer: A Renewed Appreciation* (Beverly Hills, CA: Sage, 1985).

Spencer's First Principles

In the 1860s, Spencer began to issue his general Synthetic Philosophy by subscription. The goal of this philosophy was to treat the great divisions of the universe—inorganic matter, life, mind, and society—as subject to understanding by scientific principles. The initial statement in this rather encompassing philosophical scheme was *First Principles*, published in 1862.[12] In this book, Spencer delineated the "cardinal" or "first principles" of the universe. Drawing from the biology and physics of his time, he felt that he had perceived, at the most abstract level, certain common principles that apply to all realms of the universe. Indeed, it must have been an exciting vision to feel that one had unlocked the mysteries of the physical, organic, and superorganic (societal) universe.

The principles themselves are probably not worth reviewing in detail; rather, the imagery they communicate is important. For Spencer, evolution is the master process of the universe, and it revolves around movement from simple to complex forms of structure. As matter is aggregated—whether this matter is cells of an organism, elements of a moral philosophy, or human beings—the force that brings this matter together is retained, causing the larger mass to differentiate into varying components, which then become integrated into a more complex whole. This complex whole must sustain itself in an environment, and as long as the forces that have aggregated, differentiated, and integrated the "matter" are sustained, the system remains coherent in the environment. Over time, however, these forces dissipate, with the result that the basis for integration is weakened, thereby making the system vulnerable to forces in the environment. At certain times, these environmental forces can revitalize a system, giving it new life to aggregate, differentiate, and integrate. At other times, these forces simply overwhelm the weakened basis of integration and destroy the system. Thus, evolution is a dual process of building up more complex structures through integration and the dissolution of these structures when the force integrating them is weakened.

---

[12]Herbert Spencer, *First Principles* (New York: A. L. Burt, 1880; originally published in 1862). The contents of this work had been anticipated in earlier essays, the most important of which are "Progress: Its Law and Cause," *Westminster Review* (April 1857), and "The Ultimate Laws of Physiology," *National Review* (October 1857); moreover, hints at these principles are sprinkled throughout the first edition of *Principles of Psychology* (New York: Appleton-Century-Crofts, 1880; originally published in 1855).

This is all rather vague, of course, but it gives us a metaphorical vision of how Spencer viewed evolution. Evolution revolves around the process of aggregating matter—in the case of society, populations of human beings and the structures that organize people—and the subsequent differentiation and integration of this matter. The forces that aggregate this matter—forces such as immigration, new productive forms, use of power, patterns of conquest, and all those phenomena that have the capacity to bring humans together—are retained, and as a consequence, they also become the forces that differentiate and integrate the matter. For example, if war and conquest have been the basis for aggregation of two populations, the coercive and organizational power causing their aggregation is also the force that will drive the pattern of differentiation and integration of the conquered and their conquerors. When this force is spent or proves ineffective in integrating the new society, the society becomes vulnerable to environmental forces, such as military aggression by another society.

This image of evolution helps explain the issues that most concerned Spencer when he finally turned to sociology in the 1870s. His view of evolution as the aggregation, differentiation, integration, and disintegration of matter pushed him to conceptualize societal dynamics as revolving around increases in the size of the population (the "aggregation" component), the differentiation of the population along several prominent axes, the bases for integrating this differentiated population, and the potential disintegration of the population in its environment. Evolution is thus analysis of societal movement from simple or homogeneous forms to differentiated or heterogeneous forms as well as the mechanisms for integrating these forms in their environments. This is all we need to take from Spencer's *First Principles*.

Spencer moved considerably beyond this general metaphor of evolution, however, because he proposed many specific propositions and guidelines for a science of society. Ultimately, his contribution to sociological theorizing does not reside in his abstract formulas on cosmic evolution but, rather, in his specific analyses of societal social systems—what he called *superorganic* phenomena. This contribution can be found in two distinct works, *The Study of Sociology*, which was published in serial form in popular magazines in 1872, and the more scholarly *Principles of Sociology*, which was published in several volumes between 1874 and 1896. The former work is primarily a methodological statement on the problems of bias in sociology, whereas the latter is a substantive work that seeks to develop abstract principles of evolution and dissolution and, at the same time, to describe the complex interplay among the institutions of society.

Spencer's *The Study of Sociology*

The Study of Sociology[13] was originally published as a series of articles in *Contemporary Review* in England and *Popular Science Monthly* in the United States. This book represents Spencer's effort to popularize sociology and to address "various considerations which seemed needful by way of introduction to the *Principles of Sociology*, presently to be written."[14] Most of *The Study of Sociology* is a discussion of the methodological problems confronting the science of sociology. At the same time, a number of substantive insights later formed the core of his *Principles of Sociology*. We will first examine Spencer's methodological discussion and then his more theoretical analysis, even though this division does not correspond to the order of his presentation.

The Methodological Problems Confronting Sociology

The opening paragraph of Chapter 4 of *The Study of Sociology* sets the tone of Spencer's analysis:

From the intrinsic natures of its facts, from our natures as observers of its facts, and from the peculiar relation in which we stand toward the facts to be observed, there arise impediments in the way of Sociology greater than those of any other science.[15]

He went on to emphasize that the basic sources of bias stem from the inadequacy of measuring instruments in the social sciences and from the nature of scientists who, by virtue of being members of society, observe the data from a particular vantage point. In a series of insightful chapters—far superior to any statement by any other sociologist of the nineteenth century—Spencer outlined in more detail what he termed *objective* and *subjective* difficulties.

---

[13]Herbert Spencer, *The Study of Sociology* (Boston: Routledge & Kegan Paul, 1873).
[14]Ibid., iv.
[15]Ibid., 72.

Under objective difficulties, Spencer analyzed the problems associated with the "uncertainty of our data." The first problem encountered revolves around the difficulty of measuring the "subjective states" of actors and correspondingly of investigators' suspending their own subjective orientation when examining that of others. A second problem concerns allowing public passions, moods, and fads to determine what sociologists investigate, because it is all too easy to let the popular and immediately relevant obscure from vision more fundamental questions. A third methodological problem involves the "cherished hypothesis," which an investigator can be driven to pursue while neglecting more significant problems. A fourth issue concerns the problem of personal and organizational interests influencing what is seen as scientifically important. Large-scale governmental bureaucracies, and individuals in them, tend to seek and interpret data in ways that support their interests. A fifth problem is related to the second, in that investigators often allow the most visible phenomena to occupy their attention, creating a bias in the collection of data toward the most readily accessible (not necessarily the most important) phenomena. A sixth problem stems from the fact that any observer occupies a position in society and hence will tend to see the world in terms of the dictates of that position. And seventh, depending on the time in the ongoing social process when observations are made, varying results can be induced—thereby signaling that "social change cannot be judged . . . by inspecting any small portion of it."[16]

Spencer's discussion is timely even today, and his advice for mitigating these objective difficulties is also relevant: Social science must rely on multiple sources of data, collected at different times in varying places by different investigators. Coupled with efforts by investigators to recognize their bias, their interests, and their positions in society as well as their commitment to theoretically important (rather than popular) problems, these difficulties can be further mitigated. Yet many subjective difficulties will persist.

Spencer emphasized two classes of subjective difficulty: intellectual and emotional. Under intellectual difficulties, Spencer returned to the first of the objective difficulties: How are investigators to put themselves into the subjective world of those whom they observe? How can we avoid representing another's "thoughts and feelings in terms of our own"?[17] For if investigators cannot

---

[16]Ibid., 105.
[17]Ibid., 114.

suspend their own emotional states to understand those of others under investigation, the data of social science will always be biased. Another subjective intellectual problem concerns the depth of analysis, for the more one investigates a phenomenon in detail, the more complicated are its elements and their causal connections. Thus, how far should investigators go before they are to be satisfied with their analysis of a particular phenomenon? At what point are the basic causal connections uncovered? Turning to emotional subjective difficulties, Spencer argued that the emotional state of an investigator can directly influence estimations of probability, importance, and relevance of events.

After reviewing these difficulties and emphasizing that the distinction between subjective and objective is somewhat arbitrary, Spencer devoted separate chapters to "educational bias," "bias of patriotism," "class bias," "political bias," and "theological bias." Thus, more than any other sociologist of the nineteenth century, Spencer saw the many methodological problems confronting the science of society.

Spencer felt that the problems of bias could be mitigated not only by attention to one's interests, emotions, station in life, and other subjective and emotional sources of difficulty but also by the development of "mental discipline." He believed that by studying the procedures of the more exact sciences, sociologists could learn to approach their subjects in a disciplined and objective way. In a series of enlightening passages,[18] he argued that by studying the purely abstract sciences, such as logic and mathematics, one could become sensitized to "the necessity of relation"—that is, that phenomena are connected and reveal affinities. By examining the "abstract–concrete sciences," such as physics and chemistry, one is alerted to causality and to the complexity of causal connections. By examining the "concrete sciences," such as geology and astronomy, one becomes alerted to the "products" of causal forces and the operation of lawlike relations. For it is always necessary, Spencer stressed, to view the context within which processes occur. Thus, by approaching problems with the proper mental discipline—with a sense of relation, causality, and context—one can overcome many methodological difficulties.

---

[18]Ibid., 314–326.

The Theoretical Argument

The opening chapters of *The Study of Sociology* present a forceful argument against those who would maintain that the social realm is not like the physical and biological realms. On the contrary, Spencer argued, all spheres of the universe are subject to laws. Every time people express political opinions about what legislators should do, they are admitting implicitly to regularities, which can be understood in human behavior and organization.

Given the existence of discoverable laws, Spencer stressed that the goal of sociology must be to uncover the principles of morphology (structure) and physiology (process) of all organic forms, including the superorganic (society). But, he cautioned, we must not devote our energies to analyzing the historically unique, peculiar, or transitory. Rather, sociology must look for the universal and enduring properties of social organization.[19] Moreover, sociologists should not become overly concerned with predicting future events because unanticipated empirical conditions will always influence the weights of variables and, hence, the outcomes of events. Much more important is discovering the basic relations among phenomena and the fundamental causal forces that generate these relations.

In the early and late chapters of *The Study of Sociology*, Spencer sought to delineate, in sketchy form, some principles common to organic bodies. In so doing, he foreshadowed the more extensive analysis in *Principles of Sociology*. He acknowledged Auguste Comte's influence in viewing biology and sociology as parallel sciences of organic forms and in recognizing that understanding the principles of biology is a prerequisite for discovering the principles of sociology.[20] As Spencer emphasized in all of his sociological works, certain principles of structure and function are common in all organic bodies.

Spencer even hinted at some of these principles, on which he was to elaborate in the volumes of *Principles of Sociology*. One principle is that increases in the size of both biological and social aggregates create pressures for differentiation of functions. Another principle is that such differentiation results in the creation of distinctive regulatory, operative, and distributive processes. That is, as organic systems differentiate, it becomes necessary for some units to regulate and control action, for others to produce what is necessary for system maintenance, or for

---

[19]Ibid., 58–59.
[20]Ibid., 328.

still others to distribute necessary substances among the parts. A third principle is that differentiation initially involves separation of regulative centers from productive centers, and only with the increases in size and further differentiation do distinctive distributing centers emerge.

Such principles are supplemented by one of the first functional orientations in sociology. In numerous places, Spencer stressed that to uncover the principles of social organization, it is necessary to examine the social whole, to determine its needs for survival, and to assess various structures by how they meet these needs. Although this functionalism always remained somewhat implicit and subordinate to his search for the principles of organization among superorganic bodies, it influenced subsequent thinkers, particularly Émile Durkheim.

In sum, then, *The Study of Sociology* is a preliminary work to Spencer's *Principles of Sociology*. It analyzes in detail the methodological problems confronting sociology; it offers guidelines for eradicating biases and for developing the proper "scientific discipline"; it hints at the utility of functional analysis; and, most importantly, it begins to sketch out what Spencer thought to be the fundamental principles of social organization. During the two decades after the publication of *The Study of Sociology*, Spencer sought to use the basic principles enunciated in his *First Principles* as axioms for deriving the more specific principles of superorganic bodies.

A Note on Spencer's *Descriptive Sociology*

Using his inheritance and royalties, Spencer commissioned a series of volumes to describe the characteristics of different societies.[21] These

---

[21]The full title of the work reads *Descriptive Sociology, or Groups of Sociological Facts*. The list of volumes of *Descriptive Sociology* is as follows: Vol. 1: *English* (1873); Vol. 2: *Ancient Mexicans, Central Americans, Chibchans, Ancient Peruvians* (1874); Vol. 3: *Types of Lowest Races, Negritto, and Malayo-Polynesian Races* (1874); Vol. 4: *African Races* (1875); Vol. 5: *Asiatic Races* (1876); Vol. 6: *North and South American Races* (1878); Vol. 7: *Hebrews and Phoenicians* (1880); Vol. 8: *French* (1881); Vol. 9: *Chinese* (1910); Vol. 10: *Hellenic Greeks* (1928); Vol. 11: *Ancient Egyptians* (1929); Vol. 12: *Ancient Romans* (1930); and Vol. 13: *Mesopotamia* (1934). A revised edition of Vol. 3, edited by D. Duncan and H. Tedder, was published in 1925; a second edition of Vol. 6 appeared in 1885; Vol. 14 is a redoing by Emil Torday of Vol. 4. In addition to these volumes, which are folio in size, two unnumbered works appeared: Ruben Long, *The Sociology of Islam*, 2 vols. (1931–1933); and John Garstang, *The Heritage of Solomon: An Historical Introduction to the Sociology of Ancient Palestine* (1934). For a more detailed review and analysis of these volumes, see Jonathan H. Turner and Alexandra Maryanski, "Sociology's Lost Human Relations Area Files," *Sociological Perspectives*, 31 (1988), 19–34.

volumes were, in his vision, to contain no theory or supposition; rather, they were to constitute the "raw data" from which theoretical inductions could be made or by which deductions from abstract theory could be tested. These descriptions became the data source for Spencer's sociological work, particularly his *Principles of Sociology*. As he noted in the "Provisional Preface" of Volume 1 of *Descriptive Sociology*,

> in preparation for *The Principles of Sociology*, requiring as bases of induction large accumulations of data, fitly arranged comparison, I . . . commenced by proxy the collection and organization of facts presented by societies of different types, past and present . . . the facts collected and arranged for easy reference and convenient study of their relations, being so presented, apart from hypotheses, as to aid all students of social science in testing such conclusions as they have drawn and in drawing others.[22]

Spencer's intent was to use common categories for classifying "sociological facts" on different types of societies. In this way, he hoped that sociology would have a sound database for developing the laws of superorganic bodies. In light of the data available to Spencer, the volumes of *Descriptive Sociology* are remarkably detailed. What is more, the categories for describing different societies are still useful. Although these categories differ slightly from volume to volume, primarily because the complexity of societies varies so much, there is an effort to maintain a consistent series of categories for classifying and arranging sociological facts. Volume 1, *The English*, illustrates Spencer's approach.

First, facts are recorded for general classes of sociological variables. Thus, for *The English*, "facts" are recorded on the following:

1. Inorganic environment
    a. General features
    b. Geological features
    c. Climate

---

[22] *The English*, classified and arranged by Herbert Spencer, compiled and abstracted by James Collier (New York: Appleton-Century-Crofts, 1873), vi.

2. Organic environment

    a. Vegetable

    b. Animal

3. Sociological environment

    a. Past history

    b. Past societies from which present system formed

    c. Present neighbors

4. Characteristics of people

    a. Physical

    b. Emotional

    c. Intellectual

This initial basis of classification is consistent with Spencer's opening chapters in *Principles of Sociology*. (See his section on "Critical Variables.")

Second, most of *The English* is devoted to a description of the historical development of British society, from its earliest origins to Spencer's time, divided into the following topic headings:

Division of labor

Regulation of labor

Domestic laws—marital

Domestic laws—filial

Political laws—criminal, civil, and industrial

General government

Local government

Military

Ecclesiastical

Professional

Accessory institutions

Funeral rites

Laws of intercourse

Habits and customs

Aesthetic sentiments

Moral sentiments

Religious ideas and superstitions

Knowledge

Language

Distribution

Exchange

Production

Arts

Agriculture, rearing, and so forth

Land—works

Habitations

Food

Clothing

Weapons

Implements

Aesthetic products

Supplementary materials

Third, for some volumes, such as *The English*, more detailed descriptions under these headings are represented in tabular form. *The English*, for example, opens with a series of large and detailed tables, organized under the general headings "regulative" and "operative" as well as "structural" and "functional." The tables begin with the initial formation of the English peoples around AD 78 and document through a series of brief statements, organized around basic topics (see previous list), to around AD 1850. By reading across the tables at any given period, the reader can find a profile of the English for that period. By reading down the columns of the table, the reader can note the patterns of change of this society.

The large, oversize volumes of *Descriptive Sociology* make fascinating reading. They are, without doubt, among the most comprehensive and detailed descriptions of human societies ever constructed, certainly surpassing those of Max Weber or any other comparative social scientist of the late nineteenth and early twentieth centuries. Although the descriptions are flawed by the sources of data (historical accounts and travelers' published reports), Spencer's methodology is sound, and because he employed professional scholars to compile the data, they are as detailed as they could be at the time. Had the volumes of *Descriptive Sociology* not lapsed into obscurity and had they been updated with more accurate accounts, modern social science would, we believe, have a much firmer database for comparative sociological analysis and for theoretical activity.

Spencer's *Principles of Sociology*

The Principles of Sociology is a massive work—more than 2,000 pages.[23] It is filled with rich empirical details from *Descriptive Sociology*, but the book's importance resides in the theory that Spencer developed as the successive installments of this work were released between 1874 and 1896. In *The Principles of Sociology*, Spencer defined sociology as the study of *superorganic* phenomena—that is, of relations among organisms. Thus, sociology could study nonhuman societies, such as ants and other insects, but the paramount superorganic phenomenon is human society. Spencer employed an evolutionary model; over the long haul of history, societies had become increasingly complex. Human societies had followed the basic principles, articulated in *First Principles*, of evolutionary movement from small, homogeneous masses to more complex and differentiated masses. Thus, for Spencer, evolution is the process of increasing differentiation of human populations as they grow in size.

Spencer argued that several important factors always influence this movement from small and homogeneous to large and complex social forms. One is the nature of the people involved, another is the effects of environmental conditions, and a third is what he termed *derived factors* involving the new environments created by the evolution of

---

[23]Herbert Spencer, *The Principles of Sociology*, 3 vols., 8 parts (New York: Appleton-Century-Crofts, 1885; originally initiated in 1874). This particular edition is the third and is printed in five separate books; subsequent references are all to this third edition. Other editions vary in volume numbering, although part numbers are consistent across various editions. See also, Turner's edited reprint of this edition, published by Transaction Publishers. This reprint contains a long summary and analysis of *The Principles of Sociology*.

society. This last factor is the most important because the larger and more complex societies become, the more their culture and structure shapes the environment to which people and groups must adapt. Of particular importance are the effects of (1) size and density of a population and (2) the relations of societies with their neighbors. As the size and density of a population increases, it becomes more structurally differentiated, with the result that individuals live and adapt to highly diverse social and cultural environments. As societies get larger, they begin to have contact with their neighbors, and this contact can range from cordial relations of economic exchange to warfare and conquest. As we will see, these two derived factors are related in Spencer's scheme because the nature of internal differentiation of a population is very much influenced by the degree to which it is engaged in war with its neighbors.

The Superorganic and the Organismic Analogy

Part 2 of Volume 1 of *Principles of Sociology* contains virtually all the theoretical statements of Spencerian sociology. Employing the organismic analogy—that is, comparing organic (bodily) and super-organic (societal) organization—Spencer developed a perspective for analyzing the structure, function, and transformation of societal phenomena. Too often commentators have criticized Spencer for his use of the organismic analogy, but in fairness, we should emphasize that he generally employed the analogy cautiously. The basic point of the analogy is that because both organic and superorganic systems reveal organization among component parts, they should reveal certain common principles of organization. As Spencer stressed,

> between society and anything else, the only conceivable resemblance must be due to *parallelism of principle in the arrangement of components.*[24]

Spencer began his analogizing by discussing the similarities and differences between organic and superorganic systems. Among important similarities, he delineated the following:

1. Both society and organisms can be distinguished from inorganic matter, for both grow and develop.

---

[24]Spencer, *Principles of Sociology*, 1:448 (emphasis in original).

2. In both society and organisms, an increase in size means an increase in complexity and differentiation.

3. In both, a progressive differentiation in structure is accompanied by a differentiation in function.

4. In both, parts of the whole are interdependent, with a change in one part affecting other parts.

5. In both, each part of the whole is also a micro society or organism in and of itself.

6. And in both organisms and societies, the life of the whole can be destroyed, but the parts will live on for a while.[25]

Among the critical differences between a society and an organism, Spencer emphasized the following:

1. The degree of connectedness of the parts is vastly different in organic and superorganic bodies. There is close proximity and physical contact of parts in organic bodies, whereas in superorganic systems there is dispersion and only occasional physical contact of elements.

2. The nature of communication among elements is vastly different in organic and superorganic systems. In organic bodies, communication occurs as molecular waves passing through channels of varying degrees of coherence, whereas among humans communication occurs by virtue of the capacity to use language to communicate ideas and feelings.

3. In organic and superorganic systems, there are great differences in the respective consciousness of units. In organic bodies, only some elements in only some species reveal the capacity for conscious deliberations, whereas in human societies all individual units exhibit the capacity for conscious thought.

The Analysis of Superorganic Dynamics

If Spencer had only made these analogies, there would be little reason to examine his work. The analogies represent only a sensitizing

---

[25]This particular listing is taken from Jonathan H. Turner, *The Structure of Sociological Theory* (Belmont, CA: Wadsworth, 2004).

framework, but the real heart of Spencerian sociology is his portrayal of the dynamic properties of superorganic systems. We begin by examining his general model of system growth, differentiation, and integration; then we will see how he applied this model to societal processes.

System Growth, Differentiation, and Integration

As Spencer had indicated in *First Principles*, evolution involves movement from a homogeneous state to a more differentiated state. Spencer stressed that certain common patterns of movement from undifferentiated states can be observed.

First, growth in an organism and in society involves development from initially small units to larger ones.

Second, both individual organisms and societies reveal wide variability in the size and level of differentiation.

Third, growth in both organic and superorganic bodies occurs through compounding and recompounding; that is, smaller units are initially aggregated to form larger units (compounding), and then these larger units join other units (recompounding) to form an even larger whole. In this way, organic and superorganic systems become larger and more structurally differentiated. Hence, growth in size is always accompanied by structural differentiation of those units that have been compounded. For example, small clusters of cells in a bodily organism or in a small, primitive society initially join other cells or small societies (thus becoming compounded); then these larger units join other units (thus being recompounded) and form still larger and more differentiated organisms or societies; and so on for both organic and superorganic growth.

Fourth, growth and structural differentiation must be accompanied by integration. Thus, organic and societal bodies must reveal structural integration at each stage of compounding. Without such integration, recompounding is not possible. For instance, if two societies are joined, they must be integrated before they can, as a unit, become compounded with yet another society. In the processes of compounding, growth, differentiation, and integration, Spencer saw parallel mechanisms of integration in organisms and societies. For both organic and superorganic systems, integration is achieved increasingly through the dual processes of (1) centralization of regulating functions and (2) mutual dependence of unlike parts. In organisms, for example, the nervous system and the functions of the brain become increasingly centralized, and the organs become increasingly interdependent; in superorganic systems, political processes become more and more centralized, and institutions become increasingly dependent on one another.

Fifth, integration of matter through mutual dependence and centralization of control increase the "coherence" of the system and its adaptive capacity in a given environment. Such increased adaptive capacity often creates conditions favoring further growth, differentiation, and integration, although Spencer emphasized that dissolution often occurs when a system overextends itself by growing beyond its capacity to integrate new units.

These general considerations, which Spencer initially outlined in his 1862 *First Principles*, offer a model of structuring in social systems. In this model, the basic processes are (1) forces causing growth in system size, (2) the differentiation of units, (3) the processes whereby differentiated units become integrated, and (4) the creation of a "coherent heterogeneity," which increases the level of adaptation to the environment.

Thus, for Spencer, institutionalization is a process of growth in size, differentiation, integration, and adaptation. With integration and increased adaptation, a new system is institutionalized and capable of further growth. For example, a society that grows as the result of conquering another will tend to differentiate along lines of conqueror and conquered. It will centralize authority, it will create relations of interdependence, and, as a result, it will become more adapted to its environment. The result of this integration and adaptation is an increased capacity to conquer more societies, setting into motion another wave of growth, differentiation, integration, and adaptation. Similarly, a nonsocietal social system such as a corporation can begin growth through mergers or expenditures of capital, but it soon must differentiate functions and then integrate them through a combination of mutual dependence of parts and centralization of authority. If such integration is successful, it has increased the adaptive capacity of the system, which can grow if some capital surplus is available.

Conversely, to the extent that integration is incomplete, dissolution of the system is likely. Thus, social systems grow, differentiate, integrate, and achieve some level of adaptation to the environment, but at some point, the units cannot become integrated, setting the system into a phase of dissolution. Figure 5.1 illustrates this process.

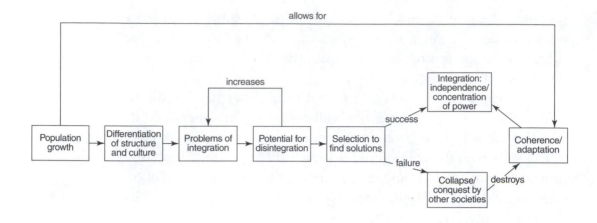

Figure 5.1   Spencer's General Model of Evolution

Thus, Spencer did not see growth, differentiation, and integration as inevitable. Rather, as differentiation increases, problems of integrating the larger social "mass" generate pressures to find solutions to these problems. For example, people will seek solutions if the roles people fill are poorly coordinated, if crime and deviance are high, if commitments to a society's values are weak, if people have no place to work, and if many other disintegrative pressures prevail. These disintegrative tendencies are a kind of "selection pressure" because, as problems of integration mount, members of a population see the problems and attempt to do something about them. If members find ways to develop relations of mutual interdependence and to regulate their actions with centralized authority, they can stave off these pressures for disintegration and prevent dissolution. Many societies, Spencer argued, had failed to respond adequately to pressures for integration, and as a result, they had collapsed or, more likely, had been conquered by a more integrated and powerful population. Indeed, Spencer argued that war has been an important force in human evolution because the more integrated and organized society will generally win wars against less integrated societies. As the conquered are integrated into the social structure and culture of their conquerors, the size and scale of society increases, and so, even as some societies dissolve or are conquered, the scale of societies had been slowly growing over the long course of human history. Spencer's famous phrase "survival of the fittest" was partly intended to communicate this geopolitical dimension of societal evolution.

Geopolitical Dynamics

Spencer's model of geopolitics is rather sophisticated for his time. As noted earlier, he argued that one of the most important forces increasing the size and scale of societies is war. Throughout *Principles of Sociology*, a theory of geopolitics is developed—a theory that, surprisingly, contemporary sociology ignores.

In this theory, Spencer posited that when power becomes centralized on its coercive base, leaders often use the mobilization of coercive power to repress conflicts within the society and, equally often, to conquer their neighbors. The reverse is also true: when leaders must deal with internal conflicts or external threats from other societies, they will centralize power to mobilize resources to deal with these sources of threat. So, for example, if there is class or ethnic conflict within a society, coercive power will be used to repress it, or if a neighboring society is seen as dangerous, political leaders will centralize coercive power to meet this perceived threat. Indeed, leaders will often use real or imagined internal and external threats as a way to legitimate their grabbing more power; once this power is consolidated, it can be used to centralize power even further.

The result is that once this cycle of threat and centralized power is initiated, it becomes self-fulfilling, for several reasons. First, when power is concentrated, it is used to usurp the wealth and resources of a population, with the result that inequality increases. Those with power simply tax or take resources from others to finance war making and supplement their privilege. And, as inequality increases, the sense of internal threat also escalates because those who have had their resources taken are generally hostile and pose a threat to elites who must then concentrate even more power to deal with this escalated threat, thereby increasing inequality and raising new threats. Over the long run, Spencer felt, this escalating cycle would potentially cause the disintegration of a society, or make it vulnerable to conquest by other societies. Second, when power is concentrated and used to make war against other societies, resources must be extracted to pay for this military effort, thus potentially causing escalated inequality and internal threat, which would compound problems of making war. As long as a society is successful in adventurism, the resentments of those who must pay for it often remain muted, but when external war making does not go well, the resentments from those who have had their resources taken will increase and pose internal threats to leaders, forcing them to mobilize more coercive power, if they can. Third, when power is concentrated to make war, and such efforts at conquest are successful, it then becomes necessary to control those who have been conquered. The need to manage a restive and resentful population pushes political leaders to concentrate more power, thus extracting increasing resources for social control. As resources are channeled to social control, inequality increases, thereby escalating internal threats, which require even more usurpation of resources to maintain social control.

For Spencer, then, concentrating power is a double-edged sword. It allows one population to conquer another and to increase the size, scale, and complexity of human societies, but it also increases inequalities and internal threats that, unless the cycle of concentrating more power is broken, causes the disintegration of the new, larger, and more complex society. This is why, Spencer argued, that military adventurism in the industrial era is ill advised; it drains a population's resources toward coercive and control activities and away from innovation and investment in domestic production. In essence, Spencer was arguing against the creation of what we would call today the *military–industrial complex*. Moreover, Spencer felt that once power is concentrated on the coercive base (military and police) of power, decision making by leaders in government is biased toward the use of coercion rather than alternatives, such as negotiation, compromise, use of incentives, and other alternatives to repression and tight control. For example, if Spencer had seen the rise of the Soviet Union through most of the twentieth century, his theory of geopolitics might have led him to predict its collapse in the 1990s.

Spencer's theory of geopolitics is woven throughout the pages of *Principles of Sociology*, and it is part of a much more general theory of evolution of societies moving from simple to more complex forms. Spencer conceptualized these movements as a series of prominent stages.

Stages of Societal Evolution

Spencer argued that increases in the size of a social aggregate necessitate the elaboration of its structure. Such increases in size are the result of high birth rates, migrations, and populations joining through conquest and assimilation. Although Spencer visualized much growth as the result of compounding and recompounding—that is, successive joining together of previously separate social systems through treaties, conquest, expropriation, and other means—he also employed the concept of compounding in another sense: to denote successive stages of internal growth and differentiation of social systems.

Spencer employed the terms *primary*, *secondary*, and *tertiary compounding*, by which he meant that a society had undergone a qualitative shift in the level of differentiation from a simpler to a more complex form.[26] These stages of compounding marked a new level of differentiation among and within what Spencer saw as three main axes of differentiation in social systems: (1) the *regulatory*, in which structures, mobilizing and using power manage relations with the external environment, while engaging in internal coordination of a society's members; (2) the *operative*, in which structures meet system needs for production of goods and commodities and for reproduction of system members and their culture; and (3) the *distributive*, in which structures move materials, people, and information. In simple societies, these three great axes of differentiation are collapsed together, but as societies grow and compound, distinctive structures emerge for each of these axes. The subsequent course of evolution then occurs with further differentiation between and within these axes.

Primary compounding occurs when the simplest structures become somewhat more complex. At first, only a differentiation of regulatory and operative processes is evident. For example, the sexual division of labor between males and females might move to one where some males have more authority than do females (regulatory functions), while females began to shoulder a greater burden in gathering food and in socializing the young (operative functions). Thus, the first big shift in the level of differentiation is along the regulatory and operative axes; only with further growth and differentiation of the population does a distinctive set of structures devoted to distribution of resources, people, and information emerge. Secondary compounding occurs, Spencer argued, when the structures involved in regulatory, operative, and distributive functions undergo further differentiation. For example, internal administrative structures might become distinguished from warfare roles in the regulative system; varieties of domestic activities, with specialized persons or groups involved in these separate activities, might become evident; or distinguishable persons or groups involved in external trade and internal commerce might become differentiated. Tertiary compounding occurs when

---

[26]Spencer, *Principles of Sociology*, 1:479–483.

these secondary structures undergo further internal differentiation, so that one can observe distinct structures involved in varieties of regulatory, operative, and distributive processes.

Figure 5.2 represents these dynamics diagrammatically as a model. This model outlines the "stages" of societal evolution in three respects. First, Spencer saw five basic stages: (1) simple without head or leadership, (2) simple with head or leadership, (3) compound, (4) doubly compound, and (5) trebly compound. Second, he visualized each stage as being denoted by (1) a given degree of differentiation *among* regulatory, operative, and distributive processes and (2) a level of differentiation *within* each process. Third, he suggested how the nature of regulation, operation, and distribution changes with each stage of compounding (as denoted by the descriptive labels in each box in Figure 5.2).

Contained within Spencer's view of the stages of evolution is a mode of functional analysis. By viewing social structures with reference to regulatory, operative, and distributive processes, Spencer implicitly argued that these three processes represent basic "functional needs" of all organic and superorganic systems. Thus, a particular structure is to be assessed by its contribution to one or more of these three basic needs. But Spencer's functionalism is even more detailed, for he argued in several places that all social structures had their own internal regulatory, operative, or distributive needs, regardless of which of the three functions they fulfilled for the larger social whole in which they were located.[27] For example, the family might be viewed as an operative structure for the society as a whole, but it also reveals its own division of labor along regulatory, operative, and distributive functions.

Sequences of Differentiation

Spencer devoted most of his attention to analyzing the regulatory system because he was primarily a theorist of power.[28] His discussion revolves around delineating those conditions under which the regulatory system (1) becomes differentiated from operative and distributive processes and (2) becomes internally differentiated. We can consider Spencer a political theorist because of this emphasis on the regulating system—that is, the center of power in society.

---

[27]Ibid., 477.
[28]Ibid., Part 2, 519–548.

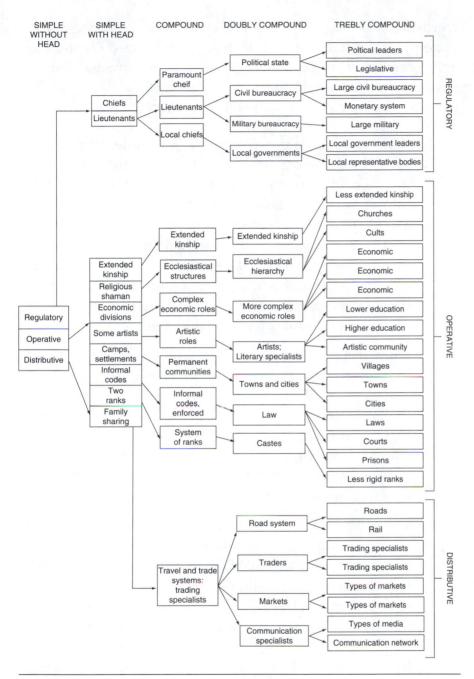

Figure 5.2   Spencer's Stage Model of Societal Evolution

If we translate differentiation between regulatory and operative functions into more modern terminology, then the first phase of differentiation is between the emergence of a political system and specialized structures involved in (a) production or the conversion of resources into usable commodities and (b) reproduction or the regeneration of people as well as their culture. Most of Spencer's sociology is devoted to the regulatory system, especially the cause and consequences of centralized power on operative and distributive processes. In general, Spencer posited the following conditions as increasing the concentration and centralization of power:

1. When productive processes become complex, they require some kind of external authority to coordinate activity to ensure that exchanges proceed smoothly, to maintain contractual obligations, to prevent fraud and corruption, and to ensure that necessary productive activities are conducted. These pressures for external authority lead to the mobilization of power. Once this capacity to regulate the economy exists, the level of production can expand further, creating new pressures for expanded use of power to coordinate more complex levels of economic activity.

2. When there are internal threats, typically arising from conflicts over inequalities, centers of power will mobilize to control the conflict. Ironically, the use of power to control conflict often increases inequality because those with power begin to usurp resources for themselves. As a result, as more power is concentrated, further inequality and conflict will ensue in a cycle of conflict, use of power to control and usurp, increased inequality, and escalated potential for conflict.

3. When there are external threats from other societies arising from economic competition or military confrontations, centers of power will mobilize coercive forces to deal with such threats. Consequently, they will also set off the dynamics described under (2), because when power is mobilized to deal with threats, it is also used to enhance the well-being of elites, thereby increasing inequality and the potential for conflict. Moreover, as noted for Spencer's theory of geopolitics, when a political system is mobilized for conflict with other societies, it will generally pursue war as the first option (rather than diplomacy), with the result that if it wins a war, this very success creates new internal threats, as specified in (2) above, revolving around the inequalities between conquerors and conquered.

As both regulatory and operative processes develop, Spencer argued, pressures for transportation, communication, and exchange among larger and more differentiated units increase. As a result of these pressures, new structures emerge as part of a general expansion of distributive functions. Spencer devoted considerable attention to the historical events causing increases in transportation, roads, markets, and communication processes, and by themselves, these descriptions make for fascinating reading. At the most general level, he concluded,

> the truth we have to carry with us is that the distributing system in the social organism, as in the individual organism, has its development determined by the necessities of transfer among inter-dependent parts. Lying between the two original systems, which carry on respectively the outer dealings with surrounding existences, and the inner dealings with materials required for sustentation [sic] its structure becomes adapted to the requirements of this carrying function between the two great systems as wholes, and between the sub-divisions of each.[29]

As the regulatory and operative systems expand, thereby causing the elaboration of the distributive system, this third great system differentiates in ways that facilitate increases in (1) the speed with which material and information circulate and (2) the varieties of materials and information that are distributed. As the capacities for rapid and varied distribution increase, regulatory and operative processes can develop further; as the latter expand and differentiate, new pressures for rapid and varied distribution are created. Moreover, in a series of insightful remarks, Spencer noted that this positive feedback cycle involved an increase in the ratio of information to materials distributed in complex, differentiating systems.[30]

In sum, then, Spencer's view of structural elaboration emphasizes the processes of structural growth and differentiation through the joining of separate systems and through internal increases in size. As an evolutionist, Spencer took the long-range view of social development as growth, differentiation, integration, and increased adaptive capacity; then, with this new level as a base, further growth, differentiation, integration, and adaptive capacity would be possible.

---

[29]Ibid., 1:518.

[30]Of course, the absolute amounts of both increase, but the processing of information—credits, accounts, ideas, purchase orders, and so on—increases as a proportion of things circulated.

His view of structural elaboration is thus highly sophisticated, and though flawed in many ways, it is the equal of any other nineteenth-century social theory.

System Dialectics and Phases

As we have emphasized, Spencer saw war as an important causal force in human societies. War pushes a society to develop centralized regulatory structures to expand and coordinate internal operative and distributive processes. Yet war can have an ironic effect on a society: once these operative and distributive processes are expanded under conditions of external conflict, they increasingly exert pressures for less militaristic activity and for less authoritarian centralization. For example, a nation at war will initially centralize along authoritarian lines to mobilize resources, but as such mobilization expands the scope of operative and distributive processes, those engaged in operation and distribution develop autonomy and begin to press for greater freedom from centralized control. In this way, Spencer was able to visualize war as an important force in societal development but, at the same time, as an impediment to development if concentrated power is used to concentrate even more power. And in an enlightening chapter on "social metamorphoses,"[31] he argued that the dynamic force underlying the overall evolution of the superorganic from homogeneous to heterogeneous states was the successive movement of societies in and out of "militant" (politically centralized and authoritarian) and "industrial" (less centralized) phases. This cyclical dynamic is presented in Figure 5.3, which views these phases somewhat more abstractly than in Spencer's portrayal.

Figure 5.3 presents one of the most interesting (and often ignored) arguments in Spencerian sociology. For Spencer, there is always a dialectical undercurrent during societal evolution (and dissolution) revolving around the relationship between regulatory and operative processes. On the one hand, each of these initial axes of differentiation encourages the growth and development of the other in a positive feedback cycle, but, on the other hand, there is an inherent tension and dialectic between the two. For example, war expands regulatory functions; increased regulatory capacity allows for more extensive coordination of operative processes; greater operative

---

[31]Spencer, *Principles of Sociology*, 1:577–585.

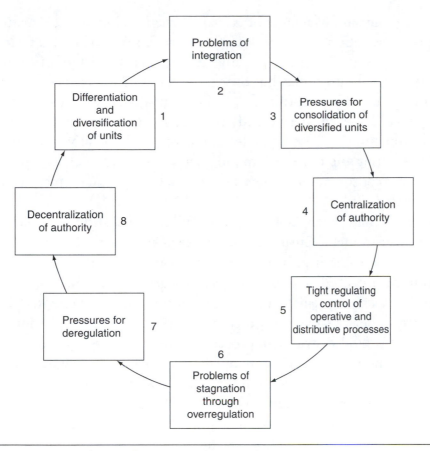

Figure 5.3   Phases of Institutionalization

capacity encourages expanded war efforts and, hence, expansion of the regulatory system. But at some point in this cycle, development of internal operative structures primarily for war making becomes counterproductive, limiting the scope and diversity of development in operative processes. Indeed, Spencer argued that too much political control of production and reproduction causes economic stagnation and, in the reproductive sphere, arouses resentments. Over time, and under growing pressures from the internal sector as mobilization against tight control increases, the warlike profile of the regulatory system is reduced. Thus, as resentments against too much power arise, it is not inevitable that political elites will continue to concentrate power to manage such threats, as we examined earlier in Spencer's theory of geopolitics. Spencer saw an alternative: Growing resentment leads political leaders to make concessions and to recognize that they must release some of their control. Spencer never specifies the conditions under which leaders will give up power; he simply assumed that it had been an important dynamic in the evolution of human societies from simple to complex forms. When power is released, operative structures expand and differentiate in many directions, but over time, these structures become too divergent, poorly coordinated, and unregulated. A war can provide, Spencer believed, the needed stimulus for greater regulation and coordination of these expanded and diversified operative processes, thus setting the cycle into motion once again. Alternatively, problems of coordination become so acute that government must step in to restore order.

Such had been the case throughout evolutionary history, Spencer thought. Curiously, he also seemed to argue that modern, industrial capitalism made the need for war and extensive regulation by a central state obsolete. No longer would it be necessary, in Spencer's capitalistic utopia, for centralized government, operating under the pressures of war, to seek extensive regulation of operative and distributive processes. These processes were, in his vision, now sufficiently developed and capable of growth, expansion, and integration without massive doses of governmental intervention. Here, Spencer's ideology clearly distorts his perceptions because advanced capitalism requires the exercise of control by government; yet the analysis of the dialectic between militant and industrial societies allowed him to see how concentrated power could be lessened without disintegration.

Classifying Social Systems

Spencer also used these models of societal evolution (Figure 5.2) and system phases (Figure 5.3) as a basis for classifying societies. His most famous typology (Table 5.1) is of what he termed *militant* and *industrial* societies—a typology that commentators have frequently misunderstood. Too often it is viewed as representing a unilinear course of evolutionary movement from traditional and militant to modern and industrial societal forms. Although Spencer often addressed the evolution of societies from a primitive to a modern profile, he did not rely heavily on the militant–industrial typology in describing types or stages of evolutionary change. Rather, as is emphasized in Figure 5.3, the militant–industrial distinction is primarily directed at capturing the difference between highly centralized authority systems where regulatory processes dominate and less centralized systems where operative processes

Table 5.1   Spencer's Typology of Militant and Industrial Societies

Basic System Processes	Militant	Industrial
1. Regulatory processes		
a. Societal goals	Defense and war	Internal productivity and provision of services
b. Political organization	Centralized, authoritarian	Less centralized; less direct authority over system units
2. Operative processes		
a. Individuals	High degrees of control by state; high levels of stratification	Freedom from extensive controls by state; less stratification
b. Social structures	Coordinated to meet politically established goals of war and defense	Coordinated to facilitate each structure's expansion and growth
3. Distributive processes		
a. Flow of materials	From organizations to state; from state to individuals and other social units	From organizations to other units and individuals
b. Flow of information	From state to individuals	Both individuals to state and state to individuals

prevail.[32] The term *industrial* does not refer to industrial production in the sense of modern factories and markets but, instead, to a reduction in centralized power and to the vitality and diversity of operative processes. Both the simplest and most modern societies can be either militant or industrial; Spencer hoped that modern industrial capitalism would be industrial rather than militaristic.

---

[32]The misinterpretation of Spencer's intent stems from his introduction of the typology at several points in *Principles of Sociology*. From its usage in his discussion of political and industrial (economic) institutions, it would be easy to see the typology as his version of the stages of evolution. But if one reads the more analytical statement in the early chapter on social types and constitutions in Vol. 1, paying particular attention to the fact that this chapter precedes the one on social metamorphoses, then our interpretation is clear. Because Spencer uses another typology for describing the long-run evolutionary trends, it seems unlikely that he would duplicate this effort with yet another typology on militant–industrial societies. See, in particular, *Principles of Sociology*, Vol. 1, Part 2, 569–580.

As we noted in the last section, however, Spencer saw societies as cycling in and out of centralized and decentralized phases. The typology is meant to capture this dynamic.

The distinction between militant and industrial societies emphasizes that during the course of social growth, differentiation, integration, and adaptive upgrading,[33] societies move in and out of militant (dominance of regulatory) and industrial (operative) phases. Militant phases consolidate the diversified operative structures of industrial phases. The causes of either a militant or industrial profile for a system at any given time are varied, but Spencer saw as critical (1) the degree of external threat from other systems and (2) the need to integrate dissimilar populations and cultures. The greater the threat to a system from external systems or the more diverse the system's population (an internal threat), the more likely it is to reveal a militant profile. Once external and internal threats have been mitigated through conquest, treaties, assimilation, and other processes, however, pressures for movement to an industrial profile increase. Such is the basic dynamic underlying broad evolutionary trends from a homogeneous to a heterogeneous state of social organization.

Spencer's other typology, which has received considerably less attention than the militant–industrial distinction, addresses the major stages in the evolution of societies. Whereas the militant–industrial typology seeks to capture the cyclical dynamics underlying evolutionary movement, Spencer also attempts to describe the distinctive stages of long-term societal development, as was modeled earlier in Figure 5.2. This typology revolves around describing the pattern and direction of societal differentiation. As such, it is concerned with the processes of compounding. As was evident in Figure 5.2, Spencer marked distinctive stages of societal growth and differentiation: simple (with and without leadership), compound, doubly compound, and trebly compound.

In Table 5.2, we have taken Spencer's narrative and organized it in a somewhat more formal way. But the listing of characteristics for simple (both those with leaders and those without), compound, doubly compound, and trebly compound societies for regulatory, operative, and distributive as well as for demographic (population characteristics) dimensions captures the essence of Spencer's intent.

---

[33]We are using Parsons's terms here because they best connote Spencer's intent. See Parsons, *Societies*, cited in Note 34.

Several points need to be emphasized. First, although certain aspects of Spencer's description are flawed, his summary of the distinctive stages of societal evolution is equal, or superior, to any that recent anthropologists and sociologists have delineated.[34] Second, this description is far superior to any developed by other anthropologists and sociologists of Spencer's time.

Spencer sought to communicate what we can term *structural explanations* with this typology. The basic intent of this mode of explanation is to view certain types of structures as tending to coexist. As Spencer concluded,

> the inductions arrived at . . . show that in social phenomena there is a general order of co-existence and sequence; and therefore social phenomena form the subject-matter of a science reducible, in some measure at least, to the deductive form.[35]

Thus, by reading down the columns of Table 5.2, we can see that certain structures are likely to coexist within a system. And by reading across the table, the patterns of change in structures with each increment of societal differentiation can be observed. Moreover, as Spencer stressed, such patterns of social evolution conformed to the general law of evolution enunciated in *First Principles*.

> The many facts contemplated unite in proving that social evolution forms a part of evolution at large. Like evolving aggregates in general, societies show *integration*, both by simple increase of mass and by coalescence and re-coalescence of masses. The change from *homogeneity* to *heterogeneity* is multitudinously exemplified; up from the simple tribe, alike in all its parts, to the civilized nation, full of structural and functional unlikenesses. With progressing integration and heterogeneity goes increasing *coherence.* We see the wandering group dispersing, dividing, held together by no bonds; the tribe with parts made more coherent by subordination to a dominant man; the cluster of tribes united in a political plexus under a chief with sub-chiefs; and so on up to the civilized nation, consolidated enough to hold together for a thousand years

---

[34]See, for example, Talcott Parsons, *Societies* (1966) and *The System of Modern Societies* (Englewood Cliffs, NJ: Prentice Hall, 1971); Gerhard Lenski, Jean Lenski, and Patrick Nolan, *Human Societies* (New York: McGraw-Hill, 1991); and Morton H. Fried, *The Evolution of Political Society* (New York: Random House, 1967).

[35]Spencer, *Principles of Sociology*, Vol. 1, Part 2, 597.

Table 5.2   Spencer's Stages of Evolution

System Dimensions	Simple Society	
	Headless	**Headed**
1. Regulatory system	Temporary leaders who emerge in response to particular problems	Permanent chief and various lieutenants
2. Operative system		
a. Economic structure	Hunting and gathering	Pastoral; simple agriculture
b. Religious structure	Individualized religious worship	Beginnings of religious specialists: shaman
c. Family structure	Simple; sexual division of labor	Large, complex; sexual and political division of labor
d. Artistic–literary forms	Little art; no literature	Some art; no literature
e. Law and customs	Informal codes of conduct	Informal codes of conduct
f. Community structure	Small bands of wandering families	Small, settled groupings of families
g. Stratification	None	Chief and followers
3. Distributive system		
a. Materials	Sharing within family and band	Intra- and interfamilial exchange and sharing
b. Information	Oral, personal	Oral, personal
4. Demographic profile		
a. Size	Small	Large
b. Mobility	Mobility within territory	Less mobility; frequently tied to territory

Compound Society	Doubly Compound	Trebly Compound (Never Formally Listed)
Hierarchy of chiefs, with paramount chief, local chiefs, and varieties of lieutenants	Elaboration of bureaucratized political state; differentiation between domestic and military administration	Modern political state
Agricultural; general and local division of labor	Agricultural; extensive division of labor	Industrial capitalism
Established ecclesiastical arrangements	Ecclesiastical hierarchy; rigid rituals and religious observance	Religious diversity in separate church structures
Large, complex; numerous sexual, age, and political divisions	Large, complex; numerous sexual, age, and political divisions	Small, simple; decreased in sexual division of labor
Artists	Artists; literary specialists; scholars	Many artistic literary specialists; scholars
Informal codes; enforced by political elites and community members	Written law and codes	Elaborate legal codes; civil and criminal
Village; permanent buildings	Large towns; permanent structures	Cities, towns, and hamlets
Five or six clear ranks	Castes; rigid divisions	Classes; less rigid
Travel and trade between villages	Roads among towns; considerable travel and exchange; traders and other specialists	Roads, rail, and other nonmanual transportation; many specialists
Oral, personal; at times, mediated by elites or travelers	Oral and written; edicts; oracles; teachers and other communications specialists	Oral and written; formal media structures for edicts; many communications specialists
Larger; joining of several simple societies	Large	Large
Less mobility; tied to territory; movement among villages of a defined territory	Settled; much travel among towns	Settled; growing urban concentrations; much travel; movement from rural to urban centers

or more. Simultaneously comes increasing *definiteness*. Social organization is at first vague; advance brings settled arrangements which
grow slowly more precise; customs pass into laws which, while gaining fixity, also become more specific in their applications to varieties of actions; and all institutions, at first confusedly intermingled,
slowly separate, at the same time that each within itself marks off
more distinctly its component structures. Thus in all respects is fulfilled the formula of evolution. There is progress towards greater size,
coherence, multiformity, and definiteness.[36]

In sum, then, Spencer provided two basic typologies for classifying
societal systems. One typology—the militant–industrial distinction—
emphasizes the cyclical phases of all societies at any stage of evolution.
The second typology is less well-known but probably more important.
It delineates the structural features and demographic profile of societies at different stages of evolution. Embedded in this typology is a
series of statements on what structures tend to cluster together during
societal growth and differentiation. This typology is, in many ways,
the implicit guide for Spencer's structural and functional analysis
of basic societal institutions, which comprises Parts 3 through 7 in
Volumes 1 and 2 of *Principles of Sociology*. We should, therefore, close
our review of *Principles of Sociology* by briefly noting some of the more
interesting generalizations that emerge from Spencer's description of
basic human institutions.

The Analysis of Societal Institutions

Fully two thirds of *Principles of Sociology* is devoted to an evolutionary
description and explanation of basic human institutions.[37] For Spencer,
institutions are enduring patterns of social organization that (1) meet
fundamental functional needs or requisites of human organization and
(2) control the activities of individuals and groups in society. Spencer
employed a "social selection" argument in his review of institutional
dynamics. The most basic institutions emerge and persist because they
provide a population with adaptive advantages in a given environment, both natural and social. That is, those patterns of organization

---

[36]Ibid., 596.

[37]See Turner, *Herbert Spencer* (cited in Note 11), for a more detailed review of Spencer's
institutional analysis.

that facilitate the survival of a population in the natural environment and in the milieu of other societies will be retained, or "selected"; as a consequence, these patterns will become institutionalized in the structure of a society. Because certain problems of survival always confront the organization of people, it is inevitable that among surviving populations a number of common institutions would be evident for all enduring societies—for example, kinship, ceremony, politics, religion, and economy. Spencer discusses more than these five institutions, but our review will emphasize only these, because they provide some of the more interesting insights in Spencerian sociology.

Domestic Institutions and Kinship

Spencer argued that kinship emerged to meet the most basic need of all species: reproduction.[38] Because a population must regulate its own reproduction before it can survive for long, kinship was one of the first human institutions. This regulation of reproduction involves the control of sexual activity, the development of more permanent bonds between men and women, and the provision of a safe context for rearing children.

Spencer's discussion of kinship was extremely sophisticated for his time. After making the previous functional arguments, he embarked on an evolutionary analysis of varying types of kinship systems. Although flawed in some respects, his approach was nonetheless insightful and anticipated similar arguments by twentieth-century anthropologists. Some of the more interesting generalizations emerging from his analysis are the following:

1. In the absence of alternative ways of organizing a population, kinship processes will become the principal mechanism of social integration.

2. The greater the size of a population without alternative ways of organizing activity, the more elaborate will be a kinship system, and the more it will reveal explicit rules of descent, marriage, endogamy, and exogamy.

---

[38]Spencer, *Principles of Sociology*, Vol. 1, Part 3, 603–757. See also Leonard Beeghley, "Spencer's Analysis of the Evolution of the Family and the Status of Women: Some Neglected Considerations," *Sociological Perspectives* (formerly *Pacific Sociological Review*) 26 (August 1983), 299–313.

3. Those societies that engage in perpetual conflict will tend to create patrilineal descent systems and patriarchic authority; as a consequence, they will reveal less equality between the sexes and will be more likely to define and treat women as property.[39]

Ceremonial Institutions

Spencer recognized that human relations were structured by symbols and rituals.[40] Indeed, he tended to argue that other institutions—kinship, government, and religion—were founded on a "preinstitutional" basis revolving around interpersonal ceremonies, such as the use of (1) particular forms of address, (2) titles, (3) ritualized exchanges of greetings, (4) demeanors, (5) patterns of deference, (6) badges of honor, (7) fashion and dress, and (8) other means for ordering interactions among individuals. Thus, as people interact, they "present themselves" through their demeanor, fashion, forms of talk, badges, titles, and rituals, and in so doing they expect certain responses from others. Interaction is thereby mediated by symbols and ceremonies that structure how individuals are to behave toward one another. Without this control of relations through symbols and ceremonies, larger institutional structures could not be sustained.

Spencer was particularly interested in the effects of inequality on ceremonial processes, especially inequalities created by centralization of power (as is the case in the militant societies depicted in Table 5.1). These interesting generalizations emerge from his more detailed analysis:

1. The greater the degree of political centralization that exists in a society, the greater the level of inequality will be and, hence, the greater the concern for symbols and ceremonials demarking differences in rank among individuals will be.

2. The greater the concern over differences in rank, (a) the more likely people in different ranks are to possess distinctive objects and titles to mark their respective ranks, and (b) the more likely interactions between people in different ranks are to be ritualized by standardized forms of address and stereotypical patterns of deference and demeanor.

---

[39]See Turner, *Herbert Spencer* (cited in Note 11), 115.
[40]Spencer, *Principles of Sociology*, Vol. 2, Part 4, 3–216.

3. Conversely, the less the degree of political centralization and the less the level of inequality, the less people are concerned about the symbols and ceremonies that demark rank and regulate interaction.[41]

Political Institutions

In his analysis of political processes in society, Spencer also developed a perspective for examining social class structures.[42] In his view, problems of internal conflict resulting from unbridled self-interest and the existence of hostility with other societies have been the prime causal forces behind the emergence and elaboration of government. Although governments reveal considerable variability, they all evidence certain common features: (1) paramount leaders, (2) clusters of subleaders and administrators, (3) large masses of followers who subordinate some of their interests to the dictates of leaders, and (4) legitimating beliefs and values that give leaders "the right" to regulate others. Spencer argued that once governmental structures exist, they are self-perpetuating and will expand unless they collapse internally for lack of legitimacy or are conquered from without. In particular, war and threats of war centralize government on the use of force to conquer additional territories and internally regulate operative processes, with the result that governmental structures expand. Moreover, the expansion of government and its centralization create or exacerbate class divisions in a society because those with resources can use them to mobilize power and political decisions that further enhance their hold on valued resources. Thus, Spencer developed a very robust political sociology, and although a listing of only a few generalizations cannot do justice to the sophistication of his approach, some of his more interesting conclusions are the following:

1. The larger the number of people and internal transactions among individuals in a society, the greater will be the size and degree of internal differentiation of government.

2. The greater the actual or potential level of conflict with other societies and within a society, the greater will be the degree of centralization of power in government.

---

[41]See Turner, *Herbert Spencer*, 122.

[42]Spencer, *Principles of Sociology*, Vol. 2, Part 5, 229–643.

3. The greater the centralization of power, the more visible class divisions will be; and the more these divisions create potential or actual internal conflict.

Religious Institutions

Spencer's analysis emphasized that all religions shared certain common elements: (1) beliefs about supernatural beings and forces, (2) organized groupings of individuals who share these beliefs, and (3) ritual activities directed toward those beings and forces presumed to have the capacity to influence worldly affairs.[43] Religions emerge in all societies, he argued, because they increase the survival of a population by (1) reinforcing values and beliefs through the sanctioning power of the supernatural and (2) strengthening existing social structural arrangements, especially those revolving around power and inequality, by making them seem to be extensions of the supernatural will.

Spencer provided an interesting scenario on the evolution of religion from primitive notions of "ancestor spirits" to the highly bureaucratized monotheistic religions that currently dominate the world. He saw the evolution and structural patterns of religion as intimately connected to political processes, leading him to propose the following generalizations:

1. The greater the level of war and conquest by a society, the greater are the problems of consolidating diverse religious beliefs, thereby forcing the expansion of the religious class of priests to reconcile these diverse religions and create polytheistic religions.

2. The greater the political centralization and the greater the level of class inequalities in a society, the more likely is the priestly class to create a coherent pantheon of ranked deities.

3. The more government relies on the priestly class to provide legitimation through a complex system of religious beliefs and symbols, the more this class extracts wealth and privilege from political leaders, thereby consolidating their distinctive class position and creating an elaborate bureaucratic structure for organizing religious activity.

---

[43]Ibid., Vol. 2, Part 6, 3–159. We should note how close this view of religious functions is to that to be developed by Durkheim.

4. The more centralized a government is and the more it relies on religious legitimation by a privileged and bureaucratized class of priests, the greater is the likelihood of a religious revolt and the creation of a simplified and monotheistic religion.

Economic Institutions

For Spencer, the long-term evolution of economic institutions revolves around (1) increases in technology or knowledge about how to manipulate the natural environment, (2) expansion of the production and distribution of goods and services, (3) accumulation of capital or the tools of production, and (4) changes in the organization of labor.[44] In turn, these related processes are the result of efforts to achieve greater levels of adaptation to the environment and to meet constantly escalating human needs. That is, as one level of economic adaptation is created, people's needs for new products and services escalate and generate pressures for economic reorganization. Thus, as new technologies, modes of production, mechanisms of distribution, forms of capital, and means for organizing labor around productive processes are developed, a more effective level of adaptation to the natural environment is achieved; as this increased adaptive capacity is established, people begin to desire more. As a result, economic production becomes less and less tied to problems of survival in the natural environment during societal evolution and increasingly the result of escalating wants and desires among the members of a society.

Spencer further argued that war decreased advances in overall economic productivity because mobilization for war distorts the economy away from domestic production toward the development of military technologies and the organization of production around military products or services. For Spencer, war depletes capital, suppresses wants and needs for consumer goods, encourages only military technologies, and mobilizes labor for wartime production (while killing off much of the productive labor force). Only during times of relative peace, then, will economic growth ensue. Such growth in the domestic economy will be particularly likely to occur when there are increases in population size. In Spencer's view, escalating population size under conditions of peace creates pressure for expanded production while increasing needs for new products and services. These and

---

[44]Ibid., Vol. 2, Part 8, 327–608.

many other lines of argument in his analysis of the economy have a highly modern flavor, but unlike his approach to other institutions, he presents few abstract generalizations, so we will not attempt to conclude with any here.

This brief summary of Spencer's analysis of basic institutions does not do justice to the sophistication of his approach. As much as any scholar of his time, or of today, he saw the complex interrelationships among social structures. One reason for this sophistication in his analysis is his in-depth knowledge of diverse societies, which he acquired through the efforts of researchers hired to construct descriptions of historical and contemporary societies. Throughout his work, his ideas are illustrated by references to diverse societies. Such familiarity with many historical and contemporary societies came from his efforts to build a "descriptive sociology."

Critical Conclusions

Herbert Spencer is, without doubt, the most neglected of the early sociological theorists. Comte is, of course, also neglected but unlike Spencer, he never really developed a theory. Spencer did articulate a theory that, for the most part, contemporary sociologists ignore. Why should this be so?

Spencer's moral philosophy clearly stigmatized him, especially his view that government should not intervene too extensively to help the unfortunate. Such a view ran counter to the expansion of the welfare state in the twentieth century. This ideology taints Spencer's sociology, and it has clearly made scholars reluctant to give it a fair reading.

Spencer's coining of the phrase "survival of the fittest" and the use of this idea in much twentieth-century conservative philosophy, and even worse, in the eugenics movement of the past century further stigmatized his sociology. Indeed, those advocating the selective breeding of humans, or alternatively, the natural death of the "less fit" have at times made appeals to Spencer, a fact that certainly has not helped our retrospective view of him.

Spencer also was the supreme generalist at a time when academic disciplines were beginning to specialize. Spencer's sociology is a part of a much larger, almost cosmic vision of evolution in all domains of the universe. Twentieth-century sociologists were less likely to embrace such grandiose and rather vague pronouncements, and this is even more the case for the discipline today where hyperspecialization is rapidly occurring.

Spencer's emphasis on evolution as the master societal process was also to get him into trouble. By the second decade of the twentieth century, evolutionary thinking was under heavy attack, and as the supreme evolutionary thinker in the social sciences, Spencer was under constant criticism. When the evolutionary paradigm collapsed and fell into obscurity in the 1930s, so did Spencer's sociology. Even with the revival of evolutionary thinking in the 1960s in sociology, Spencer was never resurrected, except by a few dedicated scholars.

Spencer probably wrote too much. The key ideas of Spencer's sociology must be extracted from thousands of pages, and most sociologists are unwilling to read all these materials. Still, if scholars will have the patience to read through these many pages, Spencer's sociology had many strong points that deserve a rehearing. First, Spencer developed a very sophisticated theory of politics in his sociology. This theory emphasizes that the concentration of power dramatically transforms all other institutional systems, as can be seen by the propositions that we have listed in the text, and it sets into motion both geopolitical and dialectical dynamics. Even by today's standards, this portion of Spencer's sociology is rather sophisticated. Indeed, Spencer should be considered a political theorist as much as a functionalist or evolutionary thinker, and if this fact were recognized, perhaps sociologists would be willing to give his work another reading. Second, Spencer's views on the dynamics of differentiation are worth revisiting. The basic relationships among system size, level of differentiation, and integration through interdependence and power do represent some of sociology's most powerful laws. Although more contemporary sociologists have worked with these ideas, they seem to forget from where they come. And third, even though the use of so much data from his *Descriptive Sociology* makes reading *The Principles of Sociology* an arduous task, much can be learned from these materials. Few sociologists have ever documented their arguments with so much ethnographic and historical detail. In some ways, Spencer can serve as a model for how this should be done.

CHAPTER 6

The Origin and Context of Karl Marx's Thought

Biographical Influences on Marx's Thought

Karl Marx, theorist and revolutionary, was born to Heinrich and Henrietta Marx on May 5, 1818, in the city of Trier. Located in the Rhineland, Trier was (and is) the commercial center of the Moselle wine-growing area of Germany. Descended from a long line of rabbis on both sides of the family, the young Marx lived in a stable bourgeois (or middle-class) household. His father, a lawyer and lover of ideas, converted to Lutheranism in 1817 to protect his position. Although Jewish by heritage, the elder Marx appears to have had little interest in organized religion, being attracted to the deism characteristic of the Enlightenment. The young Marx was apparently close to his father and learned of Voltaire, Rousseau, and other writers on individualism and human progress from him.

As Marx grew up, he was also influenced by an upper-class Prussian, Ludwig von Wesphalen, whose daughter Jenny he eventually married. Despite status differences between the two families, von Wesphalen took a liking to Marx, encouraging him to read and introducing him to works of the great German writers of the time, Johann Goethe and Friedrich Schiller, as well as to the classical Greek philosophers.

This intellectual background paved the way for Marx's subsequent study of the philosophy of G. W. F. Hegel and the political economy of Adam Smith, leading eventually to a theoretical critique of the capitalist social order. Just as important, however, these aspects of his background made Marx peculiar among nineteenth-century revolutionaries, for he was neither thwarted nor persecuted as a young man. Thus, although he was arrogant, vain, and vindictive toward enemies, Marx was also positive and self-confident throughout his adult life.[1]

Hegel and the Young Hegelians

After graduating from the Trier gymnasium (or high school), the 17-year-old Marx enrolled at the University of Bonn in 1835. After a year, however, he left for the more cosmopolitan and sophisticated University of Berlin. Here he encountered Hegel's idealism. The great philosopher, who died only a few years before, dominated intellectual life in Germany at that time. Marx also met youthful academic interpreters of Hegel, who called themselves Young Hegelians. They constituted Marx's first contact with people who did not blindly accept the dominant values and norms of German society.

The Young Hegelians, including forgotten men such as Max Stirner, Bruno Bauer, David Strauss, and Ludwig Feuerbach, saw themselves as radicals. And they were, in fact, irreligious and liberal. They questioned the established order in Prussia (where Berlin was located). Marx noted their influence on him in a now-famous letter to his father. "There are moments in one's life," he wrote, "which are like frontier posts marking the completion of a period but at the same time clearly indicating a new direction." After studying Hegel's idealism, he continued, "I arrived at the point of seeking the idea in reality itself."[2] The last phrase is important, for Marx was asserting that he had rejected Hegel's idealism in favor of studying "reality itself," as defined by the Young Hegelians. In effect, he questioned the status quo. He thus initiated the long process of transforming philosophy into social science.

---

[1]Isaiah Berlin, *Karl Marx: His Life and Environment* (New York: Oxford University Press, 1963), 33.

[2]Karl Marx, "Discovering Hegel" (Marx's letter to his father), in *The Marx-Engels Reader*, ed. Robert C. Tucker (New York: Norton, 1978), 7–9.

This transition, however, occurred in a very despotic social context. During most of the nineteenth century, Prussia was perhaps the most repressive nation in Europe, with organized religion supporting the state's activities. Those who questioned the established order, religious or political, were treated as subversive. Hence, over time the Young Hegelians saw their writings censored and found themselves dismissed from faculty positions.

Nonetheless, the young Marx prepared himself for a life in academia. In addition to studying philosophy, he wrote hundreds of poems, a novel, a play modeled after a Greek tragedy, and much more. In 1841, Marx received a doctorate based on a thesis titled "The Difference Between the Democritean and Epicurean Philosophy of Nature."[3] Unfortunately, his academic patrons had been dismissed from their posts and were unable to obtain a position for him. Marx was thus left without career prospects.

Lacking alternatives, Marx tried journalism, becoming a writer for—and eventually editor of—a liberal newspaper, the *Rheinisch Zeitung* (or *Rhineland News*). In this role, he battled the Prussian censors constantly, writing articles on the poverty of the Moselle valley winegrowers, the harsh legal treatment received by peasants who stole timber to heat their homes in winter, and the repressiveness of various European governments. Within 6 months, the Prussian authorities suppressed the paper, and Marx was out of work, a situation that recurred frequently during his life. In the aftermath, he turned again to studying Hegel. The result was "A Contribution to the Critique of Hegel's *Philosophy of Right*."[4] Although unpublished at the time, this essay constitutes Marx's decisive break with Hegel's idealism, particularly its religious and philosophical justification of the political status quo in Germany.

Paris and Brussels

Marx, now married to Jenny von Wesphalen, moved to Paris in 1843; he was 25 years old. Paris was the intellectual center of Europe

---

[3]Karl Marx, "The Difference Between the Democritean and Epicurean Philosophy of Nature," in *Activity in Marx's Philosophy*, ed. Norman D. Livergood (The Hague, Netherlands: Martinus-Nijhoff, 1967), 57–109.

[4]Karl Marx, "A Contribution to the Critique of Hegel's *Philosophy of Right*," in *Marx-Engels Reader* (see Note 2), 16–26, 53–66.

at that time, and the years Marx spent there allowed him to meet many radicals and revolutionaries: the Russian Mikhail Bakunin, the poet Heinrich Heine, and the tailor Wilhelm Weitling, among others. In addition, Marx encountered the emerging discipline of political economy during this period, reading Adam Smith, David Ricardo, Pierre Proudhon, and many more. Perhaps most important, however, in September 1844, Marx met the man who became his lifelong friend and partner: Friedrich Engels (1820–1895). The son of a wealthy German industrialist, Engels wrote the first great urban ethnography, *The Condition of the Working Class in England in 1844*, along with an essay, "Outlines of a Critique of Political Economy," during this same period.[5] These works helped Marx see the new urban working class, the proletarians, as real human beings with practical problems made worse by the systematic exploitation characteristic of capitalism at that time. One result was that Marx now rejected the ideas of the Young Hegelians as politically timid. In fact, the first product of his collaboration with Engels, a pompous and nearly unreadable tome titled *The Holy Family*, consisted of a diatribe against the Young Hegelians.[6] As we will discuss later, of all the Young Hegelians, only Feuerbach had a long-term impact on Marx's works. Another, more significant result was that Marx wrote a series of notebooks, the now famous *Economic and Philosophic Manuscripts*, in which he set forth his initial interpretation of capitalism as inherently exploitive and alienating.[7] In 1845, Marx moved to Brussels after the French government forced him to leave Paris.

Shortly after arriving in Brussels, Marx and Engels wrote *The German Ideology*, a more effective work, which they intended as a final settling of accounts with the Young Hegelians. According to Marx and Engels, the German philosophers were less concerned with "reality itself" than with ideas about reality; they had not, in other words, really rejected Hegel. Although we will describe the theoretical implications of *The German Ideology* in the next chapter, Marx and Engels used the opportunity to poke fun at Stirner, Bauer, and the others, as in the following example:

---

[5]Friedrich Engels, *The Condition of the Working Class in England* (Palo Alto, CA: Stanford University Press, 1968). The current translation omits the year 1844 from the title. Friedrich Engels, "Outlines of a Critique of Political Economy," in *The Economic and Philosophic Manuscripts*, ed. Karl Marx (New York: International, 1964), 197–228.

[6]Karl Marx and Friedrich Engels, *The Holy Family* (Moscow: Foreign Languages Publishing House, 1956).

[7]Marx, *Economic and Philosophic Manuscripts* (see Note 5).

Once upon a time an honest fellow had the idea that men were drowned in water only because they were possessed with the idea of gravity. If they were to knock this idea out of their heads, say, by stating it to be a superstition, a religious idea, they would be sublimely safe against any danger from water. His whole life long he fought against the illusion of gravity, of whose harmful results all statistics brought him new and manifold evidence. This honest fellow was the prototype of the German revolutionary philosophers of our day.[8]

In contrast with the Young Hegelians, Marx wanted to understand the practical problems people face. He also saw himself as a true revolutionary, dedicated to the overthrow of capitalist society—violently if necessary. Thus, he and Engels joined with other European émigrés and radicals in a variety of revolutionary organizations: the League of the Just, the German Workers' Educational Association, and the Communist League. Both Marx and Engels were dominating personalities, determined to lead working-class people toward a revolutionary reorganization of society. Here is a prophetic description of Marx by Paul Annenkov, a Russian who knew him during these years:

He was most remarkable in his appearance. He had a shock of deep black hair and hairy hands and his coat was buttoned wrong; but he looked like a man with the right and the power to demand respect, no matter how he appeared before you and no matter what he did. His movements were clumsy but confident and self-reliant, his ways defied the usual conventions in human relations, but they were dignified and somewhat disdainful; his sharp metallic voice was wonderfully adapted to the radical judgments that he passed on persons and things. He always spoke in imperative words that would brook no contradiction and were made all the sharper by the almost painful impression of the tone which ran through everything he said. This tone expressed the firm conviction of his mission to dominate men's minds and prescribe them their laws. Before me stood the embodiment of a democratic dictator such as one might imagine in a daydream.[9]

---

[8]Karl Marx and Friedrich Engels, *The German Ideology* (New York: International, 1947), 3.

[9]Quoted in David McClellen, *Karl Marx: His Life and Thought* (New York: Harper & Row, 1973), 452.

In 1847, Marx and Engels decided to compose a statement of revolutionary principles under the aegis of the Communist League. Accordingly, Engels wrote an initial draft in catechism form titled "Principles of Communism" and sent it to Marx.[10] During the early days of 1848, Marx completely rewrote the draft and, although the final version incorporated many of Engels's ideas, the document printed in February of that year was strikingly different and original: *The Communist Manifesto*.[11] Although it had little immediate impact, the publication of the *Manifesto* occurred during great political ferment in Europe. Many observers, not all of them radicals, believed that some form of communist revolution was inevitable in West European societies. Later that year, revolts broke out all over the continent. In Paris, for example, workers held the city against the onslaught of the French army for 6 weeks. Ultimately, however, the workers and peasants were defeated throughout Europe, often after bloody battles. In 1849, Marx returned to Paris, still (like many others) believing that a communist insurrection was imminent. Subsequently, under pressure from the French government, he left for London, where he lived the remainder of his life.

The London Years

Now 30 years old, Marx withdrew from public life altogether for about 15 years, concentrating instead on devising his theoretical analysis of capitalism. He studied and wrote copiously, producing notebook after notebook of observations about the nature of capitalist societies and criticism of economics as then practiced. These materials, almost all unpublished at the time, eventually appeared as *The Grundrisse* (or *Notebooks*), *The Theory of Surplus Value*, and *A Contribution to the Critique of Political Economy*.[12] Finally, Marx's greatest book appeared in 1867, when he was 49 years old: *Capital*, Volume 1.[13]

Although he intended to produce a multivolume work, only Volume 1 appeared at the time, and it usually stands alone as a theoretical

---

[10]Friedrich Engels, "Principles of Communism," in *Birth of the Communist Manifesto*, ed. Dirk J. Struik (New York: International, 1971), 169–192.

[11]The edition we are using is reprinted in *Birth of the Communist Manifesto*, 85–126.

[12]Karl Marx, *The Grundrisse* (New York: Random House, 1973), *The Theory of Surplus Value* (Moscow: Foreign Languages Publishing House, 1963), and *A Contribution to the Critique of Political Economy* (New York: International, 1970). Only the last was published in Marx's lifetime, in 1859.

[13]Karl Marx, *Capital*, Vol. 1 (New York: International, 1967).

analysis of capitalism. Although Engels subsequently edited and published the second and third volumes, Engels observed that the first "is in a great measure a whole in itself and has for more than twenty years ranked as an independent work."[14] As we will explain in the next chapter, *Capital* is more than a narrow work of economics; it is, rather, a theoretical analysis of capitalist social systems.

The tremendous quantity of work, however, did not bring in much money. Although Marx's income was adequate, neither he nor Jenny could manage money very well. As a result, the family lived in constant financial peril through most of these years. During much of this period, Marx served as European correspondent for the *New York Daily Tribune*, and the income from these articles constituted his main source of financial support. In addition, Engels, who benefited from an inheritance, periodically sent Marx money or ghostwrote articles for the *Tribune*. Apart from their economic circumstances and the death of two children in infancy, Marx and his family appear to have enjoyed a settled and happy life during these years. Only after the death of his mother in 1863 and the receipt of a bequest from a socialist, Wilhelm Wolff, did Marx's financial worries decline.

Although aloof from public life during the years in London, Marx, like many other radicals, still believed that economic crises would produce some form of workers' revolt. In 1864, the International Working Man's Association was formed in London. Composed of working people from most European nations, the organization proposed to destroy the capitalist system and substitute some form of collective control of the society. Abandoning his long reticence, Marx joined the group and, characteristically, quickly became its dominating force. Apart from ongoing work on *Capital*, all his energies were devoted to the International (as it was called). One side benefit, perhaps intended, was that *Capital* received considerable publicity. Unlike Marx's previous works, which had been generally ignored, *Capital* was widely read and quickly translated into French, Russian, English, and Italian—with Marx supervising these efforts. Apart from this activity, he immersed himself in political life, attempting to show how theory and revolution could be combined in practice.

In 1871, the long-awaited workers' revolt occurred in the aftermath of the Franco-Prussian War. As in 1848, however, the proletarians were suppressed, again with much loss of life. At this time, Marx

---

[14]Friedrich Engels, "Preface to the First English Edition," in Marx, *Capital*, Vol. 1, 5.

produced his last great political pamphlet, *The Civil War in France*, in which he defended Paris workers protesting the government.[15] Soon afterward, the International split apart and ceased to exist. This was Marx's last effective political role.

In the years after 1870, Marx finally achieved a comfortable lifestyle. Engels, very wealthy by this time, gave him a bequest, and Marx settled into the life of a Victorian gentleman—albeit a radical one. A famous man, revered by socialists and revolutionaries around the world, Marx was sought out for advice by those who would defend the rights of working people. But he wrote far less and without much creativity. It was as if relative prosperity had robbed him of his anger, the source of his insight.

Jenny's death in 1881 deprived Marx of his lifelong companion. His oldest daughter, also named Jenny, died in January 1883, and on March 14 of that year, Marx died in his armchair. He was 65 years old.

Karl Marx's analysis of capitalism represents one of the most striking and original achievements in the history of social thought. As we will show in Chapter 7, he constructed a theoretical analysis that sought to account for the origins of capitalism, its historical stability, and its eventual demise. In the process, he combined social theory and revolutionary action in a way that has never been duplicated. That his work is shortsighted in some respects and misbegotten in others does not detract from its evocativeness.

Like all scholars, he benefited from the legacy of concepts and ideas that others had advanced. Marx was a voracious reader, and his writings are filled with detailed analyses of the philosophers and political economists of the day. In the remainder of this chapter, we sketch the ways in which he was influenced by Hegel, Feuerbach and the other Young Hegelians, Adam Smith and the other capitalist political economists, and, of course, Engels.

G. W. F. Hegel and Karl Marx

The origin of Marx's sociological theory lies in his youthful reaction to the writings of Georg Wilhelm Friedrich Hegel (1770–1831). In

---

[15]Karl Marx, "The Civil War in France," in Karl Marx and Friedrich Engels, *Selected Works*, Vol. 2 (Moscow: Progress, 1969), 178–244.

four main books, *The Phenomenology of Mind* (1807), *The Science of Logic* (1816), *The Encyclopedia of Philosophy* (1817), and *The Philosophy of Right* (1821), Hegel developed one of the most original, complex, and obscure philosophical doctrines ever devised.[16] Marx transformed Hegel's philosophy into an empirically based social science, albeit a peculiar one, decisively rejecting Hegel's idealism while retaining his reliance on dialectical analysis and applying it to the material world. To appreciate Hegel's influence on Marx, we need to briefly discuss idealist philosophy and Marx's major criticisms of it. Only then will the continuity and discontinuity between the two men's ideas become clear.

Hegel's Idealism

In Hegel's writing, idealism is a complex philosophical doctrine that can only be superficially sketched here. Its essence consists of the denial that things in the finite world—such as trees, houses, people, or any other physical object—are ultimately real. In Hegel's words, idealism "consists in nothing else than in recognizing that the finite has no veritable being."[17] For Hegel, true reality is embodied in that which is discovered through reason. In thus emphasizing the importance of thought, he followed a philosophical tradition that originated with Plato. From this point of view, the objects perceived by the senses are not real: They are merely the phenomenal appearance of an ultimate reality of ideas. Only "logical objects," or concepts, constitute ultimate reality. As Hegel wrote, "It is *only* in thought that [an] object is truly in and for itself; in intuition or ordinary perception it is only an appearance."[18] Hegel continued by asserting that if only concepts are real, then the ultimate concept is God, and Hegel's philosophy is essentially an attempt at proving the existence of God through the application of reason. According to Hegel, previous philosophers had seen only finite things as real and had relegated the infinite (or God) to the "mere 'ideal.'" He argued that this separation was artificial and could not

---

[16]G. W. F. Hegel, *The Phenomenology of Mind* (New York: Macmillan, 1961), *The Science of Logic* (London: Allen & Unwin, 1969), *The Encyclopedia of Philosophy* (New York: Philosophical Library, 1959), and *The Philosophy of Right* (Oxford, UK: Clarendon, 1942).

[17]Hegel, *Science of Logic,* 154.

[18]Ibid., 585 (emphasis in original).

show how God existed and acted through people because it involves a logical impossibility: The infinite, which is absolute and cannot perish, is kept separate from finite things, which must inevitably perish, and is placed in an abstract and mentally conceived "beyond." If this latter were true, Hegel argued, God could not have come to earth in the form of Jesus, and the bread and wine of the Last Supper were merely bread and wine.

Hegel argued that there was an inherent dialectical relationship between God (the infinite) and people (the finite). The essence of the dialectic is contradiction: Each concept implies its opposite, or in Hegel's terms, each concept implies its negation. Thus, after proposing that "the finite has no veritable being," Hegel immediately said, "The finite is ideal"; that is, its essence lies in that which contradicts it: the infinite, God. In this way, the finite world of flesh and blood is annihilated (at least in thought), and the "infinite can pass over from the beyond to the here and now—that is, become flesh and take on earthly attire," as Jesus did a long time ago.[19] Hence, although this phrase states the issue too simply, Hegel believed that human history could be considered the autobiography of God because history only "exists" through its negation by the infinite and the latter's manifestations in this world. As in Christianity, even as the finite world of things is destroyed, it is saved. In Hegel's words, "the finite has vanished in the infinite and what *is*, is only the *infinite*," or everlasting life.[20] One implication of this analysis is a belief in the reality of transubstantiation (that the bread and wine become the body and blood of Jesus). Another implication, which is also characteristic of some forms of Christianity, is a relatively passive acceptance of the political status quo. For example, Hegel said, "All that is real is rational; and all that is rational is real."[21] Statements like this were taken by many as a sanctification of the Prussian state, with its despotism, police government, star-chamber proceedings, and censorship. Hence, the Prussian government glorified Hegel's philosophy for its own purposes and, when he died, gave him a state funeral.

---

[19]Lucio Colletti, *Marxism and Hegel* (Atlantic Highlands, NJ: Humanities, 1973), 12. This is a good Marxist source. One of the best non-Marxist commentaries is John N. Findlay, *Hegel: A Re-Examination* (London: Allen & Unwin, 1958).

[20]Hegel, *Science of Logic*, 138 (emphasis in original).

[21]Quoted in Friedrich Engels, "Ludwig Feuerbach and the End of Classical German Philosophy," in *Marx and Engels, Selected Works*, Vol. 3, 337.

Marx's Rejection of Hegel's Idealism

Marx reacted strongly against Hegel's idealism, criticizing it in a number of ways. First, and most important, he completely rejected Hegel's assertion that finite or empirical phenomena are not ultimately real. All his other criticisms follow from this basic point. Marx believed that when empirical phenomena are understood only as thoughts, people's more significant practical problems are ignored. Neither material objects nor relationships can be changed by merely thinking about them. The puerile quality of Hegel's point is evident, Marx suggested, in a simple example: If people are alienated such that they have no control over their lives or the material things produced by their labor, they cannot end their alienation by changing their perception of reality (or by praying, for that matter).[22] Rather, people must change the social structure in which they live; that is, they must make a revolution in this world rather than wait for the next world. Marx believed that life in this world posed a variety of very practical problems that people could solve only in hardheaded ways and that human reason was of little use unless it was applied to the problems that exist in the finite world.

Second, according to Marx, Hegel's emphasis on the ultimate reality of thought led him to misperceive some of the essential characteristics of human beings. For example, Marx contended that although Hegel correctly "grasps labor as the essence of man," "the only labor which [he] knows and recognizes is abstractly mental labor."[23] Yet people have physical needs, Marx noted, such as those for food, clothing, and shelter, which can be satisfied only by productive activity in the finite world. Hence, for Marx, the most significant labor is productive activity rather than mental activity. Similarly, Marx said that Hegel's belief in the unreality of finite things had led him to a position in which people were regarded as nonobjective, spiritual beings. But Marx asserted that people were "natural beings"; that is, they have physical needs that can be satisfied only in this world:

As a natural, corporeal, sensuous, objective being [a person] is a suffering, conditioned and limited creature, like animals and plants. That is to say, the objects of his instincts exist outside

---

[22]Marx, *Economic and Philosophical Manuscripts*, 175.
[23]Ibid., 177.

him, as objects independent of him; yet these objects are objects that he needs—essential objects, indispensable to the manifestation and confirmation of his essential powers. To say that man is a corporeal, living, real, sensuous, objective being full of natural vigor is to say that he has real, sensuous objects as the objects of his being or of his life, or that he can only express his life in real, sensuous objects.[24]

Marx's third criticism was also an outgrowth of the first, in that he rejected the religious motif that pervades Hegel's work. As noted earlier, Hegel denied reality to the finite world to prove the existence of God, albeit a Christian God. Nevertheless, Marx believed that when "reason" is applied to such impractical problems, people are prevented from recognizing that they are exploited and that they have an interest in changing the status quo in this world. For Marx, the next world is a religious fantasy not worth worrying about. Thus, he was particularly vitriolic, yet strangely poetic, in his denunciation of the religious implications of Hegel's philosophy:

Religion is the sigh of the oppressed creature, the sentiment of a heartless world, and the soul of soulless conditions. It is the opium of the people. The abolition of religion as the illusory happiness of men, is a demand for their real happiness. The call to abandon their illusions about their conditions is a call to abandon a condition which requires illusions. The criticism of religion is, therefore, the embryonic criticism of this vale of tears of which religion is the halo.[25]

Marx believed that one of the main functions of religion was to blind people to their true situations and interests. Religion does this by emphasizing that compensation for misery and exploitation on earth will come in the next world.

Marx's fourth criticism of Hegel was that idealism is politically conservative rather than revolutionary. Idealism creates the illusion of a community of people rather than the reality of a society riddled with opposing interests. This illusion results partly from Hegel's assertion that the state, a practical and physical entity, emerges from the Spirit, or thought. In this way, Hegel imbued the state with a

---

[24]Ibid., 181.
[25]Marx, "Contribution to the Critique of Hegel's *Philosophy of Right*," 54.

sacred quality. As Marx noted, Hegel "does not say 'with the will of the monarch lies the final decision' but 'the final decision of the will is—the monarch.'"[26] When the state is sacred, history can be seen as part of an overall divine plan that is not only reasonable but necessary. For this reason, Marx interpreted Hegel's philosophy as politically conservative.

Marx's Acceptance of Hegel's Dialectical Method

Despite his complete rejection of idealism, Marx saw a significant tool in Hegel's use of the dialectic. In Hegel's hands, however, the entire analysis is couched in terms of a mystical theology. Thus, as Marx noted in *Capital*, Hegel's dialectic "is standing on its head. It must be turned right side up again, if you would discover the rational kernel within the mystical shell."[27] As we will show in Chapter 7, the process by which Marx turned the dialectic right side up involved its application to the finite world where people make history by producing their sustenance from the environment. Rather than being concerned with the existence of God, Marx emphasized that the focus must be on concrete societies (seen as social systems) and on actual people who have conflicting interests.

The significance of turning Hegel "right side up" is that for Marx, no product of human thought or action can be final; there can be no absolute truth that, when discovered, need only be memorized. From this point of view, science can only increase knowledge; it cannot discover absolute knowledge. Moreover, there can be no end to human history, at least in the sense of attaining an unchanging utopia, a perfect society. Such social structures can exist only in the imagination. Rather, every society is only a transitory state in an endless course of human development. This development occurs as conflict is systematically generated from people's opposing interests. Although each stage of history is necessary, and hence justified by the conditions in which it originated, progress occurs as the old society inevitably loses its reason for being. In Marx's work, the dialectical method means that nothing can be final or absolute or sacred: Everything is transitory, and conflict is everywhere.

---

[26]Quoted in Sidney Hook, *From Hegel to Marx* (Ann Arbor: University of Michigan Press, 1962), 23.

[27]Marx, *Capital*, 20.

Ludwig Feuerbach and Karl Marx

The Young Hegelians also affected Marx's sociology. The most important influence among them was unquestionably Ludwig Feuerbach. In this section, we outline some of the Young Hegelians' ideas and then suggest more specifically how Feuerbach's views altered the direction of Marx's thought.

The Young Hegelians and Marx's Thought

Like Hegel, the Young Hegelians tried to understand the nature of reality and the relationship between religious beliefs and reality. However, because religion legitimated oppressive political conditions, the Young Hegelians rejected the political conservatism that seemed inherent to Hegel's thought. They reacted in this way because during most of the nineteenth century Prussia was an extremely repressive nation, with religion serving as one of the chief pillars of the repressive state. The Young Hegelians believed that the church's emphasis on the sanctity of tradition, authority, and the renunciation of worldly pleasures helped prop up an oppressive governmental apparatus. But because political agitation was not possible (without being arrested or expatriated), they sought to criticize the state indirectly by investigating the sacred texts, doctrines, and practices of Christianity.

For example, in 1835 David Strauss published *The Life of Jesus Critically Examined*, in which he tried to show that the Gospels were not accurate historical narratives.[28] This book prompted great controversy because it was thought that if the life of Jesus as portrayed by the Gospels was not to be believed, then the authority of the church would be undermined. Shortly thereafter, Bruno Bauer published a series of articles in which he denied the historical existence of Jesus altogether and tried to explain the Gospels as works of pure fiction.[29] By debunking the nature and logic of Christian tenets (and hence the church) in this way, the Young Hegelians hoped also to impugn the authority of the state. The Prussian government recognized the seditious implications of these works, and as a result, the Young Hegelians suffered varying degrees of surveillance, political harassment, and dismissal from their university posts.

---

[28]David Strauss, *The Life of Jesus Critically Examined* (London: Swan Sonneschein, 1902).
[29]On Bauer, see Hook, *From Hegel to Marx*.

Nonetheless, despite their political stance, all these men were still Hegelian in orientation, and this eventually led to Marx's split with them. For example, in *The Ego and His Own: The Case of the Individual Against Authority* (1844), Max Stirner argued that nothing was objective outside the individual.[30] According to Stirner, social institutions, such as the church, are oppressive to the individual's spirit. Like a true Hegelian, Stirner then asserted that reality was not based on people's sense perceptions. As Hegel claimed, reality is created by the imagination and will of each person and, as a corollary, there is no objective reality apart from the ego. Thus, according to Stirner, individuals should avoid participating in the society as much as possible, and in this way, they can also avoid being oppressed by authority. With this argument, he anticipated the development of anarchist thought some years later. Marx, however, believed that Stirner's position was politically futile because social institutions must be controlled rather than ignored.

As will be seen in our discussion of *The German Ideology* in Chapter 7, Marx believed that the Young Hegelians were intellectual mountebanks, and he wrote hundreds of pages of vituperation against them. For example, he and Engels made fun of Stirner, Bauer, and others by calling them "The Holy Family" and referring to them as "Saint Max" and "Saint Bruno." More generally, Marx developed four main criticisms of the Young Hegelians, all of which can be seen as variations on his criticisms of Hegel. First, their writings treated the development of theology independently of the actual activities of the church and other social institutions that theological ideas pervaded. Such an emphasis ignored the fact that the development of ideas never proceeds apart from human practices. Second, the Young Hegelians were essentially idealists, in that the origin of religious as well as other kinds of thought was to be found in the Spirit. But for Marx, religion and all other ideas emerge from people's actual social relationships and in their need to survive. As he would emphasize some years later in *The Communist Manifesto*, people's ideas, world-views, and political interests depend on their positions in society.[31] Third, the Young Hegelians' writings were fatalistic in that the historical process was seen as automatic and inexorable, either because

---

[30]Max Stirner, *The Ego and His Own: The Case of the Individual Against Authority* (New York: Libertarian Book Club, 1963).

[31]Karl Marx and Friedrich Engels, "The Communist Manifesto," in *Birth of the Communist Manifesto*, 85–125.

it was directed by the Spirit or because it was directed by individuals (e.g., the Prussian king) who were somehow seen as connected with the Spirit. For Marx, although history has direction and continuity, it is shaped by human action. Fourth, and most fundamental, the Young Hegelians foolishly believed that by changing ideas they could change human behavior. Therefore, they fought a war against the state, using words as the primary weapons. Wars must be fought with guns, Marx believed, and those who do not recognize this elementary fact are very unrealistic.

Marx made one exception to his indictment of the Young Hegelians, however. The only member of the group Marx did not vilify, even though the two men disagreed, was Feuerbach.

Feuerbach and Marx's Thought

Like the other Young Hegelians, Feuerbach was also interested in the religious implications of Hegel's philosophy, but unlike the others, he fundamentally altered the direction of Marx's thought. This alteration occurred in Marx's critique of Hegel and in the development of Marx's peculiar but highly effective version of social theory.

In his book *The Essence of Christianity* (1841), Feuerbach undercut both Hegel and the Young Hegelians by arguing that religious beliefs arose from people's unconscious deification of themselves.[32] According to Feuerbach, human beings have taken all that they believe is good in themselves and simply projected these characteristics onto God. He showed how the "mysteries" of Christianity—the Creation, the suffering God, the Holy Trinity, the Immaculate Conception, the Resurrection, and the like—all represented human ideals. Thus, he argued that theology was simply a mythical vision of human aspirations and that "what man praises and approves, that is God to him; what he blames [and] condemns is the nondivine."[33] The true essence of religion, Feuerbach believed, is to be found in anthropology, not theology, for "religion is man's earliest . . . form of self-knowledge."[34]

---

[32]Ludwig Feuerbach, *The Essence of Christianity* (New York: Harper & Row, 1957).
[33]Quoted in Hook, *From Hegel to Marx*, 246.
[34]Feuerbach, *Essence of Christianity*, 13.

This analysis reveals Feuerbach to have been the most original of the Young Hegelians. Whereas most of them were content to analyze and critique Christian theology, Feuerbach decisively rejected any analysis that treated theology as existing independently of empirical activities. Moreover, although many Young Hegelians still accepted the idea that God necessarily directed human affairs, Feuerbach argued that an abstract and amorphous Spirit could not be the guiding force in history because people were simply worshipping projections of their own characteristics and desires. Finally, although the other Young Hegelians continued to be mired in idealism, Feuerbach was a materialist in the sense that he believed that people's consciousness of the world was the product of their brains and, hence, of physical matter. To Marx and others, this position seemed clear-sighted after the obfuscations and puerile logic of Hegel, Strauss, Bauer, and Stirner.

Feuerbach's argument had yet another consequence for Marx. In Feuerbach's work, Marx found the key to criticizing Hegel and, ultimately, to developing a social theory designed to promote revolutionary action. Marx realized that Feuerbach's analysis of religion as an expression of human desires could be generalized to people's relationships to other social institutions (especially the state) and to any situation in which human beings were ruled by their own creations. Thus, following Feuerbach, Marx reversed Hegel's argument, which asserted that the state emerged from the Spirit, by arguing that the modern state emerged from capitalist social relationships (which he called "civil society"). This argument has important implications, for if the state is the product of human action, it can be changed by human action. Marx's mature social theory follows from this fundamental insight.

Adam Smith and Karl Marx

By the late eighteenth century, England had already become a relatively industrialized and commercial nation. As such, it constituted the first fully capitalist society, with the result that scholars attempted to account for the origins of capitalism, its nature, and its future development. Men such as Adam Smith, David Ricardo, and many others developed a new mode of analysis, called political economy, and sought to understand the characteristics of industrial capitalism. After being introduced to the study of political economy by Engels and others, Marx began to deal with the topics characteristic of the new discipline. For example, in *The Economic and Philosophical Manuscripts*, he analyzed (among other things) the origin of the value of commodities, the origin of profit, the role of land in a capitalist economy, and the accumulation of capital. However, his most detailed analyses and criticisms did not occur until the 1850s in his notebooks (subsequently published as *The Grundrisse*) and *A Contribution to a Critique of Political Economy*. From these efforts, Marx's great work, *Capital*, eventually emerged.

Political Economy and Marx's Thought

Marx's detailed analyses of various political economists are less important today than are his more general criticisms of their works. In his opinion, the literature in political economy displayed two fundamental defects. First, capitalist social relations were assumed to reflect "irrefutable natural laws of society." Because of this emphasis, basic types of social relations, such as exchange, exploitation, and alienation, were all assumed (at least by implication) to be historically immutable. Second, the political economists analyzed each part of society separately, as if it had no connection with anything else.[35] For example, even such strictly economic categories as production, exchange, distribution, and consumption were generally treated as if they were separate and unconnected phenomena. But Marx had learned from Hegel and Feuerbach that history moves in a dialectical pattern. As a result, Marx saw capitalism as a historically unique pattern of social relationships that would inevitably be supplanted in the future. Thus, he set himself the task of developing a scientific analysis of capitalist society that could account for both its development and eventual demise.

Although Marx regarded most political economists as simply bourgeois ideologues defending the status quo, he believed that Adam Smith and David Ricardo were the two most objective and insightful observers of the economics of capitalism. In the course of analyzing their work, Marx achieved many of his fundamental insights into the dynamics of capitalism. For illustrative purposes, we focus here on Smith's work.

---

[35]Marx, "Introduction," in *Contribution to the Critique of Political Economy*, 188–217.

Adam Smith's Influence

Adam Smith was a moral philosopher as well as a political econo-mist. In his first book, *The Theory of Moral Sentiments*, originally pub-lished in 1759, he argued that there was a natural order to the world, including both its physical and social aspects, that had been created by God and carefully balanced to benefit all species.[36] Hence, he empha-sized the beneficent qualities of the natural order and the general inad-equacy of human institutions that tried to change or alter this order. His subsequent book, *An Inquiry Into the Nature and Causes of the Wealth of Nations*, published in 1776, represented his attempt at apply-ing the principles of naturalism to the problems of political economy.[37]

The Wealth of Nations focuses on three main issues. First, Smith wanted to discover the "laws of the market" holding society together. In dealing with this issue, he hoped to show both how commodities acquired value and why this value included profit for the capitalist. Second, he wanted to understand the laws of evolution characteristic of capitalist society. Third, like most work in political economy (at least according to Marx), *The Wealth of Nations* is a thoroughgoing defense of capitalist society, a defense Marx found inadequate.

Laws of the Market

Smith's attempt at showing how the economic laws of the market hold society together begins with the assertion that people act out of self-interest when they produce commodities for other members of the society to purchase. For,

> It is not from the benevolence of the butcher, brewer, or the baker, that we expect our dinner but from their regard to their own interest. We address ourselves, not to their humanity, but to their self-love, and never talk to them of our own necessities but of their advantages."[38]

And the advantage that accrued to the butchers, bakers, and other capitalists is profit. Indeed, in Smith's view, the exchange of

---

[36]Adam Smith, *The Theory of Moral Sentiments* (Oxford, UK: Clarendon, 1976).

[37]Adam Smith, *An Inquiry Into the Nature and Causes of the Wealth of Nations* (Oxford, UK: Clarendon, 1976).

[38]Ibid., 26–27.

commodities for profit becomes a fundamental characteristic of human society whenever the division of labor and private property develop beyond a certain point. Marx believed, however, that Smith had been guilty of trying to make patterns of interaction that were characteristic of capitalist social relationships valid for all times and places. As an alternative, Marx envisioned a modern society without exchange relationships because he felt that they were inherently exploitive. Nonetheless, for Smith the origin of value and profit resided in the process of commodity exchange, and by distinguishing between the "use value" and the "exchange value" of commodities, he achieved an insight that later guided Marx's thought.

Smith went on to formulate a version of the labor theory of value in which the amount of labor time going into a product was the source of its value, a thesis Marx embraced some 90 years later. But if labor is the source of value, Smith could not account for the origin of profit because those who profit generally contribute very little labor to the creation of the product. They merely invest money and reap a return on it. Thus, although *The Wealth of Nations* displays much vacillation and confusion, Smith ultimately dropped the labor theory of value and simply argued that profit was added on to the costs of production by the capitalist. As we will see in the next chapter, Marx was able to adopt the labor theory of value and still account for the origin of profit by distinguishing between the workers' labor and their labor power (or capacity to work).

By arguing that profit was merely part of the cost of production, Smith created a potential problem: The "natural price" of a commodity is difficult to determine because nothing prevents capitalists from constantly and arbitrarily raising prices. His solution was to argue that competition prevented avaricious persons from pushing prices too high. Those capitalists who try to raise prices unduly (and Smith was very aware that they constantly try to do just that) will inevitably find other enterprising persons underselling them, thereby forcing prices back down. Similarly, capitalists who attempt to keep wages too low will find that they have no workers because others offer the workers higher wages. In this way, then, both profits and wages are more or less automatically regulated—as if by an "invisible hand." Paradoxically, people's selfish motives promote social harmony through the natural operation of the market, even though that goal is not their objective. In Smith's words,

By directing that industry in such a manner as its produce may be of the greatest value, he intends only his own gain . . . he is in this, as in many other cases, led by an invisible hand to promote an end which was no part of his intention.[39]

The final step in Smith's analysis was to argue that these laws of the market also ensured that the proper quantities of products were produced. For example, if the public prefers to own coats rather than tables, a greater number of the former will be produced because the profit involved in making tables will fall, and capitalists (and workers) will turn to the manufacture of coats. Thus, natural mechanisms inherent to the market govern the allocation of resources in the society and, hence, the production of goods. Once again, this process occurs because of people acting in their own self-interests.

Laws of Evolution

During the latter portion of the eighteenth century and well into the nineteenth, many political economists speculated that as capitalism advanced, the rate of profit on investment would fall. Smith had a rather optimistic view of the process of history, however, and he did not believe this calamity would occur. To Smith, in addition to being self-regulating, society seemed to be improving because of the operation of two relatively simple laws of evolution. The first can be called the "law of capital accumulation." Smith saw that capitalists continuously tried to accumulate their savings or profits, invest them, accumulate even more savings or profits, and invest them again. The impact is to increase both production and employment. Thus, from Smith's point of view, selfish motives can be seen once again to redound to the public good, because the expansion of production and employment helps everyone in some way. (Smith did not worry about whether savings would be invested; that became a problem for later economists.)

Some observers argued, however, that if accumulation was to continue and production to expand, more and more workers were required. When the supply of workers is exhausted, then profits will fall, and hence the rate of accumulation will also fall—just as many feared. Smith dealt with this problem by formulating a "law

---

[39]Ibid., 73.

of population," his second law of evolution. This hypothesis asserts that when wages are high, the number of workers will increase; when wages are low, the number of workers will decrease. Smith meant this statement literally, as people living and dying, not their periodic ventures into or out of the labor market. Mortality rates, especially among children, were extraordinarily high in those days; it was common for a woman to have a dozen or more children and have only one or two survive. Yet it was still possible for a higher standard of living to affect decisively people's ability to feed, clothe, and protect their children. As a result, Smith argued, higher wages would allow greater numbers of children to survive and become workers themselves. Lower wages, of course, would have the reverse effect. Thus, Smith believed that the advance of capitalism would be accompanied by an increase in population and that this increase would, in turn, allow capital accumulation to continue. Therefore, according to Smith, the rate of profit will not fall and a capitalist society will constantly improve itself, all because of the natural forces, unencumbered by rules and regulations established by the state. Although he recognized that an expanding population would always act to deflate wages, as long as capital accumulation continued, wages had to remain above the level of subsistence. Of course, Smith's argument, in Marx's view, assumes that capitalist social relations are somehow irrefutable "natural laws" of the social universe.

The Defense of Capitalism

As enunciated by Smith, the logical implication of *The Wealth of Nations* is fairly simple: Leave the market alone. From Smith's point of view, this stricture meant that the natural regulation of the market would occur as consumers' purchasing practices forced businesses to cater to their needs. Such a process could only happen, he believed, if business was not protected by the government and did not form monopolies. Hence, he opposed all efforts to protect business advantage. His analysis, however, quickly became an ideological justification for preventing government regulation in some important areas. Moreover, because any act of government could be seen as interfering with the natural operation of the market, *The Wealth of Nations* was used to oppose humanitarian legislation designed to protect workers from the many abuses already apparent in Smith's time.

For Marx, this result showed the inherent weakness in classical political economy, for there is nothing natural about the operation of the market or any other social relationship. The market is left alone by government because the capitalists, like all ruling classes, control the government. Hence, Marx argued that theory must take into account the interconnections among the parts of society, with special attention to how political power is used to justify and enforce exploitive social relationships. The capitalists, like all ruling classes, also controlled the dissemination of ideas, which suggested to Marx why they were able to use *The Wealth of Nations* for their own ideological purposes. In his theory, Marx emphasized the importance (and the difficulty) of stimulating an awareness in the working classes of their true interests.

Friedrich Engels and Karl Marx

Friedrich Engels and Karl Marx were friends and collaborators for more than 40 years. When possible, they saw each other every day; at other times, they corresponded about every other day. Despite Marx's sometimes churlish temperament, the two men never broke off their relationship. Most commentators see Engels's role in the development of Marx's theory as secondary, and with regard to their joint works, especially *The German Ideology* and *The Communist Manifesto*, this appears to be an accurate assessment. Yet two of Engels's own writings, "Outlines of a Critique of Political Economy" (1844) and his much-neglected classic, *The Condition of the Working Class in England* (1845), fundamentally influenced the development of Marx's thought at a time when he was still searching for a way of understanding and changing the world.

Engels's Critique of Political Economy

Engels's short and angry essay, "Outlines of a Critique of Political Economy," appeared in the same journal as did Marx's critique of Hegel's philosophy. In this work, which is characterized by the excessively acerbic prose of a young man, Engels indicted both the science of political economy and the existence of private property. He began by noting caustically that political economy ought to be called "private economy" because it existed only to defend the private control of the means of production. He continued (although in a quite disorganized way) by stridently attacking the institution of private property. According to Engels, a modern industrial society based on the private ownership of property is inevitably inhumane, inefficient, and alienating. In the process of his attack, Engels also suggested (albeit vaguely) that, despite these faults, capitalism was historically necessary for a communist society to emerge in the future.

From Engels's point of view, capitalism is inhumane for two reasons. First, people do not and cannot trust one another. When private property exists in an industrial context, Engels wrote, trade and competition are the center of life. And because everyone seeks to buy cheap and sell dear, people must distrust and try to exploit one another. In Engels's words, "trade is legalized fraud."[40] The second reason capitalism is inhumane is that competition generates an increased division of labor, one of the major manifestations of which is the factory system. As we will see, Engels regarded factory work and the urban lifestyle accompanying it as one of the most inhumane and exploitive forms of social organizations in history. The factory system was becoming more pervasive in the 1840s, however, and as a result, capitalist society appeared to be dividing into two groups: those who owned the means of production and those who did not.

Engels argued that capitalism was inefficient because those who dominated it could neither understand nor control the recurrent and steadily worsening economic crises that afflicted every nation. Capitalist society is, therefore, beset by a curious paradox: Although its productive power is incredibly great, overproduction periodically results in misery and starvation for the masses. "The economist has never been able to explain this mad situation," Engels wrote.[41] Moreover, he believed that people living under capitalism were inevitably alienated because they had no sense of community. In the competitive environment characteristic of capitalism, each person's interests are always opposed to every other person's. As a result, "private property isolates everyone in his own crude solitariness," with the consequence that people's lives have little meaning and

---

[40]Engels, "Outlines of a Critique of Political Economy," 202.
[41]Ibid., 217.

carry no intrinsic rewards.[42] Yet underlying this entire argument is Engels's belief that the rise of capitalism is historically necessary to make a communist society possible, for only now are people "placed in a position from which we can go beyond the economics of private property" and end the "unnatural" separation of individuals from one another and from their work.[43]

Before 1843, the still youthful Marx was relatively unfamiliar with political economy. Engels's essay, as much as any other event, introduced Marx to the topic and made him recognize its importance in developing a theory of society. Thus, after reading the essay, he began an intensive study of political economy that lasted for more than 20 years. Ultimately, he indicted the science of political economy for essentially the same reason as had Engels: It defended capitalist society. In addition, all the main ideas that we will describe subsequently appeared in a more sophisticated fashion in Marx's theory.

Engels's Analysis of the Working Class

To continue his business training at the textile mills in which his father was part owner, Engels left his native Germany for Manchester, England, in 1842. At that time, Manchester was the greatest industrial city in the most industrialized nation in the world; to many observers, it was the epitome of the new kind of society forming as a result of the rise of capitalism and the industrial revolution. Engels spent 2 years in Manchester, leading something of a double life because he not only learned the textile business but also gathered the materials for his book. During this period, nearly all his leisure time was spent walking through Manchester and the surrounding towns, talking to and drinking with working-class people and reading the many governmental reports and other descriptions of living conditions in Manchester. The result was the first urban ethnography—and a damning indictment of the English ruling class.

Engels's analysis of *The Condition of the Working Class* in England can be divided into three parts. First, he sketched an idyllic rural society that existed before industrialization and briefly suggested the factors that had destroyed that society. Second, he described the conditions of working-class life in Manchester. Third, he indicted

---

[42]Ibid., 213.
[43]Ibid., 199, 212.

the attitudes of the bourgeoisie toward the proletariat and concluded that a violent revolution was inevitable.

Peasant Life Before Industrialization

Like many other observers, Engels saw that the Industrial Revolution was utterly transforming Western society. Like other commentators, he believed that feudal society had been better for people in many ways. Consequently, he described the feudal past in an idyllic manner. Although he has been justifiably criticized for idealizing the past, it is not altogether clear how (in the middle of the nineteenth century) he could have obtained a sound or accurate portrayal of feudal society. Thus, *The Condition of the Working Class* begins with a description of simple, God-fearing peasants who lived in a stable and patriarchal society where "children grew up in idyllic simplicity and in happy intimacy with their playmates." Engels saw feudal life as "comfortable and peaceful" and believed that most peasants generally had a higher standard of living in the past than did factory workers in 1844:

> They were not forced to work excessive hours; they themselves fixed the length of their working day and still earned enough for their needs. They had time for healthy work in their gardens or smallholdings and such labor was in itself a recreation. They could also join their neighbors in various sports such as bowls and football and this too kept them in good physical condition. Most of them were strong, well-built people, whose physique was virtually equal to that of neighboring agricultural workers. Children grew up in the open air of the countryside, and if they were old enough to help their parents work, this was only an occasional employment and there was no question of an eight- or twelve-hour day.[44]

At the same time, Engels argued, these peasants were "spiritually dead" because they were ignorant, concerned only with their "petty private interests," and contented with their "plantlike existence."[45]

Although this depiction of life before industrialization is clearly not accurate, it does identify some themes that Engels used in his

---

[44]Engels, *Condition of the Working Class*, 10.
[45]Ibid., 11–12.

indictment of capitalist society: People are forced to work excessive hours, they are in chronic ill health, and child labor is pervasive. In addition, his sketch of feudal life also implied the historical inevitability of a communist revolution; according to Engels, industrialization not only shattered forever this idyllic lifestyle, it also made people aware of their subordination, exploitation, and alienation. As we will see, Marx and Engels believed that this recognition was the first necessary step to a communist revolution. Thus, Engels's portrayal of the atrocities characteristic of urban life in the 1840s should be seen in light of his optimistic vision of the historical development of a revolutionary proletariat capable of seizing the world for itself. All Marx's subsequent work was imbued with this vision, which he and Engels shared and tried to actualize in the political arena.

Having described peasant life before industrialization, Engels noted the four interrelated factors that went into making the modern working class he observed in Manchester. First, the use of water and steam power in the productive process meant that, for the first time in human history, muscle power was not the primary motive force in producing goods. Second, the massive introduction of modern machinery into the productive process signaled not only that machines rather than people set the pace of work but also that more goods were being produced than ever before. Third, the intensification of the division of labor meant that the number of tasks in the productive process increased while the requirements for each task were simplified. Fourth, the tendency in modern society for concentration of both work and ownership caused not only the rise of the factory system but also a division of society into owners and producers. According to Engels, and he was not alone, these factors were the "great levers" of the Industrial Revolution that had been used to "heave the world out of joint."[46] In *Capital,* Marx took these same ideas and placed them in a theoretical context that, in his mind, allowed him to demonstrate why a proletarian revolution was inevitable.

Working-Class Life in Manchester

The world Engels saw was indeed out of joint. His description began with a portrayal of the neighborhoods in which working-class people

---

[46]Ibid., 27–29.

were forced to live. Manchester had grown from a town of 24,000 people in 1773 to a metropolitan area of more than 400,000 in 1840. Throughout this period, it had no effective city government, little police protection, and no sewer system. Engels observed that middle-class people and the owners of the factories and mills lived apart and provided themselves with city services, police protection, and sewage disposal. In contrast, the working classes were forced to live with pigs in the slums available to them. When Engels said that human beings lived with pigs (and, unavoidably, like pigs), he meant it literally.

Because Manchester had no modern sewage facilities, people had to use public privies. In some parts of the city, more than 200 people used a single receptacle. In a city without government, there were few provisions for cleaning the streets or removing debris. Engels described the result in some detail; for example, in one courtyard, "right at the entrance where the covered passage ends, is a privy without a door. This privy is so dirty that the inhabitants can only enter or leave the court by wading through puddles of stale urine and excrement."[47] Thus, in *The Condition of the Working Class*, Engels portrayed a situation in which thousands of men, women, and children were living amid their own bodily wastes. If it can be imagined, the situation was even worse for those thousands of people living in cellars, below the waterline. As Steven Marcus has observed, "That substance [their bodily waste] was also a virtual objectification of their social condition, their place in society: that was what they were."[48]

Engels continued by describing the neighborhoods where pigs and people lived together:

> Heaps of refuse, offal and sickening filth are everywhere interspread with pools of stagnant liquid. The atmosphere is polluted by the stench and is darkened by the smoke of a dozen factory chimneys. A horde of ragged women and children swarm about the streets and they are just as dirty as the pigs which wallow happily on the heaps of garbage and in the pools of filth. In short, the horrid little slum affords as hateful and repulsive a spectacle as the worst courts to be found on the banks of the Irk [river]. The inhabitants live in dilapidated cottages, the windows of which are broken and patched with oilskin. The doors and the door posts

---

[47]Ibid., 58.

[48]Steven Marcus, *Engels, Manchester, and the Working Class* (New York: Vintage, 1975), 184–185.

are broken and rotten. The creatures who inhabit these dwellings and even their dark, wet cellars, and who live confined amidst all this filth and foul air—which cannot be dissipated because of the surrounding lofty buildings—must surely have sunk to the lowest level of humanity.[49]

It is not hard to conclude, as many did, that a society in which people have gone back to living like animals has something terribly, deeply wrong with it. For many observers, however, Manchester epitomized a new and better world, an industrial world.

The Bourgeoisie, the Proletariat, and Revolution. Engels concluded *The Condition of the Working Class* by describing the attitudes of the bourgeois toward the proletarians. In his prose, the bourgeoisie are portrayed as debased people who know nothing except greed and see all human ties as having a "cash nexus." He used the following vignette to illustrate these traits:

One day I walked with one of these middle-class gentlemen into Manchester. I spoke to him about the disgraceful unhealthy slums and drew his attention to the disgusting condition of that part of the town in which the factory workers lived. I declared I had never seen so badly built a town in my life. He listened patiently and at the corner of the street at which we parted company he remarked: "And yet there is a great deal of money made here. Good morning, Sir."[50]

Yet the proletarians were sometimes capable of responding to their condition in life. Although much self-destructive behavior always occurs among oppressed people (as in the use of drugs, alcohol, and the like), Engels noted that Manchester was "the mainspring of all working-class movements" in England.[51] He described the long history of working-class efforts at organizing in opposition to the factory owners, for only by acting together rather than competing with one another could they effectively oppose the capitalists. More generally, however, he argued that the proletarians' true interest was in establishing a noncompetitive society, which meant the abolition

---

[49]Engels, *Condition of the Working Class,* 71.

[50]Ibid., 312.

[51]Ibid., 50.

of the private ownership of the means of production (although this last point was not made explicitly):

> Every day it becomes clearer to the workers how they are affected by competition. They appreciate even more clearly than the middle classes that it is competition among the capitalists that leads to those commercial crises which cause such dire suffering among the workers. Trade unionists realize that commercial crises must be abolished, and they will soon discover *how* to do it.[52]

The Condition of the Working Class ends with Engels's prophecy of a violent proletarian revolution. Although Engels believed that this "revolution must come," he had not shown why; his work accounted for neither how capitalist society functioned nor why it would inevitably be destroyed. He had not, in short, developed a theory to explain what he had observed. But at a time when Marx was searching for the underlying dynamics of society, Engels demonstrated the significance of the proletariat. Furthermore, he recognized (although the point was not made very clearly) that the evils of capitalism were a necessary prelude to a communist revolution. Yet Marx, rather than Engels, developed a set of theoretical concepts and propositions that purported to show why a revolution would occur in capitalist societies. In developing these theoretical arguments, Marx contributed to the emergence of sociological theory.

---

[52]Ibid., 249 (emphasis in original).

CHAPTER 7

The Sociology of Karl Marx

Industrialization and capitalism destroyed feudal social relationships that had existed for a millennium, but in Karl Marx's eyes, these changes had produced a paradoxical result. Industrialization and capitalism meant that sustenance and amenities could be available for everyone, and yet only those who owned capital (income-producing assets) actually benefited. These capitalists exploited the masses, who lived in great misery and depravity. To remedy this situation, Marx proposed new forms of social arrangements in which everyone's needs could be met. He argued that change was inevitable, with the only question being when it would occur. Throughout his life, he served as a participant, organizer, and leader of revolutionary groups dedicated to ending the exploitation of the masses.

Of all the classical sociologists, Marx was unique in that he acted as a revolutionary and a social scientist, a combination that constitutes the greatest weakness in his sociology. His orientation can be summarized in the following way: As a revolutionary, he sought to overthrow the existing order and substitute collective control of society by the people so that, in a cooperative context, they could be free to develop their potential as human beings. As a social scientist, he tried to show that such collective control was historically inevitable. According to Marx, history has a direction that can be observed. This direction, he and Engels wrote in *The Communist Manifesto*, will lead inevitably to a communist society in which "the free development of each is the condition for the free development of all."[1] In such a context, Marx believed, the few will no longer exploit the many.

The German Ideology

The German Ideology was completed in 1846, when Marx was 28 years old and Engels was 26. Much of the rather lengthy book is given to heavy-handed and satirical polemics against various Young Hegelians. The publisher declined to accept the manuscript at the time, perhaps for political reasons, because Marx was already well-known as a radical and had been expelled from both Germany and France, or perhaps because of the arcane writing style. In any case, Marx later recalled, the manuscript was "abandoned to the gnawing criticism of the mice . . . since we had achieved our main purpose—self-clarification."[2]

In *The German Ideology*, Marx opens with a bitter attack on the Young Hegelians, whom he described at one point as engaging in "theoretical bubble blowing."[3] For the Young Hegelians, Marx observed, great conflicts and revolutions take place only in the realm of thought because no buildings are destroyed and no one is injured or dies. Thus, despite their excessive verbiage, Marx believed, Young Hegelians merely criticized the essentially religious nature of Hegel's work and substituted their own negative religious canons. "It is an interesting event we are dealing with," he said caustically, "the putrescence of the absolute spirit."[4] In the process of debunking the Young Hegelians' writings, however, Marx developed an understanding of social theory, a description of the characteristics of all societies, and a theoretical methodology for understanding those characteristics.

---

[1] Karl Marx and Friedrich Engels, "The Communist Manifesto," in *Birth of the Communist Manifesto*, ed. Dirk J. Struik (New York: International, 1971), 112.

[2] Karl Marx, "Preface," in *A Contribution to the Critique of Political Economy* (New York: International, 1970), 22.

[3] Karl Marx and Friedrich Engels, *The German Ideology* (New York: International, 1947), 3. Only Part 1 of the text is translated, and it is generally assumed that Engels' contribution to this portion of the book was minimal. This is mainly because the text appears to be an elaboration of Marx's "Theses on Feuerbach," which he outlined for himself in 1845; see Robert C. Tucker, ed., *The Marx-Engels Reader* (New York: Norton, 1978), 43–45. In addition, Engels stated repeatedly that Marx had already developed his conception of history before their collaboration. Therefore, in what follows we will generally refer only to Marx.

[4] Marx and Engels, *German Ideology*, 3.

The Nature of Social Theory

As an alternative to the "idealistic humbug" of the Young Hegelians, Marx argued that theoretical analyses should be empirically based. Social theory, he said, should be grounded on the "existence of living human individuals" who must survive, often in a relatively hostile environment.[5] This orientation is necessary because human beings are unlike other animals in that they manipulate the environment to satisfy their needs. They "begin to produce their means of subsistence, a step which is conditioned by their physical [i.e., social] organization."[6] This idea implies that people are "conscious"—that is, self-reflective. Thus, human beings are also unlike other animals in that they can look at themselves and their environment and then act rationally in their own interests. Consciousness thus arises from experience. Such an argument directly opposed Hegel's idealism, in which notions of morality, religion, and all other forms of awareness are considered to exist independently of human beings. Put in modern language, Marx was asserting that people produced their ideas about the world in light of the social structures in which they live and the experiences that they have in these structures. Furthermore, as social structures change, the content of people's ideas (their consciousness) changes as well. In breaking with the idealists in this way, Marx did not imply a simple-minded materialist orientation. He did not see the human mind as a passive receptacle; rather, he saw it as active, both responding to and changing the material world.

According to Marx, then, social theory should focus on how people influence and are influenced by their material conditions: for example, their degree of hunger, degree of protection from the environment, opportunity to enjoy the amenities of life, and ability to realize their creative potential. This emphasis constitutes a fundamental epistemological break with idealism. In effect, Marx stood Hegel "right side up" by transforming philosophy into an empirical social science.

The Characteristics of All Societies

Based on this vision of social theory, Marx emphasized that theoretical analyses should be oriented to what he called "the real process

---

[5]Ibid., 7.
[6]Ibid., 8.

of production."[7] The first characteristic of all societies is that human beings, unlike other animal species, produce sustenance from the environment to live and thereby "make history." Marx noted that human "life involves before anything else eating and drinking, a habitation, clothing, and many other [material] things."[8] Such needs are satisfied by employing technology to manipulate the environment in some socially organized manner. For Marx, this clearly implied that social theory has to deal with more than just ideas. It must be grounded in "the existence of living human individuals," who have material needs that must be satisfied through production. From this angle of vision, the task of social theory explains how people "produce their means of subsistence."

The second characteristic of all societies is that people create new needs over time. Need creation occurs because production (or work) always involves the use of tools or instruments of various sorts, and these tools are periodically improved, yielding more and better consumer goods. Thus, Marx said the processes of production and consumption always feed back on each other in a cumulative fashion, so that as one set of needs is satisfied, new ones emerge.[9] See Figure 7.1 for a graphic representation.

The process of need creation involves the desire not only for improved food, clothing, and shelter but also for the various amenities of life. Marx observed that in the production and consumption of goods beyond the minimum necessary for survival—what are called amenities—people become "civilized" in the sense that they can distinguish their uniquely human characteristics from those of other species. Thus, in *The Economic and Philosophic Manuscripts* (written in 1844), he described productive work as serving a dual purpose: (1) to satisfy physical needs and (2) to express uniquely human creativity. According to Marx, this duality is why other animals work only to satisfy an "immediate physical need, whilst man produces even when he is free from physical need and only truly produces in freedom therefrom."[10] Unfortunately, Marx believed, most people are prevented from expressing their human potential through work because the exploitation and alienation inherent in the division of labor prevent it.

---

[7] Ibid., 18.

[8] Ibid., 16.

[9] Marx, "Introduction," in *A Contribution to the Critique of Political Economy*, 188–217.

[10] Karl Marx, *The Economic and Philosophic Manuscripts* (New York: International, 1964), 111.

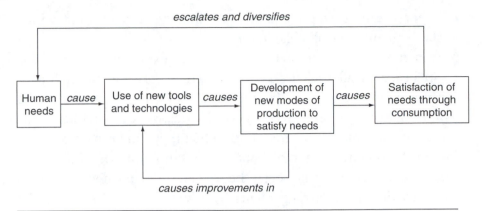

Figure 7.1   Marx's View of Human Needs, Production, and History

The third characteristic of all societies is that production is based on a division of labor, which in Marx's writings always implies a hierarchical stratification structure, with its attendant exploitation and alienation. The division of labor means the tasks that must be done in every society—placating the gods, deciding priorities, producing goods, raising children, and so forth—are divided among members of the society. But Marx observed that in all societies the basis for this division was private ownership of land or capital, which he called the *means of production*. Private ownership of the means of production produces a stratification system composed of the dominant group, the owners, and the remaining classes arrayed below them in varying degrees of exploitation and alienation. Non-owners are exploited and alienated because they cannot control either the work they do or the products produced. For example, capitalists, not employees, organize a production line to produce consumer goods, and capitalists, not employees, own the finished products. But because employees, whom Marx called *proletarians*, need these products to survive, they are forced to return their wages to the capitalists, who use the money to make more consumer goods and enrich themselves further. In this context, alienation takes the form of a fantastic reversal in which people feel themselves to be truly free only in their animal-like functions—such as eating, drinking, and fornicating. Whereas in their peculiarly human tasks, such as work, they do not feel human because they control neither the process nor the result. On this basis, Marx concluded, in capitalism "what is animal becomes human and what is human becomes animal."[11] Thus, paradoxically, the division

---

[11]Ibid., 111.

of labor means that proletarians continually re-create that which enslaves them: control of capital by the few.

In some form or another, Marx argued, exploitation and alienation occur in all societies characterized by private ownership of the means of production. That is, in all societies, members of the subordinate classes are forced to continuously exchange their labor power for sustenance and amenities so that they can keep on producing goods to benefit the members of the dominant class. For Marx, this situation implied that social theory had to focus on who benefits from existing social arrangements by systematically describing the structure of stratification that accompanies private ownership of the means of production. This situation also implied for Marx that only collective ownership could eliminate these problems.

The fourth characteristic of all societies is that ideas and values emerge from the division of labor. Put differently, ideas and values result from people's practical efforts at obtaining sustenance, creating needs, and working together. As a result, ideologies usually justify the status quo. "Ideologies" are systematic views of the way the world ought to be, as embodied in religious doctrines and political values. Thus, Marx argued, religious and political beliefs in capitalist societies state that individuals have a right to own land or capital; they have a right to use the means of production for their own rather than for the collectivity's benefit. It is perverse, he noted, for everyone to accept these values even though only a few people, such as landowners and capitalists, can exercise this right.

Marx believed that the values (or *ideologies*, to use his word) characteristic of a society are the tools of the dominant class because they mislead the populace about their true interests. This is why he described religion as "the opium of the masses."[12] Religious belief functioned to blind people to their exploitation and their real political interests. Religion does this by emphasizing that salvation, compensation for misery and alienation on earth, will come in the next world. In effect, religious beliefs justify social inequality. For Marx, the fact that ideas and values emerge from the division of labor implies that social theory must focus on both the structural sources of dominant ideas and the extent to which such beliefs influence people.

---

[12]Karl Marx, "A Contribution to the Critique of Hegel's Philosophy of Right," in *Marx-Engels Reader*, 16–26, 53–66.

Marx's Theoretical Methodology

The exposition in *The German Ideology* is an early example of Marx's dialectical materialism. Although he did not use this phrase, it expresses the discontinuity and continuity between Hegel and Marx. Marx rejected Hegel by grounding social theory in the real world, where people must satisfy their physical and psychological needs. The term *materialism* denotes this. Having rejected the substance of Hegel's idealism, however, Marx continued to use the Hegelian method of analysis. The term *dialectical* denotes this. In Marx's hands, *dialectical materialism* transforms historical analysis.

Dialectical materialism has four characteristics. First, society is a social structure, or *system*. Marx did not use this modern term, but it means that societies can be seen as having interrelated parts, such as classes, social institutions, cultural values, and so forth. These parts form an integrated whole. Thus, the observer's angle is very important when viewing a society. In tracing the connections among the parts of the stratification system, for example, it can be seen that from one angle a specific label can be applied (e.g., bourgeoisie), whereas from another angle an opposing label can be applied (for instance, proletariat). But there is an inherent connection between the two classes, which is why Marx noted in *The Communist Manifesto* that it was tautologous to speak of wage labor and capital, for one cannot exist without the other. Similarly, this is why he described production and consumption as "identical" or as occurring "simultaneously." He meant that they were parts of a coherent structure, or system, and that there was an inherent connection between them. Furthermore, the process of production and consumption (which today would be called the economy) is connected to stratification. More generally, class relations are reflected in all arenas of social behavior: the economy, kinship, illness and medical treatment, crime, religion, education, and government. Although Marx emphasized the primacy of economic factors, especially ownership of the means of production, his work is not narrowly economic; it is, rather, an analysis of how social structures function and change.

Second, social change is inherent in all societies as people make history by satisfying their ever-increasing needs. For Marx, the most fundamental source of change comes from within societies rather than from outside them. The force behind these internally generated changes is the *contradiction* inherent in the system. Not only are all the parts of society connected, they also contain their own inherent contradictions, which will cause their opposites to develop. For example, as will be described in the next section, Marx argued that feudalism contained within itself the social relations that eventually became capitalism. Similarly, in the *Manifesto* and *Capital*, Marx contended that capitalism contained within itself the social relations that would inevitably engender a new form of society: communism.

Third, social change evolves in a recognizable direction. For example, just as a flower is inherent in the nature of a seed, so the historical development of a more complex social structure, such as capitalism, is inherent in the nature of a less complex one, such as feudalism. The direction of history is from less complex to more complex social structures, which is suggested by the pattern of need creation depicted earlier. Marx was a child of the Enlightenment, and he believed in the inevitability of human progress.[13] He had a vision of evolutionary development toward a utopian end point. For Marx, this end point was a communist society.

Fourth, freely acting people decisively shape the direction of history given the predictable patterns of opposition and class conflict that develop from the contradictions in society. As with all Marx's concepts, his use of the term *class* is sometimes confusing. The key to understanding this concept lies in the idea of opposition, for he always saw classes as opposed to one another. It should be remembered, however, that this opposition occurs within a system of stratification; classes are opposed but still connected.[14]

Thus, regardless of their number or composition, the members of different classes are enemies because they have opposing interests. This is not a result of choice, but of location within the stratification system. For example, if the position of an aggregate of people makes obtaining food and shelter a constant problem and if these people cannot control their own activities or express their human potential, they are clearly in a subordinate position in relationship to others. In their alienation, they have an interest in changing the status quo, whether they are aware of it or not. On the other hand, if the position of an aggregate of people is such that their basic needs are satiated, if they can control their daily activities, and if they can devote themselves to realizing their human potential, such people have an interest

---

[13]Robert A. Nisbet, *Social Change and History* (New York: Oxford University Press, 1968).

[14]Bertell Ollman, "Marx's Use of 'Class,'" *American Journal of Sociology* 73 (March 1968), 573–580.

in preserving the status quo. Marx believed that these opposing interests could not be reconciled.

Hence, given a knowledge of the division of labor in capitalism, the differing interests and opportunities of the proletarians and capitalists are predictable, as is the generation of class conflict. The latter, however, is a matter of choice. History does not act, people do. From this point of view, Marx's theoretical task was to identify the social conditions under which people will recognize their class interests, unite, and produce a communist revolution. As will become clear later, Marx believed that he had achieved this goal. The important point to remember is that his theoretical methodology combines determinism, or direction, with human freedom: A communist revolution is a predictable historical event ushered in by freely acting people who recognize and act in their own interests.

Dialectical materialism can thus be summarized in the following way: Within any society, a way of producing things exists, both for what is produced and the social organization of production. Marx called this aspect of society the *productive forces*.[15] In all societies, the productive forces are established and maintained through a division of labor. Those few who own the means of production make up the dominant class, which benefits from the status quo. The masses make up the subordinate class (or classes). They are exploited and alienated because they have little control over their lives, and hence they have an interest in change. Over time, new ways of producing things are devised, whether based on advances in technology, changes in the way production is organized, or both. Such new forces of production better satisfy old needs and stimulate new ones. They are in the hands of a new class, and they exist in opposition to current property relationships and forms of interaction. Over the long run, the tension between these opposing classes erupts into a revolutionary conflict and a new dominant class emerges.[16]

The end point of this continuum is a communist society, a communal social organization in which there is collective control of the

---

[15]Sometimes Marx uses the phrase *forces of production* narrowly, so that it refers only to the instruments used in the productive process. Sometimes, however, he uses the phrase so that it refers to both the instruments used in production and the *social organization* that accompanies their use. By social organization is meant not only the organization of work (as in factories) but also family life, law, politics, and all other institutions. This tactic occurs with many of Marx's key concepts. See Bertell Ollman, *Alienation: Marx's Conception of Man in Capitalist Society* (New York: Oxford University Press, 1976).

[16]See Richard Appelbaum, "Marx's Theory of the Falling Rate of Profit: Towards a Dialectical Analysis of Structural Change," *American Sociological Review* 43 (February 1978), 73–92.

means of production (in today's societies, this is capital) so that people, acting cooperatively, can be free. In such a social context, Marx argued, exploitation and alienation will not exist because the division of labor will not be based on private ownership of property.

The German Ideology constitutes the first presentation of Marx's theory. It is, however, incomplete. It does not, for example, raise one of the most crucial issues: How are the oppressed proletarians to become aware of their true interests and seize control of the society for the benefit of all? This and other problems of revolutionary action are dealt with in *The Communist Manifesto*.

The Communist Manifesto

In 1847, Marx and Engels joined the Communist League, which they soon dominated. Under their influence, the League's goal was to overthrow the bourgeois society and to establish a new social order without classes and private property. To this end, Marx and Engels decided to compose a manifesto that would publicly state the Communist League's doctrines. The result constitutes one of the greatest political pamphlets ever written.

The *Manifesto* opens with a menacing phrase that immediately reveals its revolutionary intent: "A spectre is haunting Europe—the spectre of Communism. All the Powers of old Europe have entered into a holy alliance to exorcise this spectre." In a political context where opposition parties of all political orientations were called communists, Marx wrote, it was time for the communists them-selves to "meet this nursery tale of the spectre of Communism with a Manifesto of the party itself."[17] The remainder of the *Manifesto* is organized into four sections, which are summarized as follows.

Bourgeoisie and Proletarians

Marx presented his theoretical and political position early in the text when he emphasized, "The history of all hitherto existing society is the history of class struggles." He continued by observing that in every past era

---

[17]Marx and Engels, *Communist Manifesto*, 87.

oppressor and oppressed stood in constant opposition to one another [and] carried on an uninterrupted, now hidden, now open fight, a fight that each time ended either in a revolutionary reconstitution of society at large or in the common ruin of the contending classes.[18]

Put differently, Marx believed that in every social order those who own the means of production always oppress those who do not. Thus, in his view, bourgeois society merely substituted a new form of oppression and, hence, struggle in place of the old feudal form. Marx argued, however, that bourgeois society was distinctive in that it had simplified class antagonisms, because the "society as a whole is splitting up more and more into two great hostile camps, into two great classes directly facing each other: Bourgeoisie and Proletariat."[19] Because one class owns the means of production and the other does not, the two have absolutely opposing interests: the bourgeoisie in maintaining the status quo and the proletariat in a complete reorganization of society so that production can benefit the collectivity as a whole. This situation reflected a long historical process. As in *The German Ideology*, the analysis in the *Manifesto* is an example of Marx's dialectical materialism.

Historically, Marx argued, capitalism emerged inexorably from feudalism. "From the serfs of the Middle Ages sprang the chartered burghers of the earliest towns. From these burgesses the first elements of the bourgeoisie [capitalists] were developed."[20] Such changes were not historical accidents, Marx said, but the inevitable result of people acting in their own interests. The rise of trade and exchange, stimulated by the European discovery of the Americas, constituted new and powerful productive forces, which faced a feudal nobility that had exhausted itself by constant warfare. Furthermore, as they were increasingly exposed to other cultures, the members of the nobility wanted new amenities, and so they enclosed the land to raise cash crops using new methods of production. It should be recalled that production and consumption reciprocally affect each other—they are part of a social system—and they are tied to the nature of the class structure. As this historical process occurred, the serfs were forced off the land and into the cities, where they had to find work.

---

[18]Ibid., 88.
[19]Ibid., 89.
[20]Ibid., 90.

During this same period, a merchant class arose. At first, the nascent capitalists existed to serve the needs of the nobility by facilitating trade and exchange. Over time, however, capital became the dominant productive force. This process occurred as new sources of energy (such as steam) were discovered, as machines were invented and used to speed up the production process, and as the former serfs were pressed into service in new industries as wage laborers. The result, Marx noted, was that in place of feudal retainers and patriarchal ties, there was "left no other nexus between man and man than naked self-interest, than callous 'cash payment.'"[21]

The *Manifesto* summarizes the situation in the following way:

The feudal system of industry, under which industrial production was monopolized by closed guilds, now no longer sufficed for the growing wants of the new markets. The manufacturing system took its place; the guild masters were pushed on one side by the manufacturing middle class; division of labor between the different corporate guilds vanished in the face of division of labor in each single workshop.

Meantime, the markets kept ever growing, the demand ever rising. Even manufacture no longer sufficed. Thereupon steam and machinery revolutionized industrial production. The place of manufacture was taken by the giant, modern industry, the place of the industrial middle class by industrial millionaires, the leaders of whole industrial armies, the modern bourgeois.

We see then: The means of production and of exchange, on whose foundation the bourgeoisie built itself up, were generated in feudal society. At a certain stage in the development of these means of production and of exchange, the conditions under which feudal society produced and exchanged, the feudal organization of agriculture and manufacturing industry, in one word, feudal relations of property, became no longer compatible with the already developed productive forces; they became so many fetters. They had to be burst asunder, they were burst asunder.[22]

Thus, the rise of capitalism meant that the forces of production were revolutionized, and therefore, the class structure changed as well. Marx said that although these developments had been the result

---

[21]Ibid., 91.
[22]Ibid., 90, 94.

of freely acting people pursuing their self-interests, they had also been predictable—indeed, inevitable—historical events. Furthermore, because of the rise of capitalism, the class structure became simplified. Now there existed a new oppressed class, the proletarians, who had to sell their labor to survive. Because these people could no longer produce goods at home for their own consumption, they constituted a vast exploited and alienated workforce that was constantly increasing in size. Opposed to the proletarians was a new oppressor class, the bourgeoisie (or capitalists), as a few former artisans and petty burghers became entrepreneurs and eventually grew wealthy. These people owned the new productive forces on which the proletarians depended.

Marx then described the truly revolutionary nature of the capitalist mode of production. As a result of the Industrial Revolution, the bourgeoisie "has accomplished wonders far surpassing Egyptian pyramids, Roman aqueducts, and gothic cathedrals; it has conducted expeditions that put into the shade all former Exoduses of nations and crusades."[23] For the bourgeoisie to exist, Marx predicted, it must constantly develop new instruments of production and thereby create new needs that manufactured products can fill. As this process occurs, the bourgeoisie also seizes political power in each country, so that "the executive of the modern state is but a committee for managing the common affairs of the whole bourgeoisie."[24]

Having described the great historical changes accompanying the rise of capitalism, Marx then made two of his most famous predictions concerning the ultimate demise of the capitalist system. First, capitalism is inherently unstable. Periods of economic growth and high employment are followed by economic decline and unemployment. For Marx, these cycles—what today we call the "business cycle"—are endemic to capitalism. Capitalists and proletarians cannot escape them because eventually too many goods are produced relative to the demand for them, causing production to be cut back, and thereby forcing capitalists to lay off labor. Once this process begins, it accelerates as those who have been laid off can no longer afford to purchase goods, pushing capitalists to terminate the employment of even more workers in an escalating cycle that can lead to an economic depression. Capitalists try to avoid this cycle in many ways. For example, they may

---

[23]Ibid., 92.
[24]Ibid., 91.

destroy older products and sell only new ones; they may try to eliminate their competitors and thus exploit their markets more efficiently; and they may seek new markets. Try as they might, however, they cannot escape the inherent tendency of capitalist economies to experience recessions and depressions. As proletarians' lives are made more miserable by these circumstances, they begin to sense that their interests do not reside with capitalists, leading Marx to make his second great prediction.

Marx's second prediction was that "the modern working class, the proletarians" would become increasingly impoverished and alienated under capitalism. Because they could no longer be self-supporting, the proletarians had become "a class of laborers who live only so long as they find work, and who find work only so long as their labor increases capital."[25] Thus, in a context characterized by the extensive use of machinery owned by others, proletarians have no control over their daily lives or the products of their activities. Each person becomes, in effect, a necessary but low-priced appendage to a machine. In this situation, Marx said, even women and children are thrown into the maelstrom. Thus, under capitalism, human beings are simply instruments of labor whose only worth is the cost of keeping them minimally fed, clothed, and housed. Confronted with their own misery, Marx predicted, the proletarians will ultimately become class conscious and overthrow the entire system, especially as they live through cycles of recession and depression where their lives are made increasingly miserable.

The rise of the proletariat as a class proceeds with great difficulty, however, primarily because individual proletarians are forced to compete among themselves. For example, some are allowed to work in the capitalists' factories and others are not. Within the factories, a few are allowed to work at somewhat betterpaying or easier jobs, but most labor at lower paying and more difficult tasks. After work, proletarians with too little money still compete with one another for the inadequate food, clothing, and shelter that are available. Under these competitive conditions, it is difficult to create class consciousness. Marx showed, however, that as the bourgeoisie introduce improvements in education, force the proletarians to become better educated (to work the machines), and drag the proletarians into the political arena, the proletarians' ability to recognize the source of their exploitation increases.

---

[25]Ibid., 96.

But this process is slow and difficult; when workers did revolt, they usually directed their attacks against the instruments of production rather than the capitalists. When they did organize, the proletarians were often co-opted into serving the interests of the bourgeoisie.[26]

With the development of large-scale industry, the proletariat constantly increases in size. Like many other observers of nineteenth-century society, Marx predicted that the number of working-class people would continually increase as elements of the lower-middle class—artisans, shopkeepers, and peasants—were gradually absorbed into it. Furthermore, he believed that even those in professions such as medicine, law, science, and art would increasingly become wage laborers. Modern industry thus sweeps aside all the skills of the past, creating but two great classes.

The revolutionary development of the proletariat would, Marx argued, be aided by the fact that it was becoming increasingly urban, and hence its members were better able to communicate with one another. Furthermore, they were becoming better educated and politically sophisticated, partly because the bourgeoisie constantly dragged them into the political arena. Although the proletarians' efforts at organizing against the bourgeoisie were often hindered, Marx believed that they were destined to destroy capitalism because the factors mentioned here would stimulate the development of their class consciousness.

Proletarians and Communists

As Marx expressed it, the major goal of the communists could be simply stated as the abolition of private property. After all, he noted, under capitalism 9/10 of the population has no property anyway. As might be imagined, the bourgeoisie were especially critical of this position. But Marx felt that just as the French Revolution had abolished feudal forms of private property in favor of bourgeois forms, so the communist revolution would abolish bourgeois control over capital—without substituting a new form of private ownership. Marx emphasized, however, that the abolition of the personal property of the petty artisan or the small peasant was not at issue. Rather the

---

[26]See Karl Marx, "The Civil War in France," in Karl Marx and Friedrich Engels, *Selected Works* (Moscow: Progress, 1969), 178–244. Marx shows here how the proletarians actively participated in subjecting other classes to the rule of the bourgeoisie.

communists wished to abolish bourgeois "capital, i.e., that kind of property which exploits wage labor and which cannot increase except upon condition of begetting a new supply of wage labor for fresh exploitation."[27]

To change this situation, the proletarians periodically organized and rebelled during the nineteenth century. Indeed, shortly after publication of the *Manifesto*, revolts occurred throughout Europe. Even though such efforts were always smashed, Marx believed that the proletariat was destined to rise again, "stronger, firmer, mightier," ready for the final battle.

Marx viewed this process as an inevitable evolutionary development. In the *Manifesto*, Marx emphasized that "the theoretical conclusions of the Communists . . . express, in general terms, actual relations springing from an existing class struggle, from an historical movement going on under our very eyes."[28] According to Marx, just like the feudal nobility before it, "the Bourgeoisie [has] forged the weapons that bring death to itself." This process occurred because the productive forces of capitalism make it possible for all people to satisfy their needs and realize their human potential. For this possibility to occur, Marx contended, productive forces must be freed from private ownership and allowed to operate for the common good. Furthermore, the bourgeoisie has also "called into existence the men who are to wield those weapons—the modern working class—the proletarians." Marx believed that the working classes in all societies would, in their exploitation and alienation, eventually bring about a worldwide communist revolution.

Although Marx did not say much about the future, he knew that the transition to communism would be difficult, probably violent. This is because the communists aimed at destroying the core of the capitalist system: private ownership of the means of production. To achieve this goal, Marx believed that the means of production had to be "a collective product" controlled by the "united action of all members of the society." Such cooperative arrangements are not possible in bourgeois society, with its emphasis on "free" competition and its apotheosis of private property. Collective control of the society, Marx thought, is only possible under communism, where capital can be used as a means to widen, to enrich, and to promote the existence of the laborer. This drastic change required a revolution.

---

[27]Marx and Engels, *Communist Manifesto*, 104.
[28]Ibid., 103–104.

The first step in a working-class revolution, Marx argued, would be for the proletariat to seize control of the state. Once attaining political supremacy, the working class would then wrest "all capital from the bourgeoisie," "centralize all instruments of production in the hands of the state," and "increase the total of productive forces as rapidly as possible."[29] Furthermore, the following measures would also be taken in most countries:

1. Abolition of private ownership of land

2. A heavy progressive income tax

3. Abolition of all rights of inheritance

4. Confiscation of the property of emigrants and rebels

5. Centralization of credit and banking in the hands of the state

6. Centralization of communication and transportation in the hands of the state

7. State ownership of factories and all other instruments of production

8. Equal liability of all to labor

9. Combination of agricultural and manufacturing industries to abolish the distinction between town and country

10. Free public education for all children and the abolition of child labor

Marx understood perfectly that these measures could only be implemented arbitrarily, and he forecast a period of temporary communist despotism in which the Communist party acted in the interests of the proletariat as a whole. In an essay written many years after the *Manifesto*, Marx labeled this transition period the "revolutionary dictatorship of the proletariat."[30] Ultimately, however, his apocalyptic vision of the transition to communism was one in which people would become free, self-governing, and cooperative instead of alienated and competitive. They would no longer be mutilated by a division of labor over which they had no control. "The public power will lose its political character," Marx wrote. "In

---

[29]Ibid., 111.

[30]Karl Marx, "Critique of the Gotha Program," in Marx and Engels, *Selected Works*, 9–11.

place of the old bourgeois society with its classes and class antago-nisms, we shall have an association in which the free development of each is the condition for the free development of all."[31] It is a splendid vision; unfortunately, it is not that of the sorcerer, but of the sorcerer's apprentice.

Socialist and Communist Literature

In the third section of the *Manifesto*, Marx attacked the political literature of the day. He recognized that in all periods of turmoil and change, some inevitably desire to return to times past or to invent fantastic utopias as the way to solve humankind's ills. He believed that such dreams were, at best, a waste of time and, at worst, a vicious plot on the part of reactionaries. Thus, this section of the *Manifesto* is a brief critique of socialist literature as it then existed. He classi-fied this literature as (1) reactionary socialism (including here feudal socialism, petty-bourgeois socialism, and German "true" socialism); (2) conservative, or bourgeois, socialism; and (3) critical-utopian socialism.

Reactionary Socialism

Because the bourgeoisie had supplanted the feudal nobility as the ruling class in society, the remaining representatives of the aris-tocracy attempted revenge by trying to persuade the proletarians that life had been better under their rule. Marx characterized this literature as "half lamentation, half lampoon; half echo of the past, half menace of the future" and said that their efforts were misbegot-ten primarily because the mode of exploitation was different in an industrial context and a return to the past was not possible.

Petit bourgeois socialism is also ahistorical and reactionary. Although its adherents have dissected capitalist society with great acuity, they also have little to offer but a ridiculous return to the past: a situation in which corporate guilds exist in manufacturing and patriarchal relations dominate agriculture. Because they manage to be both reactionary and utopian, which is difficult, this form of social-ism always ends "in a miserable fit of the blues." Marx had previously criticized German, or "true," socialism in *The German Ideology*. In the *Manifesto*, he merely emphasized again (with typically acerbic

---

[31]Marx and Engels, *Communist Manifesto*, 112.

prose) that the Germans had written "philosophical nonsense" about the "interest of human nature, of Man in General, who belongs to no class, has no reality, who exists only in the misty realm of philosophical fantasy."[32]

Conservative, or Bourgeois, Socialism

In Marx's estimation, bourgeois socialists wanted to ameliorate the miserable conditions characteristic of proletarian life without abolishing the system itself. Today he might call such persons liberals. In any case, Marx believed that this goal was impossible to achieve, for what Proudhon and others did not understand was that the bourgeoisie could not exist without the proletariat and all the abuses inflicted on it.

Critical-Utopian Socialism

Utopian socialists had many critical insights into the nature of society, but Marx believed that their efforts were historically premature because the full development of the proletariat had not yet occurred, and so they were unable to see the material conditions necessary for its emancipation. As a result, they tried to construct a new society independent of the flux of history. For the utopian socialists, the proletarians were merely the most suffering section of society rather than a revolutionary class destined to abolish the existence of all classes.

Communist and Other Opposition Parties

In the final section of the *Manifesto*, Marx described the relationship between the Communist party, representing the most advanced segment of the working class, and other opposition parties of the time. Basically, in every nation the communists were supportive of all efforts to oppose the existing order of things, for Marx believed that the process of opposition would eventually "instill into the working class the clearest possible recognition of the hostile antagonism between the bourgeoisie and the proletariat."[33] In this regard, communists would always emphasize the practical and theoretical importance of private property as the means of exploitation in capitalist society.

---

[32]Ibid., 117.
[33]Ibid., 125.

Marx, the revolutionary, concluded the *Manifesto* with a final thundering assault on the bourgeoisie:

> The communists disdain to conceal their views and aims. They openly declare that their ends can be attained only by the forcible overthrow of all existing social conditions. Let the ruling classes tremble at a Communist revolution. The proletarians have nothing to lose but their chains. They have a world to win. WORKING MEN OF ALL COUNTRIES, UNITE![34]

Table 7.1   Marx's View of the Stages of History

Stage	*Oppressing Class*	*Oppressed Class*
Primitive communism	No classes	
Slavery	Slave owners	Slaves
Feudalism	Landowners	Serfs
Capitalism	Bourgeoisie	Proletariat
Socialism	State managers	Workers
Communism	No classes	

Marx's View of Capitalism in Historical Context

Reading *The Communist Manifesto* makes clear that Marx saw human societies as having developed through a series of historical stages, each characterized by its unique class divisions and exploitations. His vision is summarized in Table 7.1.[35]

Marx believed that humans originally lived in hunting-and-gathering societies in which everyone worked at the same tasks to subsist. Private property did not exist. Nor did a division of labor. Hence, there were no classes and no exploitation based on class. These societies, in short, were communist, with all members contributing according to their abilities and taking according to their needs. But this primitive communism collapsed, in his rendering of history, as social organization changed.

The first system of exploitation was slavery, in which ownership of other human beings determined rank and position. In slave societies,

---

[34]Ibid., 125.
[35]Marx, "Preface," in *A Contribution to the Critique of Political Economy*, 22.

the interests of owners and slaves were obviously opposed. Slaves had an interest in minimizing daily work demands, improving their living conditions, providing mechanisms by which they could work their way out of bondage, and preventing the inheritability of slave status (so their children would be born free). Slave owners had an interest in maximizing daily work (productivity), minimizing expenditures for food and other maintenance costs, making it difficult for slaves to escape bondage, and ensuring the inheritability of slave status. These conflicts of interest grew more difficult to control as the number of slaves increased and owners competed with one another in ways that increased the plight of the slaves—for example, by demanding more work while reducing food rations. The resulting conflict, in Marx's interpretation, led to a revolution in which slaves rose up and abolished the mechanism of their exploitation: the system of slavery.

Slavery was followed by feudalism, in which landless serfs and landowners represented the two great classes. Again, they had opposing interests. Those who owned the land wanted to increase productivity and, over time, to generate more cash income. Serfs were obliged to work the land under the presumption that they would share in a portion of its bounty. Their interest was to retain as much control over their crops as possible. In countries such as England, feudalism declined because landowners cleared the countryside of peasants to make room for products that would generate cash. For example, sheep were raised not for meat but as a source of raw material for the nascent wool industry. Sheep generated more profit, enabling landowners to purchase valued goods and amenities.

As described in the *Manifesto*, the feudal epoch gave way to capitalism. The name signifies that capital rather than land became the source of exploitation. The two great classes, of course, are the proletariat and the bourgeoisie (capitalists). Capitalists hire proletarians only if they generate profit, which is why capitalists are often described as leeches in Marx's writings. He believed that capitalism would grow like a giant octopus, spreading its tentacles over the entire globe, until nearly all human activity became debased because it was a commodity subject to purchase.

Marx argued that as the contradictions inherent in capitalism grew, it would collapse and be replaced by 'socialism. He described this stage as a transitory "dictatorship of the proletariat" in which the Communist party would seize control of the state in the name of the working class and expropriate private property (capital). Eventually, he believed, communism would emerge, a classless society in which all would give according to their ability and take according to their needs. The circle would be complete.

This depiction of the stages of history is superficial and, indeed, quite wrong.[36] Remember, however, that Marx did not have access to the data available to modern historians. But his vision does reveal Marx's view of history as successive systems of exploitation in which change emerges from within a society as people with competing interests attempt to satisfy their expanding needs. Thus, it reflects the use of dialectical materialism as a historical method. Moreover, despite its empirical flaws, it is possible to construct a model of stratification and conflict that remains useful.

Marx's Model of Stratification and Class Conflict

Modern readers often have two contrasting reactions when studying *The Communist Manifesto*, neither of which is very clearly articulated. On the one hand, it is easy to see how aspects of Marx's analysis can be applied to societies today. After all, exploitation does occur, and people in different classes do have opposing interests. On the other hand, Marx's political orientation seems both naive and threatening. It appears naive because a truly cooperative industrial society is hard to imagine. It appears threatening because subsequent history shows that a totalitarian government (like that in the former Soviet Union) seems to follow from any application of his ideas. Both reactions reflect Marx's peculiar combination of revolution and theory, which constitutes the greatest weakness in his writings. Nonetheless, it is possible to extrapolate a useful model of social stratification and class conflict from *The Communist Manifesto*.

Before doing so, however, we must recognize that any discussion of Marx's legacy demands a political confession: We are not Marxists. Thus, in what follows, the analysis implies nothing about the inevitability of a communist revolution or the transformation of society. Rather, it implies a concern with those ideas in Marx's writings that can still serve sociological theory.

Figure 7.2 displays a model of stratification and class conflict taken from the *Manifesto*. It illustrates some key variables to look for in studying social stratification and conflict, and it implies a modern sociological orientation. Marx asserted that in a stable social structure,

---

[36]See Fernand Braudel, *Civilization and Capitalism, 15th–18th Centuries*, Vol. 1 (New York: Harper & Row, 1981), and Immanuel Wallerstein, *The Modern World System*, Vols. 1 and 2 (New York: Academic, 1980).

THE SOCIOLOGY OF KARAL MARX

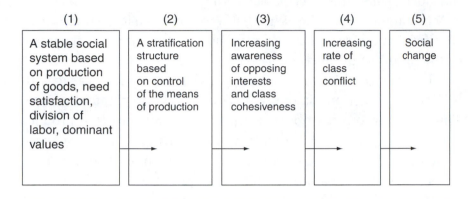

Figure 7.2   Marx's Model of the Generation of Stratification, Class Conflict, and Change

goods are produced to satisfy the material needs of people, a process necessitating a division of labor and justified in terms of dominant values. This situation is depicted in the first box in Figure 7.2.

Many past observers have construed Marx's emphasis on productive activity to be a form of economic determinism. But this is too narrow a reading. Marx's point is not that economic activity determines behavior in other areas but, rather, that all social action is conditioned by, and reciprocally related to, the type of productive activity that exists. For example, family life is likely to be different in a hunting-and-gathering society than in an industrial one, as are the forms of government, education, religious beliefs, law, cultural values, and so on. These variations occur, in part, because the way people obtain food, clothing, and shelter differs. Alternatively, in two societies at the same level of economic development, the organization of economic activity is likely to vary, because of differences in religious beliefs, law, family life, and so on.[37]

The recognition of such variation implies an essential sociological orientation: The range of options available to people is shaped by the nature of the society, its way of producing goods, its division of labor, and its cultural values. This orientation is fundamental to sociology today. Some writers like to begin with economic issues, others focus on some aspect of the division of labor (e.g., the family or criminal justice), and still others start by looking at how values circumscribe behavior. In every case, however, sociologists

---

[37]All these factors constitute what Marx called the forces of production. See Note 15.

emphasize that society is a social system with interrelated parts and that social facts circumscribe behavior.

Marx argued—and he is probably correct—that a structure of stratification emerges in all societies based, at least in part, on control of the means of production. This fact, which is depicted in the second box in Figure 7.2, means the upper class also has the capacity to influence the distribution of resources because it dominates the state. Thus, those who benefit because they control the means of production have an interest in maintaining the status quo, in maintaining the current distribution of resources, and this interest is pervasive across all institutional arenas. For example, classes in the United States today have different sources of income, they have different political resources, they are treated differently in the criminal justice system, they provide for their children differently, they worship at different churches, and so forth.[38]

In assessing what modern sociologists can learn from Marx, the use of the word *control* rather than *ownership* in Box 2 in Figure 7.2 is an important change because control over the means of production can occur in ways that he did not realize. For example, in capitalist societies the basis of social stratification is private ownership of property, whereas in communist societies the basis of social stratification is Communist party control of property. In effect, the Communist party is a new kind of dominant class ushered in by the revolution.[39] In both cases, the group controlling the means of production exploits those who do not, while acting to justify its benefits by dominating the state and promulgating its values among the masses that legitimize its exploitation.

When he looked at social arrangements, Marx always asked a simple question, one that modern sociologists also ask: Who benefits? For example, the long empirical sections of *Capital* (to be examined shortly) are designed to show how attempts at lengthening the working day and increasing productivity also increased the exploitation of the working class to benefit the capitalists. Marx also applied this question to nonobvious relationships. For example, his analysis of the "fetishism of commodities" in the early part of *Capital* shows how people's social relationships are altered by the reification (or worship)

---

[38]See Leonard Beeghley, *The Structure of Stratification in the United States*, 4th ed. (Boston: Allyn & Bacon, 2005).

[39]See Milovan Djilas, *The New Class* (New York: Praeger, 1965), and *Rise and Fall* (New York: Harcourt Brace Jovanovich, 1985). See also Michael Voslensky, *Nomenklatura: The Soviet Ruling Class* (Garden City, NY: Doubleday, 1986).

of machines and products that commonly occurs in capitalist societies, again to the benefit of capitalists. In effect, Marx teaches modern observers that an emphasis on who is benefiting from social arrangements and public policies can always improve analysis. For example, macroeconomic decisions that emphasize keeping inflation low and unemployment high benefit the middle class and rich in American society at the expense of working people. In every arena—at home, at work, in court, at church, in the doctor's office, and so forth—it is useful to ascertain who is benefiting from current social arrangements.

The second box in Figure 7.2 is important in another way as well. As emphasized in the *Manifesto*, Marx divided modern capitalist societies into two great classes: (1) bourgeoisie and (2) proletariat. Although he recognized that this basic distinction was too simplistic for detailed analyses, his purpose was to highlight the most fundamental division within these nations. Whenever he chose, Marx would depict the opposed interests and experiences of various segments of society, such as bankers, the "lower middle classes," or the *lumpenproletariat* (the very poor).

Boxes 3, 4, and 5 in Figure 7.2 outline the process of class conflict and social change. Under certain conditions, members of subordinate classes become aware that their interests oppose those of the dominant class. In such a context, Marx taught, class conflict ensues, and social change occurs.

In Marx's work, of course, this process is linked to assumptions about the direction of history and the inevitability of a communist revolution. But this need not be the case. Members of a class can become aware of their true interests and be willing to act politically without seeking a revolutionary transformation of society. This process occurs because, although classes might be opposed to one another in any ongoing social structure, they are also tied to one another in a variety of ways. As Reinhard Bendix argues, citizenship, nationalism, religion, ethnicity, language, and many other factors bind aggregates of people together despite class divisions.[40] Furthermore, to the extent that a subordinate class participates effectively in a political system, as when it obtains some class-related goals, it then acquires an interest in maintaining that system and its place within it. In the United States, at least, most mass movements composed of politically disenfranchised people have sought to get into the system rather than

---

[40]Reinhard Bendix, "Inequality and Social Structure: A Comparison of Marx and Weber," *American Sociological Review* 39 (April 1974), 149–161.

overthrow it. The labor movement, various racial and ethnic movements, and the feminist movement are all examples of this tendency. Thus, although the middle class and rich dominate the political process in the United States, subordinate classes also have resources that can influence public policy. This militates against a revolutionary transformation of U.S. society.

The emphasis on class conflict that pervades Marx's writings implies what sociologists today call a *structural* approach—that is, a focus on how rates of behavior among aggregates of people are influenced by their location in the society. Their differing locations dictate that classes have opposing interests. Moreover, Marx usually avoided looking at individual action because it is influenced by different variables. Rather, he wanted to know how the set of opportunities (or range of options) that people had influenced rates of behavior. For example, his analysis of the conditions under which proletarians transform themselves into a revolutionary class does not deal with the decision-making processes or cost–benefit calculations of individuals; rather, it shows that urbanity, education, political sophistication, and other factors are the social conditions that will produce class consciousness among the proletarians. Sociology at its best deals with structural variables. Although his work is misbegotten in many ways, Marx was a pioneer in this regard.

Capital

In *The German Ideology*, Marx attacked the Young Hegelians because they had avoided an empirical examination of social life. In *Capital*, he demonstrated the intent of this criticism by analyzing capitalist society. Using England (and copious amounts of British government data) as his primary example, he sought to show that the most important characteristic of the capitalist mode of production was the constant drive to accumulate capital using exploited and alienated labor. As a result of the need to accumulate capital, Marx argued, the processes of production are incessantly revolutionized, and over the long run, the instability and degradation of people characteristic of capitalist society will lead to its complete transformation. Thus, in contrast with the *Manifesto*, which is a call to arms, *Capital* is a scholarly attempt to show why such a transformation of capitalist society will inevitably occur. As such, *Capital* is much more than a narrow work of economics; it is an analysis of capitalist social structure and its inevitable transformation.

The Labor Theory of Value

Marx sketched the labor theory of value in the opening chapter of *Capital.* Although he approached this issue from what appears to be a strictly economic vantage point—the nature and value of commodities—his discussion turns out to have considerably broader implications. A *commodity* is "an object outside of us, a thing that by its properties satisfies human wants of some sort or another."[41] For his purposes, both the origin of people's wants and the manner in which commodities satisfy them are irrelevant. The more important problem is what makes a commodity valuable. The answer provides the key to Marx's analysis of capitalist society.

Two different sources of value are inherent to all commodities: (1) use value and (2) exchange value denote the fact that commodities are produced to be consumed. For example, people use paper to write on, autos for transportation, and so forth. Clearly, some things that have value, such as air and water, are not produced but are there for the taking (at least they were in the nineteenth century). Marx, however, was primarily interested in manufactured items. Commodities having use value are qualitatively different from one another; for example, a coat cannot be compared with a table. The *exchange value* of commodities provides a basis for comparing the labor time required to produce them. For Marx, the value of commodities is determined by the labor time necessary to produce them. He phrased this *labor theory of value* in the following way:

> That which determines the magnitude of the value of any article is the amount of labour socially necessary, or the labour-time socially necessary for its production. Each individual commodity, in this connection, is to be considered as an average sample of its class. Commodities, therefore, in which equal quantities of labour are embodied, or which can be produced in the same time, have the same value. The value of one commodity is to the value of any other, as the labour-time necessary for the production of the one is to that necessary for the production of the other. As values, all commodities are only definite masses of congealed labour-time.[42]

---

[41]Karl Marx, *Capital: A Critical Analysis of Capitalist Production*, Vol. 1 (New York: International, 1967). The original spelling is retained in all quotations.

[42]Ibid., 39–40.

Marx supplemented the labor theory of value in five ways. First, different kinds of *useful labor* are not comparable. For example, the tasks involved in producing a coat are qualitatively different from those involved in producing linen. All that is comparable is the expenditure of human labor power in the form of brains, nerves, and muscles. Thus, the magnitude of exchange value is determined by the quantity of labor as indicated by its duration in hours, days, or weeks. Marx called this quantity *simple average labor.*

Second, although different skills exist among workers, Marx recognized that "skilled labour counts only as simple labour intensified, or rather, as multiplied simple labour."[43] Thus, to simplify the analysis, he assumed that all labor was unskilled. In practice, he asserted, people make a similar assumption in their everyday lives.

Third, the value of a commodity differs according to the technology available. With mechanization, the labor time necessary to produce a piece of cloth is greatly reduced (and so, by the way, is the value of the cloth—at least according to Marx). During the initial stages of his analysis, Marx wished to hold technology constant. Therefore, he asserted that the labor time socially necessary to produce an article under the normal conditions of production existing at the time determined the value of a commodity.

Fourth—and this point will become very important later on—under capitalism, labor itself is a commodity with exchange value, just like linen and coats. Thus, "the value of labour power is determined as in the case of every other commodity, by the labour time necessary for the production, and consequently, the reproduction, of this special article."[44]

Fifth, an important implication of the labor theory of value is the development of what Marx called the *fetishism of commodities* whereby people come to believe that commodities possess humanlike attributes and that exploitation as well as alienation arise from relations with machines, as a kind of commodity, rather than from those who own the machines. In capitalist society, the fetishism of commodities manifests itself in two different ways: (1) Machines (as a reified form of capital and a commodity) are seen as exploiting workers, which is something only other people can do. Thus, products that people designed and built and that can be used or discarded at will become seen not only as having human attributes but even as

---

[43]Ibid., 44.
[44]Ibid., 170.

being independent participants in human social relationships. (2) When machines are seen to exploit workers, the social ties among people are hidden, so that their ability to understand or alter the way they live is impaired. In this context, Marx wrote, "There is a definite social relation between men, that assumes, in their eyes, the fantastic form of a relation between things."[45]

In later chapters of *Capital*, Marx illustrated what he meant by the fetishism of commodities by showing that machines rather than laborers set the pace and style of work and by showing that machines rather than their owners "needed" the night work of laborers so that they could be in continuous operation. The owners, the capitalists, are hidden behind their machines, and they are the real villains in this exploitive and alienating relationship.

Capitalists have little interest in the use value of the commodities produced by human labor. Rather, it is exchange value that interests them. Marx writes, "the restless never-ending process of profit-making alone is what [the capitalist] aims at."[46] His term for profit was *surplus value*.

Surplus Value

Because Marx believed that the source of all value was labor, he had to show how laborers create surplus value for capitalists. He did this by distinguishing between "labor" and "labor power." *Labor* is the work people actually do when they are employed by capitalists, whereas *labor power* is the capacity to work that the capitalist purchases from the worker. As Marx put it, "by labour-power or capacity for labour is to be understood the aggregate of those mental and physical capabilities existing in a human being, which he exercises whenever he produces a use-value of any description."[47] Labor power is a commodity just like any other, and it is all the workers have to sell. Marx noted that the laborer, "instead of being in the position to sell commodities in which his labour is incorporated, [is] obliged to offer for sale as a commodity that very labour-power, which exists only in his living self."[48] Furthermore, in a capitalist society the proletarians can sell their labor power only to capitalists, who own the

---

[45]Ibid., 72.
[46]Ibid., 149.
[47]Ibid., 167.
[48]Ibid., 168–169.

means of production. The two meet, presumably on an equal basis, one to sell labor power and the other to buy it. In reality, Marx saw labor as always at a disadvantage in this exchange.

The value, or selling price, of labor power is "determined, as in the case of any other commodity, by the labour-time necessary for the production, and consequently also the reproduction, of this special article."[49] Thus, labor power is, at least for the capitalist, a mass of congealed labor time—as represented by the cost of food, clothing, shelter, and all the other things necessary to keep the workers returning to the marketplace with their peculiar commodity. Because workers must also reproduce new generations of workers, the cost of maintaining entire families must be included. Having discovered that labor power is the source of surplus value, Marx wanted to calculate its rate. To do so, he distinguished between absolute and relative surplus value.

Absolute surplus value occurs when capitalists lengthen the working day to increase laborers' productivity. This issue became a matter of conflict throughout the nineteenth century. Hence, Marx spent a considerable amount of space documenting the way in which the early capitalists had forced laborers to work as many hours as possible each day.[50] The data that he presented are significant for two reasons. First, despite their anecdotal quality (by today's standards), they are clearly correct: Capitalists sought to extend the working day and keep the proletarians in an utterly depraved condition. For Marx, the effort to lengthen the number of hours that laborers worked was inherent to capitalism; and moreover, proletarians would always be helpless to resist. Second, these remarkable pages of *Capital* drew from historical and governmental data. Indeed, Marx took great satisfaction in using information that the British government had supplied to indict capitalism.

Relative surplus value occurs when capitalists increase laborers' productivity by enabling them to produce more in the same amount of time. This result can be achieved in two ways, he said. One is to alter the organization of work—for example, by placing workers together in factories. Another, more prevalent as capitalism advances, is to apply advanced technology to the productive process. By using machines, laborers can produce more goods (boots, pens,

---

[49]Ibid., 170.
[50]Ibid., 231–312.

computers, or anything else) in less time. This means that capitalists can undersell their competitors and still make a profit. Because the reorganization of the workplace and the use of machines were methods of exploiting laborers, they were also the locus of much conflict during the nineteenth century. For such changes meant that proletarians had to work either harder or in a more dehumanizing environment. As in his analysis of absolute surplus value, Marx spent much time documenting the capitalists' efforts to increase relative surplus value.[51] By using historical and governmental data, he again showed how productivity had increased steadily through greater exploitation of proletarians.

This analysis of the sources of surplus value provided Marx with a precise definition of exploitation. In his words, "the rate of surplus value is therefore an exact expression of the degree of exploitation of laborer-power by capital, or of the laborer by the capitalist."[52] In effect, surplus value is the value created by workers but skimmed off by capitalists just as beekeepers take a (large) fraction of the honey from the bees which make it.

More broadly, exploitation is not simply a form of economic injustice, although it originates the labor theory of value. The social classes that result from the acquisition of surplus value by one segment of society are also precisely defined. That class accruing surplus value, administering the government, passing laws, and regulating morals is the *bourgeoisie*, and that class being exploited is the *proletariat*.

By discovering the advantages of increasing productivity, Marx thought he had uncovered the hidden dynamic of capitalism that would lead inexorably to increasing exploitation of the proletarians, more frequent industrial crises, and, ultimately, the overthrow of the capitalist system itself. His rationale was that the capitalists' increased profits were short-lived, because other capitalists immediately copied any innovation. Thus, the extra surplus value generated by rising productivity disappeared "so soon as the new method of productivity has become general, and has consequently caused the difference between the individual value of the cheapened commodity and its social value to vanish."[53] The long-term result, Marx predicted, would be the sort of chaos originally described in *The Communist Manifesto*.

---

[51]Ibid., 336–507.
[52]Ibid., 218.
[53]Ibid., 319.

The Demise of Capitalism

Marx's description of surplus value was a systematic attempt at showing the dynamics of capitalist exploitation. His next task was to reveal the reasons why, despite its enormous productivity, capitalism contained the seeds of its own destruction. He proceeded in two steps.

The first deals with what he called *simple reproduction*. It occurs as workers continuously produce commodities that become translated into surplus value for capitalists and wages for themselves. Proletarians use their wages in ways that perpetuate the capitalist system. Because capitalists own the means of production and the commodities produced with them, proletarians must give their wages back to the capitalists as they purchase the necessities of life. The capitalists, of course, use that money to make still more money for themselves. In addition, after minimally satisfying their needs, workers return to the marketplace ready to sell their labor power and prepared once again to augment capital by creating surplus value. Over time, then, capitalist society is continuously renewed, because proletarians produce not only commodities, their own wages, and surplus value, but also capitalist social relations: exploited and alienated workers on one side and capitalists on the other.

The second step focuses on what Marx called the *conversion of surplus value into capital*. Today, we refer to the reinvestment of capital. Thus, after consuming a small part of the surplus value they obtain from proletarians, capitalists reinvest the remainder to make even more money. As Marx observed, "the circle in which simple reproduction moves, alters its form and . . . changes into a spiral."[54] The result is a contradiction so great that the demise of capitalism and its transformation into "a higher form of society" becomes inevitable.

On this basis, Marx made three now-famous predictions. The first was that proletarians would be forever separated from owning or controlling private property, even their own labor. Workers would always be at a disadvantage in labor markets, and as a result, they would sell their labor power and, thereby, give capitalists surplus value. Without this surplus value, the proletariat would never own or control private property. They would have just enough, perhaps, to survive and reproduce the next generation of exploited labor. Yet, paradoxically, the laborers have not been defrauded—at least according to capitalist

---

[54]Ibid., 581.

rules of the game—for as we saw earlier, the capitalists merely pay laborers for the value of their commodity, labor power. Moreover, because proletarians have only labor power to sell, they have little choice but to participate according to the capitalists' rules.

Marx's second prediction was that proletarians would become increasingly impoverished and that an industrial reserve army of poor people would be created. This outcome would increasingly occur as capitalists used ever more machines in the factories to make labor more productive and lower the price of goods; as a result, fewer laborers would be needed, and their labor power could be purchased at a lower price. Thus, Marx predicted not only that proletarians would continuously reproduce their relations with the capitalists— that is, selling their labor and making profits for capitalists—but also that they would produce the means by which they were rendered a superfluous population forced to work anywhere, anytime, and for any wages. Under these extreme conditions, Marx believed, proletarians will become a self-conscious revolutionary class.

Marx's third prediction was that the *rate of profit* would fall and bring on industrial crises of ever-greater severity. As capitalists compete with each other, the price of commodities would have to fall to the point where it was not possible to make a profit. Even more efficient organization of work or the adoption of new technologies reducing costs for capitalists could not, in the end, keep the profits from falling. As Marx emphasized, competitors soon copied each new innovation, thereby eroding any pricing advantages. Yet the cutthroat competition would continue, forcing capitalists to lower prices relative to costs. Eventually, an insurmountable crisis would begin to emerge: Capitalists would have increasing problems generating profits. And, the fact that capitalists had laid off workers as they adopted new technologies would aggravate this situation, thus diminishing the ability of workers to buy commodities at any price. As an outcome, capitalism would fall. The contradictions built into its very nature, Marx felt, would increasingly disrupt the operation of the capitalist system, while at the same time making the proletariat more aware of their interests in overthrowing the bourgeoisie. Indeed, capitalism is locked into several self-destructive cycles described in Table 7.2. Thus, according to Marx, the logic of capitalist development will produce the conditions necessary for its overthrow: an industrial base along with an impoverished and class-conscious proletariat. Ultimately, these dispossessed people will usher in a classless society in which production occurs for the common good.

Capitalism in Historical Context

Marx's analysis of capitalism presupposed that it was an ongoing social system. Thus, in the final pages of *Capital*, he once again sketched the origins of capitalism, which he now called the process of *primitive accumulation*. We should recall that capitalist social relations occur only under quite specific circumstances; that is, the owners of money (the means of production) who desire to increase their holdings confront free laborers who have no way of obtaining sustenance other than by selling their labor power. Thus, to understand the origins of capitalist social relations, Marx had to account for the rise of both the proletariat and the bourgeoisie. Typically, he opted for a structural explanation.

According to Marx, the modern proletariat arose because self-supporting peasants were driven from the land (and from the guilds) and transformed into rootless and dependent urban dwellers. This process began in England during the fifteenth and sixteenth centuries and then spread throughout Western Europe. Using England as his example, Marx argued that this process had begun with the clearing of the old estates by breaking up feudal retainers, robbing peasants of the use of common lands, and abolishing their rights of land tenure under circumstances he described as "reckless terrorism." In addition, Marx argued, one of the major effects of the Protestant Reformation was "the spoliation of the church's property" by its conversion into private property—illegally, of course. Finally, the widespread theft of state land and its conversion into privately owned property ensured that nowhere in England could peasants continue to live as they had during medieval times. In all these cases (although this analysis is clearly too simplistic), the methods used were far from idyllic, but they were effective, and they resulted in the rise of capitalist agriculture capable of supplying the needs of a "free" proletariat. Furthermore, given that they had nowhere to go, thousands of displaced peasants became beggars, robbers, and vagabonds. Hence, throughout Western Europe beginning in the sixteenth century, there was "bloody legislation against vagabondage" with severe sanctions against those who would not work for the nascent capitalists who were then emerging.

Marx believed that the emergence of the capitalist farmer and the industrial capitalist occurred concomitantly with the rise of the modern proletariat. Beginning in the fifteenth century, those who owned or controlled land typically had guarantees of long tenure,

Table 7.2 Marx's Views on Why Capitalism Would Collapse

1. Capitalists must exploit labor—that is, extract surplus value from labor power—to make profits. This exploitation cannot be hidden from workers, especially as capitalists continuously increase the rate of exploitation.

2. Capitalists must compete with each other, forcing them to lower prices and to find new ways to reduce costs to maintain a profit. As they seek to find new ways to lower costs, capitalists gain only a short-term advantage until competitors copy cost-cutting efforts, but they increase the longer term likelihood that the proletariat will become aware of their interests.

   a. As capitalists build larger factories to take advantage of the cost benefits that come with "economies of scale," they amass workers so that they can better communicate their grievances with each other and form a more effective revolutionary force.

   b. As capitalists adopt new technologies to reduce reliance on labor, they increase unemployment, which makes labor more hostile to capitalists but also reduces the demand for the commodities produced by capitalists.

   c. As capitalists copy each others' innovations, a new round of price competition occurs, eventually creating a declining rate of profit that begins to destroy capitalist enterprises.

3. Capitalism will always overproduce commodities relative to demand, causing recessions and depressions that make workers even more aware of their misery and of who is to blame.

could employ newly "freed" workers at very low wages, and benefited from a rise in the price of farm products. In addition, they were able to increase farm production, despite the smaller number of people working the land, through the use of improved methods and equipment, which increased cooperation among workers in the farming process and concentrated land ownership in fewer hands. Thus, primitive accumulation of capital could occur.

Marx believed that industrial capitalism had developed as the result of a variety of interrelated events. First, he emphasized, usury and commerce existed throughout antiquity—despite laws against such activity—and laid a basis for the primitive accumulation of capital to occur. Second, the exploration and exploitation of the New World brought great wealth into the hands of just a few people. In this regard, Marx pointed especially to the discovery of gold and silver, along with the existence of native populations that could be exploited. Finally, he noted the emergence of a system of public credit and its expansion into an international credit system. On this basis, he claimed, capitalism emerged in Western Europe.

Critical Conclusions

Substantive Contradictions

Marx had a utopian vision of a classless society within which people acted cooperatively for the common good and, in the process, realized their human potential. Paradoxically, he believed that this goal could be achieved through the centralization of political power in the hands of the state. It is because he had such a belief that he was described as a sorcerer's apprentice. The image is that of a leader without wisdom who inadvertently releases the power of the netherworld on the earth. Put bluntly, Marx's vision of the transition from capitalism to communism invites the establishment of a regime in which the state has strict control over all aspects of an individual's life; it invites, in other words, modern totalitarianism.

To understand why Marx proceeded in this way, we need to appreciate the dilemma he faced. As a revolutionary, he sought to overthrow a brutal and exploitive society in favor of a humane and just community. It is worth remembering that Engels's description of the living conditions of the working class was horribly accurate, and many nineteenth-century observers saw the situation as becoming steadily worse. Thus, as Marx saw it, the problem was to get from a competitive society to a communal one, which would free individuals to realize their potential as human beings.

So Marx made a series of proposals that are worth restating: the abolition of private ownership of land, confiscation of the property of emigrants and rebels, centralization of credit, communication, and transportation by the state, ownership of factories by the state, and several others. These measures imply a belief that unrestrained political power can be redemptive, that the way to freedom is through totalitarian control. As Marx put it, the transition to communism would require a temporary dictatorship of the proletariat. But experience has shown that this strategy can only mean total rule by the Communist party, which justifies its exploitation of the masses by invoking the common good. Now the political issue is not whether the ends justify the means. It is, rather, whether the means can produce the ends; that is, can power, unfettered by accountability, produce freedom for individuals? The answer is no. There is no evidence that totalitarianism can produce freedom. Despite its grandiose vision, Marx's writings had perverse political consequences.

Where Prophecy Fails

Marx's predictions or prophecies go wrong not only because he failed to recognize that power, once given, does not "wither away," but also because he assumed that it would be the proletariat who would rise up and overthrow capitalism. Yet the great communist revolutions in Russia and China were really outcomes of longer term civil wars, and the key actors were not the proletariat but peasants. The state did not wither away in either case, and ironically, only with the rise of capitalism in these countries, particularly China, can some hope for a less totalitarian regime be found. Clearly, Marx's grand predictions contain several significant miscalculations.

First, Marx saw the value of commodities as inhering in the labor power necessary to produce them (less other costs such as machines and marketing). This assumption is perhaps his most fundamental mistake, and despite efforts by contemporary Marxists[55] to stay with this idea because it offers a measure of exploitation, it is fundamentally flawed. Value inheres in what one is willing to pay, or must pay under constrained conditions, for something in a market, and though Marxists would decry this as imposing capitalist categories, it is nonetheless true. People can still be exploited when they are paid little and forced to work under terrible conditions, but we need not invoke the value theory of labor as our measure of the degree of exploitation. Rather, we invoke other values, such as fair wages, basic standards of living, and safe working conditions to assess exploitation. The notion of exploitation is thus evaluative; it cannot be an objective construct, as Marx sought to make it. We can still see capitalist profits and wealth as coming from exploitation, if we choose, but the value theory of labor is an ideology disguised as science. Like Adam Smith, who had worked with the idea, we should abandon the notion of a labor theory of value because it is not useful.

Second, Marx miscalculated the extent to which capitalists and proletarians were inexorably on a collision course. The early capitalism that Marx observed did indeed seem to be locked into a self-destructive system, but Marx simply assumed that these crises of recession/depression and labor discontent were not resolvable within

---

[55]See, for example, John A. Roemer, *A General Theory of Exploitation and Class* (Cambridge, MA: Harvard University, Press, 1982), and Erik Olin Wright, *Class Counts* (Cambridge, UK: Cambridge University Press, 1997).

the framework of capitalism. Part of the reason for this miscalculation was that Marx overestimated the extent to which the state is simply a tool of the bourgeoisie, whereas in fact, capitalism is associated with the rise of political democracies in which all citizens have some say, despite the fact that the rich certainly have more influence than the poor. Another part of the reason for Marx's miscalculations is that persistent crises force the state to seek agreements between capitalists and labor over wages and working conditions. These crises have pulled the state into regulating markets and capitalists as recessions threatened political stability. Marx assumed that such flexibility by the state and capitalists could not exist. In fact, during early capitalism, this flexibility is not so evident, but over time, masses of urban workers have been able to gain political power.

Third, Marx incorrectly assumed that workers were, and always would be, powerless in labor markets. Although this was certainly true in early capitalism as rural peasants migrated to cities (and indeed is still true for rural migrants to cities), workers were able to gain political power to force political interventions in labor markets. This gain in power was partly the result of labor unions that were far more successful than Marx could have envisioned at the time he was writing. Moreover, there is not always a perpetual shortage of labor or reserve labor force that can be drawn on when existing workers demand higher wages. Labor shortages do emerge, and under these conditions, the proletariat is in a better bargaining position. Furthermore, as investments in technology and facilities mount, the costs of unused capital investments arising from prolonged labor disputes have often forced capitalists to bargain with workers rather than leave big machines idle.

Fourth, Marx did not anticipate the rise of the middle classes, another occurrence that has posed problems for Marxist theorists.[56] Indeed, he made the opposite prediction: Most people would be pushed into the proletariat. History shows, however, that as the economy expands, especially as new technologies drive the expansion, the proportion of skilled, white-collar workers grows and eventually comes to constitute the majority of workers. These more skilled workers are in a much better bargaining position over wages and working conditions than were early industrial workers.

---

[56]Erik Olin Wright, *Classes* (London: Verso, 1985), and Erik Olin Wright and Luca Perrone, "Marxist Class Categories and Income Inequality," *American Sociological Review* 42 (1977), 32–55.

Fifth, Marx did not recognize the importance of government as a large employer. He tended to see government as the tool of the bourgeoisie, but as government intervenes in all spheres of society—from schools to economic regulation—a significant proportion of the labor force comes to work for government. As a result, it is difficult to typify the interests of government workers as part of conflicts between an exploited proletariat and capitalists.[57]

Sixth, late in his writings, Marx began to see some of the implications of joint stock companies, but he could not have predicted the revolution ushered in by the issuing of stocks in markets. Ownership was to become more diffused, with many workers having a stake in capitalism as they acquired stock. Moreover, not only was ownership diffused, but also it was separated from management such that owners would not directly manage companies and, hence, relations with labor. Under these conditions, management would increasingly be interested in rationalizing relations with labor to keep production going.

Thus, many specific forces in capitalism mitigated against Marx's predictions. Some of these forces he could not be expected to have anticipated, but he might have seen the effects of others if he had not been so committed ideologically to overthrowing capitalism. It is always hazardous to make predictions based on a historical trend, as Marx did, because specific historical events can change the trajectory of a prediction. Marx had confidence in his prophecies because his entire intellectual scheme forced these predictions, but he never questioned some of the assumptions on which this scheme was based; when some proved questionable, the entire system collapsed.

Is Marx Still Relevant?

So why should sociologists still read Marx? After all, have not most of his predictions about revolution and the spread of communism failed to materialize? The communist revolution by the proletariat never really occurred. The class structure of the capitalist system did not polarize, but instead, became ever more complex. The state did not "wither away" in communist countries (indeed, only when they turned capitalist). And the world has become more capitalist rather than communist. Some contemporary sociologists continue to hold

---

[57]Erik Olin Wright, "Rethinking, Once Again, The Concept of Class," in *The Debate on Classes*, ed. E. O. Wright (London: Verso, 1989).

out, arguing that as capitalism goes completely global, the contradictions in the system will finally emerge and usher in the communist revolution. Others have sustained an interest in exploitation and the value theory of labor, reworking these ideas to fit more contemporary conditions. Yet it must be said that much of the Marxian system of thinking, especially its more ideologically loaded portrayals of the future, has not held up.

Still, Marx anticipated and framed many of the issues that occupy discussion of the economy and society today.[58] Marx saw, more than any other scholar of the last century, that the economy is the driving force of society, and he predicted that capitalism would spread or, in today's vocabulary, become a global force. He understood that economic power and political power are highly correlated and that those with power could disproportionately influence the formation of ideologies and the other elements of culture. He explained the incredible wealth-generating capacities of free markets, but this dynamism is tempered by the inequalities, exploitation, and alienation generated by such a system, as well as by the inherent tendency of the system to cycle in and out of ever-deeper recessions and depressions. Moreover, he even anticipated the power of big capitalism to standardize activities, to impoverish small businesses and artisans, and to destroy old cultures in the relentless drive to make production more efficient and to penetrate all markets. Thus, Marx had a very good sense for many of the outcomes of capitalism, once unleashed. Why, then, did his more specific predictions about the revolution of the proletariat go wrong? The answer must reside in Marx's ideological fervor. Marx was blinded by his convictions and, hence, could not see that the state, bourgeoisie, and workers could change the capitalist system in ways that make it more benign.

---

[58]For a recent review of contemporary Marxist thinking, see Michael Burawoy and Erik Olin Wright, "Sociological Marxism" in *Handbook of Sociological Theory*, ed. J. H. Turner (New York: Kluwer Academic, 2002).

CHAPTER 8

The Origin and Context of Max Weber's Thought

Biographical Influences on Weber's Thought

Max Weber, the first of seven children, was born to Max and Helene Weber on April 21, 1864, in the city of Erfurt in Thuringia. Thuringia was located in Prussia, the most powerful of the German states at that time. Weber descended from Protestants on both sides of his family. His father's ancestors were Lutheran refugees from Austria, and his mother's forebears were Huguenot emigrants from France. As we will see, Weber's Protestantism weighed heavily on him, serving as a source of torment and eventually as motivation for one of the greatest sociological analyses ever written, *The Protestant Ethic and the Spirit of Capitalism.*[1]

The Early Years

Weber's father, a lawyer and judge in Erfurt, became a politician in Berlin, where the family moved in 1869. In Berlin, the elder Weber began his political career as a city councilor and subsequently served as a member of the Landtag (Regional Assembly) and the Reichstag (Imperial Parliament). In this context, the Weber family entertained

---

[1]Max Weber, *The Protestant Ethic and the Spirit of Capitalism* (New York: Scribner's, 1958). The original appeared in two parts, in 1904 and 1905.

a wide assortment of distinguished people. For example, the historians Theodor Mommsen and Wilhelm Dilthey lived nearby and frequently visited the Weber household.[2] This background allowed the young Weber to meet the leading politicians and scholars of the day, listen to and participate in their discussions, and become aware of the issues facing the nation.

By all accounts, Weber's father enjoyed the freewheeling lifestyle of a German politician, with its emphasis on material success, its lack of religiosity, and its rough-and-tumble world of gossip, deals, and accommodation. He was a hedonist, a man who enjoyed bourgeois living to the fullest. Within the family, however, the senior Weber ruled absolutely. He did not tolerate young people holding opinions different from his own and felt compelled, as a patriarch, to control his wife's behavior in myriad ways. The elder Weber was nonetheless devoted to his children, supervising their education and taking them on outings in the countryside. During his youth, the young Weber was close to his father, an orientation that would later change.

Weber's mother was altogether different from her husband. Helene Weber, a shy and sensitive woman, was religiously devout. When she was 16, an older friend of the family sexually attacked her; as a result of this episode, she came to hate sexuality. Marianne Weber, Max Weber's wife, reports that the physical aspect of marriage was to her not a source of joy but a heavy sacrifice and also a sin that was justified only by the procreation of children. Because of this, in her youthful happiness she often longed for old age to free her from that duty. A loving and affectionate mother, Helene Weber nonetheless adhered to strict Calvinist standards of hard work, ascetic behavior, and personal morality, which she tried to instill in her children. "She was never satisfied with herself and always felt inadequate before God," resulting in a life marked by great inward struggle.[3] Moreover, because they were so mismatched, Weber's parents became permanently estranged very early in their marriage, a conflict that affected Weber throughout his life. Indeed, he believed that he had to choose between his parents and that this choice would be decisive for his own personality development. This "choice" became a source of emotional agony throughout Weber's

---

[2]Marianne Weber, *Max Weber: A Biography* (New York: Wiley, 1975), 39. The original was published in 1926. Unless otherwise noted, all biographical material comes from this source.

[3]Ibid., 21–30.

life. In fact, some have argued that Weber's sociological writings are an attempt at working through his inner conflicts.[4]

Weber was a sickly child. He contracted a serious disease, possibly meningitis, at age 2, and the experience left him smaller and less physically capable than other children. Nonetheless, he was intellectually precocious. His youthful letters, many of which survive, are filled with reflections on the classical Greek and Roman writers as well as on the philosophers Johann Goethe, Benedict de Spinoza, and Immanuel Kant. Weber's conversations at home also ensured that he became politically sophisticated at a very young age, a characteristic that apparently made him a discipline problem in school, where he thought the level of instruction too low and the ignorance of his classmates appalling. More generally, the nature and use of authority preoccupied him throughout his life, both personally and intellectually.

In 1882, Weber graduated from the gymnasium (high school) and enrolled at the University of Heidelberg. Like his father, he chose the law as a field of study and professional training. In addition, he also studied economics, history, philosophy, and theology. Sociology was not offered at that time. Weber became active in his father's fraternity, joining in the ritual dueling and drinking bouts characteristic of German university life in those days. The large amount of beer consumed and the hedonistic lifestyle transformed the frail youth into a rather heavyset young man, complete with fencing scars on his face.

In 1883, Weber served an obligatory year of military service and, during that period, came under the influence of an aunt, Ida Baumgarten (his mother's sister), and an uncle, the historian Herman Baumgarten. It proved to be a turning point in Weber's life. Stronger and more forceful than her sister, Ida Baumgarten led a simple and ascetic religious life. In so doing, she helped Weber understand and appreciate his mother's Christian piety. As a result, Weber began to identify with his mother rather than his father.

Before the Breakdown

Weber returned in the following year to Berlin, where he enrolled at the University of Berlin and lived at home. He remained there for 7 years, financially dependent on a father whom he increasingly

---

[4]Ibid., 84. On the relationship between Weber's psychic turmoil and his scholarly work, see Randall Collins, *Max Weber: A Skeleton Key* (Beverly Hills, CA: Sage, 1986).

disliked and condemned, while completing his apprenticeship in law. Like Marx, Weber was a person with encyclopedic learning. While working for several years as a full-time unpaid legal apprentice, he completed a PhD dissertation titled "The History of Trading Companies in the Middle Ages" and a postdoctoral thesis titled "Roman Agrarian History," which qualified him to teach at the university level.[5] He also joined the Evangelical Social Union, a Protestant political group reacting against the excesses of industrialization in Germany, and the Social Political Union, an academic organization committed to researching social problems. Under the aegis of the latter, he investigated the conditions of rural peasants. The result, a 900-page book titled *The Situation of Farm Workers in Germany East of the Elbe River*, established his reputation as a young scholar.[6] To produce three books while working full-time as a junior barrister, Weber "repressed everything," living an ascetic life strictly regulated by the clock.[7] These characteristics of his own life assumed intellectual significance in his subsequent work, the *Protestant Ethic*.

Convinced that he was not a "true scholar," Weber nonetheless decided to pursue a combined academic and legal career. Thus, in 1892, he accepted an instructor's position at the University of Berlin. During this same period, he courted and married his cousin, Marianne Schnitger, whose loving biography of her husband remains the standard source about his life.

Weber had a passion for work: "Hardly was one [task] complete when his restless intellect took hold of a new one."[8] Thus, his chronic overwork and unhealthy lifestyle became a cause of concern for both his mother and wife, who urged him to slow down. Their remonstrations, however, had little effect. In 1894, the couple moved to Freiburg, where he took a position as professor of political economy. According to Marianne Weber, the workload there "surpassed everything up to then."[9] Over the next several years, Weber

---

[5]Neither of these works has been translated into English.

[6]Only a fragment of this book has been translated under the title "Development Tendencies in the Situation of East Elbian Rural Laborers," in *Reading Weber*, ed. Keith Tribe (London: Routledge, 1989), 158–187. The entire work is summarized in Reinhard Bendix, *Max Weber: An Intellectual Portrait* (Garden City, NY: Doubleday, 1962), 14–30.

[7]Weber, *Max Weber*, 149.

[8]Ibid., 195.

[9]Ibid., 195–201.

maintained a punishing academic, legal, and political schedule. He was apparently regarded as an outstanding professor, a promising lawyer, and a man with a future in public service. In addition, the Webers (who were by all accounts, not just Marianne's, happily married) maintained an unconventional lifestyle for the period. Over time Marianne Weber became a student under Heinrich Rickert, a historian and social worker and a supporter of women's rights. She apparently converted Weber because he soon became "more of a feminist than she was."[10]

Against this background, Weber's long-simmering anger toward his father erupted in 1897, with disastrous consequences for all.[11] Each year Helene Weber usually spent several weeks visiting her children and their families. The elder Weber, however, always made these trips difficult, believing that he should control his wife's every activity. During the summer, father and son clashed violently over this issue and parted without reconciliation. Shortly thereafter the old man died. Soon after that, Weber, at age 33 and now a professor of political economy at the University of Heidelberg, suffered a complete nervous breakdown, which incapacitated him for more than 5 years.

It is intriguing, of course, to speculate about the causes of Weber's psychic break.[12] Although little doubt exists that the fight with, and subsequent death of, his father constituted the precipitating incident, the more general issues contributing to Weber's psychological trauma were unresolved difficulties of identification with his parents and inner conflicts over their contradictory values. Furthermore, his chronic overwork served as both a symptom of his underlying stress and an additional cause of the breakdown. Weber did little work between 1897 and 1903. Sustained by an inheritance, he traveled widely, periodically recovering for short periods, only to collapse repeatedly. In 1900, the University of Heidelberg retired Weber. He did not teach again for nearly two decades.

---

[10]Ibid., 229.

[11]See John Patrick Diggins, *Max Weber: Politics and the Spirit of Tragedy* (New York: Basic Books, 1996), 62–63.

[12]See "Introduction: The Man and His Work" in *From Max Weber*, eds. Hans Gerth and C. Wright Mills (New York: Oxford University Press, 1946), 3–32; Arthur Mitzman, *The Iron Cage: A Historical Interpretation of Max Weber* (New York: Knopf, 1970); and Collins, *Max Weber: A Skeleton Key.*

The Transition to Sociology

Beginning in 1903, Weber found himself able to write again. He first produced a rather laborious work criticizing the German historical economists Wilhelm Roscher and Karl Knies.[13] Shortly afterward, he wrote an important methodological essay, "'Objectivity' in Social Science and Public Policy," in which he analyzed the place of values in the emerging social scientific disciplines.[14] This piece was followed in 1904 and 1905 by the seminal book for which Weber is primarily remembered, the *Protestant Ethic*, in which he outlined the historical significance of Protestantism for the development of capitalist cultural values. These works mark the beginning of Weber's self-conscious identification as a sociologist.

Between 1906 and 1914, Weber continued research and writing, now confining himself to the role of private scholar. He studied religion, the origin of cities, and social scientific methodology, producing a series of books and essays. Among them are the methodological *Critique of Stammler* (1907), *The Sociology of Religion* (1912), *The Religion of China* (1913), *The Religion of India* (which appeared in 1916–1917), and *Ancient Judaism* (which appeared in 1917).[15]

In addition to scholarly work, Weber also participated in the social life of German intellectuals.[16] Max and Marianne's home served as a meeting place for distinguished persons in many fields. The sociologists Georg Simmel and Robert Michels, the historian Heinrich Rickert, and the philosopher Karl Jaspers were among the many scholars who regularly took part in wide-ranging discussions of politics and social science. In 1910, Weber helped found the German Sociological Association, serving as its secretary for several years. In this context, he continued to press his views on the nature of sociology, especially the importance of objectivity in social research.

With the outbreak of World War I, Weber, a passionate German nationalist, became a hospital administrator in the Heidelberg area.

---

[13]Max Weber, *Roscher and Knies: The Logical Problems of Historical Economics* (New York: Free Press, 1975).

[14]Max Weber, "'Objectivity' in Social Science and Social Policy," in *The Methodology of the Social Sciences*, eds. Shils and Finch (New York: Free Press, 1949), 50–112. The original appeared in 1904.

[15]Max Weber, *Critique of Stammler* (New York: Free Press, 1977); *The Sociology of Religion* (Boston: Beacon, 1963); *The Religion of China* (New York: Free Press, 1951); *The Religion of India* (New York: Free Press, 1958); and *Ancient Judaism* (New York: Free Press, 1952).

[16]See Diggins, *Max Weber*, 110–113.

Over time, however, he began to oppose the German conduct of the war, advocating limited aims and prophesying defeat if unrestricted submarine warfare brought the United States into the conflict. Few people paid any attention.

In 1918, Weber accepted an academic position at the University of Vienna and offered a course for the first time in 20 years. In the following year, he taught at the University of Munich, giving two of his most famous addresses: "Science as a Vocation" and "Politics as a Vocation."[17] During this period, he began reworking the material from the prewar years, writing what became Part 1 of his *Economy and Society*.[18] He also gave a series of lectures that were posthumously published under the title *General Economic History*.[19]

In the twilight of his life, Weber evidently found some release from the traumas of the past. Although he had little time for relaxation, Marianne Weber says his capacity for work became steadier and his sleep more regular. During the summer of 1920, Max Weber developed pneumonia. He died on June 14.

Karl Marx and Max Weber

Despite the fact that Marx is rarely cited in Weber's works, Weber carried on a "silent dialogue" with the dead revolutionary. Some have argued that Weber's writings should be seen as an effort at "rounding out," or supplementing, Marx's interpretation of the rise and fall of capitalist society,[20] in several senses. First, in the *Protestant Ethic*, Weber showed the relationship between the cultural values associated with the Protestant Reformation and the rise of the culture of capitalism in the West, although he did not deny the importance of the material factors that Marx had previously identified. Apart from the transformative impact of Puritanism, Marx and Weber generally agreed on the structural factors involved in the rise of modern society. Second, both men can be seen as "systems theorists" in the sense that their conceptual schemes represent an attempt at mapping the connections among the situational and environmental contexts in which people act. Third, both scholars recognized the extent to

---

[17]These essays are reprinted in *From Max Weber*, 7–158.

[18]Max Weber, *Economy and Society* (New York: Bedminster, 1968).

[19]Max Weber, *General Economic History* (New York: Collier, 1961).

[20]Gerth and Mills, "Introduction," in *From Max Weber*, 3–76.

which individuals' freedom of action was limited in capitalist societies, although they did so in somewhat different ways.[21] In Marx's work, people are alienated because they do not control the means of production, whereas in Weber's work individuals often find themselves in an "iron cage" constructed by increasingly omnipresent and "rationalized" bureaucracies. Finally, despite the constraints just noted, both Marx and Weber observed the importance of human decision making in shaping history. For Marx, who was always a hopeful utopian and revolutionary, action will usher in a new era of freedom for all people; for Weber, who was less hopeful about the future, individuals have a wider range of choices in modern societies than was possible in the traditional communities of the past.

Despite these areas of similarity, Weber's work was different from Marx's in origin, purpose, and style. Marx combined revolution and theory to explain what he saw as the pattern of history. Weber helped establish an academically based sociology committed to the objective observation and understanding of historical processes, which he regarded as inherently unpredictable. These differences in orientation cannot be reconciled without obliterating the distinctiveness of each man's work. Hence, rather than "rounding out" Marx, Weber tried to refute Marxist thought as it existed at the turn of the century. For example, in the *Protestant Ethic*, Weber went out of his way to note that his findings flatly contradicted those postulated by "historical materialism," and he wondered at the naïveté of those Marxists who espoused such doctrines.[22] More generally, Weber disagreed with Marx and the Marxists (the two are not the same) on three interrelated and fundamental topics: (1) the nature of science, (2) the inevitability of history, and (3) economic determinism.

The Nature of Science

As we saw in Chapter 7, Marx combined science and revolution in such a way that theories were verified by what they led people to do (or not do). Weber, on the other hand, saw science as the search for truth and argued that observation verified knowledge. In making observations, research must be "value-free" in the sense that concepts

[21]Karl Löwith, *Marx and Weber* (London: Routledge, 1993).

[22]Weber, *Protestant Ethic*, 55, 75, 90–92, 266–277.

are clearly defined, agreed-on rules of evidence are followed, and logical inferences are made. Only in this way, Weber argued, can there be an objective science of sociology.[23]

Although recognizing that Marxists were often motivated by moral outrage at the conditions under which most people were forced to live, Weber asserted that ethical positions were not scientifically demonstrable, no matter how laudable they might be. Further, by combining science and revolution to justify their view of the future, Weber believed that Marxists inevitably confuse "what is" and "what ought to be," with the result that their ethical motives are undermined.[24] Such confusion should be eliminated as much as possible, Weber insisted, by making social science objective through an exclusive emphasis on "what is." Nonetheless, Weber recognized that social scientists' values inevitably intrude into social inquiry because they influence the topics considered important for research. This fact, Weber contended, does not preclude the possibility that the process of research can and should be objective. Thus, Weber believed that science could not tell people how to live or how to organize themselves but could provide them with the sort of information necessary to make such decisions.

The Inevitability of History

Marx posited the existence of historical laws of development, with the result that he saw feudalism as leading inevitably to capitalism and the latter leading inexorably to a more humane communist society. Against this position, Weber argued that there were no laws of historical development and that capitalism had arisen in the West as a result of a series of historical accidents, including the industrialization of production, the rise of a free labor force, the development of logical accounting methods, the expansion of free markets, the codification of modern forms of law, the use of paper instruments of ownership (e.g., stock certificates), and the emergence of what Weber called the *spirit of capitalism*.[25] Weber believed this last factor

---

[23]Weber, "Science as a Vocation." See Note 17.

[24]Guenther Roth, "[Weber's] Historical Relationship to Marxism," in *Scholarship and Partisanship: Essays on Max Weber*, eds. Reinhard Bendix and Guenther Roth (Berkeley: University of California Press, 1971), 227–252.

[25]Weber, *General Economic History*, 207–276.

to be the most significant. Further, he argued that none of these phenomena could have been predicted in advance; rather, they were all chance events.

Economic Determinism

By the beginning of the twentieth century, many Marxists were arguing that certain economic arrangements, especially the private ownership of the means of production, inevitably caused specific political forms as well as other social structures to develop. Weber attempted to refute this rather congealed form of Marx's analysis in two different ways. First, in the *Protestant Ethic*, Weber showed the importance of religious ideas in shaping the behavior of the Puritans and, by extrapolation, all Western people. Second, in *Economy and Society*, he outlined the extent to which systems of domination are maintained because they are viewed as legitimate by citizens, a commitment that generally overwhelms the class divisions that always exist. In Weber's words,

> it is one of the delusions rooted in the modern overestimation of the "economic factor" . . . to believe that national solidarity cannot survive the tensions of antagonistic economic interests, or even to assume that political solidarity is *merely* a reflection of the economic substructure.[26]

The *Methodenstreit* and Max Weber

In Germany, a rather rigid division between the natural sciences and the cultural disciplines existed. Natural phenomena—such as those studied in physics, chemistry, and biology—were seen as readily amenable to theoretical (i.e., scientific) analysis, whereas the world of the "spirit" was considered to be beyond analysis in scientific terms. Hence, studies of natural and social phenomena developed in much different directions in Germany.[27]

---

[26]Weber, quoted in Roth, "[Weber's] Historical Relationship to Marxism," 234 (emphasis in original).

[27]See Talcott Parsons, *The Structure of Social Action* (New York: Free Press, 1948), 473–486.

These views presented a problem of how to study social, especially economic, phenomena. There were two main ways of dealing with the methodological problem of how to study the social world. One was to develop better theory, and the other was to eschew science altogether and to concentrate on depicting the historical development of particular economic systems. The members of the historical school of economics chose the latter course, a position that fit comfortably with the dominant German intellectual tradition. Nonetheless, a number of scholars (although they were a minority in German academic circles) chose to develop economic theory. For the most part, these theoretical economists were non-Germans who pushed for a more scientific approach. Because the *Methodenstreit* is primarily remembered for the acrimonious and often vicious debate between Karl Menger and Gustav Schmoller during the 1870s, we will refer to them as the representatives of each school of thought.

Issues Dividing the Historical and Theoretical Schools

The historical school and the theoretical school disagreed over four fundamental issues, all stemming from the divergence between economic theory and economic reality.[28] The first involved the relative importance of deduction and induction. Gustav Schmoller and the historical economists charged that the theoreticians' use of deductive methods was faulty, chiefly because their theories could not explain reality. Hence, the historical economists emphasized as an alternative the importance of observing and describing people's concrete patterns of action (often down to the smallest details), and they spent many years compiling such data. Unlike some historians, for whom description quickly became an end in itself, Schmoller asserted that the long-run result of this descriptive work would be the discovery of economic laws by inductive methods. He believed that the resulting propositions would better describe reality because they would take the complexity of people's actual behavior into account.

---

[28]The following paragraphs have benefited from Thomas Burger, *Max Weber's Theory of Concept Formation: History, Laws, and Ideal Types* (Durham, NC: Duke University Press, 1976), 140–50; Joseph Schumpeter, *Economic Doctrine and Method* (New York: Oxford University Press, 1954), 152–201; and Charles Gide and Charles Rist, *A History of Economic Doctrine* (Lexington, MA: D. C. Heath, 1948), 383–409.

Alternatively, Karl Menger and the theoretical economists charged (correctly, as it turned out) that the historians were so immersed in data that no laws would ever be found.

The second issue dividing the two schools had to do with the universality versus the relativity of findings. Schmoller and the historical economists asserted that the theoreticians' emphasis on the universal applicability of economic laws was absurd. Rather, from the historians' points of view, empirical research had shown that economic development occurs in evolutionary stages unique to each society, which implies that it is possible to understand a society's present stage of economic advancement only by ascertaining previous stages. Menger and the theoreticians responded by observing that theory, whether in the social sciences or the natural sciences, is oriented toward what is common to all societies rather than toward what is unique. Hence, economic theories can (at least in principle) explain certain aspects of human behavior that are common to all societies, but, admittedly, not every element of social action can be explained theoretically. On this basis, Menger argued that both theory and history had a place in economics and the other social sciences.

The third issue of debate in the *Methodenstreit* dealt with the degree of rationality versus non-rationality in human behavior. Schmoller and the historical economists believed that the theoretical economists' view of humans as rational and motivated only by narrow self-interest was unrealistic. They went on to assert that there was a unity to all of social life, in the sense that people act out of a multiplicity of motives, which are not always rational. Thus, to obtain a comprehensive view of social reality, historical research often went far beyond the narrow confines of economic action, dealing with the interrelationships among economic, political, legal, religious, and other social phenomena. Although Schmoller was correct, Menger simply replied that economic theory dealt with only one side of human behavior (i.e., people's attempts at material need satisfaction) and that the other social sciences must focus on different aspects of social action. Over the long run, Menger believed, the result will be a comprehensive understanding of human behavior.

Finally, the fourth issue separating the two schools had to do with economics as an ethical discipline versus economics as a science. Schmoller and other members of the historical school unquestionably saw economics as an ethical discipline that could help solve many of the problems facing German society, with the result that their scholarly writings often had an avowedly political intent. This attitude was partly a consequence of the long-standing German division between the natural sciences and the cultural disciplines and partly a consequence of the fact that Schmoller and many others held important university and governmental positions. In opposition, Menger charged that Schmoller's political value judgments were hopelessly confused with his scholarly analyses, to the detriment of both. In science, Menger said, the two must be kept separate.

Weber's Response to the *Methodenstreit*

In economics, the *Methodenstreit* eventually dissipated, although more by the force of theoretical developments than the rhetoric of the participants. On several occasions, however, Weber appears to have used the arguments raised in the controversy as a baseline from which to develop his own methodological orientation.[29]

In regard to the first issue, the relative importance of inductive and deductive methods, Weber tried to bridge the gap between the two schools to create a historically based social science. With the historical economists, he argued that if the social sciences imitated the natural sciences by seeking to discover general laws of social behavior, then not very much useful knowledge would be produced. He reasoned that any social science oriented toward the development of timelessly valid laws would, of necessity, emphasize those patterns of action that were common from one society to another, resulting in ideographic events inevitably being omitted from consideration. Unique phenomena, such as the Protestant Reformation, are often the most significant factors influencing the development of a society. Hence, a science seeking to understand the structure of social action must necessarily focus on precisely those factors not amenable to lawlike formulations. Put differently, Weber argued that the social sciences had to make use of historical materials. Nonetheless, with the theoretical economists he asserted that the development of abstract concepts was absolutely necessary to guide empirical research. As will

---

[29]For Weber's views on Menger and the theoretical economists, see his "'Objectivity'" and his "Marginal Utility Theory and the So-Called Fundamental Law of Psychophysics," *Social Science Quarterly* 56 (June 1975), 48–159. For his views on the historical economists, see his *Roscher and Knies*.

be seen in the next chapter, his goal was an objective (i.e., scientific) comprehension of modern Western society, and for that reason he needed to develop a set of clear and precise concepts, which he called *ideal types*, that could be used in understanding historical processes.

Weber's response to the second issue dividing the two schools follows from the first. That is, a historically based social science cannot be universally applicable; rather, findings are always relative to a particular culture and society. One implication of this point of view is that although Weber tried to understand the origins of modern Western society, his findings might not have any relevance for the process of modernization in the Third World today because those societies are operating in a rather different historical context. It should be emphasized, however, that Weber strongly disagreed with the historical economists' evolutionary interpretations. Rather, he believed that economic development did not occur in evolutionary stages because unpredictable events, such as wars, ecological changes, charismatic leaders, and myriads of other phenomena, alter the course of history.

The third issue in the *Methodenstreit* became essential to Weber's sociology, for the protagonists inadvertently identified one of the fundamental characteristics of modern Western society: the tension between rational and nonrational action. Thus, Menger's argument that rational economic behavior needs to be conceptually distinguished from other modes of action seemed reasonable to Weber because he had observed that action in the marketplace was characterized by an emphasis on logic and knowledge, which was often absent in other arenas. At the same time, Schmoller's emphasis on the unity of social life and people's multiplicity of motives, some of which are based on values other than logic, also seemed reasonable. Hence, Weber tried to conceptually summarize the "types of social action" to systematically distinguish modern Western societies from the traditional ones and to show the wider range of behavioral choices available to occidental people.[30]

Weber's reaction to the fourth issue in the methodological controversy was similar to his response to Marx and the Marxists: the social sciences must be value-free. Although Schmoller and the other historical economists were generally political liberals with whom Weber was in sympathy, he believed that there could be no scientific

---

[30]Weber, *Economy and Society*, 24–26.

justification for any ethical or political point of view. Rather, he argued that objective scientific analyses could provide people with the knowledge necessary to make intelligent and ethical decisions based on their values.

Wilhelm Dilthey and Max Weber

The origin of Weber's response to the *Methodenstreit* can be found in the works of Wilhelm Dilthey and Heinrich Rickert. Weber built his sociology with the methodological tools they provided, although he went beyond each of them in a number of fundamental ways. Neither Rickert nor Dilthey is very well-known in the English-speaking world, primarily because the problems they addressed were peculiar to the German intellectual scene during the late nineteenth century. Yet we cannot fully understand Weber's sociology without some attention to these now-obscure figures.

Dilthey's Methodology of the Social Sciences

Dilthey argued that human behavior and nature could be studied scientifically, but they studied different subjects and produced different kinds of knowledge. He then went on to explore some of the implications of this argument.[31] First, and most obvious, the two sciences have different subject matters. The natural sciences are oriented toward the explanation of physical or natural events, whereas the social sciences are oriented toward the explanation of human action. Second, and as a result of the first, researchers in each field obtain quite divergent forms of data. In the natural sciences, knowledge is external in the sense that physical phenomena are affected by one another in ways that can be seen and explained by timelessly valid laws. In the social sciences, however, knowledge is internal in the sense that each person has an "inner nature" that must be

---

[31]See Wilhelm Dilthey, *Meaning and History: W. Dilthey's Thoughts on History and Society* (Winchester, MA: Allen & Unwin, 1961); and *Selected Writings* (New York: Cambridge University Press, 1976). Among secondary sources, see H. P. Rickman, *Wilhelm Dilthey: Pioneer of the Human Studies* (New York: Cambridge University Press, 1979); and Rudolph A. Makkreel, *Dilthey: Philosopher of the Human Studies* (Princeton, NJ: Princeton University Press, 1992).

comprehended in some way to explain events. Third, researchers in the two spheres must have altogether different orientations to their subject. In the natural sciences, it is enough to observe events and relationships. For example, an object falling through space can be explained by the force of gravity, and this explanation is true regardless of the cultural background of different researchers who concern themselves with this topic. In the social sciences, however, scholars must go beyond mere observation and seek to understand (*verstehen*) each person's "inner nature" to explain events and relationships. Furthermore, the explanations offered might vary depending on the cultural background of the different researchers.

For Dilthey, then, the means by which observers obtain an understanding of each person's "inner nature" is the key to the scientific knowledge of human action. In this light, he tried to classify the various fields devoted to the study of social behavior by their typical mode of analysis. The first type of analysis consists of descriptions of reality, of events that have occurred; this is the field of history. The second way of discussing human action consists of value judgments made in light of historical events; this is the field of ethics or politics. The third way of dealing with social behavior consists of formulating abstractions from history; this is the field of social sciences. This last mode of analysis is the most important for understanding action, Dilthey asserted, because abstract concepts provide the tools necessary for comprehending behavior. He was unable to face the implications of this insight, however, for he went on to argue that the systematic development of abstract concepts would not be of much long-term use in understanding people's "inner nature." He opted instead for the necessity of relying on intuition (what he called the "fantasy of the artist") in comprehending social action. Such intuitive understanding occurs when, in some unexplainable and imperfect way, observers re-experience in their own consciousness the experiences of others.

Weber's Response to Dilthey's Work

From Weber's point of view, Dilthey's methodological orientation was useful in three ways.[32] First, Dilthey was correct in noting that the

---

[32]Although Weber never wrote a formal commentary on Dilthey's work, his writings suggest an easy familiarity with Dilthey's teachings. See Diggins, *Max Weber*, 114. For Weber's analysis of *verstehen*, and its relationship to ideal types, see his *Economy and Society*, 8–20.

social sciences could obtain a quite different form of knowledge than the natural sciences. Second, social scientific statements are different from and, Weber added, must be kept separate from value judgments of any sort. Third, the key to social scientific knowledge is to *verstehen* the subjective meanings that people attach to their actions.

Weber believed that the major problem in Dilthey's work resided in his emphasis on understanding each person's "inner nature," as if an objective social science could be founded on some sort of mystical and intuitive re-experiencing of others' desires and thoughts. Hence, Weber developed a different way of emphasizing the importance of *verstehen*, one that proved to be a great deal more successful than Dilthey's. For Weber, social action can be understood only when "it is placed in an intelligible and more inclusive context of meaning," the key to such understanding is the development of a set of abstract concepts (ideal types) that classify the dimensions of social action and the properties of the social structures within which social action occurs.

Heinrich Rickert and Max Weber

Like Dilthey, Rickert was concerned with the problems created by the disjunction between the world of nature and the world of human activity. Rickert began his attempt at demonstrating that history can be an objective science by dealing with a number of relatively noncontroversial epistemological issues.[33] He argued that empirical reality is infinite in space and time, which for him meant that reality could, in principle, be divided into an infinite number of objects for study and that these objects could in turn be dissected into an unlimited number of parts. An important implication of this view is that reality can never be completely known because there will always be some other way of looking at it. The practical problem, then, becomes how people can know anything at all about the world around them, and Rickert's answer was that by formulating concepts,

---

[33]Heinrich Rickert's works remain untranslated. This account draws on H. H. Bruun, *Science, Values, and Politics in Max Weber's Methodology* (Copenhagen, Denmark: Muunksgaard, 1972), 84–99; Burger, *Weber's Theory of Concept Formation*, 3–56; and H. Stuart Hughes, *Consciousness and Society: The Reorientation of German Social Thought, 1890–1930* (New York: Vintage, 1958), 190–191.

human beings select those aspects of reality that are important to them. Thus, concepts are the means by which we know the world, for without them, people could not distinguish among its significant parts. Given this necessity, Rickert came to the peculiar conclusion that the essence of science centered on the problem of concept formation. From this point of view, a discipline can be regarded as a science if it uses a principle of concept selection that everyone agrees produces objective knowledge. Not surprisingly, Rickert said that there were two valid principles of concept selection—those used in the natural sciences and those used in history—and in this way he tried to show that history was a scientific discipline.

In the natural sciences, Rickert noted, concepts are designed to identify the common traits of the empirical objects to which they refer. This tactic allows concepts to become increasingly abstract and, hence, fit into a theory that summarizes empirical regularities (e.g., the movements of the planets and their effects on one another through the force of gravity). The result is a set of general concepts that can, at least in principle, be used in a single, all-embracing law of nature. On this basis, Rickert concluded that the principle of concept selection used in the natural sciences was valid because it succeeded in identifying regular and recurrent features of the physical environment.

In history, however, Rickert argued that scholars' interests were altogether different, which means that the principle of concept selection must differ as well. To chronicle the events of the past and their significance for the present, historians must focus on their uniqueness. With this purpose in mind, historical concepts are formulated to identify those aspects of the past that make them distinctive and different from one another (e.g., "traditional society" or the "spirit of capitalism"). Thus, historians produce concepts, which Rickert called "historical individuals," that summarize a complex set of events for their historical significance (i.e., their uniqueness). On this basis, Rickert concluded that the principle of concept selection used in history was valid because it allowed observers to understand how particular societies had developed their specific characteristics. Yet, despite these differences in concept formation, Rickert saw history as a science.

Rickert next confronted the problem of how scholars select topics for study. Rickert asserted that the researchers choose topics by "value-relevance." That is, some events are seen as worth conceptualizing based on the scientists' interpretations of what the members of a society value. This emphasis on value-relevance implies a subjective rather than objective conception of knowledge, because scientists are inevitably forced to rely on their own values in determining what topics are worth knowing about, or conceptualizing. Rickert tried to avoid this implication by postulating that a kind of "normal consciousness" characterized all human beings. On this basis, he argued, all members of every society share areas of concern—for example, religion, law, the state, customs, the physical world, language, literature, art, and the economy. But this postulate is inherently metaphysical because it assumes that values have an existence independent of human beings.

Weber's Response to Rickert

Weber's preoccupation with refuting Marxism and solving the dilemma created by the *Methodenstreit* probably allowed him to recognize what Rickert had failed to see.[34] The essence of science involves not only a coherent conceptual scheme but also, and just as important, the use of logical and systematic procedures in the interpretation of observations. Hence, even though the social sciences must deal with quite different data than the natural sciences, what unites the two as sciences is their procedural similarity. This insight pervades all Weber's writings and constitutes the basis for his response to Rickert.

First, Weber simply accepted Rickert's argument that reality is infinite and human beings can only know about reality through the selection of concepts to denote key properties of the social world.[35] Second, why a scholar chooses one topic over another is less important than assuring for study that the research process is objective.[36] Third, it is necessary in the social sciences to develop a set of concepts that captures the distinctiveness of historical processes.[37]

---

[34]See Weber, "Objectivity," 50, and *Roscher and Knies*, 211–218.

[35]Weber, "Objectivity," 78–79.

[36]Weber, "Science as a Vocation" (see Note 17) and "Critical Studies in the Logic of the Cultural Sciences," in *The Methodology of the Social Sciences*, 113–188.

[37]Weber, *Economy and Society*, 18–20, and "Objectivity," 87–112. Rickert's term *historical individuals* appears in Weber's essay on *Roscher and Knies* and (once) in the *Protestant Ethic*, 47. Weber appears to have adopted the term *ideal type* from George Jellinek; see Bendix and Roth, *Scholarship and Partisanship*, 160–164.

Weber's Theoretical Synthesis

In adapting some of the conceptual tools provided by Dilthey and Rickert, Weber was able to forge a response to Marx and the *Methodenstreit* that constitutes a continuing legacy to sociology. Foremost in Weber's mind was the necessity of being objective in the analysis of social phenomena. Values may influence which topics are selected for study, but once selected, objectivity must be maintained. In trying to understand historical processes, it is necessary to develop concepts that denote key properties of these processes. These concepts should be abstractions that emphasize the essence of the phenomena denoted by concepts. Finally, it is essential to understand the causal events that have created historical outcomes. The most robust form of causal analysis examines the social and cultural conditions that lead to historical outcomes, as well as the orientations of actors who operate within these conditions.

As we will see in the next chapter, these basic elements of Weber's methodology are used to analyze a wide variety of historical events. Yet all of Weber's sociology had a common theme: the rationalization of social structures that comes with industrialization.

CHAPTER 9

The Sociology of Max Weber

I n one of his last works, Max Weber defined the fledgling discipline of sociology in the following way:

> Sociology . . . is a science concerning itself with the interpretive understanding of social action and thereby with a causal explanation of its course and consequences. We shall speak of "action" insofar as the acting individual attaches a subjective meaning to his behavior—be it overt or covert, omission or acquiescence. Action is "social" insofar as its subjective meaning takes account of the behavior of others and is thereby oriented in its course.[1]

Weber believed that this definition would allow him to achieve two interrelated goals that, taken together, signify an altogether original approach to the study of social organization.[2] First, he wanted to understand the origin and unique characteristics of modern Western societies. Second, he wanted to construct a system of abstract concepts that would be useful in describing and, hence, understanding social action in such societies. Without a set of clear and precise concepts, Weber argued, systematic social scientific research is impossible. The result was a series of concepts designed to increase understanding of the modern world.

---

[1]Max Weber, *Economy and Society*, trans. and eds. Guenther Roth and Claus Wittich (New York: Bedminster, 1968).

[2]Wolfgang Mommsen, *The Age of Bureaucracy: Perspectives on the Political Sociology of Max Weber* (New York: Harper Torchbooks, 1974), 2.

Weber's Methodology of the Social Sciences

In 1904, Weber posed a fundamental question: "In what sense are there 'objectively valid truths' in those disciplines concerned with social and cultural phenomena?"[3] All his subsequent writings can be seen as an answer to this simple query. Indeed, Weber's goal was to show that objective research was possible in those academic disciplines dealing with subjectively meaningful phenomena. The way he pursued this goal is presented here in two parts. First, his depiction of the problem of values in sociological research is shown. This was the central methodological issue for Weber; if sociology were to be a true science of society, he believed, it has to be objective. Second, he thought every science required a conceptual map, an inventory of the key concepts describing the phenomenon being studied, and he began to develop such a system of concepts, labeling them "ideal types."

The Problem of Values

During Weber's time, many observers did not think that an objective social science was plausible because it seemed impossible to separate values from the research process. So most scholars attempting to describe human behavior infused their analyses with political, religious, and other values. Karl Marx's writings constitute an extreme example of this tactic. Weber confronted the problem of values by observing that sociological inquiry should be objective, or, to use his term, *value-free*. Having said that, he then suggested how values and economic interests were connected to social scientific analyses.

Value-Free Sociology

Weber's use of the term *value-free* is unfortunate, because it implies that social scientists should have no values at all, plainly an impossibility. What he meant is that researchers' personal values and economic interests should not affect the process of social scientific analysis. He believed that if such factors influenced the

---

[3]Max Weber, "'Objectivity' in Social Science and Social Policy," in *The Methodology of the Social Sciences*, trans. Edward A. Shils and Henry A. Finch (New York: Free Press, 1949), 51.

research process, the structure of social action could not be depicted objectively. This fundamental concern with attaining objective and verifiable knowledge links all the sciences, natural and social.[4]

In Weber's eye, sociology should not be a moral science. It is not possible to state scientifically which norms, values, or patterns of action are correct or best, but, rather, it is only possible to describe them objectively. Weber believed that such descriptions would represent a considerable achievement. After all, they did not exist then. Thus, unlike many others, Weber explicitly distinguished between "what ought to be," the sphere of values, and "what is," the sphere of science, arguing that sociology should focus only on the latter. This distinction implies Weber's view of the underlying value that ought to guide social scientific inquiry: the search for truth.[5]

Another implication of Weber's argument for a value-free sociology is that the new science reflects an ongoing historical process in which magic and other forms of inherited wisdom become less acceptable as means for explaining events. Weber referred to this change as the process of *rationalization*, and it is the dominant theme in his work. Unlike Marx, who used the dialectic as a leitmotif, Weber believed that social life is becoming increasingly "rationalized" in the sense that people lead relatively methodical lives: They rely on reason buttressed by objective evidence. The rationalization of the economy—for example, by means of improved accounting, the use of technology, and other methods—produced modern capitalism. The rationalization of government—by reliance on technical training and legal procedures, for example—resulted in the rise of the modern political state. The sciences, of course, are the archetypal methodical disciplines.[6] In a "rationalized discipline," values should not affect the research process. But they remain relevant.

---

[4] Weber, "Objectivity," 143.

[5] In general, sociologists have followed Weber's lead in making the distinction between "what is" and "what ought to be." Nonetheless, some critics of positivism argue that Weber's methodological goal of objective knowledge is not attainable, a position with which we disagree. For a discussion of these issues as they relate to Weber's work, see Alan Scott, "Value Freedom and Intellectual Autonomy," *History of the Human Sciences* 8 (1995), 69–88.

[6] Weber used the concept of rationalization in a number of different ways and, hence, subsequent scholars differ in how to interpret it. See, for example, Randall Collins, *Max Weber: A Skeleton Key* (Beverly Hills, CA: Sage, 1986); Stephen Kalberg, "Max Weber's Types of Rationality: Cornerstones for the Analysis of Rationalization Processes in History," *American Journal of Sociology* 85 (1980), 1145–1179; and John Patrick Diggins, *Max Weber: Politics and the Spirit of Tragedy* (New York: Basic Books, 1996).

The Connection Between Values and Science

Although Weber knew that the separation between values and science is difficult to maintain in practice, the distinction highlighted the relevance of values before and after the research process. The choice of topics comes before the research takes place. The only basis for making such a decision is the scientists' religious beliefs, economic interests, and other values, which lead some of them to each topic. But once having chosen a topic for study, according to Weber's dictum, scientists must follow an objective research process.

The situation is more complex when dealing with public policy issues. Given a specific political goal, Weber said sociologists could determine (1) the alternative strategies for achieving it, (2) the outcomes of using different strategies, and (3) the consequences of attaining the goal.[7] Once this is done, however, there is no scientific way of choosing public policies. Selecting one goal rather than another and one strategy rather than another ultimately depends on people's political values, their economic interests, and other nonobjective factors.

Having said that the research process must be objective and that the sphere of values and the sphere of science must be kept separate, Weber drew a unique conclusion. Unlike nearly all the other classical sociologists (except Marx), Weber rejected the search for general laws in favor of historical theories that provide an "interpretive understanding of social action and . . . a causal explanation of its course and consequences."[8] A search for universal laws necessarily excludes from consideration important and unique historical events. Weber summarized his position in the following way:

> For the knowledge of historical phenomena in their concreteness, the most general laws, because they are most devoid of content are also the least valuable. The more comprehensive the validity—or scope—of a term, the more it leads us away from the richness of reality since in order to include the common elements of the largest possible number of phenomena, it must necessarily be as abstract as possible and hence devoid of content. In the [social] sciences, the knowledge of the universal or general is never valuable in itself.[9]

---

[7]Weber, "Objectivity," 53.
[8]Weber, *Economy and Society*, 4.
[9]Weber, "Objectivity," 80.

In effect, then, Weber was most interested in focusing on the "big empirical questions," such as why capitalism had originated in the West rather than somewhere else, and he knew that an emphasis on the development of general theories would not allow for an examination of such issues. Ideal types were his method for dealing with these issues.

Ideal Types

To study social phenomena, Weber argued that it is necessary to have a description of the key elements of phenomena. The goal is to describe forms of action and patterns of social organization while seeking to identify the historical causes of these forms and patterns. The use of what he termed *ideal types* is central to this approach.[10] An *ideal type* or *pure type* summarizes the basic properties of social phenomena, which, in turn, can help the search for its historical causes. Weber tended to develop two different kinds of ideal types:[11] historical and general. Following is a summary of each.

Historical Ideal Types

Historical events can be described by analytically accentuating their key components. For example, in Weber's famous analysis of "the spirit of capitalism," he drew up a list of the features of this belief system. Once the essence or pure form of this belief system is highlighted, it then becomes possible to seek the causes for the emergences of this distinctive historical event; and in Weber's analysis, the emergence of Protestantism appears to have been the key historical cause of the spirit of capitalism, as we examine later. Thus, a historical ideal type accentuates the key properties of specific

---

[10]See Theodore Abel, "The Operation Called Verstehen," *American Journal of Sociology* 54 (1948), 211–218; Peter A. Munch, "Empirical Science and Max Weber's *Verstehen Sociologie*," *American Sociological Review* 22 (1957), 26–32; Murray L. Wax, "On Misunderstanding Verstehen: A Reply to Abel," *Sociology and Social Research* 51 (1967), 322–333; and Theodore Abel, "A Reply to Professor Wax," *Sociology and Social Research* 51 (1967), 334–336. A good recent summary is in John Patrick Diggins, *Max Weber*, 114–122. For a more general analysis of Weber's methodology, see Stephen Kalberg, *Max Weber's Historical-Comparative Sociology* (Chicago: University of Chicago Press, 1994).

[11]See Thomas Burger, *Max Weber's Theory of Concept Formation: History, Laws, and Ideal Types* (Durham, NC: Duke University Press, 1976), 130–134.

events in history, but it does more: Once the key components of a phenomenon are delineated, the search for causes is given focus and direction.

General Ideal Types

Although Weber did not believe that general laws of human organization could be produced in the social sciences, he still wanted to make generalizations about generic social phenomena. This desire led him to formulate ideal types of phenomena that are always present in human action. These ideal types do not describe historical events, but rather, they accentuate certain key properties of actors, action, and social organization in general. The most famous of these more abstract and general ideal types is Weber's conceptualization of the types of action.

According to Weber, people's actions can be classified into four analytically distinct ways.[12] The first type of action is the *instrumentally rational*, which occurs when means and ends are systematically related to each other based on knowledge. Weber knew that the knowledge that people possess might not be accurate. Thus, both the rain dance and the timing of a stock purchase are instrumentally rational acts, from the point of view of the dancers and the buyers, even though the means–end link might be based on magical beliefs or rumors. Thus, instrumentally rational action occurs in all societies. Nonetheless, Weber said, the archetypal form of instrumentally rational action is based on objective, ideally scientific, knowledge. Action buttressed by objective knowledge is more likely to be effective. Its effectiveness is one reason why the spheres in which instrumentally rational action occurs have widened over time, and its pervasiveness in modern societies reflects the historical process of rationalization. The second type of action is *value-rational*, which is behavior undertaken in light of one's basic values. Weber emphasized "value rational action always involves 'commands' or 'demands' which, in the actor's opinion are binding."[13] Religious people avoiding alcohol use because of their faith, parents paying for their children's braces and college

---

[12]Weber, *Economy and Society*, 24–26. Again, scholars have interpreted the types of social action in various ways. Compare, for example, Collins, *Max Weber*, 42–43, and Raymond Aron, *Main Currents in Sociological Thought, II* (Garden City, NY: Doubleday, 1970), 220–221.

[13]Weber, *Economy and Society*, 26.

education, politicians passing laws, and soldiers obeying orders are acting as a result of their values. The essential characteristic of value-rational action is that it constitutes an end in itself. The third type of action is *traditional*, which is behavior "determined by ingrained habituation." Weber's point is that in a context where beliefs and values are second nature and patterns of action have been stable for many years, people usually respond to situations from habit. In a sense, they regulate their behavior by customs handed down across generations. In such societies, people resist altering long-established ways of living, which are often sanctified in religious terms. As a result, when confronted with new situations or choices, they often continue in the old ways. Traditional action typifies behavior in contexts where choices are (or are perceived to be) limited. Traditional action thus characterizes people in preindustrial societies. The fourth type of action is *affectual*, which is behavior determined by people's emotions in a given situation. The parent slapping a child and the football player punching an opponent are examples. This type of behavior occurs, of course, in all societies although it constitutes a residual category that Weber acknowledged but did not explore in detail.

These types of action classify behavior by visualizing its four "pure forms." Although Weber knew that actual situations would not perfectly reflect these concepts, they provide a common reference point for comparison. That is, a variety of empirical cases can be systematically compared with one another and with the ideal type, in this case, the types of social action. This strategy is presented in Figure 9.1. Ideal types thus represent for Weber a quasi-experimental method. The "ideal" serves as the functional equivalent of the control group in an experiment. Variations or deviations from the ideal are seen as the result of causal forces (or a stimulus in a real laboratory experiment), and effort is then undertaken to find these causes. In this sense, Weber could achieve two goals: (1) to analytically accentuate the elements of social action and (2) to discover the causes of various types of action.

Weber's Image of Social Organization

Weber's analysis of social organization is detailed and complex, and indeed, it is often difficult to get a sense for how he visualized society as a whole. As noted earlier, Weber defined sociology as the study of *social action*, and as we have seen in the analysis of ideal types, he felt

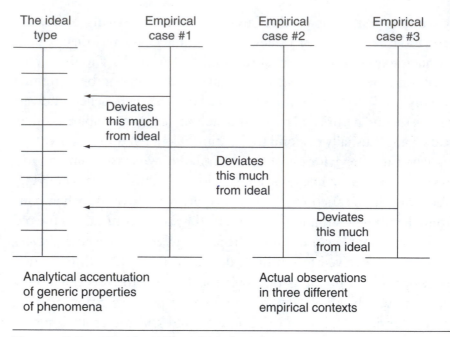

Figure 9.1   The Ideal Type of Methodology

that there are four basic types of action: instrumental-rational, value-rational, traditional, and affectual.[14] Thus, human behavior is guided or, in Weber's terms, "oriented," by considerations of rationality, tradition, or affect. These types of action, however, need not be mutually exclusive; they can be combined, although some orientations are more compatible with each other than others are. For example, affectual and value-rational are more likely to be combined than, say, are instrumental-rational and traditional. Still, even when combined, Weber implied that one type of action will generally dominate a social relationship.

As is typical of Weber, the nature of social relationships,[15] like the actions forming them, is portrayed as an ideal type. There are two basic kinds of social relationships arising out of social action: one is *communal* relationships, which are formed by individuals' feelings for each other, with such feelings based on affectual or traditional actions; the other is *associative* relationships, which are based on rationality, whether instrumental- or value-rational. Thus, in Weber's eye, the two basic types of social relationships—communal and associational—are motivated by a split in the four types of

---

[14]Ibid., 22–26.
[15]Ibid., 26–28, 40–43.

action, with one of these splits revolving around the two types of rational action (value and instrumental) and the other around affectual and traditional orientations.

Social relationships, whether communal or associative, are generally connected to what Weber termed *legitimated orders*.[16] An "order" appears to be Weber's way of conceptualizing the larger structures that are built from social relationships. Action and social relationships almost always occur within the context of an existing legitimated order. Such orders "guarantee" that actions and social relationships will be conducted in accordance with "maxims" or rules, the violation of which will bring about negative sanctions on those failing to meet their obligations. Thus, the structure connecting the more micro processes of action and social relationships to more macro levels of reality is the legitimated order. Like so many concepts in Weber's work, there is a classification of orders into two basic types. One is organized around "subjective" guarantees that social relationships will proceed in accordance with the rules of the order, with this subjectivity arising from one of three routes: (a) affect, or "emotional surrender" to the order; (b) value-rationality, or a belief in the absolute validity of the order as the most efficient means to an end; and (c) religious beliefs that salvation depends on the order. The other type of order is organized by expectations among actors for certain "external effects" that are predictable outcomes to actions undertaken; thus, because actors calculate their actions in accordance with expected outcomes, Weber implied that this kind of order is organized by instrumental-rationality.

Weber then shifted to the basis of legitimation of orders—that is, routes by which actors ascribe rights to "the order" to control their conduct. Again, as is typical with Weber, there are several basic types of legitimation: (a) tradition, or the way things have always been; (b) affectual, or emotional attachments to the ways things are organized; (c) value-rational, or the "deduction" that the current order is the best possible way of organizing actions; and (d) legal, which is composed of binding agreements (entered into by considerations of instrumental-rationality) among actors or by an external authority that is considered to have the right to impose and enforce agreements.

---

[16]Ibid., 31–39.

In Figure 9.2, we have diagrammed what we think is Weber's intent, although we must confess that, despite all the definitions and categories, Weber's analytical scheme is far from precise or clear. The subject matter of sociology is social action, whereby actors take cognizance of each other's behaviors. Actions are "oriented" to affect, tradition, value-rationality, or instrumental-rationality; here, Weber implied that these orientations are cultural or part of the values, beliefs, and ideologies of a society, but they also become motivations that push actors to behave in certain ways. Various oriented and motivated social actions then lead to the formation of more stable social relationships that can be either communal or associative, depending on the configuration of cultural orientations and motivations involved. Communal relations are guided by affectual and traditional orientations and motivations, whereas associational relations are composed from considerations of rationality, whether instrumental or value-rationality. Social relationships are typically part of an order that structures action in accordance with rules. Such orders are organized by cultural orientations

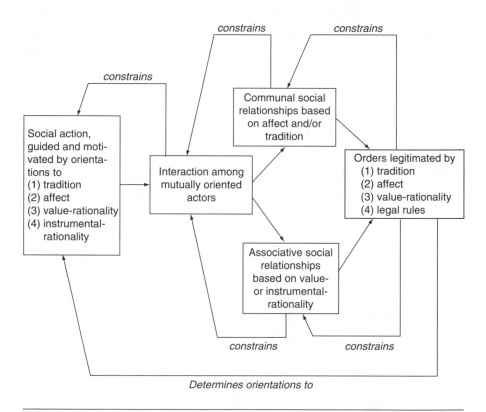

Figure 9.2   Weber's Conception of Action, Relationships, and Orders

emphasizing affect, value-rationality, religion, and rationality; the order's basic legitimation can be either traditional, affectual, value-rational, or legal.

At this point, Weber's view of social organization seems rather vague about how the model in Figure 9.2 leads us to the major topics of Weberian sociology. The definitional distinctions in the model were written rather late in Weber's career, after he had written much of his sociology; thus, the model does not provide clear guidelines back into the substantive topics addressed by Weber earlier in his career. Still, let us make an effort, if only to set the stage for our discussion in this chapter of Weber's sociology. Figure 9.3 begins where Figure 9.2 ends, with the formation of legitimated orders. Weber implies, but does not clearly state, that there are two basic types of orders: (1) *organizational orders* composed of structures revealing a division of labor and pursuing particular goals and (2) *stratification orders* composed of categories of individuals in a system of inequality. These are not mutually exclusive because organizations can sustain a system of inequality, whereas an organization can exist as the result of a particular configuration of inequality in the distribution of resources. These come together under Weber's concept of *domination*, as we will see shortly. By this term, Weber meant that

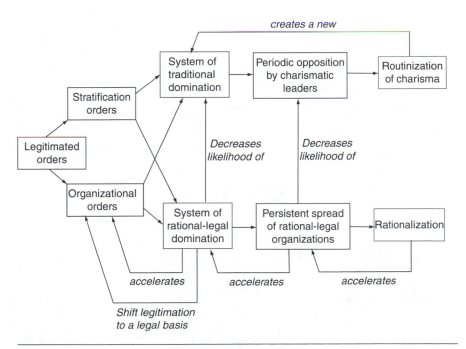

Figure 9.3   Weber's Conception of Legitimated Orders and Domination

some segments of a society have the authority to tell others what to do and, as a result, those with authority can control the distribution of resources. Legitimated orders, therefore, generate systems of domination.

In Weberian sociology, then, a society cannot be understood without inquiry into its patterns of domination. Weber saw the long-term trends as revolving around a shift in the basis of domination in human societies. For Weber, history had been typified by periods of relative stability in patterns of domination revolving around traditional authority, punctuated by periodic emergence of charismatic leaders who had mobilized opposition movements and established new patterns of domination based on their charismatic authority that, over time, tended to turn into a new form of traditional authority. With the expansion of markets during capitalism, however, domination increasingly comes from *rational-legal authority* as personified by law and bureaucratic organizations. These organizations were, in Weber's eyes, gaining control of all legitimated orders, displacing the affectual, traditional, and even value-rational legitimation of orders with the rule of law, while orienting action in all spheres of social life to instrumental-rationality. The social world was thus becoming "rationalized," as bureaucratic organizations in the state and economy became the basis for domination in society.

This was Weber's general view of the social world when he looked at historical trends and industrial capitalism as it was emerging in Germany around the turn into the twentieth century. He wanted to explain the shift in patterns of domination, and this led him to explore a variety of substantive topics—bureaucratic organizations, stratification, cities, law, religion, geopolitics, and markets—to see how these topics could help explain the shift in domination toward rational-legal authority. Alas, there is no clear theory in all of these substantive concerns, only a set of topics organized around the theme of rationalization.

Weber's Analysis of Domination

Types of Domination

A society can be typified by its system of domination. In German, the term *herrschaft* connotes both domination and authority, and

Weber probably meant this to be the case.[17] Any system of domination is ultimately built from what we termed *stratification orders* and *organizational orders*. All orders must be legitimated; so those who hold power seek to legitimate their power as "authority" in the eyes of those who are subject to this power.[18] Domination also requires organizational orders to administer and monitor conformity to directives given to subordinates. As was typical for Weber, he saw three basic types of domination—charismatic, traditional, and rational-legal—with each type relying on a different basis of legitimation and a different kind of administrative apparatus.[19]

Charismatic Domination

The first type of domination is called charismatic. The term *charisma* has a religious origin and literally means "gift of grace," implying that a person is endowed with divine powers.[20] In practice, Weber did not restrict his use of charisma to manifestations of divinity but, rather, employed the concept to refer to those extraordinary individuals who somehow identify themselves with the central facts or problems of people's lives and who, by the force of their personalities, communicate their inspiration to others and lead them in new directions. Thus, people in other than religious roles can sometimes be considered charismatic: for example, politicians, soldiers, or artists.[21]

Weber believed that charismatic leadership emerges during times of crisis, when dominant ways of confronting the problems faced by a society seem inappropriate, outmoded, or inadequate. In such a context, charismatic domination is revolutionary. People reject the past in favor of a new direction based on the master's inspiration. As Weber put it, every charismatic leader implicitly argues that "it is written . . . but I say unto you." Thus, charismatic domination is a vehicle for social change in both traditional and rational-legal contexts, which are the other two types of domination.

---

[17]Considerable controversy exists over the proper translation of *herrschaft*.

[18]Weber, *Economy and Society*, 946.

[19]Ibid., 956–958.

[20]Ibid., 241.

[21]See Reinhard Bendix, "Charismatic Leadership," in *Scholarship and Partnership: Essays on Max Weber*, eds. Reinhard Bendix and Guenther Roth (Berkeley: University of California Press, 1971), 170–187; and Edward A. Shils, "Charisma, Order, and Status," *American Sociological Review* 30 (1965), 199–213.

The legitimacy of charismatic domination lies both in the leader's demonstration of extraordinary insight and accomplishment and in the followers' acceptance of the master. It is irrelevant, from Weber's point of view, whether a charismatic leader turns out to be a charlatan or a hero; both Hitler and Gandhi were charismatic leaders. Rather, what is important is that the masses are inspired to freely follow the master. Weber believed that charisma constituted an unstable form of authority over extended periods because its legitimacy depended on the leader's claim to special insight and accomplishment. Thus, if success eludes the leader for long and crises are not resolved satisfactorily, the masses will probably reject the charismatic figure, and his or her authority will disappear.

In charismatic domination, the leader's administrative apparatus usually consists only of a band of faithful disciples who serve the master's immediate personal and political needs. Over the long run, however, every regime led by a charismatic leader faces the "problem of routinization," which involves both finding a successor to the leader and handling the day-to-day decisions that must be made.

Weber noted that the problem of succession could be resolved in a variety of ways: for example, by the masses searching for a new charismatic leader, by the leader's designation of a successor, or by the disciples' designation of a successor. But all these methods involve political instability. For this reason, either customs or legal procedures allowing the orderly transfer of power usually develop over time.

The problem of making day-to-day decisions (i.e., of governing) is usually resolved by either the development of a full-fledged administrative staff or the takeover of an already existing organization. In both cases, the typical result is the transformation of the relationship between charismatic leader and followers from one based on beliefs in the master's extraordinary qualities to one based on custom or law. "It is the fate of charisma," Weber wrote, "to recede before the powers of tradition or of rational association after it has entered the permanent structures of social action."[22] These new bases of legitimation represent the other two types of domination.

---

[22]Weber, *Economy and Society*, 1148.

Traditional Domination

The second type of domination is based on tradition. In Weber's words, "Authority will be called traditional if legitimacy is claimed for it and believed in by virtue of the sanctity of age-old rules and powers."[23] Put differently, traditional domination is justified by the belief that it is ancient and embodies an inherent (often religiously sanctified) state of affairs that cannot be challenged by reason. Weber distinguished between two forms of traditional authority. *Patriarchalism* is a type of traditional domination occurring in households and other small groups where the use of an organizational staff to enforce commands is not necessary. *Patrimonialism* is a form of traditional domination occurring in larger social structures that require an administrative apparatus to execute edicts.

In the patrimonial form of traditional domination, the administrative apparatus consists of a set of personal retainers exclusively loyal to the ruler. Weber observed that in addition to its grounding in custom, the officials' loyalties are based on either their dependence on the ruler for their positions and remuneration or their pledge of fealty to the leader, or both. As an ideal type, the essence of patrimonialism (traditional authority coupled with an administrative staff) is expressed by the following characteristics:

1. People obtain positions based on custom and loyalty to the leader.

2. Officials owe obedience to the leader issuing commands.

3. Personal and official affairs are combined.

4. Lines of authority are vague.

5. Task specialization is minimal.

In such a context, decisions are based on officials' views of what will benefit them and what the leader wants. Moreover, officials appropriate the means of production themselves or are granted them by the leader. Hence, where their jurisdiction begins and ends remains uncodified. A sheriff, for example, might both catch criminals and collect taxes (skimming off as much as possible). But how these tasks are accomplished will be idiosyncratic, subject to official whim rather than law. Thus, it should not be surprising that in *Economy*

---

[23]Ibid., 226.

and Society, Weber described traditional domination as inhibiting the development of capitalism, primarily because rules are not logically established, officials have too wide a range of personal arbitrariness, and they are not technically trained.[24] Modern capitalism requires an emphasis on logic, procedure, and knowledge.

Rational-Legal Domination

The third type of domination is that based on law, what Weber called rational-legal authority. As he phrased it, "legal domination [exists] by virtue of statute. . . . The basic conception is that any legal norm can be created or changed by a procedurally correct enactment."[25] Thus, the basis for legitimacy in a system of rational-legal domination lies in procedure. People believe that laws are legitimate when they are created and enforced in the proper manner. Similarly, people see leaders as having the right to act when they obtain positions in procedurally correct ways—for example, through election or appointment. In this context, then, Weber defined the modern state as based on the monopoly of physical coercion, a monopoly made legitimate by a system of laws binding both leaders and citizens. The rule of law, rather than of persons, reflects the process of rationalization. Nowhere is this more clearly observed than in a modern bureaucracy.

Weber called the administrative apparatus in a rational-legal system a *bureaucracy* and observed that it was oriented to the creation and enforcement of rules in the public interest. A bureaucracy is the archetypal example of instrumentally rational action. Although many people today condemn bureaucracies as inefficient, rigid, and incompetent, Weber argued that this mode of administration was the only means of attaining efficient, flexible, and competent regulation under a rule of law. In its logically pure form (as an ideal type), a bureaucratic administrative apparatus has different characteristics from those in traditional societies:[26]

---

[24]Weber, *Economy and Society*, 237–241.

[25]Quoted in Reinhard Bendix, *Max Weber: An Intellectual Portrait* (London: Heinemann, 1960), 418–419. For an analysis of Weber's views on rationality see Stephen Kalberg, "Max Weber's Types of Rationality," *American Journal of Sociology* 85 (1980), 1145–1179.

[26]Weber, *Economy and Society*, 217–220. Our interpretation of the impact of bureaucracy is more benign than is Weber's. He saw bureaucracies as encasing people in an "iron cage" of reason and thereby stifling freedom; as such, bureaucracies are the archetype of the process of rationalization. This is why Diggins subtitles his book on Weber, *Politics and the Spirit of Tragedy*.

1. People obtain positions based on knowledge and experience.

2. Obedience is owed to rules uniformly applicable to all.

3. Personal and official affairs are kept separate.

4. Lines of authority are explicit.

5. Task specialization is great.

According to Weber, bureaucratic administration in a rational-legal system is realized to the extent that staff members "succeed in eliminating from official business love, hatred, and all purely personal, irrational, and emotional elements."[27] But this is an ideal type. Weber knew that no actual bureaucracy operated in this way. People often obtain positions based on whom they know. Rules are often applied arbitrarily. Personal and official matters are often combined. Thus, the empirical task becomes one of assessing the degree to which a bureaucracy conforms to the ideal type (recall Figure 9.1). The issue is important because the bureaucratic ideal type reflects a fundamental value characteristic of modern societies: Political administration should be impersonal, objective, and based on knowledge, for only in this way can the rule of law be realized. Furthermore, Weber emphasized that although this value seems commonplace today, it is historically new. It arose in the West and has become the dominant form of authority only in the past few hundred years. Finally, Weber's definition of bureaucracy points toward a fundamental arena of conflict in modern societies: Who is to make laws, and who is to administer them through their control of the bureaucracy?

Within the context of a rational-legal system of authority, political parties are the forms in which social strata struggle for power. As Weber puts it, "a political party . . . exists for the purpose of fighting for domination" to advance the economic interests or values of the group it represents, but it does so under the aegis of statutory regulation.[28] In general, the point of the struggle is to direct the bureaucracy via the creation of law, for in this way, the goals of the various social strata are achieved. For example, the very rich, who own income-producing property, in the United States act to make sure that their economic interests are codified into law. Similarly, people in all

---

[27]Weber, *Economy and Society*, 975.
[28]Ibid., 951.

social strata act to protect their interests and values, and the needs of those who do not participate are ignored.[29] The political process in Western societies, then, reflects basic cultural values: Economic and social success are to be achieved through competition under the rule of law, and the process is rational in the sense of being pursued in a methodical manner.

Social Stratification: Class, Status Group, and Party

Weber tried to provide observers with a conceptual map outlining the parts of the stratification system. He believed that such an inventory of concepts would allow an objective description of stratification processes in modern capitalist societies. At the core of his scheme are three ideal types: class, status group, and party.

Class

For Weber, a *class* consists of those persons who have a similar ability to obtain positions in society, procure goods and services for themselves, and enjoy them via an appropriate lifestyle.[30] It should be recognized immediately that a class is defined, in part, by status considerations: the lifestyle of the stratum to which one belongs. In Weber's terminology, *classes* are statistical aggregates rather than groups. Behavior is class oriented to the extent that the process by which people obtain positions, purchase goods and services, and enjoy them is characterized by an individualistic rather than a group perspective. For example, even though investors trying to make money on the stock market might have some common interests, share certain kinds of information with one another, and even join to prevent outsiders from participating, each acts individually in seeking profits or in experiencing losses. Furthermore, in the process of seeking profits, their behavior is typically characterized by an instrumentally rational orientation—that is, action reflects a systematic calculation of means and ends based on knowledge (even if such knowledge is imperfect).

In Weber's analysis, classes are essentially economic phenomena that can exist only in a legally regulated money market where

---

[29]See Leonard Beeghley, "Social Structure and Voting in the United States: A Historical and International Analysis," *Perspectives on Social Problems* 3 (1992), 265–287.

[30]Weber, *Economy and Society*, 302, 927.

income and profit are the desired goals. In such a context, people's membership in a class can be determined objectively, based on their power to dispose of goods and services. For this reason, Weber believed that one's "class situation is, in this sense, ultimately [a] market situation."[31] The most important characteristic of a money market is that in its logically pure form it is impersonal and democratic. Thus, all that should matter in the purchase of stock, groceries, housing, or any other commodity are factors such as one's cash and credit rating. Similarly, a person's class situation is also objectively determined, with the result that people can be ranked by their common economic characteristics and life chances.

In Weber's terminology, *rentiers* are those who live primarily off fixed incomes from investments or trust funds. For example, the large German landowners of his time were rentiers because these families had controlled much of the land for several generations and received their incomes from the peasants or tenant farmers who actually worked it. As a result of their possession of capital and values that they had acquired over time, the landowners chose to lead a less overtly acquisitive lifestyle. Weber called them rentiers because they did not work to increase their assets but simply lived off them, using their time for purposes other than earning a living. For example, they might hold public office or lead lives of idleness.

According to Weber, *entrepreneurs* are those, such as merchants, shipowners, and bankers, who own and operate businesses. Weber called them a commercial, or entrepreneurial, class because they actually work their property for the economic gain that it produces, with the result that in absolute terms the members of the entrepreneurial class often have more economic power, but less social honor (or prestige), than do rentiers.

This distinction between the uses to which income-producing property is put allowed Weber to differentiate between those who work as an avocation and those who work because they want to increase their assets—that is, this distinction reflects fundamental differences in values. In most societies, there exist privileged status groups, such as rentiers, the members of which "consider almost any kind of overt participation in economic acquisition as absolutely stigmatizing" despite its potential economic advantages. Usually

---

[31]Ibid., 303, 927.

these families have possessed wealth for a long time, over several generations. Thus, even though economic-oriented (or class-oriented) action is individualistic and dominated by instrumentally rational action, value-rational behavior also occurs. Action at every stratum level varies along these two dimensions.

Weber asserted that the possession of capital by both rentiers and entrepreneurs provided them with great economic and political power and sharply distinguished them from those who did not own such property. Both rentiers and entrepreneurs can monopolize the purchase of expensive consumer items. Both pursue monopolistic sales and pricing policies, whether legally or not. To some extent, both control opportunities for others to acquire wealth and property. Finally, both rentiers and entrepreneurs monopolize costly status privileges, such as education, that provide young people with future contacts and skills. In these terms, then, rentiers and entrepreneurs can be seen to have (roughly) similar levels of power; and because they are always a small proportion of the population, they often act together to protect their lifestyles. Even though they live rather differently, their source of income (ownership of capital) sets them apart from the other social classes. The distribution of property, in short, tends to prevent non-owners from competing for highly valued goods and perpetuates the structure of stratification from one generation to another.

In constructing his conceptual map of the class structure, Weber next considered those who do not own income-producing property. Despite not possessing the means of production, such people are not without economically and politically important resources in modern societies, and they can be meaningfully differentiated into a number of classes. The main criteria Weber used in making class distinctions among those without property are the worth of their services and the level of their skills; both factors are important indicators of people's ability to obtain positions, purchase goods, and enjoy them. In Weber's classificatory scheme, the "middle classes" comprise those individuals who today would be called white-collar workers because the skills that they sell do not involve manual labor: public officials, such as politicians and administrators; managers of businesses; members of the professions, such as doctors and lawyers; teachers and intellectuals; and specialists of various sorts, such as technicians; low-level, white-collar employees; and civil servants. Because their skills are in relatively high demand in industrial societies, these people generally have more economic and political power than those who work with their hands do.[32]

The less privileged, propertyless classes comprise people who today would be called blue-collar workers because their skills primarily involve manual labor. Without explanation, Weber said that such people could be divided into three levels: skilled, semiskilled, and unskilled workers. He did not elaborate much on the lifestyles of those without property.

By means of these ideal types, Weber described the parts of a modern class structure. The key factors distinguishing one class from another are (1) the uses to which property is put by those who own it and (2) the worth of the skills and services offered by those who do not own property. These factors combine in the marketplace to produce identifiable aggregates, or classes, the members of which have a similar ability to obtain positions, purchase goods, and enjoy them via an appropriate lifestyle.

As described in Chapter 7, Marx posited that modern societies display a basic division between capitalists, those who own income-producing property, and proletarians, those who are forced to sell their labor power to survive. In his words, "society as a whole is splitting up more and more into two great hostile camps, into two great classes facing each other: Bourgeoisie and Proletarian."[33]

Marx knew that this assertion was an exaggeration. He meant that historical evolution placed these two groups at the center of a class struggle, which would inevitably produce a communist society. But when examining actual historical events, Marx often looked at specific segments of society, such as bankers or the "lower middle class" or the *lumpenproletariat* (the very poor), analyzing their different experiences and interests with great insight.[34] Unlike Weber, however, Marx did not develop a systematic model (or map) of the class structure.

Table 9.1 shows that both Marx and Weber regarded the differences between those who own capital and those who do not as fundamental divisions in the class structure. The table also shows

---

[32]Ibid., 304.

[33]Karl Marx and Friedrich Engels, *The Birth of the Communist Manifesto* (New York: International, 1975), 90.

[34]Karl Marx, *The Eighteenth Brumaire of Louis Bonaparte* (New York: International, 1963); and "Critique of the Gotha Program," in *Selected Works*, Vol. 3, eds. Karl Marx and Friedrich Engels (New York: International, 1969), 9–30.

Table 9.1   Marx's and Weber's Models of the Class Structure

Marx's Model	Weber's Model
1. Capitalists	1. Propertied
2. Proletarians	a. Rentiers
	b. Entrepreneurs
	2. Nonpropertied
	a. Middle classes
	b. Skilled workers
	c. Semiskilled workers
	d. Unskilled workers

that Weber's map of the class structure is much more detailed than Marx's. Both those who own property and those who do not can be separated into classes (or strata) in a way that is useful to observers and subjectively meaningful to ordinary people. Thus, those capitalists who do not lead acquisitive lives are rentiers and those who do are entrepreneurs. Sometimes the members of these two strata act together to preserve and protect their source of income, their property, but sometimes they do not, mainly because they have different values. Weber's distinction alerts observers to the need for specifying the conditions under which each occurs. Similarly, middle-class people see themselves as different from those who are skilled workers. As a result, they tend to live in different neighborhoods, make different friends, attend different schools, and participate in different leisure activities. Current research reveals that a semipermeable boundary separates middle-class people (white-collar workers) from working-class people (blue-collar workers) at all skill levels.

The final topic of importance in Weber's analysis of class is the possibility of group formation and unified political action by the propertyless classes. Like Marx, Weber said that this phenomenon was relatively rare in history because those who did not own property generally failed to recognize their common interests. As a result, action based on a similar class situation is often restricted to inchoate and relatively brief mass reactions. Nonetheless, throughout history perceived differences in life chances have periodically led to class struggles, although in most cases the point of the conflict focused on rather narrow economic issues, such as wages or prices, rather than on the nature of the political system that perpetuates their class situation.[35]

---

[35]Ibid., 305, 930–931.

Although Weber alluded only briefly to the conditions under which the members of the propertyless classes might challenge the existing political order, he identified some of the same variables that Marx had:

1. Large numbers of people must perceive themselves to be in the same class situation.

2. They must be ecologically concentrated, as in urban areas.

3. Clearly understood goals must be articulated by an intelligentsia. Here, Weber suggested that people had to be shown that the causes and consequences of their class situation resulted from the structure of the political system itself.

4. The opponents must be clearly identified.

When these conditions are satisfied, Weber indicated, an organized class results. We turn now to another basis for action displayed by people in each stratum: status group.

Status Group

In Weber's work, a status group comprises those individuals who share "a specific, positive or negative, social estimation of honor."[36] Weber thus used the concepts of "status" and "status group" to distinguish the sphere of prestige evaluation (expressed by people's lifestyles) from that of monetary calculation (expressed by their economic behavior). Although the two are interrelated, the distinction emphasizes that people's actions cannot be understood in economic terms alone. Rather, their values often channel action in specific directions.

The income from a person's job provides the ability to purchase goods and enjoy them; class membership is thus objectively determined by a simple monetary calculation. Status and honor are based on the judgments that people make about another's background, breeding, character, morals, and community standing; and so a person's membership in a status group is always subjectively determined. Status-oriented behavior illustrates value-rational action—that is, action based on some value or values held for their own sake. Rather than behaving for their economic interests, status-oriented people act

---

[36]Ibid., 305–306, 932.

as members of a group with whom they share a specific style of life and level of social honor. In Weber's words, "in contrast to classes, *Stände* (status groups) are normally groups. They are, however, of an amorphous kind."[37]

Status "always rests on distance and exclusiveness," in the sense that members of a status group actively express and protect their lifestyles in a number of specific ways: (1) People extend hospitality only to social equals. Thus, they tend to invite into their homes, become friends with, eat with, and socialize with others who are like themselves in that they share similar lifestyles. (2) People restrict potential marriage partners to social equals (this practice is called connubium). Thus, they tend to live in areas and send their children to schools with the children of others who are like themselves, with the result that their offspring generally marry others with similar values and ways of living. (3) People practice unique social conventions and activities. Thus, they tend to join organizations, such as churches and clubs, and spend their leisure time with others who share similar beliefs and lifestyles. (4) People try to monopolize "privileged modes of acquisition," such as their property or occupations.[38]

This last tactic is important, for those in common status positions act politically to close off social and economic opportunities to outsiders to protect their capital or occupational investments. For example, because particular skills (e.g., in doctoring or carpentry) acquired over time necessarily limit the possibility for acquiring other skills, competing individuals "become interested in curbing competition" and preventing the free operation of the market. So they join together and, despite continued competition among themselves, attempt to close off opportunities for outsiders by influencing the creation and administration of law. Such attempts at occupational closure are ever recurring at all stratum levels, and they are "the source of property in land as well as of all guild [or union] monopolies."[39]

Party

As a theorist of power, Weber added another dimension to stratification: party. For Weber, *party* denotes the "house of power" or the way

---

[37]Ibid., 932.
[38]Weber, *Economy and Society*, 306, 935.
[39]Ibid., 342–343.

in which power is organized and used to control members in a society; the distribution of power represents another dimension of stratification. In contrast to Marx, who tended to view power and status as mere reflections of who owned the means of production, Weber argued that class, status group, and party constitute separate bases of stratification, although they often highly correlate with each other; success in markets allows individuals to buy status group memberships and to exert disproportionate influence on political decisions. Still, Weber saw stratification as multidimensional. People could hold different places along the three hierarchies marking a stratification system.

In fact, Weber's analysis of stratification emphasized that when there is a high correlation among class, status group, and party—that is, those high or low on one are also high and low on the other two— the potential for political conflict increases. Thus, when economic, political, and status group elites are pretty much the same individuals, those without power, money, or honor will become resentful. And if they have very little power, money, or honor, and few chances to be upwardly mobile on any other or all of these three dimensions of stratification, they are even more likely to become angry and receptive to leaders who would advocate change in a society. Thus, the more memberships in class, status group, and party correlate, the more those high in class, status group, and party horde resources, and the more likely tensions will surface in a society. These tensions over inequalities are often the fuel energizing social change.

Weber's Model of Social Change

Weber's analysis of systems of domination, especially his distinction among the three types of authority, implies a model of social change. Like Marx, Weber saw the source of change as endogenous (or internal) to the society. Figure 9.4 depicts Weber's vision of the internal system dynamics that change societies.

Weber saw the struggle for power as continuous in all societies. Those with power are organized and try to monopolize the means of coercion while also seeking to legitimate their hold on power. Parties act strategically through use of military force, co-optation, patronage, political alliances, and many other tactics to maintain power. At the same time, other segments of a society can seek to mobilize power and displace those who control government. Societies organized by patterns of traditional domination can remain relatively stable for

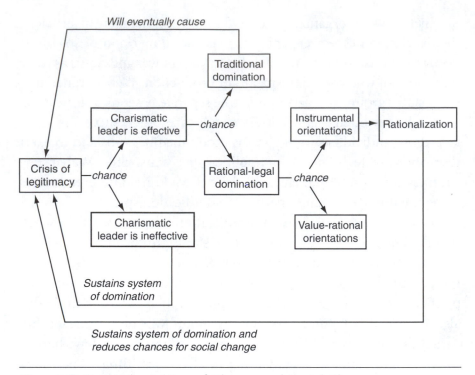

Figure 9.4   Weber's View of Chance and Social Change

many years but, eventually, tensions develop. These tensions can arise for many reasons, such as anger over unfair treatment, abuse of power, excessive taxation, lack of opportunities, inequalities in wealth and income, and just about any fault line in a stratified society. As these tensions mount, they increase the likelihood that charismatic leaders will emerge and articulate the grievances of subordinates in the system of stratification. If the charismatic leaders are successful, they face the problem of how to "routinize" their charisma, thereby setting up yet another system of traditional domination or, potentially, a new system of rational-legal domination. If charisma is routinized via traditional authority, then a new system of stratification will emerge, revealing new sources of tension that will eventually lead to the emergence of new charismatic leaders to challenge the dominant party. If, however, a rational-legal system is put into place, it will have greater capacity to resolve tensions.

Weber's Model of Stratification and Geopolitics

As a sociologist of power, seeking to explain how power is used in systems of domination, Weber was interested in the development of the state as an organizational order that could be used to administer power. Weber proposed a geopolitical theory of power, seeing both the legitimacy of political authority and the potential for the emergence of charismatic leaders as related to the relations of a society with other societies. In general, Weber argued that there is often a competition for prestige among states, with those that are successful in war and economic competition enjoying more prestige than do those that are not so successful.[40] Moreover, prestige in external relations with other states increases the legitimacy bestowed on political authority by the masses within the society. Thus, the administration of power, the degree of legitimacy given to those with power, and the potential for conflict are often tied to external, geopolitical events outside a society's borders.

Weber saw these dynamics as driven by several interrelated factors. The first was the size of the state, or the scale of the administrative structures used to exercise power. For the state to grow, production in the economy must be sufficient to create the surplus necessary to support specialized administrative personnel.

Another critical relation is between key economic actors and the state. When actors in the economy depend on the state for their right to engage in particular kinds of economic activity, as is the case with a chartered corporation or a company given a monopoly by the state, these economic actors will place pressure on the state to engage in external conflict if their interests are tied to success in the external system. For example, chartered corporations in America before the Revolutionary War gave economic actors in England a strong incentive to have the English government wage war or use coercion to protect their interests. When, however, the dependence of economic actors on the state is low but they still have interests in the external system, these economic actors are more likely, Weber believed, to exert pressures on the state to engage in co-optive strategies, such as trade agreements, rather than war. The success of the state in either war making or deal making in trade determines the prestige of society and its ruling elites not only vis-à-vis other states but also in relation to the masses within a society. For example, Japan's prestige in the world economic system has been very high since World War II because of its success in achieving favorable trade relations with other countries; this prestige has, in turn, given the dominant political

---

[40]Weber, *Economy and Society*, 901–1372; see in particular 901–920.

party prestige and legitimacy. Similarly, leaders enjoyed considerable prestige within Japan during the early phases of World War II when they had military success, but this prestige declined with each setback in the Pacific and in Asia.

Another force entering this basic relationship between prestige in the world system and the legitimacy of its ruling elites is the level of inequality. Weber recognized that when high levels of inequality exist and when memberships in classes, parties, and status groups are highly correlated (i.e., members in upper classes are also members of ruling parties and high prestige status groups, and vice versa), the potential for the emergence of charismatic leadership increases. Thus, a state that engages in diplomatic or military adventurism in relation with other states is more vulnerable if political power has been used in ways to increase the level of inequality within the society. Success in external relations will stave off the emergence of a charismatic leader, but if the state should lose prestige in external relations, then the conflict potential inhering in the stratification system increases dramatically, especially if charismatic leaders can emerge to take advantage of the state's loss of prestige.[41]

Thus, the dynamics of domination are very much tied to geopolitics, and in these, Weber can be considered an early world systems theorist. He saw clearly the connection between legitimation of a stratification order and the state, on one side, and the geopolitical position of the society in relation to its neighbors, on the other side.

Weber on Capitalism and Rationalization

As we have emphasized, Weber was very much concerned with the process of rationalization. Why had rational-legal domination spread? Part of the answer can be found in Weber's famous analysis of religion, where he argued that a change in religious beliefs (toward Protestantism) was the critical force in tipping Western European societies toward capitalism. We will examine this famous and controversial thesis in the next section, but before exploring this thesis, we address what Weber saw as a fundamental relationship between the use of money in free markets and the rationalization of orders in the

---

[41]Theda Skocpol has pursued this Weberian argument in her *States and Social Revolutions* (New York: Cambridge University Press, 1979).

political and economic arenas.[42] Weber recognized that market forces were an important precondition for the emergence of capitalism; moreover, once in place, they dramatically accelerated the process of rationalization.

For Weber, when money is introduced into exchanges, it becomes possible to engage in more precise and efficient calculations of value. That is, the worth of a good or commodity is more readily ascertained with money as a common measure of value. The use of money to mediate transactions and social relationships has slowly expanded in human history, primarily as the result of (1) the expansion of markets where money would greatly facilitate transactions and (2) the growth of the state where liquid revenues could be taxed to expand state power. Money is a generalized medium that can be used to purchase any good or commodity, and so it greatly accelerated the ease of market transactions over older patterns of barter (where one commodity is exchanged for another). As a result, it gave the state a means to purchase labor and other resources necessary to wield power. Moreover, Weber argued that rational-legal bureaucracy, whether that of the state or economic actors, would not be possible without free labor willing to sell its services in a labor market for money. Thus, rationalization depended heavily on the emergence of free markets using money.

Money also facilitates the extension of credit because a debt can be expressed with one measure—the value of money—and the interest rate can similarly be calculated. With credit, economic activity can expand, as can the activities of the state that, like any other actor, can enter credit markets. The use of credit further extends the calculability of utilities, and in so doing, money and credit rationalize market transactions. As this transition occurs, Weber believed, tradition, patronage, and other ways of regulating markets would decline. In their place come rational calculations of price, payments, debts, and interest. As older ways of organizing economic activity and exchange are pushed aside, productive units become more rational and begin to calculate their costs and profits against the yardstick of money, credit, interest notes, and market forces. Similarly, the relationship between labor and its employers shifts to one based on rational calculations rather than on patrimony or some other nonrational mechanism for organizing the work force.

---

[42]Weber, *Economy and Society*, 63–212.

Once this level of rationalization has occurred, Weber felt, it will feed on itself, constantly expanding the rationality of the state. As the state becomes dependent on market-driven productivity to finance its operations, it will introduce legal rules, and enforce these rules, to ensure that contracts and agreements are honored. Thus, the rationality of the market becomes a rational-legal domination by the state as increasingly rational actors use the law rather than tradition, affect, religion, and other nonrational bases of regulation to organize their affairs. Indeed, one of the most important bodies of law is the tax code, which specifies how, and how much, revenue the state can take from other actors to finance its operations. As the state depends more on this monetary source of revenue, coupled with its access to credit markets, it enacts more laws and expands its administrative structure to ensure a constant flow of revenue. As a result, the bureaucratized state becomes more instrumentally rational as it seeks ways to secure money (e.g., taxes, credit) to expand its functions and, hence, its capacity for domination.

Similarly, once money and credit fund economic actors and markets, markets and production expand, which further extends the use of money and credit. When the state begins to support markets through law, the use of money and credit in free markets can increase the scale of production and market distribution even more. Once a certain level of rationalization exists in the economy, organizations regulated by law and driven by instrumental rationality (for profits) come to dominate.

Thus, Weber saw a dynamism in capitalism, much as Marx had, but with a very different prediction: the disenchantment of the social world by rational-legal domination in the economic and political arenas. Rather than sowing the seeds of its own destruction, as Marx had argued, Weber felt that rationalization had planted the seeds for its own perpetuation. The capacity to oppose this monolith would be lessened, and increasing aspects of social life could be calculable, rational, efficient, and dull. Weber thus came to a very different conclusion than Marx about the liberating potential of markets and capitalism. Humans would, in Weber's words, be locked in "the iron cage" of bureaucracy and rational-legal authority.

Weber also disagreed that this rational-legal juggernaut was inevitable. He did not see history as marching inexorably anywhere, and certainly not to a liberating utopia. Rather, history was often random, moving in response to chance confluence of events, and this had been the case for the rise of capitalism and the spread of rational-legal authority. Why had history made this turn toward increasing rationalization? For Weber, the answer resided in the emergence of Protestantism.

Weber had long been interested in religion, for its own sake, and particularly for an understanding of how it worked to legitimate orders and systems of domination, but he had also been interested in religion for another reason: to understand the rise of capitalism. Perhaps his most famous work, certainly outside of sociology, is *The Protestant Ethic and the Spirit of Capitalism.* In this essay, Weber argued that the key chance event turning the historical tide toward rational-legal forms of domination had been the rise of Protestantism in the West. This controversial work was only part of a more comprehensive study of religion, but even here, Weber was interested in explaining how religion in other, equally developed societies of the East had inhibited the rise of capitalism. Thus, one of the most important reasons that Weber studied religion was to discover the critical causal event that had unleashed capitalism and rationalization.

Weber's Study of Religion

The *Protestant Ethic* is Weber's most famous and probably most important study.[43] Published in two parts, in 1904 and 1905, it was one of his first works to be translated into English, and even more significantly, it was the first application of his mature methodological orientation. As a result, the *Protestant Ethic* is neither a historical analysis nor a politically committed interpretation of history. Rather, it is an exercise in historical hypothesis testing in which Weber constructed a logical experiment using ideal types as conceptual tools.

Although the *Protestant Ethic* is the most well-known of Weber's studies in the sociology of religion, it is nonetheless only a small portion of a much larger intellectual enterprise that Weber pursued intermittently for about 15 years. In this grandiose "logical

---

[43]Max Weber, *The Protestant Ethic and the Spirit of Capitalism*, trans. Talcott Parsons (New York: Scribner's, 1958). For a more recent and better translation, see Stephen Kalberg, *The Protestant Ethic and the Spirit of Capitalism* (Los Angeles: Roxbury, 2002); see especially the Introduction.

experiment," Weber tried not only to account for the confluence of events that were associated with the rise of modern capitalism in the West but also to explain why capitalism was not likely to have developed in any other section of the world—that is, "why did not the scientific, the artistic, the political, and the economic development [of China, India, and other areas] enter upon that path of rationalization which is peculiar to the occident?"[44] Thus, the *Protestant Ethic* is the first portion of a two-stage quasi experiment. The second element in Weber's experiment is contained in a series of book-length studies on *The Religion of China* (1913), *The Religion of India* (1916–1917), and *Ancient Judaism* (1917).[45]

The Quasi-Experimental Design

Before reviewing either the *Protestant Ethic* or Weber's other work on religion, we should make explicit the implicit research design of these works. In so doing, we will describe another sense in which Weber constructed "quasi-experimental designs" for understanding the causes of historical events. Weber's basic question is "Why did modern capitalism initially occur in the West and not in other parts of the world?" To isolate the cause of this monumental historical change, Weber constructed the "quasi-experimental design" diagrammed in Figure 9.5.

In Figure 9.5, Steps 1 to 5 approximate the stages of a laboratory situation as it must be adapted to historical analysis, which is why we label it a logical experiment. The West represents the experimental group in that something stimulated capitalism, whereas China and India represent the control groups because their economic systems did not change, even though they were as advanced as the West

---

[44]Weber, "Author's Introduction," in *Protestant Ethic*, 25. It is important to recognize that Weber wrote this introduction in 1920 for the German edition of his *Collected Essays in the Sociology of Religion*. Thus, it is an overall view of Weber's work in the sociology of religion rather than an introduction to the *Protestant Ethic*. Scribner's 1976 edition of the book does not make this clear.

[45]Weber, *The Religion of China*, trans. Hans Gerth (New York: Free Press, 1951); *The Religion of India*, trans. Hans Gerth and Don Martindale (New York: Free Press, 1958); and *Ancient Judaism*, trans. Hans Gerth and Don Martindale (New York: Free Press, 1952). In addition, Part 2 of *Economy and Society* contains a book-length study, "Religious Groups (The Sociology of Religion)," which is also available in paperback under the title *The Sociology of Religion*, trans. Ephraim Fishoff (Boston: Beacon, 1963).

Figure 9.5   Weber's Quasi-Experimental Design in the Study of Religion

GROUP	STEP 1 Find "matched" societies in terms of their minimal conditions.	STEP 2 Do historical research on their properties before stimulus was introduced.	STEP 3 Examine the impact of the key stimulus, religious beliefs.	STEP 4 Use historical evidence to assess the impact of the stimulus.	STEP 5 View differences between Europe and China/India as caused by religious beliefs.
QUASI-EXPERIMENTAL GROUP	Western Europe	Descriptions of Europe (using historical ideal types)	Experiences stimulus with emergence of Protestantism	Modern capitalism	Western Europe is changed.
QUASI-CONTROL GROUP	China	Descriptions of China (using historical ideal types)	Experiences no stimulus	No capitalism	China is much the same as before.
QUASI-CONTROL GROUP	India	Descriptions of India (using historical ideal types)	Experiences no stimulus	No capitalism	India is much the same as before.

in technologies and other social forms. The stimulus that caused capitalism in the West was a set of religious beliefs associated with Protestantism (see Step 3 of Figure 9.5). Weber wrote the *Protestant Ethic* for this reason.

The Protestant Ethic and the Spirit of Capitalism

Weber opened the *Protestant Ethic* with what was a commonplace observation at the end of the nineteenth century: Occupational statistics in those nations of mixed religious composition seemed to show that those in higher socioeconomic positions were overwhelmingly Protestant. This relationship appeared especially true, Weber wrote, "wherever capitalism . . . has had a free hand."[46] Many observers in economics, literature, and history had commented on this phenomenon before Weber, and he cited a number of them.[47] Hence, in the *Protestant Ethic* Weber was not trying to prove that a relationship between Protestantism and economic success in capitalist societies existed because he took its existence as given. In his words, "it is not new that the existence of this relationship is maintained. . . . Our task here is to explain the relation."[48]

To show that Protestantism was related to the origin of *the spirit of capitalism* in the West, Weber began with a sketch of what he meant by the latter term. Like many of his key concepts, the spirit of capitalism is a historical ideal type in that it conceptually accentuates certain aspects of the real world as a tool for understanding historical processes.[49] Although he did not state what he meant very clearly, an omission that helped contribute to the tremendous controversy over the *Protestant Ethic*'s thesis, his concept of the spirit of capitalism appears to have the following components:[50]

---

[46]Weber, *Protestant Ethic*, 25.

[47]Ibid., 43–45, 191 (see Note 23). See also Reinhard Bendix, "*The Protestant Ethic*— Revisited," in *Scholarship and Partisanship: Essays on Max Weber*, eds. Reinhard Bendix and Guenther Roth (Berkeley: University of California Press, 1971), 299–310.

[48]Ibid., 191.

[49]Weber hints at his ideal type strategy but does not bother to explain it in the initial paragraphs of Chapter 2 of the *Protestant Ethic*, 47. He refers to the need to develop a "historical individual"—that is, "a complex of elements associated in historical reality which we unite into a conceptual whole from the standpoint of their cultural significance." This phrasing reveals the influence of Heinrich Rickert, as discussed in the last chapter.

[50]Weber, *Protestant Ethic*, 53–54.

1. Work is valued as an end in itself. Weber was fascinated by the fact that a person's "duty in a calling [or occupation] is what is most characteristic of the social ethic of capitalistic culture, and is in a sense the fundamental basis of it."

2. Trade and profit are taken not only as evidence of occupational success but also as indicators of personal virtue. In Weber's words, "the earning of money within the modern economic order is, so long as it is done legally, [seen as] the result and the expression of virtue and proficiency in a calling."

3. A methodically organized life governed by reason is valued not only as a means to a long-term goal—economic success— but also as an inherently proper and even righteous state of being.

4. Embodied in the righteous pursuit of economic success is a belief that immediate happiness and pleasure should be forgone in favor of future satisfaction. As Weber noted, "the *summum bonum* of this ethic, the earning of more and more money, combined with the strict avoidance of all spontaneous enjoyment of life, is above all completely devoid of an eudaemonistic, not to say hedonistic, admixture."

In sum, then, these values—the goodness of work, success as personal rectitude, the use of reason to guide one's life, and delayed gratification—reflect some of the most important cultural values in the West because they constitute perceptions of appropriate behavior that are shared by all. Weber emphasized, however, that the widespread application of such values to everyday life was historically unique and of relatively recent origin. He believed that the greatest barrier to the rise of the spirit of capitalism in the West was the inertial force of traditional values. In varying degrees, European societies before the seventeenth century were dominated by "traditional modes of action." For example, religion rather than science was used as the primary means of verifying knowledge. Bureaucracies composed of technically trained experts were unknown. Patterns of commerce and most other forms of daily life were dominated by status rather than class considerations—that is, people's economic actions were dictated by their membership in religious groups rather than by market factors. Finally, legal adjudication did not involve the equal application of law to all individuals. In short, the choice between instrumentally rational action and value-rational action did not exist. Rather, custom dictated behavior.

In such a context, of course, some individuals tried to make money. As Weber remarks, "capitalism existed in China, India, Babylon, in the classic world, and in the Middle Ages."[51] But it was traditional capitalism in which the ideal was simply to acquire enough money without spending too much time doing it so one could live as one was "accustomed to live." Weber described the traditional enterprises of the nobility as "adventurer capitalism," referring to investment in long-distance trade (e.g., in spices or silk) from which one might obtain a windfall profit sufficient to last a lifetime or the purchase of government offices (e.g., tax collector) from which one skimmed off a portion of the revenue. "Capitalistic acquisition as an adventure has been at home in all types of economic society which have known trade with the use of money."[52] Such activities, however, were not the center of these people's lives. The existence of individual adventurer capitalists, moreover, differs from a rationalized capitalist economy, based on the mass production of consumer goods, in which the entire population is oriented to making money.

In his *General Economic History*, written some years later, Weber identified the major structural changes that he believed, taken together, had caused the development of rationalized capitalist economies in Western Europe rather than elsewhere:

1. The process of industrialization through which muscle power was supplanted by new forms of energy

2. The rise of a free labor force whose members had to work for wages or starve

3. The increasing use of systematic accounting methods

4. The rise of a free market unencumbered by religious restrictions

5. The gradual imposition and legitimization of a system of calculable law

---

[51]Ibid., 52.

[52]Ibid., 57–58. See also Max Weber, "Anticritical Last Word on the Spirit of Capitalism," trans. Wallace A. Davis, *American Journal of Sociology* 83 (1978), 1127.

6. The increasing commercialization of economic life through the use of stock certificates and other paper instruments

7. The rise of the spirit of capitalism

Although all these historical developments were to varying degrees unique to the West, in the *General Economic History*, Weber still regarded the last factor as the most decisive. Thus, in attempting to understand the origin of the economic differences between Protestants and Catholics, he was not trying to deny the fundamental significance of these structural changes but to show the significance of the culture of capitalism and its unintended relationship to Protestant ethical teachings.

Weber believed that Puritanism and the other Protestant sects destroyed the cultural values of traditional society, although this was not the intent of those who adopted the new faiths, nor could this effect have been predicted in advance. In the *Protestant Ethic*, Weber focused mainly on Calvinism, with much shorter discussions of Pietism, Methodism, and Baptism appended to the main analysis. His strategy was to describe Calvinist doctrines by quoting extensively from the writings of its various theologians, then to impute the psychological consequences those doctrines had on people who organized their lives in these terms, and finally to show how they resulted in specific (and historically new) secular values and ways of living. In Weber's words, he was interested in ascertaining "those psychological sanctions which, originating in religious belief and the practice of religion, gave a direction to practical conduct and held the individual to it."[53] In this way, he could give a powerful example of the manner in which cultural phenomena influence social action and, at the same time, rebut the vulgar Marxists who thought economic factors were the sole causal agents in historical change.

Based on an analysis of Calvinist writings, such as the *Westminster Confession of 1647*, from which he quoted extensively, Weber interpreted Calvinist doctrine as having four consequences for those who accepted its tenets.

First, because the Calvinist doctrine of predestination led people to believe that God, for incomprehensible reasons, had divided the

---

[53]Ibid., 97. See also Stephen Kalberg, "The Rationalization of Action in Max Weber's Sociology of Religion," *Sociological Theory* 8 (1990), 58–84.

human population into two groups, the saved and the damned, a key problem for all individuals was to determine the group to which they belonged. Second, because people could not know with certainty whether they were saved, they inevitably felt a great inner loneliness and isolation. Third, although a change in one's relative state of grace was seen as impossible, people inevitably began to look for signs that they were among the elect. In general, Calvinists believed that two clues could be used as evidence: (a) faith, for all had an absolute duty to consider themselves chosen and to combat all doubts as temptations of the devil, and (b) intense worldly activity, for in this way, the self-confidence necessary to alleviate religious doubts could be generated. Fourth, all believers were expected to lead methodical and ascetic lives unencumbered by irrational emotions, superstitions, or desires of the flesh. As Weber put it, the good Calvinist was expected to "methodically supervise his own state of grace in his own conduct, and thus to penetrate it with asceticism," with the result that each person engaged in "a rational planning of the whole of one's life in accordance with God's will."[54] The significance of this last doctrine is that in Calvinist communities worldly asceticism was not restricted to monks and other "religious virtuosi" (to use Weber's phrase) but required of all as they conducted their everyday lives in their mundane occupations or callings.

To show the relationship between the worldly asceticism fostered by the Protestant sects and the rise of the spirit of capitalism, Weber chose to focus on the Puritan ministers' guidelines for everyday behavior, as contained in their pastoral writings. The clergy's teachings, which were set forth in books such as Richard Baxter's *Christian Directory*, tended to reflect the major pastoral problems they encountered. As such, their writings provide an idealized version of everyday life in the Puritan communities. Although it must be recognized that patterns of social action do not always conform to cultural ideals, such values do provide a general direction for people's behaviors. Most people try, even if imperfectly, to adhere to those standards of appropriate behavior dominant in their communities, and the Puritans were no exceptions. Furthermore, the use of these kinds of data suggests the broad way in which Weber interpreted the idea of "explanatory understanding" (*verstehen*): Because people's own

---

[54]Ibid., 153. As a Protestant, Weber may have overemphasized the distinction between Protestantism and Catholicism.

explanations of their actions often involve contradictory motives that are difficult to reconcile, he was perfectly willing to use an indirect means of ascertaining the subjective meaning of social action among the Puritans.

Based on Weber's analysis, it appears that the Puritan communities were dominated by three interrelated dictums, which, although a direct outgrowth of Puritan theology, eventuated over the long run in a secular culture of capitalism.

The first of these pronouncements is that God demands rational labor in a calling. As Weber noted, Puritan pastoral literature is characterized "by the continually repeated, often almost passionate preaching of hard, continuous bodily or mental labour."[55] From this point of view, there can be no relaxation, no relief from toil, for labor is an exercise in ascetic virtue, and rational, methodical behavior in a calling is taken as a sign of grace. Hence, from the Puritan's standpoint, "waste of time is . . . the first and in principle the deadliest of sins," because "every hour lost is lost to labour for the glory of God." As Weber observed, this dictum not only provides an ethical justification for the modern division of labor (in which occupational tasks are divided up efficiently) but also reserves its highest accolades for those sober, middle-class individuals who best exemplify the methodical nature of worldly asceticism. As an aside, it should be noted that members of this stratum became the primary carriers of Puritan religious beliefs precisely because they garnered immense economic, social, and political power as a result. In general, Weber emphasized that those who were able to define and sanctify standards of appropriate behavior also benefit materially.[56]

The second directive states that the enjoyment of those aspects of social life that do not have clear religious value is forbidden. Thus, from the point of view of the Puritan ministers, secular literature, the theater, and nearly all other forms of leisure-time activity were irrelevant or even morally suspect. As a result, they tried to inculcate in their parishioners an extraordinarily serious approach to life, for

---

[55]Ibid., 158.

[56]Weber, *Protestant Ethic*, 176. Although Weber's point was that religious values influenced behavior, he emphasized that values and lifestyles are interrelated. Religiosity permeated every aspect of daily life. See Robert Wuthnow, *Communities of Discourse: Ideology and Social Structure in the Reformation, the Enlightenment, and European Socialism* (Cambridge, MA: Harvard University Press, 1989).

people should direct their attention toward the practical problems dominating everyday life and subject them to rational solutions.

The third guideline specifies that people have a duty to use their possessions for socially beneficial purposes that redound to the glory of God. Thus, the pursuit of wealth for its own sake was regarded as sinful, for it could lead to enjoyment, idleness, and "temptations of the flesh." From this point of view, those who acquire wealth through God's grace and hard work are mere trustees who have an obligation to use it responsibly.

Even allowing for the usual amount of human imperfection, Weber argued, the accumulation of capital and the rise of the modern bourgeoisie were the inevitable results of whole communities sharing the values dictating hard work, limited enjoyment and consumption, and the practical use of money. Hence, modern capitalism emerged. Weber's causal argument is diagrammed in Figure 9.6. Over time, of course, Puritan ideals gave way under the secularizing influence of wealth because people began to enjoy their material possessions. Thus, although the religious roots of the spirit of capitalism died out, Puritanism bequeathed to modern people "an amazingly good, we may even say a pharisaically good, conscience in the acquisition of money."

The predominance of such a value in Western societies is historically unique. It led Weber to some rather pessimistic observations in the concluding paragraphs of the *Protestant Ethic*. He believed that the rise of modern capitalism reflected the process of rationalization

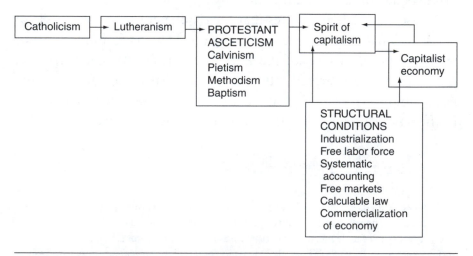

Figure 9.6   Weber's Causal Argument for the Emergence of Capitalism

we referred to earlier. People are now taught to lead methodical lives, using reason buttressed by knowledge to achieve their goals. As he put it, "the idea of duty in one's calling prowls about in our lives like the ghost of dead religious beliefs," with the result that whereas "the Puritan wanted to work in a calling; we are forced to do so." In effect, the culture of capitalism, combined with capitalist social and economic institutions, places people in an "iron cage" from which there appears to be no escape and for which there is no longer a religious justification. This recognition leads to Weber's last, sad lament: "specialists without spirit, sensualists without heart; this nullity imagines that it has attained a level of civilization never before achieved."[57]

Weber's Comparative Studies of Religion and Capitalism

During the years following publication of the *Protestant Ethic*, Weber continued his analysis of the relationship between religious belief and social structure to show why it was not very likely that capitalism as an economic system could have emerged anywhere else in the world.[58] Weber's most important works in this regard are *The Religion of China* and *The Religion of India*. They represent the extension of the "logical experiment" begun some years earlier.

Both of these extended essays are similar in format in that Weber began by assessing those characteristics of Chinese and Indian social structure that either inhibited or, under the right circumstances, could have contributed to the development of capitalism in that part of the world. For purposes of illustration, the examples used here come from *The Religion of China*. Thus, in China, during the period

---

[57]Ibid., 180–183.

[58]See Weber's "Anticritical Last Word," as well as the many explanatory footnotes in the *Protestant Ethic*. Most of these footnotes were added around 1920. The debate over Weber's "logical experiment" has continued as observers struggle to understand the origins of modernity. See Robert L. Green, ed., *Protestantism and Capitalism: The Weber Thesis and Its Critics* (Lexington, MA: D. C. Heath, 1959); S. N. Eisenstadt, ed., *The Protestant Ethic and Modernization* (New York: Basic Books, 1968); Gordon Marshall, *In Search of the Spirit of Capitalism: An Essay on Max Weber's Protestant Ethic Thesis* (New York: Columbia University Press, 1982); Hartmut Lehmann and Guenther Roth, eds., *Weber's Protestant Ethic: Origins, Evidence, Context* (New York: Cambridge University Press, 1993); Stephen Innes, *Creating the Commonwealth: The Economic Culture of Puritan New England* (New York: W. W. Norton, 1995); Stanley Lieberson, "Einstein, Renoir, and Greeley: Some Thoughts about Evidence in Sociology," *American Sociological Review* 57 (1992), 1–15.

when capitalism arose in the West, a number of structural factors existed that could have led to a similar development in the Orient. First, there was a great deal of internal commerce and trade with other nations. Second, because of the establishment and maintenance (for more than 1,200 years) of nationwide competitive examinations, there was an unusual degree of equality of opportunity in the process of status attainment. Third, the society was generally stable and peaceful, although Weber was clearly too accepting of the myth of the "unchanging China." Fourth, China had many large urban centers, and geographical mobility was a relatively common occurrence. Fifth, there were relatively few formal restrictions on economic activity. Finally, a number of technological developments in China were more advanced than those in Europe at the same time (the use of gunpowder, knowledge of astronomy, book printing, etc.). As Weber noted, all these structural factors could have aided in the development of a Chinese version of modern capitalism.

He emphasized, however, that Chinese social structure also displayed a number of characteristics that had clearly inhibited the widespread development of any form of capitalism in that part of the world. First, although the Chinese possessed an abundance of precious metals, especially silver, an adequate monetary system had never developed. Second, because of the early unification and centralization of the Chinese empire, cities never became autonomous political units. As a result, the development of local capitalistic enterprises was inhibited. Third, Chinese society was characterized by the use of "substantive ethical law" rather than calculable legal procedure. As a result, legal judgments were made considering the particular characteristics of the participants and sacred tradition rather than by the equal imposition of common standards. Finally, the Chinese bureaucracy comprised classically learned persons rather than technically trained experts. Thus, the examinations regulating status attainment "tested whether the candidate's mind was thoroughly steeped in literature and whether or not he possessed the ways of thought suitable to a cultural man."[59] Hence, the idea of the trained expert was foreign to the Chinese experience.

In sum, according to Weber, all these characteristics of Chinese social structure inhibited the development of an oriental form of modern capitalism. Nonetheless, the examples noted do suggest that

---

[59]Weber, *The Religion of China*, 156.

such a development remained possible. Yet Weber argued that the rise of capitalism as an economic system was quite unlikely in either China or India, for he found no evidence of patterns of religious beliefs that could be compatible with the spirit of capitalism. Moreover, he believed that without the transformative power of religion, the rise of new cultural values was not likely. In China before this century, the religion of the dominant classes, the bureaucrats, was Confucianism. Weber characterized Confucianism by noting that it had no concept of sin but only of faults resulting from deficient education. Furthermore, Confucianism had no metaphysic, and thus no concern with the origin of the world or with the possibility of an afterlife, and hence no tension between sacred and secular law. According to Weber, Confucianism was a rational religion concerned with events in this world but with a peculiarly individualistic emphasis. Good Confucians were less interested in the state of society than with their own propriety, as indicated by their development as educated persons and by their pious relations with others (especially their parents). In Weber's words, the educated Chinese person "controls all his activities, physical gestures, and movements as well, with politeness and with grace in accordance with the status mores and the commands of 'propriety.'"[60] Rather than seeking salvation in the next world, the Confucian accepted this world as given and merely desired to behave prudently.

On this basis, Weber asserted that Confucianism was not very likely to result in an Asian form of the culture of capitalism. He made a similar argument about Hinduism 4 years later in *The Religion of India*. Thus, by means of these comparative studies, Weber tried to show logically not only why Protestantism was associated with the rise of the culture of capitalism in the West but also why other religions could not have stimulated similar developments in other parts of the world.[61]

Weber's Outline of the Social System

In all his work, Weber employed, at least implicitly, a vision of society as a social system that consists of three analytically separable dimensions: (1) culture, (2) social structure (patterns of social action), and

---

[60]Ibid., 156.

[61]Subsequent events, however, have shown that Confucianism is congenial to capitalism. See Peter M. Berger, *The Capitalist Revolution* (New York: Basic Books, 1986).

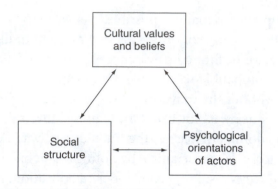

Figure 9.7   Weber's Model of the Social System

(3) psychological orientations (see Figure 9.7). Cultural values and beliefs, patterned ways of acting in the world, and the psychological states are all reciprocally related.[62] The *Protestant Ethic* provides one illustration of this model. Weber also had to consider the extent to which both social structure and people's psychological orientations were reciprocally related to the cultural values he was analyzing. Thus, he argued that the religious beliefs characteristic of the new faiths fundamentally influenced patterns of social action among people—not only among the Puritans but also among those who encountered the underlying beliefs of these faiths. Puritan values spread in part because people found them to be congenial to their own secular ambitions as they developed during a time of great change. Hence, as people adopted new beliefs and values, they altered their daily lives; conversely, as individuals began living in new ways (often because they were forced to), they changed their fundamental beliefs and values. Thus, historically, new patterns of social action reinforced the new values that had arisen.

Weber, however, concentrated on the Puritans themselves, describing the psychological consequences that their beliefs must have had for their daily lives. Because of their uncertainty and isolation, people looked for signs of their salvation and found them in the ability to work hard and maintain their faith. Hence, the Puritans'

---

[62]The basis for our interpretation is Talcott Parsons, "Introduction," in *The Theory of Social and Economic Organization*, ed. Max Weber (Glencoe, IL: Free Press, 1947), 3–86. Some scholars agree with Parsons's interpretation; see Mommsen, *The Age of Bureaucracy*, 1–21. Others disagree with it; see Reinhard Bendix, *Max Weber: An Intellectual Portrait* (Garden City, NY: Doubleday, 1962).

psychological needs led them to historically new and unique patterns of social action characterized not only by hard work (medieval peasants certainly worked as hard) but also by a methodical pursuit of worldly goods. The result was the secularization of Puritan religious values and their transformation into what he called the spirit of capitalism. Hence, it is possible to extrapolate from Weber's analysis a set of generic factors—culture, social structure, and psychological orientations—that are taken today as the fundamental features of social organization.

Weber's implicit model of the most general components of social organization has proved to be of tremendous significance in the development of sociology. For example, virtually all introductory sociology textbooks (which we will use here as a rough indicator of the state of the field) now contain a series of chapters, usually located at the beginning, titled something like "Culture," "Social Structure" or "Society," and "Personality and Socialization." The reason for this practice is that these topics provide an essential conceptual orientation to the discipline of sociology. Weber's model, then, serves as a heuristic device rather than as a dynamic analysis of the process of interaction. It can, however, lead to such an analysis—which is all Weber intended. Thus, the model is an essential first step in constructing a set of concepts that would be useful in describing and, hence, understanding modern societies.

Critical Conclusions

Weber did not believe that timeless, universal laws could ever be developed because so much that had occurred in history was the result of chance events. Even without the ability to conduct inquiry in the same way as in the natural sciences, Weber still wanted to be scientific and objective. Moreover, he sought to do more than write historical descriptions; he also wanted to provide a methodology for more abstract and analytical statements. The result was a strange compromise: the study of historical causes through the vehicle of ideal types. For each cause and effect, Weber constructs an ideal type of its essential characteristics, and some of these are among sociology's more enduring descriptions of basic social forms. In this way, Weber could be more abstract and analytical than historians, but he would not posit laws of human organization. Too much of history, he believed, was the result of random or chance confluence of events. Thus, we are given many rather ponderous descriptions of basic relationships among phenomena portrayed as ideal types, but in following Weber's methodology, we are kept from asking the most interesting question of any science: Are some of these relationships so generic and basic that they might constitute sociological laws?

Methodology aside, Weber's substantive works range widely. We have tried to give them more coherence than they actually reveal by emphasizing the theme of rationalization. Much like Herbert Spencer's work, which also is highly descriptive, Weber's presentation of details is often so convoluted that the main line of his argument becomes difficult to follow. We suspect that Weber came to the theme of rationalization rather late in his work, and he either tried to push and shove earlier works into this theme or, in many cases, did not bother. Although the result was fascinating, though dense, essays on many diverse topics, these do not hang together as did those of Herbert Spencer, Karl Marx, and Émile Durkheim. As a consequence, it is hard to extract a general theory from Weber; rather, what emerge are rich descriptions, ideal types of empirical cases, and complex causal statements on many topics without a general model to guide us. Thus, we will simply have to live with the scattered character of Weberian sociology, taking from it what we find useful.[63]

---

[63]For a recent compilation of the breadth of Weber's scholarship, see *Max Weber: The Confrontation with Modernity*, ed. Stephen Kalberg (Oxford, UK: Blackwell).

CHAPTER 10

The Origin and Context of Georg Simmel's Thought

Biographical Influences on Simmel's Thought

Simmel's Marginality

Georg Simmel was born in 1858 at the very center of Berlin.[1] His father, a successful Jewish businessman, had converted to Christianity; but still Simmel's Jewish background haunted him throughout his career. Simmel's father died when Simmel was young, and a friend of the family was appointed his guardian. Simmel appears to have had an emotionally distant relationship with his mother, and so it is reasonable to conclude that he never had any strong ties to his family.

Simmel's work was greatly influenced by this marginality not only to his family but also to the academic establishment in Germany.[2] His marginality, as we will see in the next chapter, helps account for the brilliance of Simmel's analysis of the individual in differentiated and

---

[1] This sketch of Georg Simmel's biography draws from Lewis A. Coser's *Masters of Sociological Thought* (New York: Harcourt Brace Jovanovich, 1971), 177–217. See also *Georg Simmel*, ed. Lewis A. Coser (Englewood Cliffs, NJ: Prentice Hall, 1965); Kurt H. Wolff, "Introduction," in *The Sociology of Georg Simmel* (New York: Free Press, 1950); *Georg Simmel, 1858–1918*, ed. Kurt H. Wolff (Columbus: Ohio State University Press, 1959); and Nicholas Spykman, *The Social Theory of Georg Simmel* (Chicago: University of Chicago Press, 1925).

[2] Coser, *Masters of Sociological Thought.*

cross-cutting social relationships, for there can be little doubt that he was on the edge of various intellectual worlds. It is difficult to know how embittered he was by this borderline existence. Indeed, in contrast with others of this period who tended to see modern and differentiated social structures as harmful to the individual, Simmel stressed the liberating effects of marginality. He believed that the differentiation of structure, the elaboration of markets, and the detached involvement of people in rational bureaucratic structures gave them options, choices, and opportunities not available in traditional societies. Whether or not he was justifying his own position in this argument can never be known, but one point is clear: He did not conceptualize modern society in the severe pathological terms of Karl Marx (who stressed oppression and alienation), of Émile Durkheim (who worried over anomie and egoism), or of Max Weber (who warned that the process of rationalization trapped individuals in the "iron cage" of bureaucracy). In any case, Simmel's career had a tragic quality, despite its many points of success and accomplishment.

Simmel's Intellectual Career

After graduating from secondary school, Simmel studied philosophy at the University of Berlin, where he received his doctorate in 1881. His thesis was on Immanuel Kant,[3] who, as we will see shortly, exerted enormous influence on Simmel's approach to sociological analysis. At the time of Simmel's graduation, Germany in general and Berlin in particular were undergoing a remarkable transition. The nation as a whole was industrializing in record time, and within Simmel's adult lifetime, Germany surpassed both England and France in productivity, lagging behind only the United States. This rapid industrialization revealed a critical disjuncture: Though the bourgeoisie brought about rapid economic growth, it failed to advance its claims to power, which remained in the hands of the old feudal elite.[4] This tension between the old and the new produced the

---

[3]The title of his dissertation was "The Nature of Matter according to Kant's Physical Monadology," and in this early confrontation with Kant's ideas can be seen the seeds of Simmel's "formal sociology."

[4]Ralf Dahrendorf, "The New Germanys—Restoration, Revolution, and Reconstruction," *Encounter* 23 (April 1964), 50.

disastrous policies that led to World War I and its aftermath, which ultimately created the conditions for the rise of Hitler and Nazism.

Within this broader and foreboding national context, intellectual life flourished, especially in Berlin, which in five decades grew from a city of 500,000 to 4 million on the eve of World War I. Even in this prosperous intellectual milieu, however, there was a duality between freedom and authoritarian constraint. In the lively counterculture and intellectual life around the university and in the city itself, there was a vibrant mix of activity. Within the university system, which in the earlier decades of the nineteenth century had served as the model for the research-oriented American universities, there was a conservative and at times authoritarian undercurrent. The university system was prosperous and, as a result, caught in the dilemma between encouraging academic freedom and open expression, on one side, and maintaining its comfortable position in a social and political climate charged with the tension between the capitalist bourgeoisie and the semifeudal political system, on the other side.

Many scholars did great work within this system—Max Weber being the best example in sociology. Others, especially Jews, were denied complete access to the academic system or, as was the case with many, were pushed to the provincial universities outside the main urban centers. Not just Jews but others who revealed more radical political sympathies that might disrupt the status quo also suffered this fate.[5]

Simmel was caught in this conflicting current, and early in his career, he decided to stay in Berlin and hope for the best. The result was that he became a *privatdozent*, or unpaid lecturer, who lived off student fees. The more typical pattern of this time was for academics to move from one university to another, slowly working their way into major university positions.

Perhaps Simmel saw that, as a Jew, he had the cards stacked against him, but the results of his decision in 1885 to assume a marginal position and remain in Berlin were profound. He became a popular lecturer who attracted a large lay and academic following. He lectured on a broad range of subjects—from sociology and social psychology to logic, philosophy, and ethics. But this popular success appears to

---

[5]Wilhelm Dilthey, Heinrich Rickert, and Wilhelm Windelband were among those who blocked Simmel's advancement. Despite the differences in their approach to sociology, Weber strongly supported Simmel. See John Patrick Diggins, *Max Weber: Politics and the Spirit of Tragedy* (New York: Basic Books, 1995), 138.

have antagonized the academic establishment. His popularity made many jealous, and his breadth and brilliance threatened narrow specialists. The result was that, in addition to the undercurrent of anti-Semitism, a sense of threat and envy as well as an intolerance of cross-disciplinary scholarship worked against Simmel. Moreover, his style affronted the academic establishment in many specific ways. For example, he never documented his works with footnotes and scholarly quotations in detail; he jumped from topic to topic, never pursuing a subject in great depth (except perhaps his brilliant work on *The Philosophy of Money*). He also wrote essays for popular magazines and newspapers, a tactic that always, even now, antagonizes traditional academics. Indeed, he appears to have gone out of his way to annoy the academic establishment.

In addition to his popularity among the broader intellectual and artistic community, Simmel enjoyed much academic success. With Weber and Ferdinand Tönnies, he was a cofounder of the German Society for Sociology, and his works were widely read, cited, and respected by the first generation of sociologists. Despite his marginal academic status, he did not suffer financially because his guardian left him a considerable fortune. After his marriage in 1890, he lived a comfortable upper-middle-class existence. Given his fame as a lecturer and his active association with artists, critics, commentators, journalists, and writers, Simmel enjoyed a stimulating and full life.

He still endured the stigma and frustration of being a well-known scholar and intellectual figure without a real academic position. For 15 years, Simmel remained a private lecturer, despite the efforts of friends such as Weber to secure a full-time position for him. In 1901, he was given the status of honorary adjunct professor at the University of Berlin, which confirmed his position as an outsider who was neither paid nor entitled to take part in the administrative affairs of the university. Such an appointment was, in reality, an insult for Simmel, who was now a scholar of world fame, having written six books and dozens of articles that had been translated into English, French, Italian, Polish, and Russian.

When Simmel finally received a regular academic appointment in 1914, it was at a provincial university in Strasbourg on the border between France and Germany. Moreover, he was now 56 years old, well over a decade past the normative time for promotion to full professor. To top off the frustrations in his career, he arrived at Strasbourg just at the outbreak of World War I. Border university life was suspended during the war, thereby denying him the opportunity to lecture. And, in 1915, Simmel failed in his last effort to secure a chair at the University of Heidelberg. Three years later he died of cancer.

This futility and marginality in the face of world fame must surely have contributed to Simmel's style of scholarship: He maintained a foot in both philosophy and sociology while sustaining a commitment to both formal analytical analysis and social commentary on events and topical questions.[6] The result is a lack of in-depth scholarship on sociological issues; instead, he analyzed specific sociological topics with flashes of insight and sophistication, only to move on to yet another, often disconnected topic. His most in-depth works, particularly *The Philosophy of Money*, are so heavily imbued with philosophical commentary that the sociological theory in them can easily go unnoticed.

Despite this topical character to Simmel's work, his sociology has two important themes. First, he was concerned, as were all social theorists of this early period in sociology, with the process of differentiation and its effects on the individual. Second, the methodological unity in his work revolves around trying to extract the underlying essence and form of the particular empirical topics. Moreover, although, he often shifted the substantive content of his analysis, he always sought to discover the underlying structure of social interaction and organization that linked diverse substantive areas. These themes emerged from personal and intellectual contact with a number of thinkers—particularly Max Weber, Herbert Spencer, Immanuel Kant, and Karl Marx.

Intellectual Influences on Simmel's Thought

A Note on Simmel and Weber

Simmel's sociological writings span the same three decades, 1890 to 1920, as those of his German colleague and friend, Max Weber. Despite working in similar social and cultural environments, their

---

[6]We have not mentioned Simmel's sudden burst of patriotism during the war because it is so embarrassing: Gone is the cool and analytical Simmel, and in his place is the passionate patriot. As Coser emphasizes, the latter part of Simmel's career was marked by a romantic emotionalism somewhat similar to that of Auguste Comte, who, near the end, suffered much the same fate as Simmel (see Chapter 2 of this book).

respective orientations to sociology were rather dissimilar, partly because they were trained differently and, thus, responded to somewhat different influences. Weber eschewed the development of abstract laws because he believed that such theoretical statements could not uncover the significance of those historical phenomena in which he was most interested. In contrast, Simmel was a philosopher as well as a sociologist; his published works include books and articles on diverse figures such as the philosophers Arthur Schopenhauer, Friedrich Wilhelm Nietzsche, and Kant; the writer Johann Goethe; and the painter Rembrandt. In addition, Simmel considered morals, ethics, aesthetics, and many other topics from a philosophical vantage point. As might be expected, his brand of sociology is quite different from Weber's. After an early dalliance with Spencer and some elements of social Darwinism, Simmel's mature works reflect his adaptation of some of Kant's philosophical doctrines to the study of human society. For Simmel, social processes that constitute organized and stable structures affect action in systematic and predictable ways. Hence, unlike Weber, Simmel held that sociology should focus on the development of timelessly valid laws of social organization.

Simmel and Weber were alike in at least one respect, however. Both felt compelled to react to the ideological and theoretical challenge posed by Marxism as it existed at the turn of the century. Although this interest is more central to Weber's sociology than to Simmel's, the latter's analysis is a sociologically sophisticated rejection of Marx and Marxism.

Herbert Spencer, Social Darwinism, and Simmel's Thought

Like most of the other classical social theorists, Simmel wanted to understand the nature of modern industrial societies. The title of his first sociological treatise, *Social Differentiation*, published in 1890, suggests immediately the fundamental change that he saw: Modern societies are much more differentiated (or complex) than those of the past.[7] Like Spencer (see Chapter 5), Simmel saw this change in

---

[7]Georg Simmel, *Über sociale Differenzierung* (Leipzig: Duncker & Humbolt, 1890). Although most of this book remains untranslated, two chapters, "Differentiation and the Principle of Saving Energy" and "The Intersection of Social Spheres," do appear in *Georg Simmel: Sociologist and European*, trans. Peter Laurence (New York: Barnes & Noble, 1976).

evolutionary terms and as an indication of human progress. Indeed, he labeled it an "upward development." Furthermore, just as Spencer often used organismic analogies to illustrate his argument, so did Simmel. For example, in *Social Differentiation*, he argued that just as a more complex organism could save energy in relation to the environment and use that energy to perform more difficult and complex tasks, so could a more highly differentiated society.[8] Like Spencer, Simmel never confused biological analogies with social facts, partly because he also illustrated his arguments with many other kinds of analogies and examples. Although some of Simmel's later works do not reveal much systematic concern with either the problem of evolution or the historical transition to industrialization, they display a lasting interest in understanding the structure of modern, differentiated societies and in showing how people's participation in complex social systems affects their behavior.

The evolutionary discussion in *Social Differentiation* also shows a less attractive side to the young Simmel because he embraced some of the more questionable aspects of social Darwinism that were current during the late nineteenth century. For example, he insisted on "the hereditary character of the criminal inclination" and even protested against "the preservation of the weak, who will transmit their inferiority to future generations."[9] However, his mature writings betray no trace of such views. In fact, although he generally did not comment on political events in a partisan manner, his analyses of the poor, of women, and of working people all suggest a sympathetic understanding of their plight.[10] In all these cases, his discussion reflects a more general attempt at focusing on the consequences of social differentiation in modern societies. In particular, he was concerned with *the form* of differentiated social structures and how their dynamics affect individuals independently of their purposes—a point of emphasis that Simmel took from Immanuel Kant.

---

[8]Simmel, "Differentiation and the Principle of Saving Energy."

[9]Paul Honigsheim, "The Time and Thought of the Young Simmel," in *Essays on Sociology, Philosophy and Aesthetics by Georg Simmel et al.*, ed. Kurt Wolff (New York: Harper & Row, 1965), 170.

[10]See George Simmel, "The Poor," in *Georg Simmel on Individuality and Social Forms* (Chicago: University of Chicago Press, 1971), 150–178. On working people and women, see Georg Simmel, *Conflict and the Web of Group Affiliations* (New York: Free Press, 1955); also Lewis A. Coser, "Georg Simmel's Neglected Contributions to the Sociology of Women," *Signs* 2 (Summer 1977), 869–876.

Immanuel Kant and Simmel's Thought

Kant's Basic Ideas

Kant did not finish his most significant work until the age of 51. But that book, *The Critique of Pure Reason*, published in 1781, stimulated a revolution in philosophy.[11] The book is an investigation of the potential for "pure reason" that exists apart from the mundane and disorganized sense impressions that human beings experience. Kant's definition of *pure reason* is crucial. By this term, he meant that cognitive capacities and forms of thought exist independently of, or before, sense experience, implying that pure reason is thought that is inherent to the structure of the mind. After defining the issue in this way, Kant concluded that all human conceptions of the external world are products of the activity of the mind, which shapes the unformed and chaotic succession of sense impressions into a conceptual unity that can be understood as scientific laws.

Whereas previous philosophers, such as John Locke and David Hume, had assumed that material phenomena are inherently organized and that human beings' sensations of objects and events in the world merely reflect that organization, Kant held that neither supposition was true. Rather, he asserted that people's sensations are intrinsically chaotic, reflecting nothing more than the endless succession of sights, smells, sounds, odors, and other stimuli that, in and of themselves, are disorganized and meaningless. He contended that the mind transformed this chaos of sense impressions into meaningful perceptions through a process he called the *transcendental aesthetic*. Simmel summarized this part of Kant's philosophy by observing that human sensations are "given forms and connections which are not inherent in them but which are imposed on them by the knowing mind as such."[12] This transformation of disorganized sensations into organized perceptions is accomplished by two fundamental "categories," or forms—space and time—that are inherent parts of the mind. In Kant's view, space and time are not things perceived but modes of perceiving that exist prior to, or independently of, our knowledge of the world; they are elements of pure reason. Only by using these

---

[11]Immanuel Kant, *The Critique of Pure Reason* (New York: Macmillan, 1929). For a more complete analysis, see T. E. Wilkerson, *Kant's Critique of Pure Reason: A Commentary for Students* (New York: Oxford University Press, 1976).

[12]Georg Simmel, "The Nature of Philosophy," in *Essays on Sociology*, 291.

categories are human beings able to transform the chaotic sensations that they receive from the external world into systematic perceptions.

Yet merely being able to perceive objects and events is not enough, for people's perceptions are not spontaneously organized either. Rather, like sensations, perceptions are experienced as confused sequences of observations. Thus, Kant emphasized that pure reason aimed at the establishment of higher forms of knowledge: general truths that are independent of experience. These are the laws of science, truths that are abstract and absolute. Hence, in a process Kant called *transcendental logic*, the mind transforms perceptual knowledge into conceptual knowledge—for example, the transformation of the observation of a falling apple into the law of gravity or (on a different level) the transformation of observations of action during conflict into laws stating the consequences of social conflict for human behavior. Kant held that the mind uses a set of preconceived "categories," or forms, by which to arrange perceptions. For example, the ideas of cause, unity, reciprocal relations, necessity, and contingency are modes of conceptualizing empirical processes that are inherent to the mind; like space and time, they are elements of pure reason. In Simmel's words, it is only through the activity of the mind that human perceptions "become what we call nature: a meaningful, intelligible coherence in which the diversity of things appears as a principled unity, knitted together by laws."[13] In this regard, Kant also insisted that the manner in which observations are conceptualized always depends on the purposes of the mind. For example, consider a system of thought, such as Charles Darwin's theory of evolution or Marx's theory of revolution. Kant said that these means of conceptualizing empirical data (perceptions) reveal the purposeful activity of the mind, for in neither case are the objects or events in the world prearranged in the manner conceptualized by the theory. Thus, over the long run, scientific knowledge is one result of the existence of pure reason as an intrinsic characteristic of human beings.

In this context, it is important to remember that Kant never denied the existence of the material world; he merely declared that human knowledge of external phenomena occurs through the forms imposed on it by the active mind. Put differently, the empirical world is an orderly place because the categories of thought organize our sensations, organize our perceptions, and organize our conceptions to

---

[13]Ibid., 291.

produce systematic scientific knowledge. Nonetheless, although Kant contended that such knowledge is absolute, he also indicated that it is limited to the field of actual experience. Therefore, he believed that it is impossible to know what objects and events are "ultimately like" apart from the receptivity of human senses. One of the most important implications of this point of view is that attempts at discovering the nature of ultimate reality, either through religion or science, are impossible. In Kant's phrase, "understanding can never go beyond the limits of sensibility."

Simmel's Adaptation of Kant's Ideas

The link between Kant and Simmel is most clearly explained in the latter's essay "How Is Society Possible?" which was originally inserted into the first chapter as an excursus in *Sociology: Studies in the Forms of Sociation*.[14] According to Simmel, the basic question in Kant's philosophy is "How is nature possible?" That is, how is human knowledge of nature (the external world) possible? Kant answered this query by positing the existence of certain a priori categories that observers use to shape the chaotic sensations they receive into conceptual knowledge. This point of view means that when the elements of nature are conceptualized in some manner, their unity depends entirely on the observer.

In contrast, the unity of society is both experienced by the participants and observed by sociologists. In Simmel's words, "the unity of society needs no observer. It is directly realized by its own elements [human beings] because these elements are themselves conscious and synthesizing units."[15] Thus, as people conduct their daily lives, they are absorbed in innumerable specific relationships with one another—economic, political, social, and familial, for example—and these connections give people an amorphous sense of their unity, a feeling that they are part of an ongoing and stable social structure. Weber believed that because people experience and attribute meaning to the social structures in which they participate, neither the methods nor the goals of the natural sciences are appropriate for the social sciences. So, as we saw in the last chapter, he formulated a version of sociology oriented toward the scientific understanding of historical processes.

---

[14]Georg Simmel, "How Is Society Possible?" in *Essays on Sociology*, 337–356. We have taken the liberty of translating the German title into English.

[15]Ibid., 338.

Simmel took a different view, one that has had lasting consequences for the emergence of sociological theory. Based on his study of Kant, Simmel argued that social structures (which he called *forms of interaction*) systematically influence people's behavior before and independently of their specific purposes. He used this argument to show that theoretical principles of social action could be used as proof despite the complications inherent because human beings' own experiences are the objects of study. As he put it, the entire contents of *Sociology: Studies in the Forms of Sociation* constitute an inquiry "into the processes—those which, ultimately, reside in individuals—that condition the existence of individuals in society."[16] More generally, as will be described in the next chapter, Simmel's sociology is oriented toward identifying those basic social forms—conflict, group affiliation, exchange, size, inequality, and space—that influence social action regardless of the intentions of the participants. Because these forms constitute the structure (or, as Kant would say, the "categories") within which people seek to realize their goals, knowledge of the manner in which they affect social behavior can lead to theory. In this sense, then, Simmelian sociology is thoroughly Kantian in orientation, but it deviates from Kant by seeing social forms as operating *independently* of transcendental logic or categories of the mind.

Karl Marx and Simmel's Thought

Some of Simmel's sociology constitutes a critique of Marx's major work, *Capital*, as well as a rejection of his basic revolutionary goal: the establishment of a cooperative society where people would be free to develop their human potential.[17] *Capital* is an attempt at demonstrating that the value of commodities (including human beings) results from the labor power necessary to produce them; Marx called this the labor theory of value. In *The Philosophy of Money* (1900), Simmel rejected the labor theory of value by arguing more generally that people in all societies place value on items based on their relative desirability and scarcity.[18] Simmel believed that he could better account for the value that individuals attribute to commodities in different societies (capitalist as well as socialist) by showing how

---

[16]Ibid., 340.

[17]Karl Marx, *Capital* (New York: International, 1967).

[18]Georg Simmel, *The Philosophy of Money* (Boston: Routledge & Kegan Paul, 1978).

cultural and structural phenomena systematically influence what is both scarce and desired. In this way, then, he undercut the theoretical basis for Marx's analysis.

Simmel also rejected Marx's argument by focusing on the importance of money as a medium of exchange. In *Capital*, Marx tried to show that one of the necessary consequences of capitalism was people's alienation from one another and from the commodities that they produced. In this regard, he emphasized that actors have no control over those activities that distinguish them, as human beings, from other animals. Simmel approached the problem of alienation by simply recognizing that in any highly differentiated society, some people are inevitably going to be alienated. Indeed, he saw the decline in personal and emotional contact among humans as more fundamental than the lack of control by people of their own activities. Apparently, he believed that in most societies, most individuals lack control over their daily lives. Having recognized the inevitability of alienation, however, Simmel went on to oppose Marx by arguing that the dominance of money as a medium of exchange in modern social systems reduces alienation. In contrast with Marx, Simmel argued that the widespread use of money allows exchanges between people who are spatially separated from one another, thereby creating multiple social ties and lowering the level of alienation. In addition, he suggested that the generalized acceptance of money in exchanges increases social solidarity because it signifies a relatively high degree of trust in the stability and future of the society. Finally, he concluded that the dominance of money allows individuals to pursue a wider diversity of activities than is possible in barter or mixed economies and hence gives them vastly increased options for self-expression. The result of this last factor, of course, is that people have greater control over their daily lives in money economies. As an aside, Simmel's explanation of the consequences of money in modern societies is a good example of how social processes "condition the existence of individuals in society" independently of their specific purposes. In this case, the specific ways in which money is used are less important, sociologically, than are its effects on the general nature and form of human relationships in systems where money is the modal medium of social exchange.

Finally, Simmel also discussed Marx's formulation of the problem of alienation in his essay on the functions of social conflict. In this context, Simmel reasoned that individuals probably have the best chance of developing their full human capacities in a competitive rather than a cooperative society:

> Once the narrow and naive solidarity of primitive social conditions yielded to decentralization (which was bound to have been the immediate result of the quantitative enlargement of the group), man's effort toward man, his adaptation to the other, seems possible only at the price of competition, that is, of the simultaneous fight *against* a fellow-man *for* a third one—*against* whom, for that matter, he may well compete in some other relationship *for* the former. Given the breadth and individualization of society, many kinds of interest, which eventually hold the group together throughout its members, seem to come alive and stay alive only when the urgency and requirements of the competitive struggle force them upon the individual.[19]

Simmel did not deny, of course, that competition could have "poisonous, divisive, destructive effects"; rather, he simply noted that these liabilities must be evaluated in light of the positive consequences of competition. Like money, Simmel contended, competition gives people more freedom to satisfy their needs, and in this sense, citizens of a society that is competitively organized are probably less alienated. In addition, as indicated in the quotation, he believed that competition is a form of conflict that promotes social solidarity in differentiated social systems because people establish ties with one another that involve a relatively constant "concentration on the will and feeling of fellow-men"—an argument that also implies a lessening of alienation. Finally, Simmel indicated that competition is an important means of creating values in society, a process that occurs as human beings produce objective values (e.g., commodities) for purposes of exchange; in this way, they attain satisfaction of their own subjective needs and desires. This argument not only suggests that competitive societies display less alienation than do noncompetitive ones but also implies that Marx's revolutionary goal—a fully cooperative and cohesive society—is impractical in modern, industrialized, highly differentiated social systems. On this basis, Simmel rejected socialist and communist experiments inspired by Marxist thought. He believed that they were attempts at institutionalizing,

---

[19]Simmel, *Conflict*, 6.

indeed enforcing, cooperative relationships among people to prevent the waste of energy and inequalities that inevitably occur in a competitive environment. However, he insisted that even though such results seemed positive, they could only be "brought about through a central [political] directive which from the start organizes all [people] for their mutual interpenetration and supplementation."[20] He implied that an end to alienation would not and could not occur in such an authoritarian social context. Thus, although his works do not represent a long-term debate with Marx, as was perhaps true for Weber, Simmel addressed the same issues as Marx and other early theorists—issues such as the properties of social differentiation, inequality, power, conflict, cooperation, and the procedures for understanding the nature of the social world.

The Enigmatic Simmel

In many ways, Simmel's work remains an enigma in modern sociology. Bits and pieces have exerted enormous influence on modern sociological theory; yet it is difficult to view him as inspiring a "school" of thought, as had Marx, Weber, Durkheim, and Mead. Perhaps Simmel's outsider role in the German academic establishment kept him from developing cohorts of students who could carry on his "formal sociology." The result is that his sociology is not, even now when the early masters are the subject of much commentary, fully appreciated for its breadth and brilliance.

---

[20]Ibid., 72–73.

CHAPTER 11

The Sociology of Georg Simmel

Until late in his career, Georg Simmel was never able to hold a regular academic position. As a Jew, he was subject to discrimination, and, despite efforts by Max Weber, most of his career was spent as a private scholar, lecturing to lay audiences for a fee. This marginal position between the lay and academic intellectual worlds may have prevented him from developing a coherent theoretical system. Instead, what emerges are flashes of insight into the basic dynamics of a wide variety of phenomena. Moreover, Simmel had a tendency to deal with the same topics repeatedly, each time revising and updating his thinking. If much of his work appears to be a series of lectures, that is just what it often was: lectures that prod and stimulate, often without detailed and scholarly annotation. Yet with each passing decade since the 1950s, the importance of Simmel's vision for sociology has been increasingly recognized. For despite the somewhat disjointed character of his life's work, his methodology for developing sociological theory and the substance of his insights into the form of modern society present a reasonably coherent program of sociological analysis.

Simmel's Methodological Approach to the Study of Society

In an essay titled "The Problem of Sociology," Simmel concluded as early as 1894 that an exploration of the basic and generic forms of interaction offered the only viable subject for the nascent discipline of sociology.[1] In Chapter 1 of *Sociology: Studies in the Forms of Sociation*, written in 1908, he reformulated and reaffirmed his thoughts on this issue.[2] In 1918, he revised his thinking again in one of his last works, *Fundamental Problems of Sociology*.[3] In what follows, we rely most heavily on this final brief sketch because it represents his most mature statement.

Simmel began the *Fundamental Problems* by lamenting that "the first difficulty which arises if one wants to make a tenable statement about the science of sociology is that its claim to be a science is not undisputed." In Germany after the turn of the century, many scholars still denied that sociology constituted a legitimate science; and to retain their power within the university system, these critics wanted to stop sociology from becoming an academic field. Partly for these reasons, it was proposed that sociology should be merely a label to refer to all the social sciences dealing with specific content areas—such as economics, political science, and linguistics. This tactic was a ruse, of course, for Simmel (and many others) recognized that the existing disciplines had already divided up the study of human life and that nothing would be "gained by throwing their sum total into a pot and sticking a new label on it: 'sociology.'"[4] To combat this strategy and to justify sociology as an academic field of study, Simmel argued that it was necessary for the new discipline to develop a unique and "unambiguous content, dominated by one, methodologically

---

[1]The translation appeared the following year. See Georg Simmel, "The Problem of Sociology," *Annals of the American Academy of Political and Social Science* 6 (1895), 412–423.

[2]Georg Simmel, "The Problem of Sociology," in *Essays on Sociology, Philosophy and Aesthetics by Georg Simmel et al.*, ed. and trans. Kurt Wolff (New York: Harper & Row, 1959), 310–336. This is Chapter 1 of Simmel's *Sociology: Studies in the Forms of Sociation* (1908). This book, which is Simmel's major work, has not been translated into English, but portions appear in various edited collections. See Note 17.

[3]Simmel, *Fundamental Problems of Sociology*, appears as Part 1 of *The Sociology of Georg Simmel*, trans. Kurt Wolff (New York: Free Press, 1950), 3–86.

[4]Ibid., 4.

certain, problem idea."[5] His discussion is organized around three questions: (1) What is society? (2) How should sociology study society? (3) What are the problem areas of sociology?

What Is Society?

Simmel's answer to the first question is very simple: "Society" exists when "interaction among human beings" occurs with enough frequency and intensity so that people mutually affect one another and organize themselves into groups or other social units. Thus, he used the term *society* rather loosely to refer to any pattern of social organization in which he was interested. As he put it, society refers to relatively

> permanent interactions only. More specifically, the interactions we have in mind when we talk about "society" are crystallized as definable, consistent structures such as the state and the family, the guild and the church, social classes and organizations based on common interests.[6]

The significance of defining society in this way lies in the recognition that patterns of social organization are constructed from basic processes of interaction. Hence, interaction, per se, becomes a significant area of study. Sociology, in his words, is founded on "the recognition that man in his whole nature and in all his manifestations is determined by the circumstances of living in interaction with other men."[7] Thus, as an academic discipline,

> sociology asks what happens to men and by what rules do they behave, not insofar as they unfold their understandable individual existences in their totalities, but insofar as they form groups and are determined by their group existence because of interaction.[8]

---

[5]This remark is from the preface to *Sociology: Studies in the Forms of Sociation;* it is quoted in Kurt Wolff's introduction to *The Sociology of Georg Simmel*, xxvi. For another review and analysis of Simmel's methodology, see Donald N. Levine, "Simmel and Parsons Reconsidered," *American Journal of Sociology* 96 (1991), 1097–1116, "Simmel as a Resource for Sociological Metatheory," *Sociological Theory* 7 (1989), 161–174, and "Sociology's Quest for the Classics: The Case of Simmel," in *The Future of Sociological Classics*, ed. Buford Rhea (London: Allen & Unwin, 1981), 60–80.

[6]Simmel, *Fundamental Problems*, 9.

[7]Ibid., 12.

[8]Ibid., 11.

With this statement, Simmel gave sociology a unique and unambiguous subject matter: the basic forms of social interaction.

How Should Sociology Study Society?

Simmel's answer to the second question is again very simple: Sociologists should begin their study of society by distinguishing between *form* and *content*. Subsequent scholars have often misunderstood his use of these particular terms, mainly because their Kantian origin has been ignored.[9] What must be remembered to understand these terms is that Simmel's writings are pervaded by analogies, with the distinction between form and content being drawn from an analogy to geometry. Geometry investigates the spatial forms of material objects; although these spatial forms might have material contents of various sorts, the process of abstraction in geometry involves ignoring their specific contents in favor of an emphasis on the common features, or forms, of the objects under examination. Simmel simply applied this geometric distinction between form and content to the study of society to suggest how sociology could investigate social processes independently of their content. The distinction between the forms and contents of interaction offers the only "possibility for a special science of society" because it is a means of focusing on the generic basic processes by which people establish social relations and social structures, while ignoring for analytical purposes the contents (goals and purposes) of social relations.

Thus, forms of interaction refer to the modes "of interaction among individuals through which, or in the shape of which, that content attains social reality."[10] Simmel argued that attention to social forms led sociology to goals that were fundamentally different from those of the other social scientific disciplines, especially in the Germany of his time. For example, sociology tries to discover the laws influencing small-group interaction rather than describing

---

[9]The most well-known criticism of Simmel's presumably excessive "formalism" are by Theodore Abel, *Systematic Sociology in Germany* (New York: Octagon, 1965), and Pitirim Sorokin, *Contemporary Sociological Theories* (New York: Harper & Row, 1928). The best defenses of Simmel against this spurious charge are those by F. H. Tenbruck, "Formal Sociology," in *Essays in Sociology*, 61–69, and Donald N. Levine, "Simmel and Parsons Reconsidered," as well as his *Simmel and Parsons: Two Approaches to the Study of Society* (New York: Arno, 1980).

[10]Simmel, "Problem of Sociology," 315.

particular families or marriages; it attempts to uncover the principles of formal and impersonal interaction rather than examining specific bureaucratic organizations; it seeks to understand the nature and consequences of class struggle rather than portraying a particular strike or some specific conflict. By focusing on the generic and basic properties of interaction, per se, Simmel believed that sociology could discover the underlying processes of social reality.[11] Although social structures might reveal diverse contents, they can have similar forms:

> Social groups, which are the most diverse imaginable in purpose and general significance, may nevertheless show identical forms of behavior toward one another on the part of individual members. We find superiority and subordination, competition, division of labor, formation of parties, representation, inner solidarity coupled with exclusiveness toward the outside, and innumerable similar features in the state, in a religious community, in a band of conspirators, in an economic association, in an art school, in the family. However diverse the interests are that give rise to these sociations, the *forms* in which the interests are realized may yet be identical.[12]

On this basis, then, Simmel believed that it was possible to develop "timelessly valid laws" about social interaction. For example, the process of competition or other forms of conflict can be examined in many different social contexts at different times: within and among political parties, within and among different religious groups, within and among businesses, among artists, and even among family members. The result can be some theoretical insight into how the process of competition (as a form of conflict) affects the participants apart from their specific purposes or goals. Thus, even though the terminology has changed over the years, Simmel's distinction between form and content constitutes one of his most important contributions to the emergence of sociological theory. However, the next task he faced was identifying the most basic forms of interaction; in his words, sociology must delineate its specific problem areas. Sadly, his inability to complete this task represents the most significant flaw in his methodological work.

---

[11]Simmel, *Fundamental Problems*, 18.

[12]Ibid., 22 (emphasis in original). See Levine, "Simmel and Parsons Reconsidered," for elaboration on this point of emphasis in Simmel's work.

What Are the Problem Areas of Sociology?

Unlike his responses to the other two questions, Simmel's answer to the third query has not proven to be of enduring significance for the development of sociological theory. In his initial attempts at conceptualizing the basic social forms with which sociology ought to be concerned, he referred to "a difficulty in methodology." For the present, he felt, the sociological viewpoint can be conveyed only by means of examples because only later will it be possible "to grasp it by methods that are fully conceptualized and are sure guides to research."[13]

Both the title and the organization of Simmel's *Fundamental Problems* (1918) suggest that the major impetus for writing this last little book was his recognition that the "difficulty in methodology" remained unresolved. Unfortunately, this final effort at developing systematic procedures for identifying the generic properties of the social world studied by sociology was not very successful either. In this book, Simmel identified three areas that he said constituted the fundamental problems of sociology. First is the sociological study of historical life and development, which he called *general sociology*. Second is the sociological study of the forms of interaction independent of history, which he called *pure*, or *formal, sociology*. Third is the sociological study of the epistemological and metaphysical aspects of society, which he called *philosophical sociology*. In *Fundamental Problems*, which has only four chapters, Simmel devoted a separate chapter to each of these problem areas.

General Sociology

Simmel began by noting that "general sociology" was concerned with the study "of the whole of historical life insofar as it is formed societally"—that is, through interaction. The process of historical development can be interpreted in a number of ways, however, and Simmel believed that it was necessary to distinguish the sociological from the nonsociological approach. For example, he indicated that Émile Durkheim saw historical development "as a process proceeding from organic commonness to mechanical simultaneousness," whereas Auguste Comte saw it as occurring through three distinct

---

[13]Simmel, "Problem of Sociology," 323–324.

stages: theological, metaphysical, and positive.[14] Although both claims are reasonable, Simmel remarked, neither constitutes a justification for the existence of sociology. Rather, the historical development of those observable social structures studied by the existing disciplines (politics, economics, religion, law, language, and others) must be subjected to a sociological analysis by distinguishing between social forms and social contents. For example, when the history of religious communities and labor unions is studied, it is possible to show that the members of both are characterized by patterns of self-sacrifice and devotion to ideals. These similarities can, in principle, be summarized by abstract laws.

What Simmel was apparently arguing, although this is not entirely clear, is that studies of the contents of interaction can yield valid theoretical insights only when attention is paid to the more generic properties of the social structures in which people participate. However, his chapter on general sociology, which deals with the problem of the development of individuality in society, proceeds in ways that are, at best, confusing.[15] Thus, the overall result is that readers are left wondering just what the subject of general sociology is and how it relates to the other problem areas.

Pure, or Formal, Sociology

For Simmel, "pure, or formal, sociology" consists of investigating "the societal forms themselves." Thus, when "society is conceived as interaction among individuals, the description of this interaction is the task of the science of society in its strictest and most essential sense."[16] Simmel's problem was thus to isolate and identify fundamental forms of interaction. In his earlier work, he attempted to do this by focusing on a number of less observable but highly significant social forms, which can be divided (roughly) into two general categories, although he did not use these labels: (1) generic social processes, such as differentiation, conflict, and exchange, and (2) structured role relationships, such as the role of the stranger in society. Nearly all his substantive work consists of studies of these less observable social forms. For example, a partial listing of the table of contents of

---

[14]Simmel, *Fundamental Problems*, 19–20. In general, Simmel does not cite his sources. On these two pages, however, his references are relatively clear, even though neither Durkheim nor Comte is mentioned by name.

[15]Ibid., 26–39.

[16]Ibid., 22.

Sociology: Studies in the Forms of Sociation reveals that the following topics are considered:[17]

1. The quantitative determinateness of the group

2. Superordination and subordination

3. Conflict

4. The secret and the secret society

5. Note on adornment

6. The intersection of social circles (the web of group affiliations)

7. The poor

8. The self-preservation of the group

9. Note on faithfulness and gratitude

10. Note on the stranger

11. The enlargement of the group and the development of the individual

12. Note on nobility

Yet Simmel's description of pure, or formal, sociology suffers from a fundamental defect: It does not remedy the "methodological difficulty" referred to.[18] In *Fundamental Problems*, Simmel failed to develop a precise method for either identifying the most basic forms of interaction or analyzing their systematic variation.

Philosophical Sociology

Simmel's "philosophical sociology" is an attempt to recognize the importance of philosophical issues in the development of sociology

---

[17]Items 1, 2, 4, 5, and 9 are available in *The Sociology of Georg Simmel*. Items 3 and 6 are in *Conflict and the Web of Group Affiliations*, trans. Reinhard Bendix (New York: Free Press, 1955). Item 10 is in *Essays on Sociology*. Item 8 is in the *American Journal of Sociology* 3 (March 1900), 577–603. Items 7, 11, and 12 are in *Georg Simmel on Individuality and Social Forms*, trans. Donald Levine (Chicago: University of Chicago Press, 1971). The remaining chapters, about one fourth of the book, are still untranslated. They deal with such topics as social psychology, hereditary office holding, the spatial organization of society, and the relationship between psychological and sociological phenomena.

[18]Simmel, *Fundamental Problems*, 4 0–57. See Levine, "Simmel and Parsons Reconsidered," 1107, and "Sociology's Quest for the Classics," 69–71, for an effort to extract the basic forms from Simmel's work.

as an academic discipline. As he put it, the modern scientific attitude toward the nature of empirical facts suggests a "complex of questions concerning the fact 'society.'" These questions are philosophical, and they center on epistemology and metaphysics. The epistemological problem has to do with one of the main cognitive presuppositions underlying sociological research: Is society the purpose of human existence, or is it merely a means for individual ends?[19] Simmel's explanatory chapter on philosophical sociology deals with this question by studying the relationship between the individual and society in the eighteenth and nineteenth centuries.[20] As with the other chapters in *Fundamental Problems*, however, this material is so confusing that it is of little use. Apparently, Simmel wanted to argue that questions about the purpose of society or the reasons for individual existence could not be answered in scientific terms, but even this reasonable conclusion is uncertain.[21] Ultimately, then, his vision of philosophical sociology has simply been ignored, mainly because his analysis is both superficial and unclear.

In the end, Simmel had to confess that he had failed to lay a complete methodological foundation for the new discipline. This failure stems from his uncertainty about his ability to isolate truly basic or generic structures and processes. Thus, both *Sociology* and *Fundamental Problems* contain disclaimers suggesting that his analysis of specific topics—such as the significance of group affiliations, the functions of social conflict, and the process of social exchange— can only demonstrate the potential value of an analysis of social forms.[22] We now examine Simmel's three most important studies in formal, or pure, sociology.

The Web of Group Affiliations

"The Web of Group Affiliations" is a sociological analysis of how patterns of group participation are altered with social differentiation, as well as an analysis of the consequences of such alterations for people's everyday behavior. Simmel first dealt with this topic in his

---

[19]This same issue was dealt with 10 years earlier in Georg Simmel, "Note on the Problem: How Is Society Possible?" in *Essays on Sociology*, 337–356.

[20]Simmel, *Fundamental Problems*, 58–86.

[21]Ibid., 25.

[22]Ibid., 18.

Social Differentiation (1890).[23] However, this early version is not very useful, and the text explicated here is taken from *Sociology: Studies in the Forms of Sociation.* Like all the classical sociologists, Simmel saw a general historical tendency toward increasing social differentiation in modern industrialized societies. Rather than tracing this development either chronologically or by increased functional specialization, he focused on the nature and significance of group memberships. In this way, he was able to identify a unique social form.

The Web of Group Affiliations as a Social Form

Social forms refer to the modes of interaction through which people attain their purposes or goals. In "The Web of Group Affiliations," Simmel was interested in the extent to which changes in the network of social structures making up society affect people. Indeed, he believed that the number of groups a person belongs to and the basis on which they are formed influence interaction apart from the interests that the groups are intended to satisfy.[24]

One of the most important variables influencing the number of groups to which people belong, as well as the basis of their attachment to groups, is the degree of *social differentiation*, or the number of different activities or structures organizing these activities. For example, in a hunting-and-gathering society, almost all tasks are done in and by the family (gathering and producing food, educating children, worshiping gods, making law, and the like). Thus, people have only a few roles in an undifferentiated society, as a consequence, people are similar because they play the same roles in an undifferentiated structure. In contrast, in an industrial society, many important tasks are divided up. This increase in complexity, which sociologists call differentiation, affects interaction. People still produce goods, worship, educate, and adjudicate, but they do so differently. This disparity occurs because people increasingly choose which groups to belong to based on "similarity of talents, inclinations, activities,"

---

[23]See Georg Simmel, "The Intersection of Social Spheres," in *Georg Simmel: Sociologist and European*, trans. Peter Lawrence (New York: Barnes & Noble, 1976), 95–110.

[24]The remainder of this section draws on Leonard Beeghley, "Demystifying Theory: How the Theories of Georg Simmel (and Others) Help Us to Make Sense of Modern Life," Chapter 34 in *The Blackwell Companion to Sociology*, eds. Jon Gubbay, Chris Middleton, and Chet Ballard (New York: Blackwell, 1997).

and other factors over which they have some control.[25] Thus, people play a far greater number and variety of roles and, in so doing, often interact with others different from themselves. The remainder of "The Web of Group Affiliations" explores the structural changes that result. In this way, Simmel demonstrated how a sociological analysis can reveal what happens to people "insofar as they form groups and are determined by their group existence because of interaction." He also demonstrated some implications of modernity.

Structural Changes Accompanying Social Differentiation

Simmel observed that the process of social differentiation produced two fundamental changes in patterns of interaction. First, the principle underlying group formation changed, in his words, from *organic* to *rational* criteria. As Simmel uses it, the term *organic* is a biological metaphor suggesting that a family or village is like a living organism in which the parts are inherently connected.[26] Thus, when groups have an "organic" basis, people belong to them based on birth—into a family, a religion, village—and they are so strongly identified with the group to which they belong that they are not seen as individuals in their own right. In Shakespeare's play, *Romeo and Juliet*, for example, Romeo did not have an identity apart from his family and village; they constituted who he was. This is why his banishment was so devastating. In contrast, the term *rational* suggests the use of reason and logic. Thus, as Simmel uses the term, when groups have a "rational" basis, people belong by choice. For example, Simmel noted that English trade unions had originally "tended toward local exclusiveness" and had been closed to workers who came from other cities or regions,[27] but over time workers ended their dependence on local relationships, choosing to build and join national unions to pursue their interests.[28]

Second, social differentiation also leads to an increase in the number of groups that people can join. When groups have an "organic" basis, people can only belong to a few primary groups (i.e., small,

---

[25]Simmel, "Web of Group Affiliations," in *Conflict and the Web of Group Affiliations*, 127.

[26]The classical theorists were often groping for how to communicate. Partly for this reason, they often used the same or similar concepts with quite different meanings. Thus, Simmel's notion of "organic" is the opposite of Durkheim's (considered in Chapter 13).

[27]Simmel, "Web of Group Affiliations," 129.

[28]Ibid., 137.

intimate, face-to-face groups): their family, their village, and not much more. In contrast, when groups have a "rational" basis, people can join a greater number and variety of them, based on skill, mutual interests, money, and other types of commonality. Simmel observed a trend in modern societies for people to join many groups and for such affiliations to be based on conscious reflection. This tendency applies even to intimate relationships, such as marriages. Many of these groups, however, are larger and more formal and are called *secondary groups*. Thus, people can also belong to occupational groups of various sorts, purely social groups, and a virtually unlimited number of special-interest groups. Furthermore, individuals might also identify themselves as members of a social class and a military reserve unit. Finally, they might see themselves as citizens of cities, states, regions, and nations. Not surprisingly, Simmel concluded,

> This is a great variety of groups. Some of these groups are integrated. Others are, however, so arranged that one group appears as the original focus of an individual's affiliation, from which he then turns toward affiliation with other, quite different groups on the basis of his special qualities, which distinguish him from other members of his primary group.[29]

Put differently, group affiliations in differentiated societies are characterized by a superstructure of secondary groups that develops beyond primary group membership. From Simmel's point of view, the most important sociological characteristics of these groups—both primary and secondary—are that individuals choose to affiliate, everyone belongs to different groups, and people are often treated as individuals with unique experiences. These attributes mean that in many important respects, every person differs from every other.

The Consequences of Differentiation

The implications of this change are profound. Simmel suggests, for example, that when groups are formed by choice and people belong to a large number of them, the possibility of role conflict arises because membership in diverse groups places competing demands on people. "As the individual leaves his established position within one primary

---

[29]Ibid., 137.

group, he comes to stand at a point at which many groups 'intersect.'" As a result, "external and internal conflicts arise through the multiplicity of group affiliations, which threaten the individual with psychological tensions or even a schizophrenic break."[30] Thus, it is now common for people to have multiple obligations. Sometimes these duties lead to hard choices; this happens, for example, when obligations to one's employer compete with obligations to one's family. Usually, Simmel says, people try to balance their competing responsibilities by keeping them spatially and temporally separate. Nonetheless, the impact of conflicting expectations can lead to psychological stress and, hence, influence behavior.

Simmel's analysis also leads to insights about some of the positive consequences of modernity. For example, if it is accurate, people now play many different roles: spouse, parent, son or daughter, athlete, employee, political activist, among other roles. This list, which could be extended, gives each of them a distinct identity in relationship to other people. These others also have a unique set of characteristics (roles) that make them distinct. Thus, Simmel's theory implies that the changes produced by social differentiation lead to greater individuality (what he called a "core of inner unity") that makes each person discrete. In Simmel's words, "the objective structure of society provides a framework within which an individual's non-interchangeable and singular characteristics may develop and find expression."[31] Such a result is impossible when everyone resembles everyone else. Ironically, then, modernity not only produces role conflict and psychological stress but also creates the conditions under which individuality emerges.

Such individuality emerges precisely because people in modern societies can, indeed must, make choices. Moreover, they must adjust their behavior to different people in different situations—an insight that carries many implications. For example, as people choose and become aware of their uniqueness they enjoy greater personal freedom. As Simmel put it, although "the narrowly circumscribed and strict custom of earlier conditions was one in which the social group as a whole . . . regulated the conduct of the individual in the most varied ways," such regulation is not possible in differentiated societies because people belong to so many different groups.[32] It is not accidental, from this

---

[30]Ibid., 141.

[31]Simmel, "Web of Group Affiliations," 150; see also 139, 149, 151.

[32]Ibid., 165.

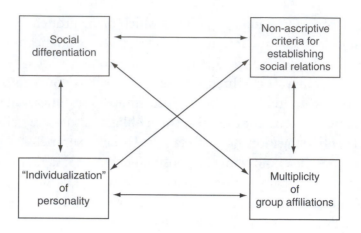

Figure 11.1   Simmel's Image of Group Affiliations

point of view, that the ideology of personal freedom as an inalienable right of every adult arose during the past two centuries. Its structural basis, Simmel said, lies in social differentiation.

These insights lead to others. For example, when people play many roles and face conflicting expectations, they develop the capacity for empathy—the ability to identify with and understand another's situation or motives.[33] This capacity can sometimes reduce the level of conflict between people. Thus, the increasing complexity of modern societies provides a structural basis for an important personality characteristic. Note two implications of this argument: First, role conflict now appears to be a positive feature of modern societies. Second, the distribution of psychological characteristics in a population (e.g., people's sense of individuality and empathy) does not happen by chance; they reflect the social structure. In addition, although role conflict burdens individuals, it also forces them to make choices and thereby encourages creativity.[34] After all, in a complex society, roles cannot be taken for granted; they must be negotiated; and so, people have to consider both their own and others' situations and be creative. Moreover, the aptitude for thinking imaginatively and originally extends to all arenas of life as people confront problems. The logic of this analysis suggests that modernity results from and, at the same time, produces a spiral effect such that as societies become more differentiated, more people become creative, and as more people become creative, societies become more complex (see Figure 11.1).

[33]Robert K. Merton, *Social Theory and Social Structure* (New York: Free Press, 1968), 436.
[34]Rose Laub Coser, *In Defense of Modernity* (Stanford, CA: Stanford University Press, 1991).

Conflict

Although his initial sketch of "The Sociology of Conflict" appeared in 1903, the basis for our commentary is a much-revised version that was included as a chapter in *Sociology: Studies in the Forms of Sociation*.[35] Simmel began the latter essay by remarking that although the social "significance of conflict has in principle never been disputed," it has most commonly been seen as a purely destructive factor in people's relationships, one that should be prevented from occurring if possible. He believed that this orientation stemmed from an emphasis on exploring the contents of interaction; people observe the destructive consequences of conflict on other individuals (both physically and psychologically) and assume that it must have a similar effect on collectivities. In Simmel's view, this emphasis is shortsighted because it fails to recognize that conflict often serves as a means of maintaining or increasing integration within groups. In his words, "it is a way of achieving some kind of unity." For example, people's ability to express their hostilities toward one another can give them a sense of control over their destinies and thereby increase social solidarity within a group.

Conflict as a Social Form

Human beings, Simmel observed, have an "*a priori* fighting instinct"—that is, they have an easily aroused sense of hostility toward others. Although this fighting instinct is probably the ultimate cause of social conflict, he said, humans are distinguished from other species because, in general, conflicts are means to goals rather than merely instinctual reactions to external stimuli. This fundamental principle in Simmel's discussion means that conflict is a vehicle by which individuals achieve their purposes in innumerable social contexts, such as marriage, work, play, politics, and religion. As such, conflict reveals certain common properties in all contexts, and hence it can be viewed as a basic social form.

Moreover, conflict is nearly always combined with cooperation: people agree on norms that regulate when, where, and how to fight

---

[35]Georg Simmel, "The Sociology of Conflict," *American Journal of Sociology* 9 (1903–1904), 490–525, 672–689, 798–811.

with one another, and this is true in marriage, business, games, war, and theological disputes. As Simmel wrote,

> there probably exists no social unit in which convergent and divergent currents among its members are not inseparably interwoven. An absolutely centripetal and harmonious group . . . not only is empirically unreal, it could show no real life process.[36]

The importance of this fusion of conflict and cooperation can be seen most clearly in those instances where a cooperative element appears to be lacking, for example, interaction between muggers and their victims or when conflict is engendered exclusively by the lust to fight. Simmel believed that these examples are clearly limiting cases, however, for if "there is any consideration, any limit to violence, there already exists a socializing factor, even though only as the qualification of violence."[37] This is why he emphasized that social conflict is usually a means to a goal; its "superior purpose" implies that people can change or modify their tactics depending on the situation.

In his essay on conflict, Simmel sketched some of the alternative forms of conflict, the way in which they are combined with regulatory norms, and the significance that this form of interaction has for the groups to which people belong. He first examined how conflict within groups affects the reciprocal relations of the parties involved, then he turned to the consequences that conflict with an out-group has for social relations within a group. The following sections deal with each of these topics.

Conflict Within Groups

Simmel's investigation of the sociological significance of conflict within groups revolves around three forms: (1) conflicts in which the opposing parties possess common personal qualities, (2) conflicts in which the opposing parties perceive each other as a threat to the existence of the group, and (3) conflicts in which the opposing parties recognize and accept each other as legitimate opponents.

---

[36]Simmel, "Conflict," in *Conflict and the Web of Group Affiliations*, 15. See Levine, "Sociology's Quest for the Classics," 68, for an effort to extract the formal properties of conflict in Simmel's essay.

[37]Simmel, "Conflict," 26.

Conflict Among Those With Common Personal Qualities[38]

Simmel noted that "people who have many common features often do one another worse or 'wronger' wrong than complete strangers do," mainly because they have so few differences that even the slightest conflict is magnified in its significance. As examples, he referred to conflict in "intimate relations," such as marriages, and to the relationship between renegades and their former colleagues. In both cases, the solidarity of the group is based on the parties possessing many common (or complementary) characteristics. As a result, people are involved with one another as whole persons, and even small antagonisms between them can be highly inflammatory, regardless of the content of the disagreements. Thus, when conflict does occur, the resulting battle is sometimes so intense that previous areas of agreement are forgotten. Most of the time, Simmel observed, participants develop implicit or explicit norms that keep conflicts within manageable bounds. When emotions run high or when group members see the conflict as transcending their individual interests, however, the fight can become violent. At that point, he suggested, the very existence of those who differ might be taken as a threat to the group.

Conflict as a Threat to the Group[39]

Conflict sometimes occurs among opponents who have common membership in a group. Simmel argued that this type of conflict should be treated as a distinct form because when a group is divided into conflicting elements, the antagonistic parties "hate each other not only on the concrete ground which produced the conflict but also on the sociological ground of hatred for the enemy of the group itself." Such antagonism is especially intense and can easily become violent because each party identifies itself as representing the group and sees the other as a mortal enemy of the collective.

Conflicts Among Recognized and Accepted Opponents

Simmel distinguished two forms of conflict among parties who recognize and accept each other as opponents. When a conflict is "direct," the opposing parties act squarely against each other to

---

[38]Ibid., 43–48.
[39]Ibid., 48–50.

obtain their goals.[40] When a conflict is "indirect," the opponents interact only with a third party to obtain their goals. Simmel referred to this latter form of conflict as *competition*.[41] Yet both forms share certain distinguishing characteristics that differentiate them from the forms of conflict noted previously: opponents are seen to have a right to strive for the same goal; conflict is pursued mercilessly yet nonviolently; personal antagonisms and feelings of hostility are often excluded from the conflict; and the opponents either develop agreements among themselves or accept the imposition of overriding norms that regulate the conflict.

The purest examples of direct conflict are antagonistic games and conflicts over causes. In the playing of games, "one *unites* [precisely] in order to fight, and one fights under the mutually recognized control of norms and rules."[42] Similarly, in the case of conflicts over causes, such as legal battles, the opponents' essential unity is again the underlying basis for interaction because, to fight in court, the opponents must always follow agreed-on normative procedures. Thus, even as parties confront each other, they affirm their agreement on larger principles. The analysis of direct conflict within groups was, however, of less interest to Simmel, with the result that he did not devote much space to it. Rather, he emphasized the sociological importance of competition because this form of fighting most clearly illustrates how conflict can have positive social consequences. By proceeding indirectly, competition functions as a vital source of social solidarity within a group.

Although recognizing the destructive and even shameful aspects of competition to which Marx and other observers had pointed, Simmel argued that even after all its negative aspects were taken into account, competition has positive consequences for the group because it forces people to establish ties with one another, thereby increasing social solidarity. Because competition between parties proceeds by the opponents trying to win over a third party, each of them is implicated in a web of affiliations that connects them with one another.[43]

With some exceptions, Simmel noted, the process of competition is restricted because unregulated conflict can too easily become

---

[40]Ibid., 34–43.

[41]Ibid., 57–86.

[42]Ibid., 35 (emphasis in original).

[43]Ibid., 62.

violent and lead to the destruction of the group itself.[44] Hence, all collectivities that allow competition usually regulate it in some fashion, either through interindividual restrictions, in which regulatory norms are simply agreed on by the participants, or through superindividual restrictions, in which laws and other normative principles are imposed on the competitors.[45] Indeed, the existence of competition often stimulates normative regulation, thereby providing a basis of social integration.

Finally, Simmel recognized instances in which groups or societies try to eliminate competition in the name of a higher principle. For instance, in socialist or communist societies, competition is suspended in favor of an emphasis on organizing individual efforts in such a way as to (1) eliminate the wasted energy that accompanies conflict and (2) provide for the common good. Nonetheless, Simmel appears to have regarded a competitive environment as more useful than a noncompetitive one in modern, highly differentiated societies, not only in economic terms but also in most other arenas of social life. He believed that such an environment provides an outlet for people's "fighting instincts" that redounds to the common good and provides a stimulus for regulatory agreements that also contribute to the common good.

Conflict Between Groups

In the final section of his essay, Simmel examined the consequences that conflict between groups has "for the inner structure of each party itself."[46] Put differently, he was concerned with understanding the effect that conflict has on social relationships within each respective party to the conflict. To make his point, Simmel identified the following consequences of conflict between groups: (1) it increases the degree of centralization of authority within each group; (2) it increases the degree of social solidarity within each group and, at the same time, decreases the level of tolerance for deviance and dissent; and (3) it increases likelihood of coalitions among groups having similar opponents.

---

[44]Ibid., 68–70. Simmel recognized that within families and to some extent within religious groups, the interests of the group often dictate that members refrain from competing with one another.

[45]Ibid., 76.

[46]Ibid., 87.

Conflict and Centralization[47]

Just as fighters must psychologically "pull themselves together," Simmel observed, so must a group when it is engaged in conflict with another group. There is a "need for centralization, for the tight pulling together of all elements, which alone guarantees their use, without loss of energy and time, for whatever the requirements of the moment may be." This necessity is greatest during war, which "needs a centralistic intensification of the group form." In addition, Simmel noted, the development and maintenance of a centralized group is often "guaranteed best by despotism," and he argued that a centralized and despotic regime was more likely to wage war precisely because people's accumulated energies (or "hostile impulses") needed some means of expression. Finally, Simmel remarked that centralized groups generally preferred to engage in conflict with groups that were also centralized. For despite the conflict-producing consequences of fighting a tightly organized opponent, conflict with such an opponent can be more easily resolved, not only because the boundaries separating each side are clearly demarcated but also because each party "can supply a representative with whom one can negotiate with full certainty." For example, in conflicts between workers and employers or between nations, Simmel argued, it is often "better" if each side is organized so that conflict resolution can proceed in a systematic manner.

Conflict, Solidarity, and Intolerance[48]

Simmel argued that conflict often increased social solidarity within each of the opposing groups. As he phrased it, a "tightening of the relations among [the party's] members and the intensification of its unity, in consciousness and in action, occur." This is especially true, he asserted, during wars or other violent conflicts. Moreover, increasing intolerance also accompanies rising solidarity, for whereas antagonistic members can often coexist during peacetime without harm to the group, this luxury is not possible during war. As a result, "groups in any sort of war situation are not tolerant" of deviance and dissent because they often see themselves as fighting for the existence of the group itself and demand total loyalty from members. Thus, in general, conflict between groups means that members must develop solidarity

---

[47]Ibid., 88–91.
[48]Ibid., 17–19, 91–98.

with one another, and those who cannot are often either expelled or punished. As a result of their intolerance toward deviance and dissent, Simmel remarked, groups in conflict often become smaller, as those who would compromise are silenced or cast out. This tendency can make an ongoing conflict more difficult to resolve, because "groups, and especially minorities, which live in conflict and persecution, often reject approaches or tolerance from the other side." The acceptance of such overtures would mean that "the closed nature of their opposition without which they cannot fight on would be blurred." Finally, Simmel suggested that the internal solidarity of many groups depends on their continued conflict with other parties and that their complete victory over an opponent could result in a lessening of internal social solidarity.

Conflict, Coalitions, and Group Formation[49]

Under certain conditions, Simmel wrote, conflict between groups can lead to the formation of coalitions and ultimately to new solidarities among groups where none had existed before. In his words, "each element in a plurality may have its own opponent, but because this opponent is the same for all elements, they all unite—and in this case, they may, prior to that, not have had anything to do with each other." Sometimes such combinations are only for a single purpose, and the allies' solidarity declines immediately at the conclusion of the conflict. However, Simmel argued, when coalitions are engaged in wars or other violent conflicts and when their members become highly interdependent over a long period, more cohesive social relations are likely to ensue. This phenomenon is even more pronounced when a coalition is subjected to an ongoing or relatively permanent threat. As Simmel wrote,

> the synthetic strength of a common opposition may be determined, not [only] by the number of shared points of interest, but [also] by the duration and intensity of the unification. In this case, it is especially favorable to the unification if instead of an actual fight with an enemy, there is a permanent *threat* by him.

Like so much of Simmel's work, the essay on conflict does not embody a unified conceptual perspective; rather, we get a series of

---

[49]Ibid., 98–107.

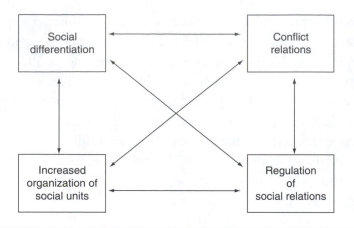

Figure 11.2   Simmel's Image of Social Conflict

provocative insights. In addition, as always with discursive writings, problems arise in presenting his insights. Nonetheless, we can extrapolate a model of the process of differentiation in Figure 11.2. As societies differentiate (become more complex), the number of organized units and their potential for conflict increases. Increased numbers of units, per se, create pressures for regulation of social relations by mechanisms such as centralization of power, laws, courts, mediating agencies, and coalitions among varying social units. Conflict escalates these pressures while unifying or consolidating social units structurally (centralization of authority, normative clarity, increased sanctioning) and ideologically (increased salience of beliefs and values). If conflicts are sufficiently frequent, low in intensity, and regulated, they release tensions, thereby encouraging further differentiation and elaboration of regulative structures. Such structures also encourage further differentiation by providing the capacity to coordinate increased numbers of units, manage tensions among them, and reduce their respective sense of threat when in potential conflict.

The Philosophy of Money

Simmel's *The Philosophy of Money* is a study of the social consequences of exchange relationships among human beings, with special emphasis on those forms of exchange in which money is used as an abstract measure of value. Like all his other work, *The Philosophy of Money* is an attempt at exposing how the forms of interaction affect the basic nature of social relations independently of their specific content. Although Simmel first considered this issue as early as 1889 in an untranslated article titled "The Psychology of Money," the final formulation of his ideas did not appear until the second edition of *The Philosophy of Money* was published in 1907.[50] Unlike the works reviewed earlier, *The Philosophy of Money* is both a sociological and philosophical treatise,[51] forcing us to extract the more sociological ideas from a philosophical text.

Exchange as a Social Form

The Philosophy of Money represents Simmel's effort to isolate another basic social form. Not all interaction is exchange, but exchange is a universal form of interaction.[52] In analyzing social exchange, Simmel concentrated on "economic exchange" in general and on money exchanges in particular. Although not all economic exchanges involve the use of money, money has historically come into increasing use as a medium of exchange. This historical trend, Simmel emphasized, reflects the process of social differentiation. But it does much more: Money is also a major cause and force behind this process. Thus, the sociological portions of *The Philosophy of Money* are devoted to analyzing the transforming effects on social life of the ever-increasing use of money in social relations.

In analyzing differentiation from an exchange perspective, Simmel developed a number of philosophical assumptions and linked these to a sociological analysis of the modern world. Much like his friend and intellectual defender, Max Weber, Simmel was interested in understanding not just the forms of modern life but also their historical origins.[53] But unlike Weber, Simmel did not engage in detailed historical analyses, nor was he interested in constructing elaborate taxonomies. Rather, his works always sought to link certain philosophical views about humans and the social universe to understanding the properties

---

[50]Georg Simmel, "Psychologie des Geldes," *Jahrbücher für Gesetzgebung, Verwaltung und Volkswirtschaft* 23 (1889), 1251–1264. *The Philosophy of Money*, 2nd ed., trans. Tom Bottomore and David Frisby (Boston: Routledge, 1990).

[51]It is often forgotten that Simmel was a philosopher as well as a sociologist. As noted in Chapter 9, he wrote books and articles on the works of Kant, Goethe, Schopenhauer, and Nietzsche and considered more general philosophical issues and problems as well.

[52]Simmel, *The Philosophy of Money*, 82.

[53]As noted in Chapter 9, Simmel was excluded from senior academic positions for much of his career, and his work was often attacked. Weber was one of his most consistent defenders and apparently helped him maintain at least a marginal intellectual standing in Germany. But Weber revealed some ambivalence toward Simmel; see Weber's "Georg Simmel as a Sociologist," with an introduction by Donald N. Levine, *Social Research* 39 (1972), 154–165.

of a particular social form. Thus, before explicating Simmel's specific analysis of money and exchange, it is necessary to place his analysis in philosophical context.

Simmel's Assumptions About Human Nature

In *The Philosophy of Money*, Simmel presented a vision of human nature that is implicit but less visible in his sociological works. He began by asserting that people are teleological beings; that is, they act on the environment in the pursuit of anticipated goals. In the essay on conflict, Simmel emphasized that this characteristic made human conflict different from that occurring among other animals. In *The Philosophy of Money*, Simmel took the position that although people's goals would vary in accordance with their biological impulses and social needs, all action reflected humans' ability to manipulate the environment in an attempt to realize goals. In doing so, individuals use a variety of "tools," but not just in the obvious material sense. Rather, people use more subtle, symbolic tools, such as language and money, to achieve their goals. In general, Simmel argued that the more tools people possessed, the greater would be their capacity to manipulate the environment, and hence, the more they could causally influence the flow of events. Moreover, the use of tools allows many events to be connected in chains that can form more extended social relations, as when money is used to buy a good. Money, for example, pays the salary of the seller, becomes profit for the manufacturer, and is transformed into wages for the worker, and so on, in a chain of social relations. Thus, Simmel thought all action reveals the properties presented in Figure 11.3. (As an interesting aside, compare Simmel's model with George Herbert Mead's analysis of the phases of "the act," reviewed in Chapter 15.)

Money, Simmel asserted, is the ultimate social tool because it is generalized; that is, people can use it in many ways to manipulate the environment to obtain their goals. This means that money can potentially connect many events and persons who would not otherwise be related. In an indirect way, then, the use of money allows a vast increase in the number of groups to which individuals can belong; thus, it is a prime force behind social differentiation.

A related assumption is that humans have the capacity to divide their world into an internal, subjective state and an external, objective state. This division occurs only when impulses are not immediately satisfied—that is, when the environment presents barriers and obstacles. When such barriers exist, humans separate their subjective

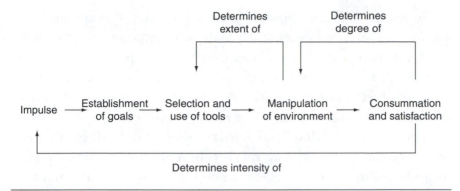

Figure 11.3   Simmel's Model of the Dynamics of Human Action

experiences from the objects of the environment that are the source of need or impulse satisfaction. As Simmel emphasized,

> we desire objects only if they are not immediately given to us for our use and enjoyment; that is, to the extent that they resist our desire. The content of our desire becomes an object as soon as it is opposed to us, not only in the sense of being impervious to us, but also in terms of its distance as something not enjoyed.[54]

Value inheres in this subject–object division. In contrast with Marx, Simmel stressed that the value of an object existed not in the "labor power" required to produce it but in the extent to which it was both desired and unattainable; that is, value resides in the process of seeking objects that are scarce and distant. Value is thus tied to humans' basic capacity to distinguish a subjective from an objective world and in the relative difficulty in securing objects. Patterns of social organization, Simmel emphasized, perform much of this subject–object separation: they present barriers and obstacles; they create demands for some objects; and they determine how objects will circulate. The economic production of goods and their sale in a market is only a special case of the more general process of subject–object division among humans. Long before money, markets, and productive corporations existed, humans desired objects that were not easily obtainable. Thus, whether in the economic marketplace or the more general arena of life, value is a positive function of the extent to which an object of desire is difficult to obtain.[55]

---

[54]Simmel, *Philosophy of Money*, 66.
[55]Ibid., 80–98.

Money, as Simmel showed, greatly increases the creation and acceleration of value because it provides a common yardstick for a quick calculation of values ("how much" a commodity or service is "worth"). Moreover, as a "tool," money greatly facilitates the acquisition of objects; as money circulates and is used at each juncture to calculate values, all objects in the environment come to be assessed by their monetary value. Unlike Marx, Simmel did not see this as a perverse process but as a natural reflection of humans' innate capacity and need to create values for the objects of their environment.

Another assumption about human nature is to be found in Simmel's discussion of "worldview."[56] People naturally seek stability and order in their world, he argued. They seek to know the place of objects and of their relationship to these objects. For example, Simmel observed, humans develop totems and religious rituals to regularize their relations to the supernatural; similarly, the development of money as a standardized measurement of value is but another manifestation of this tendency for humans to seek order and stability in their view of the world. By developing money, they can readily compare objects by their respective value and can therefore develop a "sense of order" about their environment.

In sum, then, Simmel believed that the development of money is an expression and extension of basic human nature. Money is a kind of tool in teleological acts; it is a way to express the value inherent in humans' capacity for subject–object division; and it is a means for attaining stability and order in people's worldview. All these innate tendencies are the driving force behind much human action, and this is why exchange is such a basic form of social interaction. For exchange is nothing more than the sacrificing of one object of value for the attainment of another. Money greatly facilitates this process because it provides a common reference point for calculating the respective values of objects that are exchanged.

Money in Social Exchange

For Simmel, social exchange involves the following elements:

1. The desire for a valued object that one does not have

2. The possession of the valued object by an identifiable other

---

[56]Ibid., 102–110.

3. The offer of an object of value to secure from another the desired object

4. The acceptance of this offer by the possessor of the valued object[57]

Contained in this portrayal of social exchange are several additional points that Simmel emphasized. First, value is idiosyncratic and is ultimately tied to an individual's impulses and needs. Of course, what is defined as valuable is typically circumscribed by cultural and social patterns, but how valuable an object is will be a positive function of both the intensity of a person's needs and the scarcity of the object. Second, much exchange involves efforts to manipulate situations so that the intensity of needs for an object is concealed and the availability of an object is made to seem less than it actually is. Inherent in exchange, therefore, is a basic tension that can often erupt into other social forms, such as conflict. Third, to possess an object is to lessen its value and to increase the value of objects that one does not possess. Fourth, exchanges will occur only if both parties perceive that the object given is less valuable than the one received.[58] Fifth, collective units as well as individuals participate in exchange relations and, hence, are subject to the four processes listed. Sixth, the more liquid the resources of an actor are in an exchange—that is, the more resources that can be used in many types of exchanges—the greater that actor's options and power will be. If an actor is not bound to exchange with any other and can readily withdraw resources and exchange them with another, that actor has considerable power to manipulate any exchange.

Economic exchange involving money is only a special case of this more general social form. But it is a very special case. When money becomes the predominant means for establishing value in social relationships, the properties and dynamics of social relations are transformed. This process of displacing other criteria of value, such as logic, ethics, and aesthetics, with a monetary criterion is precisely the long-term historical trend in societies. This trend is, as we

---

[57]Ibid., 85–88.

[58]Surprisingly, Simmel did not explore in any detail the consequences of unbalanced exchanges, in which people are forced to give up a more valuable object for a less valuable one. He simply assumed that at the time of exchange, one party felt that an increase in value had occurred. Retrospectively, a redefinition might occur, but the exchange will not occur if at the moment people do not perceive that they are receiving more value than they are giving up.

mentioned earlier, both a cause and an effect of money as the medium of exchange. Money emerged to facilitate exchanges and to realize even more completely humans' basic needs. Once established, however, the use of money has the power to transform the structure of social relations in society. In seeking to understand how money has this power to alter social relations, Simmel's *The Philosophy of Money* becomes distinctly sociological.

Money and Its Consequences for Social Relations

In much of Simmel's work, there is an implicit functionalism. He often asked, "What are the consequences of a social form for the larger social whole, or what functions does it perform?" This functionalism is most evident in Simmel's analysis of conflict, but it is also found in his analysis of money. He asked two related questions in tracing the consequences of money for social patterns: (1) What are the consequences of money for the structure of society as a whole? (2) What are the consequences of money for individuals?

In answering these two questions, Simmel added to his lifelong preoccupation with several issues. We mention these to place his specific analysis of the consequences of money for society and the individual into context. One prominent theme in all Simmel's work is the dialectic between individual attachments to, and freedom from, groups. On the one hand, he praised social relations that allow individuals freedom to choose their options, but on the other hand, he was somewhat dismayed at the alienation of individuals from the collective fiber of society (although not to the extent of other theorists during his time). This theme is tied to another prominent concern in his work: the growing rationalization of society, or as he phrased the matter, the "objectification" of social life. As social relations lose their traditional and religious content, they become mediated by impersonal standards—law, intellect, logic, and money. The application of these standards increases individual freedom and social justice, but it also makes life less emotional and involving. It reduces relations to rational calculations, devoid of the emotional bonds that come with attachments to religious symbols and long-standing traditions. Simmel's analysis of the "functions" of money for individuals and the social whole must be viewed in the context of these two themes.

Money and the Social Whole

Much like Weber, but in a less systematic way, Simmel was concerned with the historical trend toward rationalization, or objectification, of social relations. In general, humans tend to symbolize their relations, both with one another and with the natural environment. In the past, this was done with religious totems and then with laws. More recently, Simmel believed, people expressed their relationships with physical entities and with one another in monetary terms, with the result that they have lost intimate and direct contact with others as well as with the objects in their environment. Thus, money represents the ultimate objective symbolization of social relations—unlike material entities, money has no intrinsic value. Money merely represents values, and it is used to express the value of one object in relation to another. Although initial forms of money, such as coins of valuable metals and stones that could be converted into jewelry, possessed intrinsic value, the evolutionary trend is toward the use of paper money and credit, which merely express values in exchanges. As paper money and credit dominate, social relations in society are profoundly altered, in at least the following ways:

1. The use of money enables actors to make quick calculations of respective values. People do not have to bargain and haggle over the standards to be used in establishing the respective values of objects—whether commodities or labor. As a result, the "velocity" of exchange dramatically increases. People move through social relations more quickly.[59]

2. Because money increases the rate of social interaction and exchange, it also increases value. Simmel felt that people did not engage in exchange unless they perceived that they would get more than they gave up. Hence, the greater the rate of exchange is, the greater people's accumulation of value will be—that is, the more they will perceive that their needs and desires can be realized.[60]

3. The use of money as a liquid and nonspecific resource allows for much greater continuity in social relations. It prevents

[59]Simmel, *Philosophy of Money*, 143, 488–512.
[60]Ibid., 292.

gaps from developing in social relations, as is often the case when people have only hard goods, such as food products or jewelry, to exchange in social relations. Money gives people options to exchange almost anything because respective values can be readily calculated. As a result, there is greater continuity in social relations because all individuals can potentially engage in exchanges.[61]

4. In a related vein, money also allows the creation of multiple social ties. With money, people join groups other than those established at birth and thereby interact with many more others than is possible with a more restrictive medium of exchange.[62]

5. Money also allows exchanges among human beings located at great distances. As long as interaction involves exchange of concrete objects, there are limits to how distant people can be from one another and how many actors can participate in a sequence of exchanges. With money, these limitations are removed. Nations can engage in exchanges; individuals who never see one another—such as a factory worker and consumers of goods produced in the factory—can be indirectly connected in an exchange sequence (because some of the payment for a good or commodity will ultimately be translated into wages for the worker). Thus, money greatly extends the scope of social organization; money allows organization beyond face-to-face contact or beyond the simple barter of goods. With money, more and more people can become connected through direct and indirect linkages.[63]

6. Money also promotes social solidarity, in the sense that it represents a "trust"; that is, if people take money for goods or services, they believe that it can be used at a future date to buy other goods or services. This implicit trust in the capacity of money to meet future needs reinforces people's faith in and commitment to society.[64]

---

[61]Ibid., 124.
[62]Ibid., 307.
[63]Ibid., 180–186.
[64]Ibid., 177–178.

7. In a related argument, money increases the power of central authority, for the use of money requires that there be social stability and that a central authority guarantees the worth of money.[65] As exchange relations rely on government to maintain the stability of money, government acquires power. Moreover, money makes it much easier for a central government to tax people.[66] As long as only property could be taxed, there were limitations on the effectiveness of taxation by a remote central government because knowledge of property held would be incomplete and because property, such as land, is not easily converted into values that can be used to increase the power of central government. (How can, e.g., property effectively buy labor services in the army of the administrative staff of a government?) As a liquid resource, however, tax money can be used to buy those services and goods necessary for effective central authority.

8. The creation of a tax on money also promotes a new basis of social solidarity. Because all social strata and other collectivities are subject to a monetary taxation system, they have at least one common goal: control and regulation of taxes imposed by the central government. This commonality laces diverse groupings together because of their common interest in the taxing powers of government.

9. The use of money often extends into virtually all spheres of interaction. As an efficient means for comparing values, money replaces other, less efficient ways to calculate value. As money begins to penetrate all social relations, resistance to its influence in areas of personal value increases. Efforts to maintain the "personal element" in transactions increase, and norms about when it is inappropriate to use money become established. For example, traditions of paying a bride price vanish, using money to buy influence is considered much more offensive than personal persuasion, paying a price as punishment for certain crimes decreases, and so on.[67]

---

[65]Ibid., 171–184.
[66]Ibid., 317.
[67]Ibid., 369–387.

10. While these efforts are made to create spheres where the use of money declines, there is a general "quantification" and "objectification" of social relations.[68] Interactions become quantified as their value is expressed as money. As a result, moral constraints on what is possible decrease because anything is possible if one just has the money. Money releases people from the constraints of tradition and moral authority; money creates a system in which it is difficult to restrain individual aspirations and desires. Deviance and "pathology" are, therefore, more likely in systems where money becomes the prevalent medium of interaction.[69]

Money and the Individual

For Simmel, the extensive use of money in social interaction has several consequences for individuals. Most of these reflect the inherent tension between individual freedom from constraint, on the one hand, and alienation and detachment from social groups, on the other. Money gives people new choices and options, but it also depersonalizes their social milieu. Simmel isolated the following consequences of money for individuals:

1. As a "tool," money is nonspecific and thus gives people an opportunity to pursue many diverse activities. Unlike less liquid forms of expressing value, money does not determine how it can be used. Hence, individuals in a society that uses money as its principal medium of exchange enjoy considerably more freedom of choice than is possible in a society that does not use money.[70]

2. In a similar vein, money gives people many options for self-expression. To the degree that individuals seek to express

---

[68]Ibid., 393.

[69]Ibid., 404. Many analysts of Simmel emphasize these pathologies, especially when factoring in his analysis in other works, such as those translated by Peter Etzkorn in *The Conflict in Modern Culture and Other Essays* (New York: Teacher's College Press, 1980) and famous essays such as "The Metropolis and Mental Life." See, for example, David Frisby, *Sociological Impressionism: A Reassessment of Simmel's Social Theory* (London: Heinemann, 1981), and *Georg Simmel* (Chichester, UK: Ellis Horwood, 1984). For a balanced assessment that corresponds to the one offered here, see Donald R. Levine, "Simmel as Educator: On Individuality and Modern Culture," *Theory, Culture and Society* 8 (1991), 99–117.

[70]Simmel, *Philosophy of Money*, 307.

themselves through the objects of their possession, money allows unlimited means for self-expression. As a result, the use of money for self-expression leads to, and indeed encourages, diversity in a population that is no longer constrained in the pursuit of its needs (except, of course, by the amount of money its members have).[71]

3. Yet money also creates a distance between one's sense of self and the objects of self-expression. With money, objects are easily acquired and discarded, and hence long-term attachments to objects do not develop.[72]

4. Money allows a person to enter many different types of social relations. One can, for example, buy such relationships by paying membership dues in organizations or by spending money on various activities that ensure contacts with particular types of people. Hence, money encourages a multiplicity of social relations and group memberships. At the same time, however, money discourages intimate attachments. Money increases the multiplicity of individuals' involvements, but it atomizes and compartmentalizes their activities and often keeps them from emotional involvement in each of their segregated activities. This trend is, Simmel felt, best personified by the division of labor that is made possible by money wages but that also compartmentalizes individuals, often alienating them from others and their work.[73]

5. Money also makes it less necessary to know people personally because their money "speaks" for them. In systems without money, social relations are mediated by intimate knowledge of others, and adjustments among people are made through the particular characteristics of each individual. As money begins to mediate interaction, the need to know another personally is correspondingly reduced.

Thus, in Simmel's analysis of consequences, money is a mixed blessing for both the individual and society. Money allows greater freedom and provides new and multiple ways for connecting individuals. Money also isolates, atomizes, and even alienates individuals

---

[71]Ibid., 326–327.
[72]Ibid., 297.
[73]Ibid., 454.

from the persons and objects in their social milieu. As a result, money alters the nature of social relations among individuals in society, and therefore an analysis of its consequences is decidedly a sociological topic.

Embedded in this descriptive analysis of the consequences of money is a more general model of exchange, differentiation, and individualization of the person. Social differentiation increases the volume, rate, velocity, and potential scope of social ties among individuals and groups because there are more different kinds of units and hence more opportunities for multiple and varied social contacts. Increases in the number of social relations create pressures for the use of objective or rational symbolic media, such as money, to facilitate exchange transactions; reciprocally, the use of money allows an ever-increasing volume of social ties because money makes it easy to determine the value of each actor's resources and to conduct social transactions. Increases in social exchanges mediated by money feed back on differentiation, encouraging further differentiation, which in turn increases the volume, rate, velocity, and scope of social ties mediated by money. Such processes cause ever more individualization of people—that is, increased involvement of only small parts of one's personality in groups, increased group affiliations, and greater potential alienation from society. Yet these trends toward individualization are important contributors to the increased volume and rates of interaction, as well as the escalated use of money, on which social differentiation depends.

Critical Conclusions

In evaluating Simmel's work as a whole, his major theoretical contribution to sociology resides in his concern with the basic forms of interaction. By looking beyond differences in the "contents" of diverse social relations and by attempting to uncover their more generic forms, he was able to show that seemingly diverse situations reveal basic similarities. He implicitly argued that such similarities could be expressed as abstract models or laws, although we can criticize Simmel for not explicitly stating these laws.

Thus, although Simmel did not employ the vocabulary of abstract theory, his many essays on different topics reveal a commitment to formulating abstract statements about basic forms of human relationships. This orientation, however, is not always clear because Simmel tended to argue by example. His works tend to focus on a wide variety of empirical topics, and even when he explored a particular type of social relation, such as conflict and exchange, the discussion proceeds with many illustrations. He would, for instance, talk about conflicts among individuals and wars among nation-states in virtually the same passage. Such tendencies give his work an inductive and descriptive flair, but a more careful reading indicates that he clearly held a deductive view of theory in sociology.[74] For example, if conflict between such diverse entities as two individuals and two nations reveals certain common forms, diverse empirical situations can be understood by the same abstract law or principle.

Many might criticize Simmel for his implicit functionalism. He tended to ask, "What are the consequences of a phenomenon—for example, differentiation, conflict, exchange, money—for the social whole?" Such questions are functional because they analyze social processes in terms of their outcomes. Simmel did not fall into the functionalist trap of seeing outcomes as the causes of these very outcomes, but his work does tend to emphasize the positive outcomes. True, he recognized the atomizing and alienating effects of differentiation of structure and objectification (rationalization) of social patterns, but in general, he tends to see conflict, money, and differentiation in terms of their positive outcomes. In some ways, this orientation is refreshing because most German theorists tended to see modernity as evil and as doing harmful things to people. In contrast, Simmel argued that the great events that were making society more complex, impersonal, and objectified could free individuals from constraints and give them options not available in simpler societies. Moreover, he saw the potential for low-intensity, frequent, and regulated conflicts in differentiated societies as potentially increasing their integration. In a sense, then, Simmel's work stands as a corrective to the rather dreary prognosis of Max Weber about rationalization or to the polemical views of Karl Marx on the evils of capitalism.

Simmel has enjoyed a great rebirth recently because he recognized historical trends that have been picked up by scholars within contemporary "postmodern" theory. Simmel saw that differentiation and the spread of exchanges using money created a new kind of person, one with potentially as many identities as affiliations in

---

[74]That is, explanation occurs by deduction to empirical cases from abstract laws, which are universal and context-free.

diverse groups. This theme has been used to condemn late capitalist society as destroying a unified self; Simmel recognized this potential, but unlike postmodernists, he saw the liberating effects of being able to fashion one's own group affiliations and, hence, one's identity. Simmel more than any other theorist of the classical founders saw the transforming effects of money and markets on society. For postmodernists, everything is "commodified"—people, self, group culture, sacred symbols, affiliations—and they see this power of money and markets to create a world of unstable group structures whose culture is marketed and bought by people seeking to purchase an identity. Simmel saw this potential, but again, he came down on the more positive side, emphasizing that people are freed of the oppressive constraints associated with traditional, communal societies. Thus, because Simmel addressed the issues of interest to postmodernism, he has moved from a more minor place in sociology's pantheon to a plane just below that of Marx, Weber, and Durkheim.

CHAPTER 12

The Origin and Context of Émile Durkheim's Thought

Biographical Influences on Durkheim's Thought[1]

Émile Durkheim was born in Épinal, France, in 1858. Because his Jewish family was deeply religious, the young Durkheim studied Hebrew, the Old Testament, and the Talmud, apparently intending to follow his father's example and become a rabbi. He began to move away from religion in his early teens, however, and he eventually abandoned personal religious involvement and proclaimed himself an agnostic. As will become evident in the next chapter, he never lost interest in religion as a topic of intellectual inquiry; perhaps equally important, the high sense of morality that his family and early religious training instilled in him fueled his passion for creating a new "civil morality" in France.

Durkheim was an excellent student, and in 1879, he was admitted to the École normale supérieure, the traditional training ground for the intellectual elite of France in the nineteenth century. In the new environment, he became indifferent, apparently finding the literary, esthetic, and rhetorical thrust of the instruction unappealing. Instead, he preferred the disciplined logic of philosophical arguments and the hard facts and findings of the sciences. Several teachers at

---

[1]In this section, we have drawn heavily from Lewis A. Coser's *Masters of Sociological Thought* (New York: Harcourt Brace Jovanovich, 1977); Steven Lukes's *Émile Durkheim: His Life and Work* (London: Allen Lane, 1973); and Robert Alun Jones's *Émile Durkheim* (Beverly Hills, CA: Sage, 1986).

the École did influence Durkheim, however. The great French historian Fustel de Coulanges provided him with a firm appreciation for careful assessment of historical causes, and the philosopher Émile Boutroux instilled in him an understanding of how reality consists of discontinuous levels that reveal emergent properties that distinguish them from one another. As we will see, these concerns for historical cause and emergent realities became central to Durkheim's sociology, and he acknowledged his debt by later dedicating his two doctoral theses to these teachers at the École.

Between 1882 and 1887, Durkheim taught in various schools around Paris, except for a year in Germany, where he studied German academic life and wrote a series of reports on German sociology and philosophy. These reports gave him some visibility in academic circles and promoted contacts with important officials in the educational establishment in France. More significantly, in the 1880s, his sociological orientation took on a more coherent form. This orientation represented a mixture of moral commitment to creating an integrated and cohesive society, on the one hand, and the application of rigorous analysis of social processes, on the other. Much like Auguste Comte before him, Durkheim believed that the observations of facts and the development of theories to explain these facts would lead to a body of knowledge that could be used to create a "better society." To achieve this goal, Durkheim had to re-create sociology in an era when Comte's ideas were not highly regarded and the traditional academic structure was hostile to any "science of society." Thus, it is to Durkheim's credit that he could use his powers of persuasion as well as his personal contacts to secure a position at the University of Bordeaux in the department of philosophy, where he was allowed to teach a social science course, heretofore an unacceptable subject in French universities.

During this period at Bordeaux, Durkheim wrote the three works that made him famous and placed him in a position to change the structure and content of the French educational system from primary schools to the universities themselves. Indeed, at no other time in the history of sociology has a sociologist exerted this degree of influence in a society.

At Bordeaux, Durkheim wrote *The Division of Labor in Society, The Rules of the Sociological Method,* and *Suicide.*[2] These three books

---

[2]Émile Durkheim, *The Division of Labor in Society* (New York: Free Press, 1947; originally published in 1893); *The Rules of the Sociological Method* (New York: Free Press, 1938; originally published in 1895); and *Suicide* (New York: Free Press, 1951; originally published in 1897).

established the power of sociological analysis, generating enormous controversy and begrudging respect for Durkheim as a scholar. Perhaps more significant for his ultimate influence on French intellectual thinking was his creation of *L'Année Sociologique* in 1898. This journal soon became the centerpiece of an intellectual movement revolving around his approach to sociology. Each annual issue contained contributions by Durkheim and a diverse group of young and creative scholars who, though from varying disciplines, were committed to defending his basic position.

In 1902, Durkheim's stature allowed him to move to the Sorbonne in Paris, and in 1906, he became a professor of science and education. In 1913, by a special ministerial decree, the name of his chair was changed to Science of Education *and Sociology*. As Lewis Coser notes of this event,[3] "after more than three-quarters of a century, Comte's brainchild had finally gained entry at the University of Paris." In Paris, Durkheim continued to edit *L'Année* and inspire a new generation of gifted scholars. Moreover, he was able to help reform the French educational system. At the time he rose to prominence, the government had embarked on a difficult process of secularizing the schools and creating a state system of public education that rivaled and then surpassed the Catholic school system, which until the early decades of the twentieth century, dominated the education of children. Through his contacts in high-level government positions, Durkheim created a new kind of curriculum in the public schools and a revolutionary program of teacher education. Emphasis was on secular topics, with the schools serving as a functional substitute for the church. In essence, the school was to teach reverence for "society," and the teacher was to be the "priest" who guided this worship of civil society. Durkheim's desire was to create a "civil morality" under which students became committed to the institutions of society and, at the same time, developed the secular skills and knowledge to analyze and change society for the better. Although he was very cautious in dictating the precise nature of the school curriculum and in proposing the desirable direction of society, no social scientist has ever exerted more influence on the general profile of such a major institutional structure in a society.

This concern with a civil morality was, of course, inherited from Comte, who in turn had merely carried forth the banner of earlier

---

[3]Coser, *Masters of Sociological Thought*, 147.

French philosophers—Charles Montesquieu and Jean Jacques Rousseau being the most prominent. For Durkheim, the central question of all sociological analysis is this: What forces integrate society, especially as it undergoes rapid change and differentiation? Durkheim believed that integration will always involve a "morality" or set of values, beliefs, and norms that guide the cognitive orientations and behaviors of individuals. Durkheim approached the analysis of moral integration in many different ways, but the need for a common morality permeates his work—from his first great work, *The Division of Labor in Society*, to his last major book, *The Elementary Forms of Religious Life*.[4] Thus, the young boy who was to have been a rabbi developed into the secular academic who was to preach for societal integration.

World War I disrupted the "Année School," as it had come to be known. Indeed, it destroyed many of its most promising members, including Durkheim's son, André, who would no doubt have had a distinguished career as a sociological linguist. Durkheim never recovered emotionally from this blow because he had hoped his son would carry on his work in the social sciences. In 1917, 2 years after his son's death, Durkheim died at the age of 59. Emotionally drained and physically declining, he simply did not care to live any longer.

Durkheim died at the height of his intellectual and political prominence. As we will see in the next chapter, he left an intellectual legacy that is as influential on sociological theorizing today as it was at the turn of the twentieth century. Durkheim's work represents the culmination of the French intellectual tradition that began with the Enlightenment. At the same time, his sociology is a response to both the perceived strengths and weaknesses of German and English sociology. The result is an approach that is true to its French pedigree—especially the works of Charles Montesquieu, Jean Jacques Rousseau, Auguste Comte, and Alexis de Tocqueville. Yet the pedigree is conditioned by Durkheim's reaction against Herbert Spencer and, to a lesser extent, Karl Marx. Let us now turn to this list of influential thinkers and observe how they influenced Durkheim's thinking. In this way, we can place in a broader intellectual and historical context the works to be examined in the next chapter.

---

[4]Émile Durkheim, *The Elementary Forms of Religious Life* (New York: Free Press, 1947; originally published in 1912).

Charles Montesquieu and Durkheim

As mentioned in our analysis of Auguste Comte's work, Montesquieu marked the beginning of a French intellectual line that came to a climax with Durkheim. To appreciate many of Durkheim's concepts and points of emphasis and his methodological approach, we must return to Montesquieu, one of the giant intellects of the eighteenth century.

Montesquieu as the First Social Scientist

Montesquieu introduced an entirely new approach to the study of society. If we look at any number of scholars whose thought was prominent in his time, we can immediately observe dramatic differences between their approach to the study of society and Montesquieu's. Many scholars of the eighteenth century were philosophers who were primarily concerned with the question, "What is the ultimate origin of society?" Their answer to this question was more philosophical than sociological and tended to be given in two parts. First, humans once existed in a "natural state" before the first society was created. Theory about society thus began with speculations about "the state of nature"—whether this state be warlike (Thomas Hobbes), peaceful (John Locke), or idyllic (Rousseau). Second, in this state of nature humans formed a "social contract" and thereby created "society." People agreed to subordinate themselves to government, law, values, beliefs, and contracts.

In contrast with these philosophical doctrines, Montesquieu emphasized that humans have never existed without society. In his view, humans are the product of society, and thus speculation about their primordial state does not represent an analysis of the facts of human life. He was an empiricist, concerned with actual data rather than speculation about the essence of humans and the ultimate origins of their society. In many ways, he was attracted to the procedures employed by Newton in physics: observe the facts of the universe and from these make statements about their basic properties and lawlike relations. Although it was left to Comte in the following century to trumpet the new science of "social physics," Montesquieu was the first to see that a science of society, molded after the physical sciences, was possible.

Durkheim saw Montesquieu as positing that society was a "thing" or "fact" in the same sense that physical matter constitutes a thing or fact. Montesquieu was the first to recognize, Durkheim believed, that "morals, manners, customs," and the "spirit of a nation" are subject to scientific investigation. From this initial insight, it is a short step to recognizing, as Comte did, that a discipline called sociology can study society. Durkheim gave explicit credit to Montesquieu for recognizing that a "discipline may be called a science only if it has a definite field to explore. Science is concerned with things, realities. Before social science could begin to exist, it had to be assigned a subject matter."[5]

Montesquieu never completely carried through on his view that society could be studied in the same manner as phenomena in the other sciences, but his classic book, *The Spirit of Laws*, represents one of the first sociological works with a distinctly scientific tone. Although he had become initially famous for other works, *The Spirit* had the most direct influence on Durkheim.[6] Indeed, Durkheim's Latin doctoral thesis was on *The Spirit* and was published a year before his famous French thesis, *The Division of Labor in Society*.[7] From *The Spirit*, Durkheim took both methodological and substantive ideas, as is emphasized in the following review of Montesquieu's work and its influence on Durkheim.

Montesquieu's View of "Laws"

The opening lines of *The Spirit* read,

Laws, in their most general signification, are the necessary relations arising from the nature of things. In this sense all beings have their laws: the Deity His laws, the material world its laws, the intelligences superior to man their laws, the beasts their laws, man his laws.[8]

There is an ambiguity in this passage that is never clarified, for Montesquieu used the term *law* in two distinct senses: (1) law as a

---

[5]Émile Durkheim, *Montesquieu and Rousseau* (Ann Arbor: University of Michigan Press, 1960), 3.

[6]Montesquieu's major works include *The Persian Letters* (New York: Meridian, 1901; originally published in 1721); and *Considerations on the Grandeur and Decadence of the Romans* (New York: Free Press, 1965; originally published in 1734). In many ways, these two early books represented a data source for the more systematic analysis in *The Spirit of Laws*, 2 vols. (London: Colonial, 1900; originally published in 1748).

[7]In academic circles of Durkheim's time, two doctoral dissertations were required, one in French and another in Latin. The Latin thesis, on Montesquieu, was published in 1892, and the French thesis, on the division of labor, was published in 1893.

[8]Montesquieu, *Spirit of Laws*, 1.

commandment, or rule, created by humans to regulate their conduct and (2) law as a scientific statement of the relations among properties of the universe in its physical, biological, and social manifestations. The first is a substantive conception of law—that of the jurist and political scientist. The second is a conception of scientific laws that explains the regularities among properties of the natural world. Durkheim incorporated this distinction implicitly in his own work. On the one hand, his first great work, *The Division of Labor in Society*,[9] is about law, for he used variations in laws and the penalties for their violation as concrete indicators of integration in the broader society. On the other hand, *The Division of Labor* involves a search for the scientific laws that explain the nature of social integration in human societies.

Montesquieu also proposed an implicit "hierarchy of laws," an idea that may have suggested to Comte the hierarchy of the sciences (see Chapter 3). For Montesquieu, "lower order" phenomena, such as physical matter, cannot deviate from the scientific laws that govern their operation, but higher order beings with intelligence can violate and transgress laws, giving the scientific laws of society a probabilistic rather than absolute character. Durkheim, who was to view statistical rates as social facts in many of his works, also adopted this idea of probabilistic relations among social phenomena.

Montesquieu's Typology of Governments

To search for the scientific laws of the social world, Montesquieu argued, classification and typology are necessary. The enormous diversity of social patterns can easily obscure the common properties of phenomena unless the underlying type is exposed. The first 13 books of *The Spirit* are thus devoted to Montesquieu's famous typology of governmental forms: (1) republic, (2) monarchy, and (3) despotism. Both the methodological and substantive facets of Montesquieu's typology influenced Durkheim. On the methodological side, Durkheim saw as significant the way in which Montesquieu went about constructing his typology. Durkheim stressed the more strictly methodological technique of using "number, arrangement, and cohesion of their component parts" for classifying social structures. In many ways, he was making assumptions about Montesquieu's views on this matter because Montesquieu was

---

[9]Durkheim, *Division of Labor*.

never very explicit. Yet Montesquieu's classification of governmental forms apparently inspired Durkheim's lifelong advocacy of typology and his use of the number, arrangement, and cohesion of parts as the basis for constructing typologies.

Another methodological technique that Durkheim appears to have borrowed from Montesquieu is the notion that laws enacted by governments will reflect not only the "nature" (structural form) of government but also its "principle" (underlying values and beliefs). Moreover, laws will reflect the other institutions that the nature and principle of government influence. Law is thus a good indicator of the culture and structure of society. This premise became the central methodological tenet of Durkheim's first major work on the division of labor.

On the substantive side, Montesquieu's view of government as composed of two inseparable elements, nature and principle, probably influenced Durkheim more than he acknowledged. For Montesquieu, each government's nature, or structure, is a reflection of both who holds power and how power is exercised. Each government also reveals a principle, leading to the classification of governments by structural units and cultural beliefs. For a republic, the underlying principle is "virtue," in which people have respect for law and for the welfare of the group; for a monarchy, the guiding principle is respect for rank, authority, and hierarchy; and for despotism, the principle is fear. The specifics of Montesquieu's political sociology are less important than the general insight they illustrate: Social structures are held together by a corresponding system of values and beliefs that individuals have internalized. Moreover, as Montesquieu emphasized, when a government's nature and principle are not in harmony—or, more generally, when social structures and cultural beliefs are in contradiction—social change is inevitable. Durkheim wrestled with these theoretical issues for his entire intellectual career. Yet one finds scarce notice in his thesis of Montesquieu's profound insight into this aspect of social reality.

Another substantive issue, for which Montesquieu is most famous, is the "balance of powers" thesis. The basic argument is that a separation, or division, of powers among the elements of government is essential for a stable government. Power must be its own corrective, for only counterpower can limit the abuse of power. Thus, Montesquieu saw the two branches of the legislature (one for the nobility, the other for commoners) as they interact with each other and with the monarch as providing checks and balances on each other.[10] The judiciary, the third element of government, was not considered by Montesquieu to be an independent source of power, as it became in the American governmental system. Several points in this analysis no doubt influenced Durkheim. First, Montesquieu's distrust of mass democracy, in which the general population directly influences political decisions, was retained in Durkheim's analysis of industrial societies. In Durkheim's eye, representation is always to be mediated to avoid instability in political decisions. Second, Durkheim shared Montesquieu's distrust of a single center of power. Montesquieu feared despotism, whereas Durkheim distrusted the monolithic and bureaucratized state, but both recognized that to avoid the danger of highly centralized power, counter-power must be created.

The Causes and Functions of Governments

In addition to the notion of social types and scientific laws, the most conspicuous portions of Durkheim's Latin doctoral thesis are those on the "causes" and "functions" of government, a distinction that became central to his sociology.

Montesquieu's *The Spirit* is often a confused work, and commentators have frequently misunderstood his analysis of causes. After the typology of governments in the first 13 books of *The Spirit*, Montesquieu suddenly launched into a causal analysis that could appear to undermine his emphasis on the importance of "the principle" in shaping the "nature," or structure, of government. For suddenly, in Books 14 through 25, a variety of physical and moral causes of governmental forms is enumerated: Climates, soil fertility, manners, morals, commerce, money, population size, and religion are introduced one after another as causes of governmental and social forms.

The confusion often registered in this discussion of causes can be mitigated by recognizing Montesquieu's underlying assumptions. First, these causes do not directly affect governmental forms. Rather, each affects people's behavior, temperament, and disposition in ways

---

[10]If one computes these balances, they consistently work out in favor of the nobility and against the common people. The nobility and commoners unite to check the monarch, and the nobility and monarch check the commoners. But the monarch cannot, as an elevated figure, unite with the commoners. Montesquieu's aristocratic bias is clearly evident.

that create a "general spirit of the nation," an idea that was not far from Durkheim's conceptualization of the "collective conscience" and "collective representations" or Comte's similar notions. Thus, "physical causes," such as climate, soil, and population size, as well as "moral causes," such as commerce, morals, manners, and customs, all constrain how people act, behave, and think. From the collective life constrained and shaped by these causes comes the "spirit of a nation," which is a set of implicit ideas that bind people to one another and give them a sense of their common purpose.[11]

Once it is recognized that these causes do not operate directly on the structure of government, a second point of clarification is possible. According to Montesquieu, the underlying principle of government is linked to the general spirit that emerges from people's actions and thoughts as this list of causes constrains them. Montesquieu was ambiguous on this issue, but this interpretation is the most consistent with how Durkheim probably viewed his argument. Curiously, despite the similarity of their views on the importance of collective ideas or "spirits" for social relations, Durkheim did not give Montesquieu much credit for this aspect of his sociology.

Durkheim did give Montesquieu explicit credit, however, for recognizing that a society must assume a "definite form" because of its "particular situation" and that this form stems from "efficient causes." In particular, Durkheim indicated that Montesquieu's view of ecological and population variables stimulated his concern with "material density" and how it influences "moral density." Durkheim recognized that to view social structures and ideas as the result of identifiable causes marked a dramatic breakthrough in social thought, especially because many social thinkers of the time were often locked in discussions of human nature and the "origins" of the first social contract.

Durkheim was, however, highly critical of Montesquieu's causal analysis in one respect: He saw Montesquieu as arguing for "final causes"—that is, the ends served by a structure such as law cause it to emerge and persist. As Durkheim stressed, "anyone who limits his inquiry to the final cause of social phenomena loses sight of their origins and is untrue to science. This is what would happen to sociology

---

[11]This argument is derived from Louis Althusser, *Politics and History* (Paris: Universities of Paris, 1959).

if we followed Montesquieu's method."[12] Durkheim recognized that Montesquieu had been one of the first scholars to argue for what is now termed *cultural relativism*. Social structures must be assessed not in relation to some absolute, ethnocentric, or moralistic standard but in their own terms and in view of the particular context in which they are found. For example, Montesquieu could view slavery not so much as a moral evil but as a viable institution in certain types of societies in particular historical periods. Implicit in this kind of argument is the notion of "function": A structure must be assessed by its functions for the social whole; if a social pattern, even one like slavery, promotes the persistence and integration of a society, it cannot be deduced to be an evil or good pattern. Durkheim felt that Montesquieu too easily saw the consequence of structures—that is, integration—as their cause, with the result that Montesquieu's functional and causal analyses frequently became confused. Yet Montesquieu might have suggested to Durkheim a critical distinction between causal and functional analysis.

In sum, Durkheim gave Montesquieu credit for many insights that became a part of his sociology: the social world can be studied as a "thing"; it is best to develop typologies; it is necessary to examine the number, arrangement, and relations among parts in developing these typologies; it is important to view law as an indicator of broader social and cultural forces; and it is wise to employ both causal and functional analyses.

Despite Durkheim's praise of Montesquieu, it is interesting to note what he did not acknowledge in Montesquieu's work: the view that laws, like those of physics, can be formulated for the social realm (in the thesis, Durkheim gave Comte credit for this insight);[13] the recognition that social morphology and cultural symbols are interconnected; the position that causes of morphological structures are mediated through, and mitigated by, cultural ideas; the notion that causes, and the laws that express relations among events, are probabilistic in nature; and the view that power in social relations must be checked by counterpower. These ideas became an integral part of

---

[12]Durkheim, *Montesquieu and Rousseau*, 44.

[13]As Durkheim noted, no further progress could be made until it was recognized that the laws of societies are no different from those governing the rest of nature and that the method by which they are discovered is identical with that of the other sciences. This was Auguste Comte's contribution." (*Montesquieu and Rousseau*, 63–64)

Durkheim's thinking, and thus much of Montesquieu's theoretical legacy lived in Durkheimian sociology.[14]

Jean Jacques Rousseau and Durkheim

Writing his major works in the decade following the 1748 publication of Montesquieu's *The Spirit*, Jean Jacques Rousseau produced a philosophical doctrine that contains none of Montesquieu's sense for social science but much of his sense for the nature of social order.[15] Although not greatly admired in his time, Rousseau's ideas were, by the beginning of the nineteenth century, viewed in a highly favorable light. Indeed, in retrospect, Rousseau was considered the leading figure of the Enlightenment, surpassing Hobbes, Locke, Voltaire, and certainly Montesquieu. It is not surprising, therefore, that Durkheim read with interest Rousseau's philosophical doctrine and extracted many ideas.

Rousseau's Doctrine

Rousseau's doctrine was a unique combination of Christian notions of the fall that came with original sin and Voltaire's belief in the progress of humans.[16] Rousseau first postulated a pre-societal "state of nature" in which individuals were dependent on nature and had only simple physical needs, for "man's"[17] desires "do not go beyond his physical needs; in all the universe the only desirable things he knows are food, a female, and rest." In the "state of nature,"

---

[14]For further commentary on Montesquieu's work, see Althusser, *Politics and History*, 13–108; Raymond Aron, *Main Currents in Sociological Thought*, Vol. 1 (Garden City, NY: Doubleday, 1968), 13–72; W. Stark, *Montesquieu: Pioneer of the Sociology of Knowledge* (Toronto, Ontario, Canada: University of Toronto Press, 1961); and Thomas L. Pangle, *Montesquieu's Philosophy of Liberalism: A Commentary on "The Spirit of Laws"* (Chicago: University of Chicago Press, 1973).

[15]Jean-Jacques Rousseau, *The Social Contract and Discourses*, trans. G. D. H. Cole (New York: Dutton, 1950). This book is a compilation of Rousseau's various *Discourses* and *The Social Contract*—his most important works—which were written separately between 1750 and 1762. Durkheim analyzed *The Social Contract*, and it appears, along with his Latin thesis on Montesquieu, in Durkheim, *Montesquieu and Rousseau*, 65–138.

[16]J. H. Broome, *Rousseau: A Study of His Thought* (New York: Barnes & Noble, 1963), 14.

[17]Rousseau's phraseology uses the term *the natural state of man*, which is retained here.

humans had little contact with or dependence on one another, and they had only crude "sensations" that reflected their direct experiences with the physical environment.

The great "fall" came from this natural state. The discovery of agriculture, the development of metallurgy, and other events created a new and distinct entity: society. People formed social relations; they discovered private property; they appropriated property; they competed; those with property exploited others; they began to feel emotions of jealousy and envy; they began to fight and make war; and in other ways they created the modern world. Rousseau felt that this world not only deviated from humans' natural state but also made their return to this state impossible.

As an emergent reality that destroys the natural state, modern society poses a series of problems that make life an agonizing misery. In particular, humans feel no limit to their desires and passions, self-interest dominates, and one human exploits another. For Rousseau, society is corrupt and evil, destroying not only the natural controls on passions and self-interest but also the liberty from exploitation by one's fellows that typified the natural state.

Rousseau's solution to this evil was as original as it was naive, and yet it exerted considerable influence on Durkheim. Rousseau's solution was to eliminate self-interest and inequality by creating a situation in which human beings would have the same relation to society as they once had to nature. That is, people should be free from one another and yet equally subject to society. In Rousseau's view, only the political state could ensure individual freedom and liberty, and only when individuals totally subordinated their interest to what he termed the *general will* could inequality, exploitation, and self-interest be eliminated. If all individuals subjugate themselves equally to the general will and the state, they are equal. If the state can ensure individual freedom and maintain equal dependence of individuals on the general will, then the basic elements of nature are re-created: freedom, liberty, and equal dependence on an external force (society instead of nature).

What is the general will? And how is it to be created? Rousseau was never terribly clear about just what constituted the general will, but it appears to have referred to an emergent set of values and beliefs embodying "individual wills." The general will can be created and maintained, Rousseau asserted, only by several means: (1) the elimination of otherworld religions, such as Christianity, and their replacement by a "civil religion" with the general will as the supreme being; (2) the elimination of family socialization and its replacement by common socialization of all the young into the general will (presumably through schools); and (3) the creation of a powerful state that embodies the general will and the corresponding elimination of groups, organizations, and other "minor associations" that deflect the power of general will and generate pockets of self-interest and potential dissensus among people.[18]

Specific Influences on Durkheim

Society as an Emergent Reality

In his courses, Durkheim gave Rousseau credit for the insight that society comprises a moral reality, sui generis, that could be distinguished from individual morality.[19] Although Montesquieu had reached a similar understanding, Rousseau phrased the matter in a way that Durkheim emulated on frequent occasions. For Rousseau as well as for Durkheim, society is "a moral entity having specific qualities [separate] from those of the individual beings who compose it, somewhat as chemical compounds have properties that they owe to none of their elements."[20]

Thus, Durkheim took from Rousseau the view of society as an emergent and moral entity, much like emergent physical phenomena. Like Rousseau, Durkheim abhorred a society in which competition and exchange dominated a common morality. Indeed, for Durkheim, society was not possible without a moral component guiding exchanges among individuals.

Social Pathology

Durkheim viewed Rousseau's discussion of the natural state as a "methodological device" that could be used to highlight the

---

[18]For more detailed analyses of Rousseau's doctrines, see Broome, *Rousseau;* Ernst Cassirer, *The Question of Jean-Jacques Rousseau* (Bloomington: Indiana University Press, 1963); Ronald Grimsley, *The Philosophy of Rousseau* (New York: Oxford University Press, 1973); John Charvet, *The Social Problem in the Philosophy of Rousseau* (Cambridge, UK: Cambridge University Press, 1974); and David Cameron, *The Social Thought of Rousseau and Burke: A Comparative Study* (Toronto, Ontario, Canada: University of Toronto Press, 1973).

[19]Durkheim's essay on Rousseau in *Montesquieu and Rousseau* was drafted from a course he taught at Bordeaux. It was published posthumously in 1918.

[20]Durkheim, *Montesquieu and Rousseau*, 82. Durkheim took this quote from Rousseau.

pathologies of contemporary society and to provide guidelines for the remaking of society. Although many others in the eighteenth and nineteenth centuries had also emphasized the ills of the social world, Durkheim appeared to be drawn to three central conditions emphasized by Rousseau. Durkheim termed these (1) *egoism*, (2) *anomie*, and (3) *the forced division of labor*, but his debt to Rousseau is clear. For Durkheim, egoism is a situation in which self-interest and self-concern take precedence over commitment to the larger collectivity. Anomie is a state of deregulation in which the collective no longer controls people's desires and passions. The forced division of labor is a condition in which one class can use its privilege to exploit another and to force people into certain roles. Indeed, the inheritance of privilege and the use of privilege by one class to exploit another were repugnant to Durkheim. Like Rousseau, he felt that inequalities should be based on "natural" differences that spring from "a difference of age, health, physical strength, and mental and spiritual qualities."[21]

Thus, Durkheim was highly sympathetic to Rousseau's conception of what ailed society: people force others to do their bidding, they are deregulated, and they are unattached to a larger purpose. Hence, the social order should be structured in ways that mitigate these pathologies.

The Problem of Order

Durkheim accepted the dilemma of modern society as Rousseau saw it: How is it possible to maintain individual freedom and liberty, without also releasing people's desires and encouraging rampant self-interest, while creating a strong and cohesive social order that does not aggravate inequality and oppression?

For Rousseau, this question could be answered with a strong political state that ensured individual freedom and a general will that emulated nature. Like Rousseau, Durkheim believed that the state was the only force that would guarantee individual freedom and liberty, but he altered Rousseau's notion of society as the equivalent of the physical environment in the state of nature. For Durkheim, society and the constraints it imposes must be viewed as natural, with the result that people must be taught to accept the constraints and barriers of society in the same way that they accept the limitations of their biological

---

[21]Ibid., 86.

makeup and the physical environment. Only in this way can both egoism and anomie be held in check. Durkheim believed that constraint by the moral force of society is in the natural order of things.

Like Rousseau, Durkheim argued for a view of society as "sacred" and for the transfer of the same sentiments toward civil and secular society that people had traditionally maintained toward the gods (which, Durkheim later emphasized, are only symbolizations of society).[22] Moreover, like Rousseau, Durkheim stressed the need for a moral education outside of the family in which children could be taught in schools to understand and accept the importance of commitment to the morality of the collective. Such a commitment could be achieved, he argued, through a unified "collective conscience" or a set of "collective representations" that could regulate people's desires and passions. This view represented a reworking of Rousseau's view of absolute commitment to the general will. In sharp contrast with Rousseau, however, Durkheim came to believe that only through attachment to cohesive subgroups, or what Rousseau had called "minor associations," could egoism be mitigated. Such groups, Durkheim felt, can attach individuals to the remote collective conscience and give them an immediate community of others. Moreover, like Montesquieu, he distrusted an all-powerful state, and hence he came to view these subgroups as a political counterbalance to the powers of the state.

Thus, Durkheim borrowed many ideas from Rousseau. Some of his central concepts about social pathologies—anomie, egoism, and the forced division of labor—owed much to Rousseau's work. Durkheim's vision of society as integrated by a strong state and by a set of common values and beliefs reflected Rousseau's vision of how to eliminate these pathologies. Rousseau also inspired Durkheim's desire to use schools to provide moral education for the young and to rekindle the spirit of commitment to secular society that people once had toward the sacred.

Yet Durkheim could never accept Rousseau's trust of the state. Durkheim believed that the state's power must be checked and balanced. People must be free to associate and to join groupings that encourage diversity based on common experiences and that create

---

[22]Many of the specifics of Durkheim's ideas about religion as the symbolization of society were borrowed from Roberton Smith. See Lukes, *Émile Durkheim*, 450. For a further documentation of the influences on Durkheim's sociology of religion, see Robert Alun Jones and Mariah Evans, "The Critical Moment in Durkheim's Sociology of Religion," paper read at the meeting of the American Sociological Association, September 1978.

centers of counter-power to mitigate the state's power. Durkheim thus internalized Rousseau's vision of an integrated society in which individual freedom and liberty prevail. Durkheim accepted the challenge of proposing ways to achieve that society, but he could never abide by Rousseau's vision of an all-powerful state and its oppressive general will.[23]

Rousseau's impact on Durkheim was, no doubt, profound, but the extremes of Rousseau's philosophy are mitigated in Durkheim's work. Montesquieu's emphasis on the balancing of power with counter-power, and his emphasis on empirical facts rather than on moral precepts, represented one tempering influence on Durkheim. Still another moderating influence came from Comte, whose work consolidated many intellectual trends into a clear program for a science that could be used to create the "good society."

Auguste Comte and Durkheim

It is difficult to know how much of the French intellectual tradition of the eighteenth century came to Durkheim through Comte, because Durkheim did not always acknowledge his debt to the titular founder of sociology. This difficulty is compounded because, like Durkheim's work, Comte's intellectual scheme represents a synthesis of ideas from Montesquieu, Rousseau, Saint-Simon,[24] and others in the French lineage. Many of the specific features of Durkheimian sociology owed much to Comte's grand vision for the science of society. We reviewed Comte's thought in Chapter 3, and so we will focus here only on the specific aspects of his intellectual scheme that appear to have exerted the most influence on Durkheim.

The Science of Positivism

Comte must have reinforced for Durkheim Montesquieu's insistence that "facts" and "data," rather than philosophical speculation,

---

[23]For a discussion of Durkheim's differences with Rousseau, see Lukes, *Émile Durkheim*, Chapter 14.

[24]Many have noted how much Comte took from his teacher, Saint-Simon. We can argue, however, that Saint-Simon's more scientific concerns reached Durkheim via Comte's reinterpretation, although Durkheim rejected Saint-Simon's utopian socialism.

should guide the science of society. Borrowing Comte's vision of a science of "social facts," Durkheim agreed with Comte's view that the laws of human organization could be discovered. These laws, as Montesquieu stressed, will not be as "rigid" or "deterministic" as in sciences lower in the hierarchy, but they will be the equivalent of those laws in physics, chemistry, and biology in that they will allow for the understanding of phenomena. Thus, Comte cemented in Durkheim's mind the dictum that empirical facts must guide the search for sociological laws, and conversely, theoretical principles must direct the gathering of facts.

The Methodological Tenets of Positivism

Collecting facts requires a methodology, and Comte was the first to make explicit the variety of methods that could guide the new science of society. As he indicated, four procedures are acceptable: (1) "observation" of the social world by the use of human senses (best done, he emphasized, when guided by theory); (2) "experimentation," especially as allowed by social pathologies; (3) "historical" observation, in which regular patterns of change in the nature of society—especially in the nature of its ideas—can be seen; and (4) "comparison," in which human and animal societies, coexisting human societies, and different elements of the same society are compared to isolate the effects of specific variables. Durkheim employed all of these methods in his sociology, and hence, we can conclude that Comte's methodological approach influenced Durkheim's methodology.

Another methodological aspect of Comte's thought revolves around the organic analogy. As we saw in Chapter 3, Comte often compared society to a biological organism, with the result that a part, such as the family or the state, could be understood by what it did for or contributed to the "body social." Montesquieu had made a similar point, although Comte first drew the clear analogy between the social and biological organisms. The functional method Durkheim developed thus owed much to Comte's biological analogy. Indeed, as Durkheim emphasized, complete understanding of social facts is not possible without assessing their functions for maintaining the integration of the social whole.[25]

---

[25]For a more complete analysis of Comte's organicism and its impact on Durkheim's functionalism, see Jonathan H. Turner and Alexandra Maryanski, *Functionalism* (Menlo Park, CA: Benjamin/Cummings, 1979).

Much less prominent in Comte's scheme than in Montesquieu's was the emphasis on typology; yet Comte recognized that the construction of somewhat "idealized" types of social phenomena could help in sociological analysis. Although many intermediate cases will not conform to these extreme types, their deviations from the types allow their comparison against a common yardstick—that is, the idealized type.[26] In his early work, Durkheim developed typologies of societies; thus, we can assume that Montesquieu's emphasis on types, as reinforced by Comte's emphasis on the use of types as an analytical device for comparison, must have shaped Durkheim's approach. Throughout his career, Durkheim insisted that classification of phenomena by their "morphology," or structure, must precede either a causal or functional analysis.

Social Statics and Dynamics

Durkheim was also influenced by the substance of Comte's scheme. Comte divided sociology into "statics" and "dynamics," a distinction that Durkheim implicitly maintained. Moreover, Durkheim adopted the specific concepts Comte used to understand statics and dynamics.

With regard to social statics, Durkheim shared Comte's concern with social solidarity and with the impact of the division of labor on this solidarity. In particular, Durkheim asked the same question as Comte: How can *consensus universalis*, or what Durkheim termed the *collective conscience*, be a basis for social integration given the growing specialization of functions in society? How can consensus about ideas, beliefs, and values be maintained at the same time that people are differentiated and pulled apart by their occupational specialization? *The Division of Labor in Society*, Durkheim's first major work, addressed these questions, and though Rousseau in the eighteenth century and a host of others in the nineteenth century had also tried to address these same issues, Durkheim's approach owed more to Comte than to any other thinker.[27]

With respect to social dynamics, Comte held an evolutionary vision of human progress. Societies, especially their ideas, are moving from theological through metaphysical to positivistic modes of thought. Durkheim adopted this specific view of the evolution of ideas late in his career in his work on religion. More fundamentally,

---

[26]This approach obviously anticipated by a half-century Max Weber's ideal type method.

[27]Durkheim, *Division of Labor*.

however, he retained the evolutionary approach to studying social change held by Comte and a host of other thinkers. Durkheim saw societies as moving from simple to complex patterns of social structure and, correspondingly, from religious to secular systems of ideas. Almost everything he examined was couched in these evolutionary terms, which, to a very great extent, he adopted from Comte.

Science and Social Progress

Like his teacher and collaborator, Saint-Simon, Comte saw the development of sociology as a means of creating a better society. Although Durkheim's sense of pathology in the modern world probably owes more to Rousseau than to either Saint-Simon or Comte, Durkheim accepted the hope of the two latter thinkers for a society based on the application of sociological laws. Durkheim was much less extreme than either Saint-Simon or Comte, who tended to make a religion of science and to advocate unattainable utopias, but Durkheim retained Comte's view that a science of society could be used to facilitate social progress. Indeed, Durkheim never abandoned his dream that applying the laws of sociology could create a just and integrated social order.

In sum, then, Durkheim's debt to Rousseau was mitigated by his exposure to Comte. His view of science as reliant on data and as generating laws of human organization came as much from Comte as from any other thinker, as did his adoption of explicit methodological techniques. His substantive view of society similarly reflected Comte's emphasis: a concern for social integration of differentiated units and for determining how ideas (values, beliefs, and norms) are involved in such integration. Comte's insistence that science be used to promote the betterment of the human condition translated Rousseau's passionate and moralistic assessment of social ills into a more rational concern with constructing an integrated society employing sociological principles.

Alexis de Tocqueville and Durkheim

In 1835, Alexis de Tocqueville, a young member of an elite family, published the first two volumes of a book based on his observations of American society. *Democracy in America* was an almost immediate success, propelling Tocqueville into a lifelong position of intellectual and political prominence in France. The third and fourth volumes of

Democracy in America appeared in 1840,[28] and after a short political career culminating in his abbreviated appointment as foreign minister for France, he retired to write what he saw as his major work, *The Old Regime and the French Revolution,* the first part of which appeared in 1857.[29] His death in 1859 cut short the completion of *The Old Regime,* but the completed volumes of *Democracy in America* and the first part of *The Old Regime* established him as the leading political thinker in France, one who carried the tradition of Montesquieu into the nineteenth century and one whom Durkheim read carefully.

Tocqueville probably never read Comte, but his effort to emulate Montesquieu's method of analysis must have had considerable influence on Durkheim. Indeed, from Tocqueville's analysis of democracy in America, Durkheim got many of the ideas that mitigated the extremes of Rousseau's political solutions to social pathologies.

Tocqueville's Democracy in America

Tocqueville saw the long-term trend toward democracy as the key to understanding the modern world. In *Democracy in America,* the young Tocqueville attempted to discover why individual freedom and liberty were being preserved in the United States and, implicitly, why French efforts toward democracy had experienced trouble (a theme more explicitly developed in *The Old Regime*). In this effort, he isolated two trends that typified democracies:

1. *The trend toward a leveling of social status:* Although they preserve economic and political ranks, democratic societies bestow equal social status on their members—creating, in Tocqueville's eye, an increasingly homogeneous mass.

2. *The trend toward centralization of power:* Democratic governments tend to create large and centralized administrative bureaucracies and to concentrate power increasingly in the hands of legislative bodies.

Tocqueville saw a number of potential dangers in these two trends. First, as differences among people are leveled, the only avenue for social

---

[28]Alexis de Tocqueville, *Democracy in America* (New York: Knopf, 1945; originally published in 2 vols. in 1835 and 1840, respectively).

[29]Alexis de Tocqueville, *The Old Regime and the French Revolution* (Garden City, NY: Doubleday, 1955; originally published in 1857).

recognition becomes ceaseless material acquisition motivated by blind ambition. Tocqueville felt that traditional status and honor distinctions had kept ambition and status striving in check. As the old hereditary basis for bestowing honor is destroyed, the individual is released and freed from the constraints imposed by traditional social patterns. This point—the releasing of individuals from social control—is reminiscent of Rousseau's analysis and, no doubt, stimulated Durkheim's conceptualization of egoism and anomie.

Second, the centralization of administrative power can become so great that it results in despotism, which then undermines individual freedom and liberty. Moreover, centralized governments tend to rely on external war and to suppress internal dissent in an effort to promote further consolidation of power.

Third, the centralization of decision making in the legislative branch can make government too responsive to the immediate, short-lived, and unreasoned sentiments of the social mass. Under these conditions, government becomes unstable as it is pulled one way, and then another, by public sentiment.

Montesquieu's influence is evident in these concerns. Unlike Montesquieu, however, Tocqueville saw another side of democracy, a side in which individual liberty and freedom could be preserved even with the centralization of power, and where people's ambitions and atomization could be held in check even as the old system of honor and prestige receded. The democratic pattern in America, Tocqueville believed, provided an illustration of conditions that could promote this other side of democracy.

It is not surprising that Tocqueville, as a student of Montesquieu, made references in his analysis of American democracy to historical causes, placing emphasis on geography, unique historical circumstances, the system of laws (in particular the Constitution), and, most important, the "customs, manners, and beliefs" of the American people. From these causes, Tocqueville described several conditions that mitigated the concentration of political power and the over-atomization of individuals:

1. The system of checks and balances in government, with power in the federal government divided into three branches

2. The federalist system, in which state and local governments, with their own divisions of power, check each other's power as well as that of the federal government

3. A free and independent press

4. A strong commitment of the people to use and rely on local institutions

5. The freedom to form and use political and civil associations to achieve individual and collective goals

6. A powerful system of values and beliefs stressing individual freedom

The power and subtlety of Tocqueville's description of America cannot be captured with a short list like this. Yet this list probably best communicates what Durkheim pulled out of Tocqueville's work. Rousseau and Tocqueville had both highlighted the ills of the modern world—unregulated passions and rampant self-interest. Rousseau's solution to these problems was too extreme for the liberal Durkheim. In contrast, Tocqueville's analysis of America provided a view of a modern and differentiated social structure in which freedom and individualism could be maintained without severe pathologies and without recourse to a dictatorial state.

Specific Influences on Durkheim

Durkheim viewed modern social structure as integrated when (1) differentiated functions were well coordinated, (2) individuals were attached to collective organizations, (3) individual freedom was preserved by a central state, (4) the central state set broad collective goals and reinforced common values, and (5) the state's broad powers were checked and balanced by countersources of power.

It is not hard to find these themes in Tocqueville's work. In particular, Durkheim found the idea of "civil and political" associations appealing. These associations can provide people with a basis for attachment and identification, and they can serve as a mechanism for mediating between their members and the state. Durkheim termed these associations *occupational*, or *corporate* groups, and he took much from Tocqueville's analysis of voluntary civil and political associations. Moreover, in adopting Montesquieu's emphasis on customs, manners, and beliefs that promote strong commitments to freedom and liberty, without also promoting atomization, he recognized in Tocqueville's work the importance of general values and beliefs (Rousseau's *general will* and Comte's *consensus universalis* and *general spirit*) for promoting integration among the diversified groupings of modern societies. For even if these values and beliefs emphasize individual freedom and liberty, they can be used to unite people by stressing a collective respect for the rights of the individual.

Thus, Tocqueville gave to Durkheim a sense for some of the general conditions that could mitigate the pathologies of modern societies. These conditions became a part of Durkheim's practical program as well as of his more strictly theoretical analysis.

Herbert Spencer and Durkheim

Montesquieu, Rousseau, Comte, and Tocqueville represent the French intellectual heritage from which Durkheim took many of his more important concepts.[30] His criticism of these thinkers is not severe, and we can sense that he never reacted against their thought. He took what was useful and ignored obvious weaknesses. Such is not the case with Spencer, for throughout his career, Durkheim singled out Spencer for very special criticism.

Durkheim and Spencerian Utilitarianism

Durkheim reacted vehemently against any view of social order that ignored the importance of collective values and beliefs. Utilitarian doctrines stress the importance of competition and exchange in creating a social order held together by contracts among actors pursuing their own self-interests. Durkheim did not ignore the importance of competition, exchange, and contract, but he saw blind self-interest as a social pathology. A society could not be held together by self-interest and legal contracts alone; a "moral" component or an underlying system of collective values and beliefs must also guide people's interactions in the pursuit of "collective" goals or interests.

Durkheim was thus highly critical of Spencer, who as we saw in Chapters 4 and 5, coined phrases such as "survival of the fittest"

---

[30]This is not to deny the influence of specific teachers and less well-known scholars. But we think that the degree to which Durkheim took from the giants of French thought has been underemphasized in commentaries. There is too much similarity in the combined legacy of Montesquieu, Rousseau, Comte, and Tocqueville, on the one hand, and Durkheim's thought, on the other, for the impact of these prominent social thinkers to be ignored.

and emphasized that modern society was laced together by contracts negotiated from the competition and exchange of self-interested actors. In fact, Durkheim's works are so filled with references to the inadequacies of Spencerian sociology that we might view Durkheimian sociology as a lifelong overreaction to the imputed ills in Spencerian sociology.[31]

Durkheim and Spencerian Organicism

Spencer wore two intellectual hats: (1) the moralist, who was a staunch individualist and utilitarian, and (2) the scientist, who sought to develop laws of both organic and superorganic forms. Moreover, in attempting to realize the latter, Spencer took Comte's organic analogy and converted it into an explicit functionalism: system parts function to meet the needs of the "body social." Durkheim clearly drew considerable inspiration from this mode of analysis because one of his major methodological tenets is to stress the importance of assessing the functions of social phenomena. We might even speculate that had Spencer not formulated functionalism, it is unlikely that Durkheim would have adopted this mode of sociological analysis.

Durkheim and Spencerian Evolutionism

Spencer also had an evolutionary view of societies as moving from a simple to a treble-compound state. Although perhaps deficient in some respects, Spencer's description was far more attuned than was Comte's to the structural and cultural aspects of social evolution. Comte's evolutionism had been vague, with references to the movement of systems of thought and the view of the social organism as embracing all of humanity. In contrast, Spencer's analysis was far more sociological and emphasized explicit variables that could distinguish

---

[31]For a more detailed analysis of Durkheim and Spencer, see Turner and Maryanski, *Functionalism*, Chapter 1. Indeed, if Durkheim's and Spencer's actual theories of social differentiation are compared, side by side, they are virtually identical. For further analysis and commentary, see Jonathan H. Turner, *Herbert Spencer: Toward a Renewed Appreciation* (Beverly Hills, CA: Sage, 1985); "Durkheim's and Spencer's Principles of Social Organization: A Theoretical Note," *Sociological Perspectives* 27 (January 1984), 21–32; and "The Forgotten Giant: Herbert Spencer's Theoretical Models and Principles," *Revue Européene des Sciences Sociales* 29 (no. 59, 1981), 79–98.

types of societies from one another and that could provide a view of the dimensions along which evolutionary change could be described. Thus, it is difficult to imagine that Durkheim was unimpressed with Spencer's analysis of the broad contours of social evolution.[32] Indeed, Durkheim's first major work was to explore social evolution from simple to complex societies, a task that had initially occupied Spencer in Volume 1 of his *Principles of Sociology*.

Karl Marx and Durkheim

Durkheim analyzed socialist and communist doctrines in his courses, especially in a course on the history of social thought. He was often critical, as can be seen in posthumously published essays taken from his lectures.[33] Some evidence indicates that Durkheim wanted to devote a full course to Marx's thought, but apparently he never found the time. Durkheim was thus aware of Marx but was generally dismayed by socialism's "working-class bias" and by the emphasis on revolution and conflict. He felt that the problems of alienation, exploitation, and class antagonism were relevant to all sectors of society and that revolution caused more pathology than it resolved. Yet in his first work, he discussed the forced division of labor, the value theory of labor, and the problems of exploitation—points highly reminiscent of Marx's conceptualization.

On balance, however, Marx's influence was negative. Durkheim reacted against Marx's insistence that integration in capitalist societies could not be achieved because of their "internal contradictions." What for Marx were the "normal" conflict-generating forms of capitalism were for Durkheim "abnormal forms," which could be eliminated without internal revolution. Indeed French social thought in the aftermath of the French Revolution and the lesser revolution of 1848 was decidedly conservative and did not consider revolutionary conflict as a productive and constructive way to bring about desired

---

[32]Some commentaries, surprisingly those by British scholars, have tended to underemphasize Spencer's impact on Durkheim. Although all commentaries note the positive reaction of Durkheim to the German organicist Albert Schäffle, they fail to note that Schäffle was simply adopting Spencer's ideas. We suspect that Durkheim knew he was restating Spencer's ideas.

[33]See, for example, Émile Durkheim, *Socialism and Saint-Simon* (Yellow Springs, OH: Antioch, 1959; originally published in 1928).

change. Thus, although Marx's influence on Durkheim is evident, it is not profound. Unlike Weber, for whom the "ghost of Marx" was ever present, Durkheim considered Marx's thought, reacted against Marx's ideas in his first works, and eventually rejected and ignored Marx in later works.

Anticipating Durkheimian Sociology

A scholar's ideas are the product of multiple influences, some obvious and others more subtle. We have mentioned some biographical influences on Durkheim's thought, but our emphasis has been on those scholars from whom he took concepts and methods. Our view is that simply looking at the key elements of Durkheim's thought and then examining the major figures of his intellectual milieu make the sources of his basic concepts and concerns rather clear.

The influence of various scholars on Durkheim's sociology is evident at different points in his career, which will become clear in the next chapter. By way of anticipating this discussion, we close this chapter with a brief listing of the elements of his sociology. All these elements were derived from the scholars discussed in this chapter, but his unique biography led him to combine them in ingenious ways, creating a distinctive sociological perspective. His sociology can be seen as (1) a series of methodological tenets, (2) a theory-building strategy, (3) a set of substantive topics, and (4) a host of practical concerns. Each is briefly summarized in an effort to anticipate the detailed analysis of the next chapter.

Methodological Tenets

From Montesquieu and Comte, Durkheim came to view a science of society as possible only if social and moral phenomena were considered as distinct realities. Moreover, a science of the social world must be like that of the physical and biological worlds; it must be based on data, or facts. Montesquieu initially emphasized this point, but Comte articulated the methods to be employed by the science of society. Historical, comparative, experimental, and observational techniques must all be used to discover the social facts.

Theoretical Strategy

Durkheim took from Montesquieu and Comte the vision that sociological laws could be discovered. In particular, causal analysis came to be an integral part of Durkheim's approach. Like Montesquieu, Durkheim believed that theory should seek the general causes of phenomena, for only in this way can the abstract laws of social organization be uncovered. Yet without a corresponding, but nonetheless separate, analysis of the functions served by social phenomena, these laws will remain hidden, a point implicit in Montesquieu's and Comte's work that became explicit in Spencer's sociology. Thus, for Durkheim, the laws of sociology will come from the causal and functional analysis of social facts.

Substantive Interests

Durkheim believed that the basic task for sociology was to understand the forces that hold society together. At a substantive level, this question involves the examination of (1) social structures; (2) symbolic components, such as values, beliefs, and norms; and (3) the complex relations between (1) and (2). From Montesquieu, Tocqueville, and Spencer, Durkheim acquired a sense for social structure. From Montesquieu's *spirit of a nation*, Rousseau's *general will*, and Comte's *consensus universalis*, Durkheim came to understand the significance of cultural symbols for integrating social structures. The specific topics of most concern to Durkheim—religion, education, government, the division of labor, intermediate groups, and collective representations—come from all the scholars discussed in this chapter and from specific intellectual and academic concerns of his time. The emphasis on symbolic and structural integration connected his examination of specific topics, which will become increasingly clear in the next chapter.

Practical Concerns

Like Rousseau and Comte, Durkheim wanted to create a well-integrated society. Such a goal could be achieved only by recognizing the pathologies of the social order, which were first articulated with a moral passion in Rousseau's work and then reinforced in

Tocqueville's more dispassionate analysis of American democracy. As Durkheim came to view the matter, the solution to these pathologies involved the creation of a system of constraining ideas (Comte, Rousseau, and Montesquieu), integration in intermediate subgroups (Tocqueville), coordination of differentiated functions through exchange and contract (Comte and Spencer), and the creation of a central state that provided overall coordination while maintaining individual freedom (Rousseau, Tocqueville, and Comte).

In sum, then, these methodological, theoretical, substantive, and practical concerns mark the critical elements of Durkheim's sociology. We now explore the specific bodies of work through which Durkheim's theoretical insights evolved.

CHAPTER 13

The Sociology of Émile Durkheim

S ix decades after Auguste Comte proposed a field of inquiry called sociology, Émile Durkheim pulled together the long French lineage of social thought into a coherent theoretical approach. Throughout Durkheim's illustrious career, his theoretical work revolved around one fundamental question: What is the basis for integration and solidarity in human societies?[1] At first, he examined this question from a macro perspective, looking at society as a whole. Later, he shifted his attention to the micro bases of solidarity, examining ritual and interaction of people in face-to-face contact. In all his works, he not only brought past theorizing together into a coherent scheme but also stimulated a number of twentieth-century intellectual movements that persist to this day.[2]

---

[1]Commentators have disagreed about whether Durkheim's work changed fundamentally from a macro perspective to a micro one, or from structural to social–psychological, between 1893 and 1916. For relevant commentary on this issue and on Durkheim's approach in general, see Anthony Giddens, *Capitalism and Modern Theory: An Analysis of the Writings of Marx, Durkheim, and Max Weber* (Cambridge, UK: Cambridge University Press, 1971); Anthony Giddens, ed. and trans., *Émile Durkheim: Selected Writings* (Cambridge, UK: Cambridge University Press, 1972); Talcott Parsons, *The Structure of Social Action* (New York: McGraw-Hill, 1937); Steven Lukes, *Émile Durkheim, His Life and Work: A Historical and Critical Study* (London: Allen Lane, 1973); and Robert Alun Jones, *Émile Durkheim* (Beverly Hills, CA: Sage, 1985).

[2]For an extensive bibliography of Durkheim's published works, see Lukes, *Émile Durkheim*, 561–590. See also Robert A. Nisbet, *The Sociology of Émile Durkheim* (New York: Oxford University Press, 1974), 30–41, for an annotated bibliography of the most important works forming the core of Durkheim's theoretical system.

The Division of Labor in Society

Durkheim's first major work was the published version of his French doctoral thesis, *The Division of Labor in Society*.[3] The original subtitle of this thesis was *A Study of the Organization of Advanced Societies*.[4] On the surface, the book is about the causes, characteristics, and functions of the division of labor in modern societies, but, as we will explore, the book presents a more general theory of social organization, one that can still inform sociological theorists.[5] In this great work, Durkheim stressed a number of issues that will guide our review: (1) social solidarity,[6] (2) the collective conscience, (3) social morphology,[7] (4) mechanical and organic solidarity, (5) social change, (6) social functions, and (7) social pathology.

Social Solidarity

The Division of Labor is about the shifting basis of social solidarity as societies evolve from an undifferentiated and simple profile[8] to a complex and differentiated one.[9] Today, this topic would be termed *social integration* because the concern is with how units of a social system are coordinated. Durkheim posited that the question of social solidarity, or integration, turns on several related issues: (1) How are individuals made to feel part of a larger social collective? (2) How are their desires and wants constrained in ways that allow them to participate in the collective? (3) How are the activities of individuals and other social units coordinated and adjusted to one another? These

---

[3]Émile Durkheim, *The Division of Labor in Society* (New York: Free Press, 1947; originally published in 1893).

[4]See Lukes, *Émile Durkheim*, Chapter 7, for a detailed discussion.

[5]Our view of Durkheim's *The Division of Labor* underemphasizes the social evolutionism contained in this work because we think that too much emphasis is placed on the model of social change and not enough is placed on the implicit theory of social organization.

[6]Alternatively, social integration.

[7]Or the nature of social structure.

[8]Durkheim described such simple societies as based on mechanical solidarity. *Mechanical* was a term intended to connote an image of society as a body in which cohesion is achieved by each element revealing a similar cultural and structural form.

[9]Such societies were seen as based on organic solidarity. *Organic* was intended to be an analogy to an organism in which the elements are distinctive in form and operate independently but for the welfare of the more inclusive social organism.

questions, we should emphasize, not only dominated *The Division of Labor* but also guided all of Durkheim's subsequent substantive works.

These questions take us into the basic problem of how patterns of social organization are created, maintained, and changed. It is little wonder, therefore, that Durkheim's analysis of social solidarity contains a more general theory of social organization; we should explore those concepts that he developed to explain social organization in general. One of the most important of these concepts is the *collective conscience.*

The Collective Conscience

Throughout his career, Durkheim was vitally concerned with "morality," or *moral facts.* Although he was often somewhat vague on what constituted a moral fact, we can interpret the concept of morality to embody what sociologists now call culture. That is, Durkheim was concerned with the systems of symbols—particularly the norms, values, and beliefs—that humans create and use to organize their activities.

Durkheim had to assert the legitimacy of the scientific study of moral phenomena because other academic disciplines, such as law, ethics, religion, philosophy, and psychology, all laid claim to symbols as their subject matter. Thus, he insisted, "moral facts are phenomena like others; they consist of rules of action recognizable by certain distinctive characteristics. It must, then, be possible to observe them, describe them, classify them, and look for laws explaining them."[10]

We should emphasize that Durkheim in his early work often used the concept of *moral facts* to denote structural patterns (groups, organizations, communities, etc.) as well as systems of symbols (values, beliefs, laws, norms). In *The Division of Labor,* however, we can find clear indications that he wanted to separate analytically the purely structural from the symbolic aspects of social reality. This isolation of cultural or symbolic phenomena can best be seen in his formulation

---

[10]Durkheim, *Division of Labor,* 32. This idea owes its inspiration to Comte. As Durkheim noted in his Latin thesis on Montesquieu, "no further progress could be made until it was recognized that the laws of societies are no different from those governing the rest of nature. . . . This was Auguste Comte's contribution." Émile Durkheim, *Montesquieu and Rousseau* (Ann Arbor: University of Michigan Press, 1960; originally published in 1892), 63–64.

of another, somewhat ambiguous, concept that suffers in translation: the *collective conscience*. He later dropped extensive use of this term in favor of *collective representations*, which, unfortunately, adds little clarification. But we can begin to understand his meaning with the formal definition provided in *The Division of Labor*: "The totality of beliefs and sentiments common to average citizens of the same society forms a determinate system which has its own life; one may call it the *collective* or *common conscience*."[11] He went on to indicate that although the terms *collective* and *common* were "not without ambiguity," they suggest that societies reveal a reality independent of "the particular conditions in which individuals are placed." Moreover, people are born into the collective conscience or the culture of a society, and this culture regulates their perceptions and behaviors. What Durkheim was denoting with the concept of collective conscience, then, is that aspects of culture—systems of values, beliefs, and norms—constrain the thoughts and actions of individuals.

In the course of his analysis of the collective conscience, Durkheim conceptualized its varying states as having four variables: (1) volume, (2) intensity, (3) determinateness, and (4) religious versus secular content.[12] *Volume* denotes the degree to which the values, beliefs, and rules of the collective conscience are shared by the members of a society; *intensity* indicates the extent to which the collective conscience has the power to guide and constrain a person's thoughts and actions; *determinateness* denotes the degree of clarity in the components of the collective conscience; and *content* pertains to the ratio of religious to purely secular symbolism in the collective conscience.

Social Morphology

Durkheim saw social structure (or as he termed it, *morphology*) as involving an assessment of the "nature," "number," "arrangement," and "interrelations" among parts, whether these parts are individuals or corporate units, such as groups and organizations. Their *nature* is usually assessed by variables such as size and functions (economic, political, familial, etc.). *Arrangement* concerns the distribution of parts in relationship to one another; *interrelations* deal

---

[11]Durkheim, *Division of Labor*, 79–80 (emphasis in original).

[12]Ibid., 152 for 1, 2, and 3 and throughout the book for 4. For interesting secondary discussions, see Lukes, *Émile Durkheim*, and Giddens, *Selected Writings*.

with the modes of communication, movement, and mutual obligations among the parts.

Although Durkheim's entire intellectual career involved an effort to demonstrate the impact of social structures on the collective conscience as well as on individual cognitions and behaviors, he never made explicit use of these variables—that is, nature, number, arrangement, and interrelations—for analyzing social structures. In his more methodological statements, he argued for the appropriateness of viewing social morphology by nature, size, number, arrangement, and interrelations of specific parts. Yet his actual analysis of social structures in his major substantive works left these more formal properties of structure implicit.[13]

Mechanical and Organic Solidarity

With these views on the collective conscience and structural morphology, Durkheim developed a typology of societies based on their modes of integration or solidarity. One type is termed *mechanical*, and the other, *organic*.[14] As we will show later, each of these types rests on different principles of social integration, involving different morphologies, different systems of symbols, and different relations between social and symbolic structures. Durkheim's distinction between mechanical and organic is both a descriptive typology of traditional and modern societies and a theoretical statement about the changing forms of social integration that emerge with increasing differentiation of social structure.

At a descriptive level, mechanical solidarity is based on a strong collective conscience regulating the thought and actions of individuals located within structural units that are alike. Of the four variables by which Durkheim conceptualized the collective conscience, the cultural system is high in volume, intensity, determinateness, and religious content. Legal codes, which in his view are the best

---

[13]The concern for "social morphology" was, no doubt, an adaptation of Comte's idea of social statics, as these were influenced by the German organicist Albert Schäffle, with whom Durkheim had been highly impressed. See Lukes, *Émile Durkheim*, 86–95.

[14]Such typologizing was typical in the nineteenth century. Spencer distinguished societal types, but more influential was Tönnies's distinction between *Gemeinschaft* and *Geselleschaft*. Durkheim spent a year in Germany as a student in 1885–1886, and although Tönnies's famous work had not yet been published, his typology was well-known and influenced Durkheim's conceptualization of mechanical and organic solidarity.

empirical indicator of solidarity, are repressive, and sanctions are punitive. The reason for such repressiveness is that deviation from the dictates of the collective conscience is viewed as a crime against all members of the society and the gods. The morphology, or structure, of mechanical societies reveals independent kinship units that organize relatively small numbers of people who share strong commitments to their particular collective conscience. The interrelations among kin units are minimal, with each unit being like the others and autonomously meeting the needs of its members. Not surprisingly, then, individual freedom, choice, and autonomy are low in mechanical societies. People are dominated by the collective conscience, and their actions are constrained by its dictates and by the constraints of cohesive kin units.

In contrast, organically structured societies are typified by large populations, distributed in specialized roles in many diverse structural units. Organic societies reveal high degrees of interdependence among individuals and corporate units, with exchange, legal contracts, and norms regulating these interrelations. The collective conscience becomes "enfeebled" and "more abstract," providing highly general and secular value premises for the exchanges, contracts, and norms regulating the interdependencies among specialized social units. This alteration is reflected in legal codes that become less punitive and more "restitutive," specifying non-punitive ways to redress violations of normative arrangements and to reintegrate violators back into the network of interdependencies that typify organic societies. In such societies, individual freedom is great, and the secular and highly abstract collective conscience becomes dominated by values stressing respect for the personal dignity of the individual.

This descriptive contrast between mechanical and organic societies is summarized in Table 13.1.[15] At the more theoretical level, Durkheim's distinction between mechanical and organic solidarity posits a fundamental relationship in the social world among "structural differentiation," "value generalization," and "normative specification." Let us explore this relationship in more detail. As societies differentiate structurally, values become more abstract.[16] The collective conscience changes its nature as societies become more

---

[15]This table is similar to the one developed by Lukes, *Émile Durkheim*, 151.

[16]Durkheim, *Division of Labor*, 171.

Table 13.1   Descriptive Summary of Mechanical and Organic Societies

Morphological (Structural) Features	Mechanical Solidarity	Organic Solidarity
1. Size	Small	Large
2. Number of parts	Few	Many
3. Nature of parts	Kinship based	Diverse: dominated by economic and governmental content
4. Arrangement	Independent, autonomous	Interrelated, mutually interdependent
5. Nature of interrelations	Bound to common conscience and punitive law	Bound together by exchange, contract, norms, and restitutive law

Collective Conscience (Culture)	Mechanical Solidarity	Organic Solidarity
1. Volume	High	Low
2. Intensity	High	Low
3. Determinateness	High	Low
4. Content	Religious, stressing commitment and conformity to dictates of sacred powers	Secular, emphasizing individuality

voluminous. Because these societies are spread over a vaster surface, the common conscience or culture rises above local diversities and consequently becomes more abstract. Only by becoming general can culture be common to distinctive environments.[17]

As basic values lose their capacity to regulate the specific actions of large numbers of differentiated units, normative regulations arise to

---

[17]Ibid., 287.

compensate for the inability of general values to specify what people should do and how individuals as well as corporate units should interact:

> If society no longer imposes upon everybody certain uniform practices, it takes greater care to define and regulate the special relations between different social functions and this activity is not smaller because it is different.[18]

> It is certain that organized societies are not possible without a developed system of rules which predetermine the functions of each organ. In so far as labor is divided, there arises a multitude of occupational moralities and laws.[19]

Thus, in his seemingly static comparison of mechanical and organic societies, Durkheim was actually proposing lawlike relationships among structural and symbolic elements of social systems.

Social Change

Durkheim's view of social change revolves around an analysis of the causes and consequences of increases in the division of labor:

> The division of labor varies in direct ratio with the volume and density of societies, and, if it progresses in a continuous manner in the course of social development, it is because societies become regularly denser and generally more voluminous.[20]

Some translation of terms is necessary if this "proposition," as Durkheim called it, is to be understood. *Volume* refers to population size and concentration; *density* pertains to the increased interaction arising from escalated volume. Thus, the division of labor arises from increases in the concentration of populations whose members increasingly come into contact with one another. Durkheim also termed the increased rates of interaction among those thrust into contact *dynamic* and *moral density*. He then analyzed those factors that increase the material density of a population. Ecological boundaries (rivers, mountains, oceans, etc.), migration, urbanization, and

---

[18]Ibid., 205.
[19]Ibid., 302.
[20]Ibid., 262.

population growth all directly increase volume and thus indirectly increase the likelihood of dynamic density (increased contact and interaction). Technological innovations, such as new modes of communication and transportation, directly increase the rates of contact and interaction among individuals. But all these direct and indirect influences are merely lists of empirical conditions influencing the primary explanatory variable, dynamic or moral density.

How, then, does dynamic density cause the division of labor? Dynamic density increases competition among individuals who, if they are to survive the "struggle," must assume specialized roles and then establish exchange relations with each other. The division of labor is thus the mechanism by which competition is mitigated:

> Thus, Darwin says that in a small area, opened to immigration, and where, consequently, the conflict of individuals must be acute, there is always to be seen a very great diversity in the species inhabiting it. . . . Men submit to the same law. In the same city, different occupations can co-exist without being obliged mutually to destroy one another, for they pursue different objects.[21]

Figure 13.1 outlines these causal connections. To recapitulate, Durkheim saw migration, population growth, and ecological concentration as causing increased *material density*, which in turn caused increased *moral* or *dynamic density*—that is, escalated social contact and interaction. Such interaction could be further heightened by varied means of communication and transportation, as is illustrated in the model in Figure 13.1. The increased rates of interaction characteristic of a larger population within a confined ecological space cause increased competition, or "struggle," among individuals. Such competition allows those who have the most resources and talents to maintain their present positions and assume high-rank positions, whereas the "less fit" seek alternative specialties to mitigate the competition. From this competition and differentiation comes the division of labor, which, when "normal," results in organic solidarity.

The major problem with the model is the implicit argument about "final causes": The function of the division of labor is to promote social solidarity. Durkheim implied that the need for social solidarity

---

[21]Ibid., 266–267.

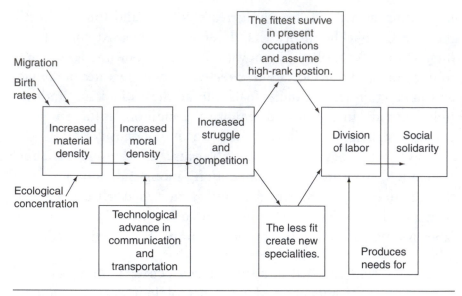

Figure 13.1   Durkheim's Implicit Model of Social Statics

caused the struggle to be resolved by the division of labor; yet he never specified how the needs met by the division of labor (i.e., social solidarity) caused it to emerge. Still, the model in Figure 13.1 contains some suggestive ideas, particularly the notions that material density causes moral density, that moral density causes competition, that competition causes differentiation, and that differentiation causes new mechanisms of integration. On the other hand, without specifying the conditions under which these causal connections are generated, the model is vague.

Social Functions

Herbert Spencer had clearly formulated the notions of structure and function, with functions assessed by the needs of the social organism being met by a structure. Durkheim appears to have borrowed these ideas and, indeed, opened *The Division of Labor* with an assessment of its functions.[22] The function of the division of labor is to promote social solidarity, or societal integration. Such functional analysis, Durkheim argued, must be kept separate from causal analysis.

---

[22]For a more detailed analysis of Durkheim's debt to Spencer and of his contribution to functionalism, see Jonathan H. Turner and Alexandra Maryanski, *Functionalism* (Menlo Park, CA: Benjamin/Cummings, 1979); and Jonathan H. Turner, "Durkheim's and Spencer's Principles of Social Organization," *Sociological Perspectives* 9 (1984), 283–291.

Nonetheless, functional analysis was critical to Durkheim's desire to be the "physician" to society. By assessing what a structure "does for" a society of a particular type or at a specific stage of evolution, Durkheim felt that he was in a better position to determine what was "normal" and "abnormal" for that society—a point that Comte had first made in his advocacy of the experimental method as it could be used in sociology. The concept of function allowed Durkheim to judge whether a structure, such as the division of labor, was functioning normally for a particular type of society. Hence, based on the degree to which the division of labor fails to promote societal integration or social solidarity in a society, he viewed this society to be in a "pathological" state and in need of alterations to restore "normality" to the "body social." These considerations led him to analyze "abnormal forms" of the division of labor at the close of this first major sociological work because the abnormality of structures can be determined only in reference to their "normal functions."

Pathology and Abnormal Forms

Durkheim opened his discussion of abnormal forms with the following statement:

> Up to now, we have studied the division of labor only as a normal phenomenon, but, like all social facts, and, more generally, all biological facts, it presents pathological forms which must be analyzed. Though normally the division of labor produces social solidarity, it sometimes happens that it has different, and even contrary results.[23]

Durkheim isolated three abnormal forms: (1) the anomic division of labor, (2) the forced division of labor, and (3) the inadequately coordinated division of labor. In discussing these abnormal forms, he drew considerable inspiration from his French predecessors, particularly Jean-Jacques Rousseau and Alexis de Tocqueville, while carrying on a silent dialogue with Karl Marx and other socialists. Thus, his analysis of abnormal forms represents his effort to address issues that had been discussed and contested for several previous generations of intellectuals. Indeed, individuals' isolation, their detachment from society, their sense of alienation, their exploitation by the powerful,

---

[23]Durkheim, *Division of Labor*, 353.

and related issues had been hotly debated in both intellectual and lay circles. Yet, although Durkheim's selection of topics is not unique, his conclusions and their theoretical implications are highly original.

The Anomic Division of Labor

The concept of anomie was not well developed in *The Division of Labor*. Only later, in the 1897 work *Suicide*, did this concept become theoretically significant. Durkheim's discussion in *The Division of Labor* is explicitly directed at Comte, who had noted the essence of the basic dilemma confronting organic social systems. As Comte stated,

> from the moral point of view, while each individual is thus made closely dependent on the mass, he is naturally drawn away from it by the nature of his special activity, constantly reminding him of his private interests, which he only very dimly perceives to be related to the public.[24]

For Durkheim, this dilemma was expressed as maintaining individuals' commitment to a common set of values and beliefs while allowing them to pursue their specialized interests. At this stage in his thinking, anomie represented insufficient normative regulation of individuals' activities, with the result that individuals do not feel attached to the collectivity.

Anomie is inevitable, Durkheim believed, when the transformation of society from a mechanical to an organic basis of social solidarity is rapid and causes the "generalization," or "enfeeblement," of values. With generalization, individuals' attachment to, and regulation by, values are lessened. The results of this anomic situation are diverse. One result is that individuals feel alienated because their only attachment is to the monotony and crushing schedule dictated by the machines of the industrial age. Another is the escalated frustrations and the sense of deprivation, manifested by increased incidence of revolt, that come in a state of under-regulation.

Unlike Marx, however, Durkheim did not consider these consequences inevitable. He rejected the notion that there were inherent contradictions in capitalism, for "if, in certain cases, organic solidarity is not all it should be . . . [it is] because all the conditions for the existence of organic solidarity have not been realized."[25] Nor would

---

[24]Quoted in Lukes, *Émile Durkheim*, 141.
[25]Durkheim, *Division of Labor*, 364–365.

he accept Comte's or Rousseau's solution to anomie: the establishment of a strong and somewhat dictatorial central organ, the state.

Yet in the first edition of *The Division of Labor*, Durkheim's own solution is vague; the solution to anomie involves reintegration of individuals into the collective life by virtue of their interdependence with other specialists and the common goals that all members of a society ultimately pursue.[26] In many ways, this argument substitutes for Adam Smith's invisible hand the "invisible power of the collective" without specifying how this integration into the collective is to occur.

Durkheim recognized the inadequacy of this solution to the problem of anomie. Moreover, his more detailed analysis of anomie in *Suicide* (1897) must have further underscored the limitations of his analysis in *The Division of Labor*. Thus, the second edition of *The Division of Labor*, published in 1902, contained a long preface that sought to specify the mechanism by which anomie was to be curbed. This mechanism is the "occupational," or "corporate," group.[27]

Durkheim recognized that industrialism, urbanization, occupational specialization, and the growth of the bureaucratized state all lessened the functions of family, religion, region, and neighborhood as mechanisms promoting the integration of individuals into the societal collectivity. With the generalization and enfeeblement of the collective conscience, coupled with the potential isolation of individuals in an occupational specialty, Durkheim saw that new structures would have to evolve to avoid anomie. These structures promote social solidarity in several ways: (1) they organize occupational specialties into a collective, (2) they bridge the widening gap between the remote state and the specific needs and desires of the individual, and (3) they provide a functional alternative to the old loyalties generated by religion, regionalism, and kinship. These new intermediate structures are not only occupational but also political and moral groupings that lace together specialized occupations, counterbalance the power of the state, and provide specific interpretations for the more abstract values and beliefs of the collective conscience.

Durkheim had taken the idea of "occupational groups" from Tocqueville's analysis of intermediate organizations in America (see Chapter 12). He extended the concept considerably, however, and in doing so, he posited a conception of how a society should

---

[26]Ibid., 373.
[27]Ibid., 1–31.

be economically, politically, and morally organized.[28] Economically, occupational groups would bring together related occupational specialties into an organization that could set working hours and wage levels and that could bargain with the management of corporations and government.

Politically, the occupational group would become a kind of political party whose representatives would participate in government. Like most French scholars in the post-revolutionary era, Durkheim distrusted mass democracy, feeling that short-term individual passions and moods could render the state helpless in setting and reaching long-range goals. He also distrusted an all-powerful and bureaucratized state on the ground that its remote structure was too insensitive and cumbersome to deal with the specific needs and problems of diverse individuals. Moreover, Durkheim saw that unchecked state power inevitably led to abuses, an emphasis that comes close to Montesquieu's idea of a balance of powers in government. Thus, the power of the state must be checked by intermediate groups, which channel public sentiment to the state and administer the policies of the state for a particular constituency.[29]

Morally, occupational groups are to provide many of the recreational, educational, and social functions formerly performed by family, neighborhood, and church. By bringing together people who are likely to have common experiences because they belong to related occupations, occupational groups can provide a place where people feel integrated into the society and where the psychological tensions and monotony of their specialized jobs can be mitigated. Moreover, these groups can make the generalized values and beliefs of the entire society relevant to the life experiences of each individual. Through the vehicle of occupational groups, then, an entire society of specialists can be reattached to the collective conscience, thereby eliminating anomie.

Inequality and the Forced Division of Labor

Borrowing heavily from Rousseau, Claude-Henri de Saint-Simon, and Comte, but reacting to Marx,[30] Durkheim saw inequalities

---

[28]We are supplementing Durkheim's discussion of occupational groups with additional works; see Émile Durkheim, *Professional Ethics and Civil Morals* (Boston: Routledge & Kegan Paul, 1957), and *Socialism and Saint-Simon* (Yellow Springs, OH: Antioch, 1958).

[29]Durkheim, *Division of Labor*, 28.

[30]Durkheim rarely addressed Marx directly. Though he wanted to devote a special course to Marx's ideas in addition to his course on Saint-Simon and socialism, he never got around to doing so. Much as with Weber, however, one suspects that Durkheim's discussion of "abnormal forms" represented a silent dialogue with Marx.

based on ascription and inheritance of privilege as "abnormal." He advocated an inheritance tax that would eliminate the passing of wealth across generations, and indeed, he felt that in the normal course of things, this change would come about. Unlike Marx, however, Durkheim had no distaste for the accumulation of capital and privilege, as long as it was earned and not inherited.

What Durkheim desired was for the division of labor and inequalities in privilege to correspond to differences in people's ability. For him, it was abnormal in organic societies for wealth to be inherited and for this inherited privilege to be used by one class to oppress and exploit another. Such a situation represents a "forced division of labor," and in the context of analyzing this abnormality, Durkheim examined explicitly Marxian ideas: (1) the labor theory of value and exploitation and (2) the domination of one class by another. Let us examine each briefly:

1. Durkheim felt that the price one pays for a good or service should be proportional to the "useful labor which it contains."[31] To the degree that this is not so, he argued, an abnormal condition prevails. What is necessary, and inevitable in the long run, is for buyers and sellers to be "placed in conditions externally equal"[32] in which the price charged for a good or service corresponds to the "socially useful labor" in it and where no seller or buyer enjoys an advantage or monopoly that would allow prices to exceed socially useful labor.

2. Durkheim recognized that as long as there is inherited privilege, especially wealth, one class can exploit and dominate another. He felt that the elimination of inheritance was inevitable, because people could no longer be duped by a strong collective conscience into accepting privilege and exploitation (a position that parallels Marx's notion of *false consciousness*). For as religious and family bonds decrease in salience and as individuals are liberated from mechanical solidarity, people can free themselves from the beliefs that have often been used to legitimate exploitation.

Durkheim was certainly naive in his assumption that these aspects of the forced division of labor would, like Marx's state, "wither away."

---

[31]Durkheim, *Division of Labor*, 382.
[32]Ibid., 383.

What he saw as normal was a situation that sounds reminiscent of Adam Smith's utilitarian vision of an "invisible hand of order."[33]

Lack of Coordination

Durkheim termed the lack of coordination *another abnormal form* and did not devote much space to its analysis.[34] At times, he noted, specialization of tasks is not accompanied by sufficient coordination, creating a situation where energy is wasted and individuals feel poorly integrated into the collective flow of life. In his view, specialization must be "continuous," with functions highly coordinated and individuals laced together through their mutual interdependence. Such a state, he argued, will be achieved as the natural and normal processes creating organic solidarity become dominant in modern society.

On this note, *The Division of Labor* ends. Durkheim's next major work, published 2 years after *The Division of Labor*, sought to make more explicit assumptions and methodological guidelines that were implicit in *The Division of Labor*. *The Rules of the Sociological Method* (1895) represents a methodological interlude that clarifies Durkheim's approach to sociological analysis.

The Rules of the Sociological Method

The Rules of the Sociological Method is both a philosophical treatise and a set of guidelines for conducting sociological inquiry.[35] Durkheim appears to have written the book for at least three reasons.[36] First, he sought intellectual justification for his approach to studying the social world, especially as evidenced in *The Division of Labor*. Second, he wanted to persuade a hostile academic community of the legitimacy of sociology as a distinctive science. Third, because he wanted to found a school of scholars, he needed a manifesto to attract and guide potential converts to the science of sociology. The chapter titles of *The Rules* best communicate Durkheim's intent:

---

[33]Ibid., 377.

[34]Ibid., 389–395; see also Charles H. Powers, "Durkheim and Regulatory Authority," *Journal of the History of the Behavioral Sciences* 21 (1985), 26–36.

[35]Émile Durkheim, *The Rules of the Sociological Method* (New York: Free Press, 1938; originally published in 1895).

[36]Lukes, *Émile Durkheim*, Chapter 10.

(1) "What Is a Social Fact?" (2) "Rules for the Observation of Social Facts," (3) "Rules for Distinguishing Between the Normal and the Pathological," (4) "Rules for the Classification of Social Types," (5) "Rules for the Explanation of Social Facts," and (6) "Rules Relative to Establishing Sociological Proofs." We will examine each of these.

What Is a Social Fact?

Durkheim was engaged in a battle to establish the legitimacy of sociology. In *The Division of Labor*, he proclaimed "moral facts" to be sociology's subject, but in *The Rules* he changed his terminology to that employed earlier by Comte and argued that "social facts" were the distinctive subject of sociology. For Durkheim, a social fact "consists of ways of acting, thinking, and feeling, external to the individual, and endowed with power of coercion, by which they control him."[37]

In this definition, Durkheim lumped behaviors, thoughts, and emotions together as the subject of sociology. The morphological and symbolic structures in which individuals participate are thus to be the focus of sociology, but social facts are, by virtue of transcending any individual, "external" and "constraining." They are external in two senses:

1. Individuals are born into an established set of structures and an existing system of values, beliefs, and norms. Hence, these structural and symbolic "facts" are initially external to individuals, and as people learn to play roles in social structures, to abide by norms, and to accept basic values, they feel and sense "something" outside of them.

2. Even when humans actively and collaboratively create social structures, values, beliefs, and norms, these social facts become an emergent reality that is external to their creators.

This externality is accompanied by a sense of constraint and coercion. The structures, norms, values, and beliefs of the social world compel certain actions, thoughts, and dispositions. They impose limits, and when deviations occur, sanctions are applied to the deviants. Moreover, social facts are "internalized" in that people want

---

[37]Durkheim, *The Rules*, 3.

and desire to be a part of social structures and to accept the norms, values, and beliefs of the collective. In the 1895 edition of *The Rules*, this point had been underemphasized, but in the second edition Durkheim noted,

> Institutions may impose themselves upon us, but we cling to them; they compel us, and we love them.[38]

> [Social facts] dominate us and impose beliefs and practices upon us. But they rule us from within, for they are in every case an integral part of ourself.[39]

Durkheim thus asserted that when individuals come into collaboration, a new reality consisting of social and symbolic structures emerges. This emergent reality cannot be reduced to individual psychology, because it is external to, and constraining on, any individual. And yet, like all social facts, it is registered on the individual and often "rules the individual from within." Having established that sociology has a distinct subject matter—social facts—Durkheim devoted the rest of the book to explicating rules for studying and explaining social facts.

Rules for the Observation of Social Facts

Durkheim offered several guidelines for observing social facts: (1) Personal biases and preconceptions must be eliminated. (2) The phenomena under study must be clearly defined. (3) An empirical indicator of the phenomenon under study must be found, as was the case for "law" in *The Division of Labor*. (4) Social facts must be considered "things." Social facts are things in two different, although related, ways. First, when a phenomenon is viewed as a thing, it is possible to assume "a particular mental attitude" toward it. We can search for the properties and characteristics of a thing, and we can draw verifiable conclusions about its nature. Such a position was highly controversial in Durkheim's time because moral phenomena—values, ideas, morals—were not often considered proper topics of scientific inquiry, and when they were, they were seen as a subarea in the study of individual psychology. Second, Durkheim asserted, phenomena such as morality, values, beliefs, and dogmas constitute a distinctive

---

[38]Ibid., Footnote 5, 3.
[39]Ibid., 7.

metaphysical reality, not reducible to individual psychology. Hence, they can be approached with the same scientific methods as any material phenomenon in the universe.[40]

Rules for Distinguishing Between the Normal and the Pathological

Throughout his career, Durkheim never wavered from Comte's position that science is to be used to serve human ends: "Why strive for knowledge of reality if this knowledge cannot serve us in life? To this we can reply that, by revealing the causes of phenomena, science furnishes the means of producing them."[41] To use scientific knowledge to implement social conditions requires knowledge of what is normal and pathological. Otherwise, one would not know what social facts to create and implement, or one might actually create a pathological condition. To determine normality, the best procedure, Durkheim argued, is to discover what is most frequent and typical of societies of a given type or at a given stage of evolution. That which deviates significantly from this average is pathological.

Such a position allowed Durkheim to make some startling conclusions for his time. In regard to deviance, for example, a particular rate of crime and some other form of deviance could be normal for certain types of societies. Abnormality is present only when rates of deviance exceed what is typical of a certain societal type.

Rules for the Classification of Social Types

Durkheim's evolutionary perspective, coupled with his strategy for diagnosing normality and pathology in social systems, made inevitable a concern with social classification. Although specific systems reveal considerable variability, it is possible to group them into general types on the basis of (1) the "nature" and "number" of their parts and (2) the "mode of combination" of parts.

In this way, Durkheim believed, societies that reveal superficial differences can be seen as belonging to a particular class or type.

---

[40]Many commentators, such as Giddens, *Capitalism and Modern Theory*, and Lukes, *Émile Durkheim*, emphasize that Durkheim was not making a metaphysical statement. We think that he was making both a metaphysical and a methodological statement.

[41]Durkheim, *The Rules*, 48.

Moreover, by ignoring the distracting complexities of a society's "content" and "uniqueness," it is possible to establish the stage of evolutionary development of a society.

Rules for the Explanation of Social Facts

Durkheim emphasized again a point he had made in *The Division of Labor:* "When the explanation of social phenomena is undertaken, we must seek separately the efficient cause which produces it and the function it fulfills."[42] Causal analysis involves searching for antecedent conditions that produce a given effect. Functional analysis is concerned with determining the consequences of a social fact (regardless of its cause) for the social whole or larger context in which it is located. Complete sociological explanation involves both causal and functional explanations, as Durkheim had sought to illustrate in *The Division of Labor.*

Rules for Establishing Sociological Proofs

Durkheim advocated two basic procedures for establishing "sociological proofs"—proofs being documentation that causal and, by implication, functional explanations are correct. One procedure involves comparing two or more societies of a given type (as determined by the rules for classification) to see if one fact, present in one but not in the other(s), leads to differences in these otherwise similar societies.

The second procedure is the method of concomitant variation. If two social facts are correlated and one is assumed to cause the other, and if all alternative facts that might also be considered causative cannot eliminate the correlation, it can be asserted that a causal explanation has been "proved." If an established correlation, and presumed causal relation, can be explained away by the operation of another social fact, the established explanation has been disproved and the new social fact can, until similarly disproved, be considered "proved." The logic of Durkheim's method of concomitant variation, then, was similar in intent to modern multivariate analyses: to assert a relation among variables, controlling for the impact of other variables.[43]

---

[42]Ibid., 95.

[43]Durkheim made other assertions: A social fact can only have one cause, and this cause must be another social fact (rather than an individual or psychological fact).

The Rules marks a turning point in Durkheim's intellectual career. It was written after his thesis on the division of labor, while he was pondering the question of suicide in his lectures. Yet it was written before his first public course on religion.[44] He had clearly established his guiding theoretical interests: the nature of social organization and its relationship to values, beliefs, and other symbolic systems. He had developed a clear methodology: asking causal and functional questions within a broad comparative, historical, and evolutionary framework. He had begun to win respect in intellectual and academic circles for the fact that social organization represents an emergent reality, sui generis, and is the proper subject matter for a discipline called sociology.

Durkheim's next work appears to have been an effort to demonstrate the utility of his methodological and ontological advocacy. For he sought to understand sociologically a phenomenon that, at the time, was considered uniquely psychological: that is, suicide. In this work, he attempted to demonstrate the power of sociological investigation for seemingly psychological phenomena, employing social facts as explanatory variables. Far more important than the specifics of suicide, we believe, is his extension of concepts introduced in *The Division of Labor*.

Suicide

In *Suicide*, Durkheim appears to follow self-consciously the "rules" of his sociological method.[45] He was interested in studying only a social fact, and hence he did not study individual suicides but rather the general pervasiveness of suicide in a population—that is, a society's aggregate tendency toward suicide. In this way, suicide could be considered a social rather than an individual fact, and it could be approached as a "thing." Suicide is clearly defined as "all causes of death resulting directly or indirectly from a positive or negative act of the victim himself which he knows will produce this result."[46] The statistical rate of suicide is then used as the indicator of this

---

[44]Lukes, *Émile Durkheim*, 227.

[45]Émile Durkheim, *Suicide: A Study in Sociology* (New York: Free Press, 1951; originally published in 1897).

[46]Ibid., 44.

social fact.[47] Suicide is classified into four types: (1) egoistic, (2) altruistic, (3) anomic, and (4) fatalistic. The cause of these types is specified by the degree and nature of individual integration into the social collective. A variant of modern correlational techniques is employed to demonstrate, or "prove," that other hypothesized causes of suicide are spurious and that integration into social and symbolic structures is the key explanatory variable.

The statistical manipulations in *Suicide* are important because they represent the first systematic effort to apply correlational and contingency techniques to causal explanation. Our concern, however, is with the theoretical implications of this work, and hence the following summary will focus on theoretical rather than statistical issues.

Types of Suicide

As noted, Durkheim isolated four types of suicide by varying causes. We should emphasize that despite his statistical footwork, isolating types by causes and then explaining these types by the causes used to classify them is a suspicious, if not spurious, way to go about understanding the social world. These flaws aside, Durkheim's analysis clarifies notions of social integration that are somewhat vague in *The Division of Labor*. Basically, Durkheim argued that suicides could be classified by the nature of an individual's integration into the social fabric. There are, in Durkheim's eye, two types of integration:

1. *Attachment* to social groups and their goals. Such attachment involves the maintenance of interpersonal ties and the perception that one is a part of a larger collectivity

2. *Regulation* by the collective conscience (values, beliefs, and general norms) of social groupings. Such regulation limits individual aspirations and needs, keeping them in check

In distinguishing these two bases of integration, Durkheim explicitly recognized the different "functions" of the structural and cultural elements of the social world. Interpersonal ties that bind individuals to the collective keep them from becoming too "egoistic"—a concept

---

[47]Ibid., 48. It should be emphasized that suicide had been subject to extensive statistical analysis during Durkheim's time, and thus he was able to borrow the data compiled by others.

borrowed from Tocqueville and widely discussed in Durkheim's time. Unless individuals can be attached to a larger collective and its goals, they become egoistic, or self-centered, in ways that are highly destructive to their psychological well-being. In contrast, the regulation of individuals' aspirations, which are potentially infinite, prevents anomie. Without cultural constraints, individual aspirations, as Rousseau[48] and Tocqueville had emphasized, escalate and create perpetual misery for individuals who pursue goals that constantly recede as they are approached. These two varying bases of individual integration into society, then, form the basis for Durkheim's classification of the four types of suicide denoted above.

Egoistic Suicide

When a person's ties to groups and collectivities are weakened, there is the potential for excessive individualism and, hence, egoistic suicide. Durkheim stated this relation as a clear proposition: "Suicide varies inversely with the degree of integration of social groups of which the individual forms a part."[49] And as a result,

> the more weakened the groups to which he belongs, the less he depends on them, the more he consequently depends only on himself and recognizes no other rules of conduct than what are founded on private interest. If we agree to call this state egoism, in which the individual ego asserts itself to excess in the face of the social ego and at its expense, we may call egoistic the special type of suicide springing from excessive individualism.[50]

Altruistic Suicide

If the degree of individual integration into the group is visualized as a variable continuum, ranging from egoism on the one pole to a complete fusion of the individual with the collective at the other pole, the essence of Durkheim's next form of suicide can be captured. Altruistic suicide is the result of individuals being so attached to the group that, for the good of the group, they commit suicide. In such a situation, individuals count for little; the group is paramount,

---

[48]This view of humans, we should note, is very similar to that of Marx.

[49]Durkheim, *Suicide*, 209.

[50]Ibid., 209.

with individuals subordinating their interests to those of the group. Durkheim distinguished three types of altruistic suicide:

1. *Obligatory altruistic suicide*, in which individuals are obliged, under certain circumstances, to commit suicide

2. *Optional altruistic suicide*, in which individuals are not obligated to commit suicide, but it is the custom for them to do so under certain conditions

3. *Acute altruistic suicide*, in which individuals kill themselves "purely for the joy of sacrifice, because, even with no particular reason, renunciation in itself is considered praiseworthy"[51]

In sum, then, egoistic and altruistic suicides result from either overintegration or underintegration into the collective. Altruistic suicide tends to occur in traditional systems—what Durkheim termed *mechanical* in *The Division of Labor*—and egoistic suicide is more frequent in modern, organic systems that reveal high degrees of individual autonomy. At the more abstract level, Durkheim posited a critical dimension of individual and societal integration: the maintenance of interpersonal bonds within coherent group structures.

Anomic Suicide

In *The Division of Labor*, Durkheim's conceptualization of anomie was somewhat vague. In many ways, he incorporated both anomie (deregulation by symbols) and egoism (detachment from structural relations in groups) into the original definition of anomie. In *Suicide*, Durkheim clarified this ambiguity: Anomic suicide came to be viewed narrowly as the result of deregulation of individuals' desires and passions. Although both egoistic and anomic suicide "spring from society's insufficient presence in individuals,"[52] the nature of the disjuncture or deficiency between the individual and society differs.[53]

Fatalistic Suicide

Durkheim discussed fatalistic suicide in a short footnote. Just as altruism is the polar opposite of egoism, so fatalism is the opposite of anomie. Fatalistic suicide is the result of "excessive regulation, that of

---

[51]Ibid., 223.
[52]Ibid., 258.
[53]Ibid., 258.

persons with futures pitilessly blocked and passions violently choked by oppressive discipline."[54] Thus, when individuals are overregulated by norms, beliefs, and values in their social relations, and when they have no individual freedom, discretion, or autonomy in their social relations, they are potential victims of fatalistic suicide.

Suicide and Social Integration

These four types of suicide reveal a great deal about Durkheim's conception of humans and the social order. The study of suicide allows us a glimpse of how he conceived human nature. Reading between the lines in *Suicide*, the following features are posited:

1. Humans can potentially reveal unlimited desires and passions, which must be regulated and held in check.

2. Total regulation of passions and desires creates a situation where life loses all meaning.

3. Humans need interpersonal attachments and a sense that these attachments connect them to collective purposes.

4. Excessive attachment can undermine personal autonomy to the point where life loses meaning for the individual.[55]

These implicit notions of human nature, it should be emphasized, involve a vision of the "normal" way in which individuals are integrated into the structural and cultural structures of society. Indeed, Durkheim was unable even to address the question of human nature without also talking about the social order. Durkheim believed that the social order is maintained only to the degree that individuals are attached to, and regulated by, patterns of collective organization. This belief led him later in his career to explore in more detail an essentially social–psychological question: In what ways do individuals become attached to society and become willing to be regulated by its symbolic elements?

Suicide and Deviance

Durkheim made an effort to see if other forms of deviance, such as homicide and crime, were related to suicide rates, but the details

---

[54]Ibid., 276, in footnote.
[55]See also Lukes, *Émile Durkheim*, Chapter 9, for a somewhat different discussion.

of his correlations are not as important as the implications of his analysis for a general theory of deviance. As he had in *The Division of Labor*, he recognized that a society of a certain type would reveal a "typical," or "average," level of deviance, whether of suicide or some other form. However, when rates of suicide, or deviance in general, exceed certain average levels for a societal type, a "pathological" condition might exist.

Durkheim's great contribution is his recognition that deviance is caused by the same forces that maintain conformity in social systems. Moreover, he specified the two key variables in understanding both conformity and deviance: (1) the degree of group attachment and (2) the degree of value and normative regulation. Thus, excessive or insufficient attachment and regulation will cause varying forms of deviance in a social system. Moreover, the more a system reveals moderate degrees of regulation and attachment, the less likely are the pathological rates of deviance and the greater is the social integration of individuals into the system.

Thus, Durkheim's analysis in *Suicide* is much more than a statistical analysis of a narrowly defined topic. It is also a venture into understanding how social organization is possible. This becomes particularly evident near the end of the book, where Durkheim proposes his solution to the high rates of suicide and other forms of deviance that typify modern or "organically" structured societies.

Suicide and the Social Organization of Organic Societies[56]

At the end of *Suicide*, Durkheim abandoned his cross-sectional statistical analysis and returned to the evolutionary perspective contained in *The Division of Labor*. During social change, as societies move from one basis of social solidarity to another, deregulation (anomie) and detachment (egoism) of the individual from society can occur, especially if this transition is rapid. Deregulation and detachment create not only high rates of deviance but also problems in maintaining the social order. If these problems are to be avoided and if social "normality" is to be restored, new structures that provide attachment and regulation of individuals to society must be created.

---

[56]Durkheim dropped the term *organic societies*, but we have retained it here to emphasize the continuity between *Suicide* and *The Division of Labor*.

In a series of enlightening pages, Durkheim analyzed the inability of traditional social structures to provide this new basis of social integration. The family is an insufficiently encompassing social structure, religious structures are similarly too limited in their scope and too oriented to the sacred, and government is too bureaucratized and hence remote from the individual. For Durkheim, the implications are that modern social structures require intermediate groups to replace the declining influence of family and religion, to mediate between the individual and state, and to check the growing power of the state. He saw the occupational group as the only potential structural unit that could regulate and attach individuals to society.

Thus, in *Suicide*, the ideas that were later placed in the 1902 preface to the second edition of *The Division of Labor* found their first forceful expression. The analysis in suicide allowed Durkheim to explore further the concept of social integration, and for this reason, *Suicide* represents both an application of the method advocated in *The Rules* and a clarification of substantive ideas contained in *The Division of Labor*. It also represents an effort to incorporate social psychology[57] into structural sociology.

The Elementary Forms of the Religious Life

Although Durkheim turned to the study of religion in his last major work, it had been an important interest for a long time. Indeed, his family background ensured that religion would be a central concern, and from 1895 on, he had taught courses on religion.[58] Regardless of any personal reasons for his interest, we suspect that Durkheim pursued the study of religion through most of his career, because it allowed him to gain insight into the basic theoretical problem that guided all of his work: the nature of symbols and their reciprocal effects on patterns of social organization. In *The Division of Labor*, he had argued that in mechanical societies, the collective conscience or culture is predominately religious in content and that it functions to integrate the individual into the collective. He had recognized that in organic systems,

---

[57]Durkheim would, of course, not admit to this label.

[58]Émile Durkheim, *The Elementary Forms of the Religious Life* (New York: Free Press, 1947; originally published in 1912).

the collective conscience becomes "enfeebled" and that religion as a pervasive influence recedes. The potential pathologies that can occur with the transition from mechanical to organic solidarity—particularly anomie—became increasingly evident to Durkheim. Indeed, the naive optimism that these pathologies would "spontaneously" wither away became increasingly untenable, and as is evident in *Suicide*, he began to ponder how to create a social system in which individuals are both regulated by a general set of values and attached to concrete groups. As he came to view the matter, these concerns revolve around the more general problem of "morality."

Durkheim never wrote what was to be the culmination of his life's work: a book on morality. In many ways, however, his study of religion represents the beginning of his formal work on morality. Although he had lectured on morality in his courses on education[59] and had written several articles on morality,[60] he saw in religion a chance to study how interaction among individuals leads to the creation of symbolic systems that (1) lace together individual actions into collective units, (2) regulate and control individual desires, and (3) attach individuals to both the cultural (symbolic) and structural (morphological) facets of the social world. Given the rise of anomie and egoism in modern societies, he thought that an understanding of religious morality in primitive social systems would help explain how such morality could be created in modern, differentiated systems. Thus, we could retitle *The Elementary Forms of the Religious Life*, "the fundamental forms of moral integration" and be close to his purpose in examining religion in aboriginal societies, particularly the Arunta aborigines of Australia.[61]

---

[59]The work on "moral education" will be examined later in this chapter in a discussion of Durkheim's more general concern with "morality."

[60]See, for example, Émile Durkheim, "The Determination of Moral Facts," in *Sociology and Philosophy*, trans. D. F. Poccock (New York: Free Press, 1974; this article was originally published in 1906).

[61]Baldwin Spencer and F. J. Gillian, in *The Native Tribes of Central Australia* (New York: Macmillan, 1899), present the first collection of "accounts" of these aboriginal peoples, which was in itself fascinating to urbane Europeans. Sigmund Freud, in *Totem and Taboo* (New York: Penguin Books, 1938; originally published in 1913), and two anthropologists, Bronislaw Malinowski, in *The Family among the Australian Aborigines* (New York: Schocken, 1963, originally published in 1913), and A. R. Radcliffe-Brown, in "Three Tribes of Western Australia," *Journal of Royal Anthropological Institute of Great Britain and Ireland* 43 (1913), were all preparing works on the aborigines of Australia at the same time that Durkheim was writing *The Elementary Forms of the Religious Life*.

In the course of writing what was his longest work, however, Durkheim introduced many other intellectual issues that occupied his attention over the years. Thus, *Elementary Forms* is more than a study of social integration; it is also an excursion into human evolution, the sociology of knowledge, functional and causal analyses, the origin and basis of thought and mental categories, the process of internalization of beliefs and values, and many other issues. Between the long descriptive passages on life among the Australian tribes, new ideas burst forth and give evidence of the wide-ranging concerns of Durkheim's intellect.

Elementary Forms is thus a long, complex, and—compared with earlier works—less coherently organized book. This requires that our analysis be divided into a number of separate topics. After a brief overview of the argument in *Elementary Forms*, we will examine in more detail some of its implications.

An Overview of Durkheim's Argument

By studying the elementary forms of religion among the most primitive[62] peoples, it should be possible, Durkheim felt, to understand the essence of religious phenomena without the distracting complexities and sociocultural overlays of modern social systems.[63] As dictated in *The Rules*, a clear definition of the phenomenon under study was first necessary. Thus, Durkheim defined religion as "a unified system of beliefs and practices relative to sacred things, that is to say, things set apart and forbidden—beliefs and practices which unite into one single moral community called a Church, all those who adhere to them."[64]

Durkheim believed that religiosity had emerged among humans when they occasionally assembled in a larger mass. From the mutual stimulation and "effervescence" that comes from animated interaction,

---

[62]Obviously Durkheim was wrong on this account, but this was one of his assumptions.

[63]This strategy was the exact opposite of that employed by Max Weber, who examined the most complex systems of religion with his ideal-type methodology.

[64]Durkheim, *Elementary Forms*, 47. His earlier definition of religious phenomena emphasized the sacred—beliefs and ritual—but did not stress on the morphological units of community and church. For example, an early definition read, "Religious phenomena consist of obligatory beliefs united with divine practices which relate to the objects given in the beliefs" (quoted in Lukes, *Émile Durkheim*, 241). His exposure to the compilation in Spencer and Gillian, *Native Tribes*, apparently alerted him to these morphological features.

people came to perceive a force, or "mana," that seemed superior to them. The mutual stimulation of primitive peoples thus made them "feel" an "external" and "constraining" force above and beyond them.[65] This force seemed to be imbued with special significance and with a sense that it was not part of this world. It was, then, the first notion of a "sacred" realm distinct from the routine or "secular" world of daily activities. The distinction between sacred and secular was thus one of the first sets of mental categories possessed by humans in their evolutionary development.

As humans came to form more permanent groupings, or clans, the force that emerged from their interaction needed to be more concretely represented.[66] Such representation came with "totems," which are animals and plants that symbolize the force of mana. In this way, the sacred forces could be given concrete representation, and groups of people organized into "cults" could develop "ritual" activities directed toward the totem and indirectly toward the sacred force that they collectively sensed.

Thus, the basic elements of religion are (1) the emergence of beliefs in the sacred, (2) the organization of people into cults, and (3) the enactment of rituals, or rites, toward totems that represent the forces of the sacred realm. What the aboriginals did not recognize, Durkheim argued, is that in worshipping totems, they were worshipping society. Totemic cults are nothing but the material symbolization of a force created by their interaction and collective organization into clans.

As people first became organized into clans and associated totemic cults, and as they perceived a sacred realm that influenced events in the secular world, their first categories of thought were also formed. Notions of causality, Durkheim argued, could emerge only after people perceived that sacred forces determined events in the secular world. Notions of time and space could exist only after the organization of clans and their totemic cults. According to Durkheim, the basic categories of human thought—cause, time, space, and so on— emerged only after people developed religion. Thus, in an ultimate sense, science and all forms of thought have emerged from religion, an argument, we might note, reminiscent of Comte's law of the three

---

[65]Durkheim clearly borrowed the ideas of crowd behavior developed by Gustave LeBon and Gabriel Tarde, even though the latter was his lifelong intellectual enemy.

[66]Durkheim, in both *The Division of Labor* and *The Rules*, had stressed that the segmental clan was the most elementary society. He termed the presocietal "mass" from which the clan emerges as the *horde*.

stages. Before religion, humans experienced only physical sensations[67] from their physical environment, but with religion, their mental life became structured by categories. In Durkheim's view, mental categories are the cornerstone of all thought, including scientific thought and reasoning. In looking back on *Elementary Forms* a year after its publication, Durkheim was still moved to conclude,

> The most essential notions of the human mind, notions of time, of space, of genus and species, of force and causality, of personality, those in a word, which the philosophers have labeled categories and which dominate the whole logical thought, have been elaborated in the very womb of religion. It is from religion that science has taken them.[68]

For Durkheim, the cause of religion is the interaction among people created by their organization into the simplest form of society, the clan. The functions of religion are (1) to regulate human needs and actions through beliefs about the sacred and (2) to attach people, through ritual activities (rites) in cults, to the collective. Because they are internalized, religious beliefs generate needs for people to belong to cults and participate in rituals. As people participate in rituals, they reaffirm these internalized beliefs and, hence, reinforce their regulation by, and attachment to, the dictates of the clan. Moreover, the molding of basic mental categories such as cause, time, and space by religious beliefs and cults function to give people a common view of the world, thus facilitating their interaction and organization.

This argument is represented in Figure 13.2, which delineates Durkheim's model on the origins of functions of religion. Regarding origins, he had an image of aboriginal peoples periodically migrating and concentrating themselves in temporary gatherings. Once they have gathered, increased interaction escalates collective emotions, which produce a sense that there is something external and constraining to each individual. This sense of constraint is given more articulate expression as a sacred force, or mana. This causal sequence occurs, Durkheim maintained, each time aboriginals gathered in their periodic

---

[67]As will be recalled, Durkheim took this idea from Rousseau and his description of the "natural state of man."

[68]Quoted in Lukes, *Émile Durkheim*, 445 (taken from *L'Année Sociologique*, 1913). This line of thought is simply Comte's idea of the movement of thought from the theological through the metaphysical to the positivistic.

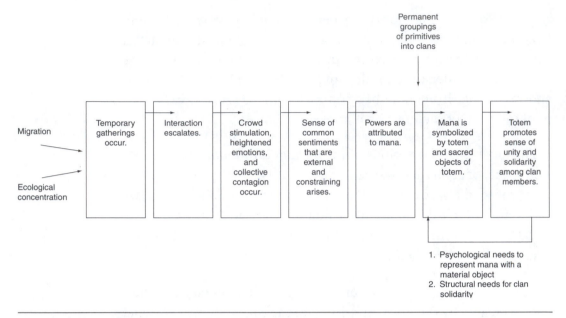

Figure 13.2   Durkheim's Model of Religious Evolution

festivals. Once they form more permanent groupings, called clans, the force of mana is given more concrete expression as a sacred totem. The creation of beliefs about, and rituals toward, the totem function to promote clan solidarity.

This model is substantively inaccurate, as are all of Durkheim's intellectual expeditions into the origins of society. For example, the clan was not the first kinship structure, and many hunter-gatherers like the aborigines do not worship totems. These errors can be attributed to Durkheim's reliance on Australian aborigine kinship and religious organization, which in many ways deviate from modal patterns among hunting-and-gathering peoples. Apart from these factual errors, the same problems evident in the model of the division of labor resurface. First, the conditions under which any causal connection holds true are not specified. Second, the functions of religious totems (for social solidarity) are also what appear to promote their very creation. In addition, a psychological need— the "primitive need" to make concrete and symbolize "mana"—is invoked to explain why totems emerge.

Because of these problems, it must be concluded that the model does not present any useful information in its causal format. But as a statement of relationships among rates of interaction—structural arrangements, emotional arousal, and symbolic representation—Durkheim's statements are suggestive and emphasize that (1) highly concentrated interactions increase collective sentiments, which mobilize actors' actions; (2) small social structures tend to develop symbols to represent their collective sentiments; and (3) these structures evidence high rates of ritual activity to reinforce their members' commitment.

Some Further Implications of Elementary Forms

Practical Concerns

Durkheim's analysis of pathologies in *Suicide*, along with other essays, forced the recognition that a more active program for avoiding egoism and anomie might be necessary to create a normal "organic" society. Religion, he thought, offers a key to understanding how this can be done. Early in his career, however, he rejected the idea that religion could ever again assume major integrative functions. The modern world is too secular and individualistic for the subordination of individuals to gods. He also rejected, to a much lesser degree, Saint-Simon's and Comte's desire to create a secular religion of humanity based on science and reason. Although Durkheim saw a need to maintain the functions and basic elements of religion, he had difficulty accepting Comte's ideal of positivism, which, as Robert Nisbet noted, was "Catholicism minus Christianity." For Comte, the Grand Being was society, the church was the hierarchy of the sciences, and the rites were the sacred canons of the positive method.[69] Durkheim also rejected Max Weber's pessimistic view of a secular, rational world filled with disenchantment and lacking in commitments to a higher purpose.

The "solution" implied in *Elementary Forms* and advocated elsewhere in various essays is for the re-creation in secular form of the basic elements of religion: feelings of sacredness, beliefs and values about the sacred, common rituals directed toward the sacred, and cult structures in which these rituals and beliefs are reaffirmed. Because society is the source and object of religious activity anyway, the goal must be to make explicit this need to "worship" society. Occupational groups and the state would become the church and cults, nationalistic beliefs would become quasi-sacred and would provide underlying symbols, and activities in occupational groups, when seen as furthering the collective goals of the nation, would assume the functions of religious ritual in (1) mobilizing individual

---

[69]Nisbet, *Émile Durkheim*, 159.

commitment, (2) reaffirming beliefs and values, and (3) integrating individuals into the collective.

Theoretical Concerns

Contained in these practical concerns are several important theoretical issues. First, integration of social structures presupposes a system of values and beliefs that reflects and symbolizes the structure of the collective. Second, these values and beliefs require rituals directed at reaffirming them as well as those social structures they represent or symbolize. Third, large collectivities, such as a nation, require subgroups in which values and beliefs can be affirmed by ritual activities among a more immediate community of individuals. Fourth, to the degree that values and beliefs do not correspond to actual structural arrangements and to the extent that substructures for the performance of actions that reaffirm these values and beliefs are not present, a societal social system will experience integrative problems.

We can see, then, that Durkheim's practical concerns follow from certain theoretical principles he had tentatively put forth in *The Division of Labor*. The study of religion seemingly provided him with a new source of data to affirm the utility of his first insights into the social order. There are, however, some noticeable shifts in emphasis, the most important of which is the recognition that the "collective conscience" cannot be totally "enfeebled"; it must be general but also strong and relevant to the specific organizations that make up a society. Despite these refinements, *Elementary Forms* affirms the conclusion contained in the preface to the second edition of *The Division of Labor*.

The most interesting aspect of the analysis is perhaps the social–psychological emphasis of *Elementary Forms*. Although Durkheim, in courses and essays, had begun to feel comfortable with inquiry into the social–psychological dynamics of social and symbolic structures, these concerns are brought together in his last major book.

Social–Psychological Concerns

Elementary Forms contains the explicit recognition that morality—that is, values, beliefs, and norms—can integrate the social order only if morality becomes part of an individual's psychological structure. Statements in *Elementary Forms* mitigate the rather hard line taken in the first edition of *The Rules*, where social facts are seen as external and constraining things. With the second edition of *The Rules*, Durkheim felt more secure in verbalizing the obvious internalization of values, beliefs, and other symbolic components of society into the human psyche. In *Elementary Forms*, he revealed even fewer reservations:

> For the collective force is not entirely outside of us; it does not act upon us wholly from without; but rather, since society cannot exist except in and through individual consciousnesses, this force must also penetrate us and organize itself within us, it thus becomes an integral part of our being.[70]

Durkheim hastened to add in a footnote, however, that although society was an "integral part of our being," it could not ever be seen as reducible to individuals.

Another social–psychological concern in *Elementary Forms* is the issue of human thought processes. For Durkheim, thought occurs in categories that structure experience for individuals:

> At the roots of all our judgments there are a certain number of essential ideas which dominate all our intellectual life; they are what philosophers since Aristotle have called the categories of the understanding: ideas of space, class, number, cause, substance, personality, etc. They correspond to the most universal properties of things. They are like the solid frame which encloses all thought.[71]

Durkheim sought in *Elementary Forms* to reject the philosophical positions of David Hume and Immanuel Kant. Hume, the staunch empiricist, argued that thought was simply the transfer of experiences to the mind and that categories of thought were merely the codification of repetitive experiences. In contrast with Hume, Kant argued that categories and mind were inseparable; the essence of mind is categorization. Categories are innate and not structured from experience. Durkheim rejected both of these positions; in their place he wanted to insert the notion that categories of thought—indeed, all thinking and reflective mental activity—were imposed on individuals by the structure and morality of society. Indeed, this imposition

---

[70]Durkheim, *Elementary Forms*, 209.
[71]Ibid., 9.

of society becomes a critical condition not just for the creation of mind and thought but also for the preservation of society.[72] Thus, Durkheim believed that the basic categories of thought, such as cause, time, and space, were social products, in that the structure of society determines them in the same way that values and beliefs also structure human "will," or motivations. For example, the idea of a sacred force, or mana, beyond individuals that could influence events in the mundane world became, in the course of human evolution, related to ideas of causality. Similarly, the idea of time emerged among humans as they developed calendrical rituals and related them to solar and lunar rhythms. The conception of space was shaped by the structure of villages, so that if the aboriginal village is organized in a circle, the world will be seen as circular and concentric in nature. These provocative insights were at times taken to excessive extremes in other essays, especially in one written with his nephew and student, Marcel Mauss, on "primitive classification."[73] Here, mental categories are seen to be exact representations of social structural divisions and arrangements. Moreover, Durkheim and Mauss appear to have selectively reported data from aboriginal societies to support their excessive claims.[74]

Durkheim is often viewed as the "father of structuralism," a school of thought in the twentieth century that embraced social science, linguistics, and literature. In Durkheim's *Elementary Forms* and other works of this period can be found an implicit model that appears to have inspired this structuralist reasoning. Figure 13.3 outlines the contours of this model. In Durkheim's view, the morphology of a society (the number, nature, size, and arrangement of parts—see Table 13.1) determines the structure of the collective conscience or culture (the volume, density, intensity, and content of values, beliefs, and norms). Reciprocally, the collective conscience reinforces social morphology. Both morphology and collective conscience circumscribe each individual's cognitive structure by determining the nature of basic categories of thought with respect to time, space, and causality. In turn, these categories mediate between morphology and the collective conscience, on the one hand, and the nature of rituals that

---

[72]Ibid., 17–18.

[73]Émile Durkheim and Marcel Mauss, *Primitive Classification*, trans. Rodney Needham (Chicago: University of Chicago Press, 1963; originally published in 1903).

[74]See the introduction to the translation for the documentation of this fact.

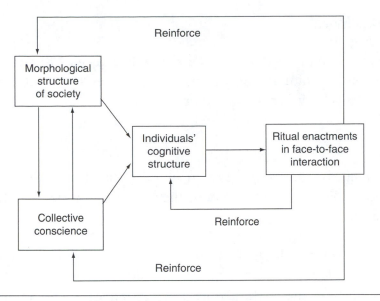

Figure 13.3   Durkheim's Structuralism

individuals emit in face-to-face interaction, on the other. The reverse causal loops in the model are crucial to Durkheim's argument: The enactment of rituals reinforces not only cognitive categories but also the structure and idea systems of society. In this way, the macrostructural features of society—morphology and idea systems—are conceptually tied to the microstructural dimensions of reality—that is, the internal psychological structure of thought and the face-to-face interactions among individuals in concrete settings.

A Science of "Morality"

As early as *The Division of Labor*, Durkheim defined sociology as the science of "moral facts," and he always wanted to write a book on morality. In light of this unfulfilled goal, perhaps we should close our analysis by extracting from his various works what would have been the core ideas of this uncompleted work.[75]

---

[75]See, in particular, Émile Durkheim, *Moral Education: A Study in the Theory and Application of the Sociology of Education*, trans. E. K. Wilson and H. Schnurer (New York: Free Press, 1961; originally published in 1922). This is a compilation of lectures given in 1902–1903; the course was repeated in 1906–1907.

What Is Morality?

In only two places did Durkheim provide a detailed discussion of morality.[76] For him, morality consists of (1) rules, (2) attachment to groups, and (3) voluntary constraint.

Rules

Morality is ultimately a system of rules that guides the actions of people. For rules to be moral, they must reveal two additional elements:

1. *Authority:* Moral rules are invested with authority—that is, people feel that they ought to obey them and they want to abide by them. Moral rules are a "system of commandments."

2. *Desirability:* Moral rules also specify the "desirable" ends toward which a collectivity of people should direct its energies. They are more than rules of convenience; they carry conceptions of the good and desirable and must therefore be distinguished from strictly utilitarian norms.

Attachment to Groups

Moral rules attach people to groups. They are the product of interactions in groups, and as they emerge, they bind people to groups and make individuals feel a part of a network of relations that transcends their individual being.

Durkheim termed these two facets of morality *the spirit of discipline.* Morality provides a spirit of self-control and a commitment to the collective. In terms of the concepts developed in *Suicide*, morality reduces anomie and egoism to the degree that it regulates desires and attaches people to the collective. True morality in a modern society must do something else, however: It must allow people to recognize that the constraints and restraints imposed on them are in the "natural order of things."

---

[76]One is Durkheim, *Moral Education*, the other is an article, published in 1906, on "The Determination of Moral Facts." Reprinted in Émile Durkheim, *Sociology and Philosophy* (New York: Free Press, 1974), from papers originally collected and translated in 1924.

Voluntary Constraint

Modern morality must allow people to recognize that unlimited desires (anomie) and excessive individualism (egoism) are pathological states. Durkheim felt that these states violate the nature of human society and can be corrected only by morality. In simple societies, morality seems to operate automatically, but "the more societies become complex, the more difficult [it becomes] for morality to operate as a purely automatic mechanism."[77] Thus, morality must be constantly implemented and altered to the changing conditions. Individuals must also come to see that such alteration is necessary and essential because to fail to establish a morality and to allow people to feel free of its power is to invite the agonies of anomie and egoism.

Durkheim then resumed an argument first made by Rousseau: Morality must be seen as a natural constraint in the same way that the physical world constrains individuals' options and actions. So it is with morality; humans can no more rid themselves of its constraint than they can eliminate the physical and biological world on which their lives depend. The only recourse is to use science, just as we use the physical and biological sciences, to understand how morality works.[78]

Thus, Durkheim never abandoned his original notion, first given forceful expression in *The Division of Labor*, that sociology is the science of moral facts. His conception of morality had become considerably more refined, however, in three senses:

1. Morality is a certain type of rule that must be distinguished from both the morphological aspects of society and other, nonmoral, types of normative rules.

2. Morality is therefore a system of rules that reflects certain underlying value premises about the desirable.

3. Morality is not only external and constraining; it is also internal. It calls people to obey from within. For although morality "surpasses us it is within us, since it can only exist by and through us."[79]

---

[77]Durkheim, *Moral Education*, 52.

[78]Ibid., 119–120.

[79]Durkheim, "Determination of Moral Facts," 55.

By the end of Durkheim's career, the study of morality involved a clear separation between two types of norms and rules: those vested with value premises and those that simply mediate and regularize interactions. Moreover, an understanding of these types of rules could come only by visualizing their relationship to the morphological or structural aspects of society—nature, size, number, and relations of parts—and to the process by which internalization of symbols or culture occurs. Durkheim had thus begun to develop a clear conception of the complex relations among normative systems, social structures, and personality processes of individuals.

What would Durkheim have said in his last work—the book on morality—if he had lived to write it? *Moral Education*, when viewed in the context of his other published books, can perhaps provide some hints about the direction of his thought—for *Moral Education* offers a view of how a new secular morality can be instilled.

For a new secular morality to be effective, the source of all morality must be recognized: that is, society. This means that moral rules must be linked to the goals of the broader society, but they must be made specific through the participation of individuals in occupational groups. The commitment to the common morality must be learned in schools, where the teacher operates as the functional equivalent of the priest. The teacher gives young students an understanding of and a reverence for the nature of the society and the need to have a morality that regulates passions and provides attachments to groupings organized to pursue societal goals. Such educational socialization must assure that the common morality is a part of students' motivational needs (their "will," in Durkheim's language), their cognitive orientations ("categories of mind"), and their self-control processes ("self-mastery").

A modern society that cannot meet these general conditions, Durkheim would have argued in this unwritten work, is a society that will be rife with pathologies revolving around (1) the failure to limit individual passions, desires, and aspirations and (2) the failure to attach individuals to groups with higher purposes and common goals.

Durkheim must have felt that the implicit theory of social organization contained in this argument had allowed him to realize Comte's dream of a science that could create "the good society." Although Durkheim was cautious in implementing his proposals, they were often simplistic, if not somewhat reactionary. At the same time, one can find the germ of a theory of human organization in his work.

Critical Conclusions

Émile Durkheim is, along with Karl Marx and Max Weber, one of the "holy trinity" of sociology's early masters. He enjoys this high place in sociology's pantheon because he addressed issues that have long fascinated sociologists. Although he borrowed a great deal from Herbert Spencer in his early work, he nonetheless presented what is now termed an *ecological model*, emphasizing population growth, competition for resources, and differentiation—a model that is widely used in sociology today. More fundamentally, he isolated in *The Division of Labor* some of the key mechanisms by which complex systems sustain integration: structural interdependence, abstract and general values and beliefs, more specific beliefs and norms to regulate relations within and between differentiated groups and organizations, and networks of subgroups forming larger coalitions and confederations with common interests. Moreover, his analysis of the pathologies, such as anomie, that arise from the failure to achieve integration, are some of sociology's more enduring concepts.

Durkheim's later work, where questions of how individuals become integrated into society became increasingly important, has also had an enormous impact on sociology. The analysis in *Suicide*, emphasizing the individual's integration into social structures and culture, has been widely used in sociological studies of deviance, crime, and other social "pathologies." Perhaps more significant is Durkheim's recognition in his last major work, *The Elementary Forms of the Religious Life*, that rituals directed at symbolic representations of groups constitute the basis of integration at the micro level of social organization.

Finally, in his insistence on analyzing one set of social facts by another, Durkheim made a very strong case for sociology as a distinctive kind of enterprise. He was trying to make a place for sociology in the academic and broader intellectual worlds, and he argued for sociology in a way reminiscent of Comte's advocacy. Perhaps he argued too much, but he did gain an academic beachhead for sociology in France during the last decade of the nineteenth century.

Still, there are problems in Durkheim's approach. Functional reasoning almost always gets a theorist into trouble, and Durkheim is no exception. He often argued that, in seemingly mysterious ways, the need for social integration brought about the cultural and structural arrangements that would meet this need for integration. Arguing for a separate causal analysis (as distinct from a functional analysis) did not obviate this problem of seeing outcomes as the cause of these very outcomes. Such reasoning usually becomes rather circular, explaining very little.

Durkheim was at his best when making causal arguments, but even here, there are problems. First, he never gave Spencer much credit for presenting the key ideas on the causes on the division of labor some 20 years before *The Division of Labor.* Second, he never really indicated the causal sequences by which new forms of integration are to be achieved with differentiation; he simply assumes that these forms will emerge without specifying causality. As with Spencer, we can invoke a selection argument—that is, problems of integration generate selection pressures for new types of cultural symbols and social structures—but this too is vague.

More substantively, Durkheim ignored the importance of power and stratification in society. He assumed that the "forced division of labor" would simply go away, and he never addressed adequately the conflict potential in systems of stratification, assuming that this too would go away as new bases of integration were achieved. Like Marx before him, but in the opposite direction, Durkheim's ideological commitments to finding a new basis of integration led him to mistake what he wanted to occur from what would actually transpire in differentiated societies. Complex societies always reveal points of tension and conflict, but through Durkheim's rose-colored glasses, we would hardly know that this was the case.

Another substantive problem is Durkheim's overemphasis on cultural forces to the detriment of recognizing the importance of power and mutual interdependence as mechanisms of integration. Durkheim addressed these topics, to be sure, but one really does not get a sense for how power integrates complex societies or how markets and other mediators of interdependence operate. Rather, values, beliefs, and norms seem to do most of the integrative work, and although this point of emphasis has added a great deal to sociology's understanding of cultural processes, the more structural dimensions of integration are underemphasized—a rather remarkable conclusion given Durkheim's emphasis on studying "social facts."

Yet some of the most important models and principles in sociology today owe their origins to Durkheim's analysis. For all their problems, then, Durkheim's collective works continue to inspire sociology in the twenty-first century.

CHAPTER 14

The Origin and Context of George Herbert Mead's Thought

Biographical Influences on Mead's Thought

George Herbert Mead was born in South Hadley, Massachusetts, in 1863.[1] His father was a minister in a long line of Puritan farmers and clergymen. His mother, who eventually became president of Mount Holyoke College, came from a background similar to her husband's, although perhaps with a more intellectual than religious bent. In 1870, the family moved to Ohio, where Mead's father assumed a position at Oberlin College as a chair of homiletics, or the art of preaching. In 1881, Mead's father died, forcing his mother to sell their house and move into rented rooms. To make ends meet, Mead's mother taught at the college, while he waited on tables to support himself as a student at Oberlin. In 1883, Mead graduated from Oberlin with a major in philosophy, and for the next 4 years, he appeared to be at loose ends. He taught for a while, but for the most part, he tutored students and worked as a surveyor on railroad construction in the Northwest. During this period, he read voraciously; and as was evident throughout his career, he was a widely read intellectual.

In 1887, Mead decided to enroll in Harvard and pursue further study in philosophy. Here, he was exposed to a fuller range of ideas

---

[1]As Lewis Coser notes, biographical materials on Mead are rather scarce; so much of the information in this chapter relies primarily on his excellent review in Lewis A. Coser, *Masters of Sociological Thought* (New York: Harcourt Brace Jovanovich, 1977).

than at Oberlin, which at the time was still a religious school, despite its history of involvement in progressive social affairs. Mead's reading of Charles Darwin brought his growing disenchantment with his father's religion to its culmination. More important, the substance of Darwin's work had considerable impact on his philosophy and social psychology, as we will explore shortly. Moreover, he read and studied Adam Smith, whose utilitarian position remained an implicit theme in Mead's theorizing. Perhaps an even more important influence was his direct contact with the Harvard psychologist, William James, whose pragmatic philosophy also became a prominent theme in Mead's work.

In his second year of graduate study, Mead went abroad to Leipzig, Germany. There he became familiar with the laboratory work of Wilhelm Wundt, whose psychological experiments and theorizing further moved Mead's philosophical interests toward social psychology. Subsequently, Mead went to Berlin in 1889, where, Lewis Coser speculates, he might have listened to lectures by Georg Simmel and come to appreciate more completely the importance of status positions and roles in the dynamics of interaction.

In 1891, Mead married and became an instructor of philosophy at the University of Michigan. Here, he encountered Charles Horton Cooley and John Dewey, both of whom provided him with critical concepts in his eventual theoretical synthesis. But he did not stay long; in 1894, he followed his friend and colleague Dewey to the new and ambitious University of Chicago. Mead remained there until his death in 1931.

At Chicago, Mead was always in the shadow of the charismatic Dewey. More significantly, he had great difficulty writing and publishing, and as a result, much of his most important work comes to us as composite transcriptions of his lectures. These lectures exerted considerable influence among students at Chicago, and the recognition that something important and revolutionary was being said led students to take virtually verbatim notes. In his lifetime, however, Mead never perceived that he had achieved a great theoretical synthesis, one that was to become the conceptual base on which all subsequent theorizing about social interaction would be laid. Indeed, although he was an active and confident man who was very much involved in local efforts, especially social reform, he saw himself in very modest terms as an intellectual. As we will describe in detail in the next chapter, his modesty was misplaced because he stands as one of the giants of sociological theory.

Before exploring the details of Mead's theory, however, we should pause and further examine the influences on his work. In particular, we will initially explore the various schools of thought, such as utilitarianism, pragmatism, behaviorism, and Darwinism, that shaped his thinking; then we will turn to the key individuals in his intellectual biography and examine the specific concepts he drew from scholars such as Wundt, James, Cooley, and Dewey.

Mead's Synthesis of Schools of Thought

As a philosopher, Mead was attuned to basic philosophical issues and to currents in many diverse intellectual arenas. His broader philosophical scheme reflects this, but, even more significantly, his seminal theoretical synthesis on social psychology also pulls together the general metaphors contained within the four dominant intellectual perspectives of his time: (1) utilitarianism, (2) Darwinism, (3) pragmatism, and (4) behaviorism.[2]

Utilitarianism

In England during the eighteenth and nineteenth centuries, the economic doctrine that became known as utilitarianism dominated social thought.[3] Mead had read prominent thinkers such as Adam Smith, David Ricardo, John Stuart Mill, Jeremy Bentham, and, to the extent that he can be classified as a utilitarian, Thomas Malthus. Mead absorbed several key ideas from utilitarian doctrines.

First, utilitarians saw human action as being carried out by self-interested actors seeking to maximize their "utility" or benefit in free and openly competitive marketplaces. Although this idea was expressed somewhat differently by various advocates of utilitarianism, Mead appears to have found useful the emphases on (1) actors as seeking rewards, (2) actors as attempting to adjust to a competitive situation, and (3) actors as goal directed and instrumental in their behaviors. Later versions of utilitarianism stressed "pleasure" and

---

[2]See also Jonathan H. Turner, *The Structure of Sociological Theory*, 7th ed. (Belmont, CA: Wadsworth, 2004).

[3]See Chapter 2 of this book.

"pain" principles, which captured the essence of the behaviorism that emerged in Mead's time and exerted considerable influence on his theoretical scheme.

Second, utilitarians often tended to emphasize—indeed, to over-emphasize—the rationality of self-seeking actors. From a utilitarian perspective, actors are rational in that they gather all relevant information, weigh various lines of conduct, and select an alternative that will maximize their utilities, benefits, or pleasures. Mead never accepted this overly rational view of human action, but the utilitarian position partially inspired his view of the human "mind" as a process of reflective thought in which alternatives are covertly designated, weighed, and rehearsed.

Thus, although utilitarianism only marginally influenced Mead, his scheme corresponded to its central points. He probably borrowed these points both directly and indirectly because utilitarianism influenced the other schools of thought that more directly shaped Mead's philosophical scheme. As we will see, early behaviorism and pragmatism, although rejecting extreme utilitarianism, nonetheless incorporated some of its basic tenets.

Darwinism

Darwin's formulation of the theory of evolution influenced not only biological theory[4] but also social thought.[5] The view that a species' profile is shaped by the competitive struggle with other species attempting to occupy an environmental niche was highly compatible with utilitarian theories. As a result of this superficial compatibility, Darwinism was carried to absurd extremes in the late nineteenth and early twentieth centuries by a group of thinkers who became known as social Darwinists.[6] From their viewpoint, social life is a competitive struggle in which the "fittest" will be the best able to "survive" and prosper.[7] Hence, those who enjoy privilege in a society deserve these benefits

---

[4]Charles Darwin, *On the Origin of Species* (London: John Murray, 1859).

[5]See, for example, William G. Sumner, *What Social Classes Owe Each Other* (New York: Harper & Row, 1883).

[6]Richard Hofstadter, *Social Darwinism in American Thought, 1860–1915* (Philadelphia: University of Pennsylvania Press, 1945).

[7]Spencer first used the phrase *survival of the fittest*, which apparently influenced Darwin, as he acknowledged in *On the Origin of Species*. Other early American sociologists, such as William Graham Sumner, took this idea to extremes. Spencer's utilitarianism was recessive in his sociological works, however, so it is unfair to count Spencer as a social Darwinist.

because they are the "most fit," whereas those who have the least wealth are less fit and worthy. Obviously, social Darwinism was a gross distortion of the theory of evolution, but its flowering illustrates the extent to which Darwin's theory represented an intellectual bombshell in Europe and America.

Other social theorists borrowed Darwin's ideas more cautiously. Mead used the theory of evolution as a broad metaphor for understanding the processes by which the unique capacities of humans emerge. Mead believed all animals, including humans, must seek to adapt and adjust to an environment; hence, many of the attributes that organisms reveal are the products of efforts to adapt to a particular environment. In the distant past, therefore, the unique capacities of humans for language, for mind, for self, and for normatively regulated social organization emerged as a result of selective pressures on the ancestors of humans for these unique capacities.

Mead was not as much interested in the origins of humans as a species as in the infant's development from an asocial to a social creature. At birth, Mead argued, an infant is not a human. It acquires the unique behavioral capacities of humans only as it adapts to a social environment. Thus, just as the species as a whole acquired its distinctive characteristics through a process of "natural selection," so the infant organism develops its "humanness" through a process of "selection." Because the environment of a person is other people who use language, who possess mind and self, and who live in society, the young must adapt to this environment if they are to survive. As they adapt and adjust, they acquire the capacity to use language, to reveal a mind, to evidence a sense of self, and to participate in society. Thus, Mead borrowed from Darwinian theory the metaphor of adaptation, or adjustment, as the key force shaping the nature of humans.[8] This metaphor was given its most forceful expression in the works of scholars who developed a school of thought known as pragmatism.

Pragmatism

Mead is frequently grouped with pragmatists such as Charles Peirce, William James, and John Dewey. Yet, although Mead was

---

[8]Mead also reacted to Darwin's later efforts to understand emotions in animals. See Charles Darwin, *The Expression of Emotions in Man and Animals* (London: John Murray, 1872). Mead used this analysis as his straw man in developing his own theory of gestures and interaction.

profoundly influenced by James and Dewey, his theoretical scheme is only partially in debt to pragmatism.[9]

Charles Peirce, an American scientist and philosopher, first developed the ideas behind pragmatism in an article titled "How to Make Our Ideas Clear," which appeared in *Popular Science Monthly* in 1878.[10] Pragmatism did not become an acknowledged philosophical school, however, until William James delivered a lecture in 1898 titled "Philosophical Conceptions and Practical Results."[11] As John Dewey developed his "instrumentalism," pragmatism became a center of philosophical controversy in the United States during the early decades of the twentieth century. Pragmatism was primarily concerned with the process of thinking and how it influences the action of individuals, and vice versa. Although pragmatists carried their banner in different directions, the central thrust of this philosophical school is to view thought as a process that allows humans to adjust, adapt, and achieve goals in their environment.

Thus, pragmatists became concerned with symbols, language, and rational thinking as well as with the way humans' mental capacities influenced action in the world. Peirce saw pragmatism as concerned with "self-controlled conduct," which was guided by "adequate deliberation," and hence, pragmatism was based on

> a study of that experience of the phenomena of self-control which is common to all grown men and women; and it seems evident that to some extent, at least, it must always be so based. For it is to conceptions of deliberate conduct that pragmatism would trace the intellectual purpose of symbols; and deliberate conduct is self-controlled conduct.[12]

For Peirce, then, pragmatism stresses the use of symbols and signs in thought and self-control, a point that Mead later adopted. James and Dewey supplemented Peirce's emphasis by stressing that the process of thinking is intimately connected to the process of adapta-

---

[9]For relevant summaries of pragmatism, see Charles Morris, *The Pragmatic Movement in American Philosophy* (New York: George Braziller, 1970); and Edward C. Moore, *American Pragmatism: Peirce, James, and Dewey* (New York: Columbia University Press, 1961).

[10]For Peirce's general works, see Charles Sanders Peirce, *The Collected Papers of Charles Sanders Peirce*, 8 vols. (Cambridge, MA: Harvard University Press, 1931–1958). Peirce's "How to Make Our Ideas Clear" is in Vol. 5, 248–271.

[11]This lecture was delivered at Berkeley, California. See also William James, *Pragmatism* (Cambridge, MA: Harvard University Press, 1975).

[12]Morris, *Pragmatic Movement*, 11.

tion and adjustment. James stressed that "truth" is not absolute and enduring; rather, he argued, scientific as well as lay conceptions of truth are only as enduring as their ability to help people adjust and adapt to their circumstances.[13] Truth, in other words, is determined only by its "practical results." Dewey similarly emphasized the significance of thinking for achieving goals and adjusting to the environment—thought, whether lay or scientific, is an "instrument" that can be used to achieve goals and purposes.[14]

Pragmatism emerged as a reaction to, and an effort to deal with, a number of scientific and philosophical events of the nineteenth century. First, the ascendance of Newtonian mechanics posed the question of whether all aspects of the universe, including human thought and action, could be reduced to invariant and mechanistic laws. To this challenge, pragmatists argued that such laws do not make human action mechanistic and wholly determinative but, rather, that these laws are instruments to be used by humans in achieving their goals.[15] Second, the theory of evolution offers the vision of continuity in life processes. Pragmatists added the notion that humans as a species, and as individuals, are engaged in a process of constant adjustment and adaptation to their environment and that thought represents the principal means for achieving such adjustment. Third, the doctrines of utilitarians present a calculating, rational, and instrumental view of human action. Pragmatists were highly receptive to this perspective, although their concern was with the process of thought and how it is linked to action. Fourth, the ascendance of the scientific method with its emphasis on the verification of conceptual schemes with data presented a consensual view of "proper" modes of investigation. To this point, the pragmatists responded that all action involves an act of verification as people's thoughts as conceptions are "checked" against their experiences in the world. For the pragmatist, human life is a continuous application of the "scientific method" as people seek to cope with the world around them.[16]

Pragmatism thus represents the first distinctly American philosophical system. Mead was personally associated with several of its advocates while being intellectually involved in the debate sur-

---

[13]William James, *The Meaning of Truth: A Sequel to "Pragmatism"* (New York: Longmans, Green, 1909).

[14]John Dewey, *Human Nature and Conduct* (New York: Holt, Rinehart & Winston, 1922).

[15]In particular, see John Dewey, *The Quest for Certainty* (New York: Minton, Balch, 1925), or James, *The Meaning of Truth*.

[16]See Morris, *Pragmatic Movement*, 5–11.

rounding the system and its critics. He was clearly influenced by the pragmatists' concern with the process of thinking and with the importance of symbols in thought. He accepted the metaphor that thought and action involve efforts to adjust and adapt to the environment. He embraced the notion that such adaptation is a continuous process of experiential verification of thought and action. In many ways, utilitarianism and Darwinism came to Mead through pragmatism, and hence, to some extent, he must be considered a pragmatist. He was also a behaviorist, and if his social psychology is to be given a label, it is more behavioristic than pragmatic.

Behaviorism

As a psychological perspective, behaviorism began from the insights of the Russian physiologist Ivan Petrovich Pavlov (1849–1936), who discovered that experimental dogs associated food with the person bringing the food.[17] He observed, for instance, that dogs would secrete saliva not only when presented with food but also when they heard their feeder's footsteps approaching. After considerable delay and personal agonizing,[18] Pavlov undertook a series of experiments on animals to understand such "conditioned responses." From these experiments, he developed several principles that were later incorporated into behaviorism. These include the following:

1. A stimulus consistently associated with another stimulus producing a given physiological response will, by itself, elicit that response.

2. Such conditioned responses can be extinguished when gratifications associated with stimuli are no longer forthcoming.

3. Stimuli that are similar to those producing a conditioned response can also elicit the same response as the original stimulus.

4. Stimuli that increasingly differ from those used to condition a particular response will decreasingly be able to elicit this response.

---

[17]For relevant articles, lectures, and references, see I. P. Pavlov, *Selected Works*, ed. K. S. Kostoyants, trans. S. Belsky (Moscow: Foreign Languages Publishing House, 1955); and *Lectures on Conditioned Reflexes*, 3rd ed., trans. W. H. Gantt (New York: International, 1928).

[18]I. P. Pavlov, "Autobiography," in *Selected Works*, 41–44.

Thus, Pavlov's experiments exposed the principles of conditioned responses, extinction, response generalization, and response discrimination. Although Pavlov clearly recognized the significance of these findings for human behavior, his insights were rediscovered in North America by Edward Lee Thorndike and John B. Watson—the founders of behaviorism.[19]

Thorndike conducted the first laboratory experiments on animals in North America. He observed that animals retain response patterns for which they are rewarded.[20] For example, in experiments on kittens placed in a puzzle box, he found that they engage in trial-and-error behavior until they emit the response allowing them to escape. With each placement in the box, the kittens engage in less trial-and-error behavior, indicating that the gratifications associated with a response allowing them to escape cause them to learn and retain this response. From these and other studies, which were conducted at the same time as Pavlov's, Thorndike formulated three principles, or laws: (1) the "law of effect" holds that acts in a situation producing gratification will be more likely to occur in the future when that situation recurs, (2) the "law of use" states that the situation–response connection is strengthened with repetition and practice, and (3) the "law of disuse" argues that the connection will weaken when the practice is discontinued.[21]

These laws overlap with those presented by Pavlov, but there is one important difference. Thorndike's experiments were conducted on animals engaged in free trial-and-error behavior, whereas Pavlov's work was on the conditioning of physiological—typically glandular—responses in a tightly controlled laboratory situation. Thorndike's work could thus be seen as more directly relevant to human behavior in natural settings.

Watson was only one of several thinkers to recognize the significance of Pavlov's and Thorndike's work,[22] but he soon became

---

[19]For an excellent summary of their ideas, see Robert I. Watson, *The Great Psychologists*, 3rd ed. (Philadelphia: Lippincott, 1971), 417–446.

[20]Edward L. Thorndike, "Animal Intelligence: An Experimental Study of the Associative Processes in Animals," *Psychological Review Monograph*, Supplement 2 (1898).

[21]See Edward L. Thorndike, *The Elements of Psychology* (New York: Seiler, 1905); *The Fundamentals of Learning* (New York: Teachers College Press, 1932); and *The Psychology of Wants, Interests, and Attitudes* (New York: Appleton-Century-Crofts, 1935).

[22]The others included Max F. Meyer, *Psychology of the Other-One* (Columbus, OH: Missouri Books, 1921); and Albert P. Weiss, *A Theoretical Basis of Human Behavior* (Columbus, OH: Adams, 1925).

the dominant advocate of what was becoming explicitly known as "behaviorism." His opening shot for the new science of behavior was fired in an article titled "Psychology as the Behaviorist Views It":

> Psychology as the behaviorist views it is a purely objective experimental branch of natural science. Its theoretical goal is the prediction and control of behavior. Introspection forms no essential part of its methods, nor is the scientific value of its data dependent upon the readiness with which they lend themselves to interpretation in terms of consciousness. The behaviorist, in efforts to get a unitary scheme of animal response, recognizes no dividing line between man and brute.[23]

Watson thus became the advocate of the extreme behaviorism against which Mead vehemently reacted.[24] For Watson, psychology is the study of stimulus–response relations, and the only admissible evidence is overt behavior. Psychologists are to stay out of the "mystery box" of human consciousness and to study only observable behaviors as they are connected to observable stimuli. Mead rejected this assertion and argued that just because an activity such as thinking is not directly observable does not mean that it is not behavior. Mead argued that covert thinking and the capacity to view oneself in situations are nonetheless behaviors and hence subject to the same laws as overt behaviors.

Mead thus rejected extreme behaviorism but accepted its general principle: Behaviors are learned as a result of gratifications associated with them. In accordance with the views of pragmatists, and consistent with Mead's Darwinian metaphor, the gratifications of humans typically involve adjustment to a social environment. Most important, some of the most distinctive behaviors of humans are covert, involving thinking, reflection, and self-awareness. In contrast

---

[23]J. B. Watson, "Psychology as the Behaviorist Views It," *Psychological Review* 20 (1913), 158–177. For other basic works by Watson, see *Psychology from the Standpoint of a Behaviorist*, 3rd ed. (Philadelphia: Lippincott, 1929); and *Behavior: An Introduction to Comparative Psychology* (New York: Holt, Rinehart & Winston, 1914).

[24]For example, in his *Mind, Self, and Society* (Chicago: University of Chicago Press, 1934), Mead has 18 references to Watson's work and is highly critical of the latter's extreme methodological position. Nonetheless, Mead considered himself a behaviorist. For further documentation of this conclusion, see Jonathan H. Turner, "A Note on G. H. Mead's Behavioristic Theory of Social Structure," *Journal for the Theory of Social Behavior* 12 (July 1982), 213–222; and John D. Baldwin, *George Herbert Mead* (Beverly Hills, CA: Sage, 1986).

with Watson's behaviorism, Mead postulated what some have called a *social behaviorism*. From this perspective, both covert and overt behaviors are to be understood through their capacity to produce adjustment to society.

In sum, we can conclude that Mead borrowed the broad assumptions from a number of intellectual perspectives, particularly utilitarianism, Darwinism, pragmatism, and behaviorism. Utilitarians and pragmatists emphasized the process of thinking and rational conduct; utilitarians and Darwinists stressed the importance of competitive struggle and selection of attributes; Darwinists and pragmatists argued for the importance of adaptation and adjustment to an understanding of thought and action; and behaviorists presented a view of learning as the association of behaviors with gratification-producing stimuli. Each of these general ideas became a part of Mead's theoretical scheme, but as he synthesized these ideas, they took on new meaning.

Mead was not only influenced by these general intellectual perspectives, but he also borrowed specific concepts from a variety of scholars, only some of whom worked within these general perspectives. By taking specific concepts, reconciling them, and then incorporating them into the metaphors of these four general perspectives, he was able to produce the theoretical breakthrough for which he is deservedly given credit.

Wilhelm Wundt and Mead

Even a casual reading of Mead's written work and posthumously published lectures reveals numerous citations to the German psychologist Wilhelm Wundt.[25] Wundt is often given credit for being the father of psychology because by the 1860s he had conducted a series of experiments that could be clearly defined as psychological in nature. In the 1870s, he was one of the first, along with William James at Harvard, to establish a psychological laboratory.

Mead studied briefly in Germany, although not in Heidelberg, where Wundt had established his laboratory and school of loyal followers.

---

[25]*Mind, Self, and Society* alone contains more than 20 references to Wundt's ideas.

Wundt's eminence prompted Mead to read his works carefully.[26] At first glance, it might appear that Mead, the philosopher, would find little of interest in Wundt's voluminous output. Most of Wundt's laboratory work deals with efforts to understand the structure of consciousness, an emphasis not conducive to Mead's insistence on mind as a process. However, Wundt was also a philosopher, social psychologist, and sociologist. Although he would write strictly psychological books such as *Physiological Psychology*, he also founded the journal *Philosophical Studies*, in which he published his laboratory studies. Indeed, he saw little reason to distinguish psychology from philosophy. He also devoted many pages in his *Outlines of Psychology* to issues such as gestures, language, self-consciousness, mental communities, customs, myths, and child development, all topics likely to interest Mead. Moreover, Wundt's *Elements of Folk Psychology* was one of the first distinctly social psychological studies, examining the broad evolutionary development of human thought and culture. Thus, he was a scholar of great range and enormous productive energy. Mead would apparently find much in the work of Wundt to stimulate his own thought.

Wundt's View of Gestures

In much of his work, Mead devoted considerable space to Wundt's view of "gestures" and "speech."[27] Mead argued that Wundt had been the first to recognize that gestures represent signs marking the course of ongoing action and that animals use these signs as ways of adjusting to one another. Human language, Wundt argued, represents only an extension of this basic process in lower animals because, over the course of human evolution, common and consensual meanings were given to signs. As human mental capacities grew, such gestures could be used for deliberate communication and interaction.

---

[26]For basic references on Wundt's work, see Wilhelm Wundt, *Principles of Physiological Psychology* (New York: Macmillan, 1904; originally published in 1874); *Lectures on Human and Animal Psychology*, 2nd ed. (New York: Macmillan, 1894; originally published in 1892); *Outlines of Psychology*, 7th ed. (Leipzig, Germany: Engelman, 1907; originally published in 1896); and *Elements of Folk Psychology: Outlines of a Psychological History of the Development of Mankind* (London: George Allen, 1916).

[27]For a more complete discussion, see Wilhelm Wundt, *The Language of Gestures* (The Hague, Netherlands: Mouton, 1973).

All these points, although greatly distorted by Wundt's poor ethnographic accounts, were incorporated in an altered form in Mead's scheme.[28] Gestures were viewed as the basis for communication and interaction, and language was defined as gestures that carry common meanings. As Wundt implied, humans are unique creatures, and society is possible only by virtue of language and its use to create customs, myths, and other symbol systems.

Wundt's View of "Mental Communities"

Mead did not give Wundt credit for inspiring a more sociological vision of gestures and language. Yet sprinkled throughout Wundt's work are ideas that bear considerable resemblance to those developed by Mead. One such idea is what Wundt termed the *mental community*.[29] Wundt saw the development of speech, self-consciousness, and mental activity in children as emerging from interaction with the social environment. Such interaction, he argued, makes possible the identification with a mental community that guides and directs human action and interaction in ways functionally analogous to the regulation of lower animals by instincts. Mental communities can vary in their nature and extensiveness, producing great variations in human action and patterns of social organization. Just as Durkheim in France had emphasized the significance of the collective conscious, Wundt saw humans as regulated by a variety of mental communities. Mead was to translate this notion of mental community into his vision of "generalized others" or "communities of attitudes" that regulate human action and organization.

In sum, then, Mead appears to have taken from Wundt two critical points. First, interaction is a process of gestural communication, with language being a more developed form of such communication. Second, social organization is more than a process of interaction among people; it is also a process of socialization in which humans acquire the ability to create and use mental communities to regulate their actions and interaction. As we will see, these two points are at the core of Mead's theory of mind, self, and society.

---

[28]See, for example, Wundt, *Folk Psychology.*
[29]Wundt, *Outlines of Psychology*, 296–298.

William James and Mead

By 1890, William James was the most prominent psychologist in America, attracting students and worldwide attention. He was also a philosopher who, along with Dewey, became the foremost advocate of pragmatism. Mead borrowed from both James's philosophy and his psychology, incorporating the general thrust of James's philosophy and his specific views on consciousness and self-consciousness.

James's Pragmatism

In many ways, James was the most extreme of the pragmatists, advocating that there was no such thing as "absolute truth."[30] Truth is temporary and lasts only as long as it works—that is, only as long as it allows adjustment and adaptation to the environment. James thus rejected the notion that truth involved a search for isomorphism between theoretical principles and empirical reality and that science represented an effort to increase the degree of isomorphism. For James, theories were merely "instruments" to be used for a time in an effort to facilitate adjustment. Hence, objective, permanent, and enduring truth cannot be found.

Mead never completely accepted this extreme position. Indeed, much of his work was directed at discovering some of the fundamental principles describing the basic relationship between individuals and society. He did, however, accept and embrace the pragmatic notion that human life was a constant process of adjustment and that the faculty for consciousness is the key to understanding the nature of this adjustment.

James's View of Consciousness

James defined psychology as the "science of mental life."[31] As a science, psychology aims to understand the nature of mental processes—that is, the nature of "feelings, desires, cognitions, reasons, decisions, and the like."[32] His classic 1890 text, *The Principles of Psychology*, became the most important work in American psychology at the time

---

[30]James, *The Meaning of Truth.*

[31]William James, *The Principles of Psychology* (New York: Holt, Rinehart & Winston, 1890), 1.

[32]Ibid., 1.

because it sought to summarize what was then known about mental life. It also contained James's interpretations of mental phenomena, and by far the most important of these interpretations is his conceptualization of consciousness as a process. For James, consciousness is a "stream" and "flow," rather than a structure of elements, as Wundt had proposed.[33] Thus, "mind" is simply a process of thinking, and with this simple fact, psychological investigation must begin: "The only thing which psychology has a right to postulate at the outset is the fact of thinking itself, and that must be taken up and analyzed."[34]

James then went on to list five characteristics of thought: (1) thought is personal and always, to some degree, idiosyncratic to each individual; (2) thought is always changing; (3) thought is continuous; (4) thought to the individual appears to deal with objects in an external world; and (5) thought is selective and focuses on some objects to the exclusion of others.[35] Of these characteristics, Mead appears to have been most influenced by the last two. For him, mind is selectively denoting objects and responding to these objects. Although the details of his conceptualization of thinking reflect Dewey's influence more than that of James, this early discussion by James probably shaped Mead's emphasis on selective perception of objects in the environment.

Far more influential on Mead's thought than James's view of consciousness in general was his conceptualization of self-consciousness.[36] Here, Mead borrowed much and was directly influenced by James's recognition that one object in the flow of consciousness is oneself.

James's View of Self-Consciousness

James's examination of self began with the assertion that people recognized themselves as objects in empirical situations. He called this process the *empirical self,* or *me*—the latter term being adopted by Mead in his examination of self-images. James went on to describe various types of empirical selves that all people have (1) the material self, (2) the social self, and (3) the spiritual self. Moreover, James saw each type, or aspect, of self as involving two dimensions: (1) self-feeling (emotions about oneself) and (2) self-seeking (actions

---

[33]James had also developed the notion of a "stream of consciousness" in his *The Varieties of Religious Experience* (New York: Longmans, Green, 1902).

[34]James, *Principles of Psychology,* 224.

[35]Ibid., 225–290.

[36]Ibid., 291–401.

prompted by each self). Thus, for James, there are types of selves, revealing variations with respect to self-feelings and self-seeking, and there is a hierarchy among the various selves.

Types of Empirical Selves

For James, the material self embraces people's conceptions of their bodies as well as their other possessions because one's actual body and possessions both evoke similar feelings and actions. The social self is, in reality, a series of selves that people have in different situations. Thus, one can have somewhat different self-feelings and action tendencies depending on the type of social situation—whether work, family, club, or community. For Mead, this vision of a social self became most important. People's self-feelings and actions are, he argued, most influenced by their conception of themselves in various social gatherings. James did not clearly describe the spiritual self, but it appears to embody those most intimate feelings people have about themselves—that is, their worth, talents, strengths, and failings. In *The Principles of Psychology*, James summarized his conceptualization of empirical selves and their constituent dimensions with a table, which is shown in Table 14.1.[37]

Table 14.1   James's Conceptualization of Empirical Selves

	Types of Empirical Self		
Dimensions	**Material**	**Social**	**Spiritual**
Self-seeking	Bodily appetites and instincts Love of adornment, foppery, acquisitiveness, constructiveness Love of home and so on	Desire to please, be noticed, admired, and so on Sociability, emulation, envy, love, pursuit of honor, ambition, and so on	Intellectual, moral and religious aspirations, conscientiousness
Self-estimation	Personal vanity, modesty, and so on Pride of wealth, fear of poverty	Social and family pride, vainglory, snobbery, humility, shame, and so on	Sense of moral or mental superiority, purity, and so on Sense of inferiority or of guilt

[37]Ibid., 329.

The Hierarchy of Empirical Selves

James felt that some empirical selves are more important than others. As he noted,

> a tolerably unanimous opinion ranges the different selves of which a man may be "seized and possessed," and the consequent different orders of his self-regard, in an *hierarchical scale, with the bodily Self at the bottom, the spiritual Self at Top, and the extracorporeal material selves and the various social selves between.*[38]

Thus, some degree of unity among a person's selves is achieved through their hierarchical ordering, with self-feelings and action tendencies being greatest for those selves high in the hierarchy. A further source of unity comes from the nonempirical self, or what James termed the *pure ego.*

The Pure Ego and Personal Identity

Above empirical selves, James argued, is a unity. People have "a personal identity," or *pure ego,* in that they have a sense of continuity and stability about themselves as objects. Humans take their somewhat diverse empirical selves and integrate them, seeing in them continuity and sameness.[39] Mead was probably greatly influenced by this conception of a stable and unified self-conception. As he argued, humans develop over time, from their experiences in the empirical world, a more "unified" or "complete" self—that is, a stable self-conception. This stable self-conception, Mead emphasized, gives individuals a sense of personal continuity and their actions in society a degree of stability and predictability.

In sum, then, James's work greatly influenced Mead's view of self as one of the distinctive features of humans. James was not as concerned as Mead was with understanding the emergence of self or its consequences for the social order. But James provided Mead with several critical insights about the nature of self: (1) self is a process of seeing oneself as an object in the stream of conscious awareness, (2) self varies from one empirical situation to another, yet (3) self also reveals unity and stability across situations. Mead never adopted

---

[38]Ibid., 313 (emphasis in original).
[39]Ibid., 334.

James's taxonomy, but he took the broad contours of James's outline and demonstrated their significance for understanding the nature of human action, interaction, and organization.

Charles Horton Cooley and Mead

Mead and Charles Horton Cooley were contemporaries and, as we noted, colleagues in their early careers at the University of Michigan. Their direct interaction was, no doubt, significant, but Cooley's influence extended beyond their period of collegial contact. Indeed, Mead adopted from Cooley several critical insights into the origins and nature of self as well as its significance for social organization.

Cooley's sociology is often vague, excessively mentalistic, and highly moralistic. Yet we can observe several lines of influence on Mead in Cooley's recognition that (1) society is constructed from reciprocal interaction; (2) interaction occurs through the exchange of gestures; (3) self is created from, and allows the maintenance of, patterns of social organization; and (4) social organization is possible by virtue of people's attachment to groups that link them to the larger institutions of society. We should therefore examine these lines of influence in more detail.

Cooley's View of Social Organization

Cooley held the view that society is an organic whole in which specific social processes work to create, maintain, and change networks of reciprocal activity.[40] Much as Mead later argued, Cooley saw the "vast tissue" of society as constructed from diverse social forms, from small groups to large-scale social institutions. The cement holding these diverse forms together is the capacity of humans to interact and share ideas and conceptions. Such interaction depends on the unique capacities of humans to use gestures and language.

Cooley's View of Interaction

Cooley saw the human ability to assign common meanings and interpretations to gestures—whether words, bodily countenance,

---

[40]Charles Horton Cooley, *Social Process* (New York: Scribner's, 1918), 28.

facial expressions, or other gestural emissions—as the central mechanism of interaction. In this way, humans can communicate, and from this communication, they establish social relations: "By communication is here meant the mechanism through which human relations exist and develop—all the symbols of the mind, together with the means of conveying them through space and preserving them in time."[41]

Mead accepted Cooley's view of social organization as constructed from gestural communication. More important, however, Cooley helped Mead understand how gestural communication leads to interaction and organization. By reading one another's gestures, people are able to see and interpret the dispositions of others. Hence, "society is an interweaving and interworking of mental selves. I imagine your mind. . . . I dress my mind before yours and expect that you will dress yours before mine."[42]

Mead took this somewhat vague idea and translated it into an explicit view of interaction and social organization as a process of reading gestures, placing oneself mentally into the position of others, and adjusting conduct so as to cooperate with others. Moreover, he accepted Cooley's recognition that self is the critical link in the creation and maintenance of society from patterns of reciprocal communication and interaction.

Cooley's View of Self

Cooley emphasized the human capacity for self-consciousness. This capacity emerges from interaction with others in groups, and once this ability to see self as an object exists, it allows people to organize themselves into society. Mead adopted the general thrust of this argument, although he made it considerably more explicit and coherent. He appears to have taken three distinct elements from Cooley's somewhat vague and rambling discussion: (1) self as constructed from the *looking glass* of other people's gestures, (2) self as emerging from interaction in groups, and (3) self as a basis for self-control and, hence, social organization.

---

[41]Charles Horton Cooley, *Social Organization: A Study of the Larger Mind* (New York: Scribner's, 1916), 61.

[42]Charles Horton Cooley, *Life and the Student* (New York: Knopf, 1927), 200.

The "Looking-Glass Self"

Cooley adopted James's view of self as the ability to see and recognize oneself as an object. But he added a critical insight: Humans use the gestures of others to see themselves. The images people have of themselves are similar to reflections from a looking glass, or mirror; they are provided by the reactions of others to one's behavior. Thus, by reading the gestures of others, humans see themselves as objects:

> As we see our face, figure, and dress in the glass, and are interested in them because they are ours . . . so in imagination we perceive in another's mind some thought of our appearance, manners, aims, deeds, character, friends, and so on, and are variously affected by it.[43]

As people see themselves in the looking glass of other people's gestures, they then (1) imagine their appearance in the eyes of others, (2) sense the judgment of others, and (3) have self-feelings about themselves. Thus, during the process of interaction, people develop self-consciousness and self-feelings. Although Cooley did not develop the idea in detail, he implied that humans develop, over time and through repeated glances in the looking glass, a more stable sense of self.

The Emergence of Self

Cooley argued that the life history of an individual is evolutionary. Because their ability to read gestures is limited, infants cannot initially see themselves as objects in the looking glass. With time, practice, biological maturation, and exposure to varieties of others, children come to see themselves in the looking glass, and they develop feelings about themselves. Such a process, Cooley felt, is inevitable as long as the young interact with others, because as they act on their environment, others will react, and this reaction will be perceived and responded to by the young.[44] Through this process, as it occurs during infancy, childhood, and adolescence, an individual's "personality" is formed. As Mead argued, the existence of a more

---

[43]Charles Horton Cooley, *Human Nature and the Social Order* (New York: Scribner's, 1902), 184.

[44]Ibid., 137–211.

stable set of self-feelings gives human action stability and predict-ability, thereby facilitating cooperation with others.

Self and Social Control

Cooley saw self as only one aspect of consciousness in general. Thus, he divided consciousness into three aspects: (1) "self-consciousness," or self-awareness of and feelings about oneself; (2) "social conscious-ness," or a person's perceptions of and attitudes toward other people; and (3) "public consciousness," or an individual's view of others as organized in a "communicative group."[45] Cooley saw all three aspects of consciousness as "phases of a single whole."

Cooley never developed these ideas to any great degree, but Mead apparently saw much potential in these distinctions. For Mead, the capacity to see oneself as an object, to perceive the dispositions of others, and to assume the perspective of a broader "public" or "com-munity" gives people a basis for stable action and cooperative inter-action. Because of these capacities, society is possible.

Cooley's View of Primary Groups

Cooley argued that the most basic unit of society is the "primary group," which he defined as those associations characterized by "inti-mate face-to-face association and cooperation":

> They are primary in several senses but chiefly in that they are fundamental in forming the social nature and ideals of individu-als. The result of intimate association, psychologically, is a cer-tain fusion of individualities in a common whole, so that one's very self, for many purposes at least, is the common life and purpose of the group.[46]

Thus, the looking glass of gestures emitted by those in one's pri-mary group are the most important in the emergence and mainte-nance of self-feelings. Moreover, the link between individuals and the broader institutional structure of society is the primary group. Institutions cannot, Cooley stressed, be maintained unless past

---

[45]Cooley, *Social Organization*, 12.
[46]Ibid., 23.

traditions and public morals are given immediate relevance to individuals through the intimacy characteristic of primary groups. Indeed, for Cooley, primary groups "are the springs of life, not only for the individual but for social institutions."[47]

Cooley's concept of the primary group appears to have influenced Mead in two ways. First, Mead retained Cooley's position that self emerges, in large part, by virtue of an individual's participation in face-to-face, organized activity. Second, Mead implicitly argued that one of the bridges between the individual and broader institutional structure of society is the small group, although Cooley's emphasis on this point was much greater than was Mead's.

Thus, Mead was enormously influenced by the work of Cooley. Mead saw the full implications of Cooley's ideas for understanding the nature of the relationship between the individual and society. As we will appreciate in the next chapter, Mead borrowed, extended, and integrated into a more coherent theory Cooley's views on gestures, interaction, self and its emergence, and social organization.

John Dewey and Mead

John Dewey and Mead were initially young colleagues at the University of Michigan, and when Dewey moved to the new University of Chicago in 1894, he invited Mead to join him in the departments of philosophy and psychology. Mead and Dewey were thus colleagues until 1905, when Dewey left for Columbia University. They engaged in much dialogue; therefore, it is not surprising that their thought reveals many similarities. Yet, Dewey was the intellectual star of Chicago, and he wrote on many diverse areas and generated much attention, inside and outside the academic world.[48] In contrast, the retiring Mead, who had great difficulty writing, was constantly in Dewey's shadow. Ironically, Mead made the more important, long-term intellectual contribution to sociology and philosophy.

---

[47]Ibid., 27.

[48]Dewey's bibliography is more than 75 pages long, indicating his incredible productivity.

Dewey's Pragmatism

Dewey's[49] pragmatism attacked the traditional dualisms of philosophy: knower and known, objects and thought of objects, and mind and external world. He thought that this dualism was false, that the act of knowing and the "things" to be known were interdependent. Objects can exist in a world external to an individual, but their existence and properties are determined by the process of acting toward these objects. For Dewey, the basic process of human life consists of organisms acting on, and making inquiry into, their environment. Indeed, the history of human thought has been a quest for greater certainty about the consequences of action. In a scheme that resembles Auguste Comte's law of the three stages, Dewey argued that religion had represented the primitive way to achieve certainty, that the classical world had classified experience to achieve certainty, and that the modern world seeks to control nature through the discovery of its laws of operation.[50] With the development of modern science, Dewey argued, a new problem emerges: Moral values can no longer be legitimized by God or by appeals to the natural order.[51]

Such is the philosophical dilemma Dewey proposed and then resolved with his pragmatism. Values, morality, and other evaluative ideas are to be found in the action of people as they cope with their environment. Value is discovered and found as people try to adjust and adapt to a problematic situation. Thus, when humans do not know the morality of a situation, they will construct one and use it

---

[49]Dewey's most important works, in addition to those cited earlier, include *Outlines of a Critical Theory of Ethics* (Ann Arbor, MI: Register, 1891); *The Study of Ethics* (Ann Arbor, MI: Register, 1894); *The School and Society* (Chicago: University of Chicago Press, 1900); *Studies in Logical Theory* (Chicago: University of Chicago Press, 1903); with James H. Tufts, *Ethics* (New York: Holt, Rinehart & Winston, 1908); *How We Think* (Boston: D. C. Heath, 1910); *The Influence of Darwin on Philosophy* (New York: Holt, Rinehart & Winston, 1910); *Democracy and Education* (New York: Macmillan, 1916); *Essays in Experimental Logic* (Chicago: University of Chicago Press, 1916); *Reconstruction in Philosophy* (New York: Holt, Rinehart & Winston, 1920); *Experience and Nature* (La Salle, IL: Open Court, 1925); *Philosophy and Civilization* (New York: Minton, Balch, 1931); *Art as Experience* (New York: Minton, Balch, 1934); *A Common Faith* (New Haven, CT: Yale University Press, 1934); *Logic: The Theory of Inquiry* (New York: Holt, Rinehart & Winston, 1938); *Theory of Valuation* (Chicago: University of Chicago Press, 1939); *Problems of Men* (New York: Philosophical Library, 1946); and with A. F. Bentley, *Knowing and the Known* (Boston: Beacon, 1949).

[50]Dewey, *Quest for Certainty.*

[51]Dewey, *Influence of Darwin*, 22.

as an "instrument" to facilitate their adjustment to that situation. Value-oriented action is like all other thought and action: It emerges from people's acts in a problematic situation. Mead never absorbed the details of Dewey's "instrumentalism" or Dewey's almost frantic efforts to create the "good society,"[52] but he did adopt the view that thinking and thought arise from the process of dealing with problematic situations.

Dewey's View of Thinking

Dewey's pragmatism led him to view thinking as a process involving (1) blockage of impulses, (2) selective perception of the environment, (3) rehearsal of alternatives, (4) overt action, and (5) assessment of consequences. Then, if a situation is still problematic, this sequence is repeated until the problematic situation is eliminated.[53]

Mead adopted two aspects of this vision. First, he saw thinking as part of a larger process of action. Thinking occurs when an organism's impulses are blocked and when it is in maladjustment with its environment.[54] This argument became part of Mead's theory of motivation and "stages of the act." Second, for Mead, thinking involves selective perception of objects, covert and imaginative rehearsal of alternatives, anticipation of the consequences of alternatives, and selection of a line of conduct. He termed these behavioral capacities *mind*, and they were clearly adapted from Dewey's discussion of human nature and conduct.[55]

Mead's Synthesis

We can now appreciate Mead's intellectual world. The convergence of utilitarianism, pragmatism, Darwinism, and behaviorism gave him a general set of assumptions for understanding human behavior. The specific concepts of Wundt, James, Cooley, and Dewey gave Mead

---

[52]However, Mead's ideals paralleled those of Dewey, and he was occasionally drawn into various reform causes.

[53]See, for example, Dewey, *Human Nature and Conduct* and *How We Think*.

[54]Indeed, Mead appears to have borrowed Dewey's exact terms in *Human Nature and Conduct*.

[55]Dewey, *Human Nature and Conduct*.

the necessary intellectual tools to understand that humans are unique by virtue of their behavioral capacities for mind and self. Conversely, mind and self emerge from gestural interaction in society. Once they emerge, however, mind and self make a distinctive form of gestural interaction and an entirely revolutionary creation: symbolically regulated patterns of social organization. In broad strokes, such is the nature of Mead's synthesis. We can now examine the details of this synthesis in the next chapter.

CHAPTER 15

The Sociology of George Herbert Mead

Because Mead wrote relatively little in his lifetime, his major works are found in the published lecture notes of his students. As a result, the four posthumous books that constitute the core of his thought are somewhat long and rambling. Moreover, with the exception of *Mind, Self, and Society*, his ideas are distinctly philosophical rather than sociological in tone.[1] Our goal in this chapter, therefore, is to pull from his philosophical works key sociological insights, while devoting most of our analysis to the explicitly social–psychological work, *Mind, Self, and Society*.

Mead's Broader Philosophy

Much of Mead's sociology is only a part of a broader philosophical view. This view was never fully articulated, nor was it well integrated, but two posthumous works, *Movements of Thought in the Nineteenth Century* and *The Philosophy of the Present*, provide a glimpse of his broader vision.

---

[1]The philosophical tone of Mead's posthumously published lectures is revealed in the titles of the four books: *The Philosophy of the Present* (La Salle, IL: Open Court, 1959; originally published in 1932); *Mind, Self, and Society* (Chicago: University of Chicago Press, 1934); *Movements of Thought in the Nineteenth Century* (Chicago: University of Chicago Press, 1936); and *The Philosophy of the Act* (Chicago: University of Chicago Press, 1938). *Mind, Self, and Society* contains a bibliography of Mead's published work (see pp. 390–392).

Many fascinating themes are contained in these works, but one of the most persistent is that all human activity represents an adjustment and adaptation to the social environment. In *Movements of Thought*, Mead traced the development of social thought from its early, prescientific phases to the contemporary, scientific stage. In a way reminiscent of Auguste Comte's law of the three stages (see Chapter 3), Mead saw the great ideas of history as moving toward an increasingly rational or scientific profile because, with the emergence of scientific thought, a better level of adaptation and adjustment to the world could be achieved.

The Philosophy of the Present contains a somewhat disjointed series of essays that represent a more philosophical treatment of ideas contained in Mead's social psychology, particularly in *Mind, Self, and Society*. Here again, he emphasized that what was uniquely human is nothing but a series of particular behavioral capacities that have evolved from adaptations to the ongoing life process. Much of the discussion addresses purely philosophical topics about the ontological status of consciousnesses in the past, present, and future. But between the lines he stressed that the capacities of humans for thought and self-reflection do not necessitate a dualism between mind and body because all the unique mental abilities of humans are behaviors directed toward facilitating their adjustment to the environment as it is encountered in the present.

Mind, Self, and Society

Mead's "book," *Mind, Self, and Society*, consists of a compilation of verbatim transcripts from his famous course on social psychology at the University of Chicago. Although the notes come from the 1927 and 1930 versions of the course, the basic ideas on social interaction, personality, and social organization had been developed a decade earlier.

At the time Mead was addressing his students, behaviorists like J. B. Watson had simply abandoned any serious effort to understand consciousness, personality, and other variables in the "black box" of human cognition. Mead felt that such a "solution" to studying psychological processes was unacceptable.[2] He also felt that the opposite

---

[2]As he observed with respect to Watson's efforts to deal with subjective experience, "John B. Watson's attitude was that of the Queen in *Alice in Wonderland*—Off with their heads!— there were no such things." Mead, *Mind, Self, and Society*, 2–3.

philosophical tendency to view "mind," "spirit," "will," and other psychological states as a kind of spiritual entity was untenable. What is required, he argued, is for mind and self, as the two most distinctive aspects of human personality, and for "society" as maintained by mind and self, to be viewed as part of ongoing social processes.

Mead's View of the "Life Process"

The Darwinian theory of evolution provided Mead with a view of life as a process of adaptation to environmental conditions. The attributes of a species, therefore, are the result of selection for those characteristics allowing for adaptation to the conditions in which a species finds itself. This theory provided Mead with a general metaphor for analyzing human behavior and society. Pragmatism, as a philosophical doctrine developed in great detail by John Dewey, represents one way of translating the Darwinian metaphor into principles for understanding human behavior: Humans are "pragmatic" creatures who use their facilities for achieving "adjustment" to the world; conversely, much of what is unique to any individual arises from making adjustments to the social world.

John Dewey's pragmatism, termed *instrumentalism*, stressed the importance of critical and rational thought in making life adjustments, and it gave Mead a view of thinking as the basic adjustment by which humans survive. Behaviorism, as a prominent psychological school of thought, converges with this element in pragmatism because it emphasizes that all animals tend to retain those responses to environmental stimuli that are rewarded or reinforced. Although behaviorists like Watson regarded the processes of thinking as too "psychical," the stress on the retention of reinforced behaviors was consistent with Darwinian notions of adaptation and survival as well as with pragmatist ideas of response and adjustment.

Mead even saw utilitarianism—especially that of such thinkers as Jeremy Bentham, who emphasized the pleasure and pain principles—as compatible with the theories of evolution, behaviorism, and pragmatism. The utilitarian emphasis on "utility," "pleasure," and "pain" was certainly compatible with behaviorist notions of reinforcement; the utilitarian concern with rational thought and the weighing of alternatives was compatible with Dewey's instrumentalism and its concept of critical thinking; and the utilitarian view that order emerges from competition among free individuals seemed to parallel Darwinian notions of struggle as the underlying principle of the biotic order.

Thus, the unique attributes of humans, such as their capacity to use language, their ability to view themselves as objects, and their facility to reason, must all be viewed as emerging from the life processes of adaptation and adjustment. Mind and self cannot be ignored, as behaviorists often sought to do, nor can they be seen as a kind of mystical and spiritual force that elevates humans out of the basic life processes influencing all species. Humans as a species evolved like other life forms, and, hence, their most distinctive attributes—mind, self, and society—must be viewed as emerging from the basic process of adaptation. Furthermore, each individual member of the human species is like the individuals of other species: What they are is the result of the common biological heritage of their species as well as their adjustment to the particulars of a given environment.

Mead's Social Behaviorism

Mead did not define his work as *social* behaviorism, but subsequent commentators have used this term to distinguish his work from Watsonian behaviorism. In contrast with Watson, who simply denied the distinctiveness of subjective consciousness, Mead felt that it was possible to use broad behavioristic principles to understand "subjective behavior":

> Watson apparently assumes that to deny the existence of mind or consciousness as a psychical stuff, substance, or entity is to deny its existence altogether, and that a naturalistic or behavioristic account of it as such is out of the question. But, on the contrary, we may deny its existence as a psychical entity without denying its existence in some other sense at all; and if we then conceive of it functionally, and as a natural rather than a transcendental phenomenon, it becomes possible to deal with it in behavioristic terms.[3]

If subjective experiences in humans are viewed as behaviors, it is possible to understand them in behavioristic terms. The unique mental capacities of humans are a model of behavior that arises from the same reinforcement processes that explain directly observable behaviors. Of particular importance for understanding the attributes of

---

[3]Mead, *Mind, Self, and Society*, 10.

humans, then, is the reinforcement that comes from adaptation and adjustment to environmental conditions. At some point in the distant past, the unique mental capacities of humans, and the creation of society dependent on these capacities, emerged by the process of natural selection under natural environmental conditions. Once the unique patterns of human organization are created, however, the "environment" for any individual is social; that is, it is an environment of other people to whom an individual must adapt and adjust.

Thus, social behaviorism stresses the processes by which individuals acquire a certain behavioral repertoire by virtue of their adjustments to ongoing patterns of social organization. Analysis must begin with the observable fact that organized activity occurs, and then attempt to understand the particular actions of individuals as they adjust to cooperative activity:

> We are not, in social psychology, building up the behavior of the social group in terms of the behavior of separate individuals composing it; rather, we are starting out with a given social whole of complex group activity, into which we analyze (as elements) the behavior of each of the separate individuals composing it. We attempt, that is, to explain the conduct of the individual in terms of the organized conduct of the social group, rather than to account for the organized conduct of the social group in terms of the conduct of the separate individuals belonging to it.[4]

The behavior of individuals—not just their observable actions but also their internal behaviors of thinking, assessing, and evaluating—must be analyzed within a social context. For what is distinctively human emerges from adjustment to ongoing social activity, or "society." Thus, Mead's social behaviorism must be distinguished from the behavioristic approach of Watson[5] in two ways. First, the existence of inner subjective experiences is not denied or viewed as methodologically irrelevant;[6] rather, these experiences are viewed as behavior. Second, the behaviors of humans, including those distinctly human behaviors that Mead called *mind* and *self*, arise from adaptation and adjustment to ongoing and organized social activity.

---

[4]Ibid., 7.

[5]And, of course, the more recent version of B. F. Skinner and others of this stripe.

[6]That is, because they cannot be directly observed, they cannot be studied.

Reinforcement is thus equated with the degree of adjustment and adaptation to society.

Mead's Behavioristic View of Mind

For Mead, "mind" is a type of behavioral response that emerges from interaction with others in a social context. Without interaction, mind could not exist:

> We must regard mind, then, arising and developing within the social process, within the empirical matrix of social interactions. We must, that is, get an inner individual experience from the standpoint of social acts which include the experiences of separate individuals in a social context wherein those individuals interact. The processes of experience which the human brain makes possible are made possible only for a group of interacting individuals: only for individual organisms which are members of a society; not for the organism in isolation from other individual organisms.[7]

Gestures and Mind

The social process in which mind emerges is one of communication with gestures. Mead gave the German psychologist Wilhelm Wundt credit for understanding the central significance of the gesture to communication and interaction. In contrast with Charles Darwin, who had viewed gestures as expressions of emotions, Wundt recognized gestures as that part of the ongoing behavior of one organism that stimulates the behavior of another organism.[8] Mead took this basic idea and extended it in ways that became the basis not only for the emergence of mind and self but also for the creation, maintenance, and change of society.

Mead formulated the concept of the "conversation of gestures" to describe the simplest form of interaction. One organism emits gestures that stimulate a response from a second organism. In turn, the second organism emits gestures that stimulate an "adjusted response"

---

[7]Mead, *Mind, Self, and Society*, 133.

[8]As Mead observed, "the term gesture may be identified with these beginnings of social acts which are stimuli for the response of other forms." *Mind, Self, and Society*, 43.

from the first organism. Then, if interaction continues, the adjusted response of the first organism involves emitting gestures that result in yet another adjustment of behavior by the second organism, and so on, as long as the two organisms continue to interact. Mead frequently termed this conversation of gestures the *triadic matrix*, because it involves three interrelated elements:

1. Gestural emission by one organism as it acts on its environment

2. A response by another organism that becomes a gestural stimulus to the acting organism

3. An adjusted response by the acting organism that takes into account the gestural stimuli of the responding organism

This triadic matrix constitutes the simplest form of communication and interaction among organisms. This form of interaction, Mead felt, typifies "lower animals" and human infants. For example, if one dog growls, indicating to another dog that it is about to attack, the other will react, perhaps by running away, requiring the growling dog to adjust its response by chasing the fleeing dog or by turning elsewhere to vent its aggressive impulses. Or, to take another example, a hungry infant cries, which in turn arouses a response in its mother (e.g., the mother feeds the infant), which in turn results in an adjusted response by the infant (and mother).

Much of the significance of Mead's discussion of the triadic matrix is that the mentalistic concept of "meaning" is lodged in the interaction process rather than in "ideas" or other mentalistic notions that might reside outside interaction. If a gesture "indicates to another organism the subsequent behavior of a given organism, then it has meaning."[9] Thus, if a dog growls and another dog uses this gesture to predict an attack, this gesture of growling has meaning. Meaning is thus given a behavioristic definition: It is a kind of behavior—a gesture—of one organism that signals to another subsequent behavior of this organism. Meaning, therefore, need not involve complex cognitive activity. A dog that runs away from another growling dog, Mead would assert, is reacting without "ideas" or "elaborate deliberation"; yet the growl has meaning to

---

[9]Mead, *Mind, Self, and Society*, 76.

the dog because it uses the growl as an early indicator of what will follow. Thus, *meaning* is

> not to be conceived, fundamentally, as a state of consciousness, or as a set of organized relations existing or subsisting mentally outside the field of experience into which they enter; on the contrary, it should be conceived objectively, as having its existence entirely within this field itself.[10]

The significance of the conversation of gestures for ongoing activity resides in the triadic matrix, and associated meanings, allowing organisms to adjust their responses to one another. Thus, as organisms use one another's gestures as a means for adjusting their respective responses, they become increasingly capable of organized and concerted conduct. Yet such gestural conversations limit the capacity of organisms to organize themselves and to cooperate. Among humans, Mead asserted, a qualitatively different form of communication evolved. This is communication involving *significant symbols* that mean the same thing to all parties. He felt that the development of the capacity to use significant symbols distinguished humans from other species. *Mind* arises in a maturing human infant as the capacity to use significant symbols increases. In turn, as we will show, the existence of mind ensures the development of self and the perpetuation of society.

Significant Symbols and Mind

The gestures of "lower organisms," Mead felt, do not evoke the same response in the organism emitting a gesture and the one interpreting the gesture. As he observed, the roar of the lion does not mean the same thing to the lion and its potential victim. When organisms become capable of using gestures that evoke the same response in each other, then they are employing what he termed *significant*, or *conventional*, gestures. As he illustrated, if a person shouts "Fire!" in a movie theater, this gesture evokes the same response tendency (to escape, and flee) in the person emitting the gesture and in those receiving it. Such gestures, he felt, are unique to humans and make possible their capacities for mind, self, and society.[11]

------

[10]Ibid., 78.

[11]However, the evidence is now clear that other higher primates can use such "significant gestures."

Significant symbols are, as Mead emphasized, the basis for language. Of particular significance are vocal significant symbols because sounds can be readily heard by both sender and receiver, thus evoking a similar behavioral tendency. Other nonvocal gestures, however, are also significant in that they can come to mobilize similar tendencies to act. A frown, glare, clenched fist, rigid stance, and the like can all become significant because they serve as a stimulus to similar responses by senders and receivers. Thus, humans' capacity for language—that is, communication by significant symbols—allows the emergence of their unique capacities for mind and self. An infant of the species cannot have a mind until it acquires the rudimentary capacity for language.

In what ways, then, does language make mind possible? Mead borrowed Dewey's vision of "reflective" and "critical" thinking, as well as the utilitarian's vision of "rational choice," in formulating his conceptualization of mind. For Mead, mind involves the behavioral capacities to do the following:

1. Denote objects in the environment with significant symbols

2. Use these symbols as a stimulus to one's own response

3. Read and interpret the gestures of others and use these as a stimulus for one's response

4. Suspend temporarily or inhibit overt behavioral responses to one's own gestural denotations or those of others

5. Engage in "imaginative rehearsal" of alternative lines of conduct, visualize their consequences, and select the response that will facilitate adjustment to the environment

Mind is thus a behavior, not a substance or entity. It is a behavior that involves using significant symbols to stimulate responses but, at the same time, to inhibit or delay overt behavior so that potential responses can be covertly rehearsed and assessed. Mind is thus an "internal conversation of gestures" using significant symbols because an individual with mind talks to oneself. The individual uses significant symbols to stimulate a line of response; the individual visualizes the consequences of this response; if necessary, the individual inhibits the response and uses another set of symbols to stimulate alternative responses; and the individual persists until he or she is satisfied with the response and overtly pursues a given line of conduct.

This capacity for mind, Mead stressed, is not inborn; it depends on interaction with others and the acquisition of the ability to interpret and use their significant symbols (as well as biological maturation). As Mead noted, feral children who are raised without significant symbols do not seem "human" because they have not had to adjust to an environment mediated by significant symbols and, hence, have not acquired the behavioral capacities for mind.

Role-Taking and Mind

Mind emerges in an individual because human infants, if they are to survive, must adjust and adapt to a social environment—that is, to a world of organized social activity. At first, an infant is like a "lower animal" in that it responds reflexively to the gestures of others and emits gestures that do not evoke similar responses in it and those in the environment. Such a level of adjustment, Mead implied, is neither efficient nor adaptive. A baby's cry does not indicate what it wants, whether food, water, warmth, or whatever, and by not reading accurately the vocal and other gestures emitted by others in their environment, the young can frequently create adjustment problems for itself. Thus, in a metaphor that is both Darwinian and behavioristic, there is "selective pressure" for acquiring the ability to use and interpret significant gestures. Hence, those gestures that bring reinforcement—that is, adjustment to the environment—are likely to be retained in the response repertoire of the infant.

A critical process in using and interpreting significant gestures is what Mead termed "taking the role of the other," or *role-taking*. An ability to use significant symbols means that the gestures emitted by others in the environment allow a person to read or interpret the dispositions of these others. For example, an infant who has acquired the rudimentary ability to interpret significant symbols can use its mother's tone of voice, facial expressions, and words to imagine her feelings and potential actions—that is, to "take on" her role or perspective. Role-taking is critical to the emergence of mind, for unless the gestures of others, and the disposition to act that these gestures reveal, can become a part of the stimuli used to covertly rehearse alternative lines of conduct, overt behavior will often produce maladjustment to the environment. For without the ability to assume the perspective of others with whom one must deal, it is difficult to adjust to, and coordinate responses with, these others.

The Genesis of Mind

Mead saw mind as developing in a sequence of phases, as is represented in Figure 15.1. Because an infant depends on others and, in turn, these others depend on society for their survival, mind develops from the forced dependency of an infant on society. Because society is held together by actors who use language and who can role-take, the infant must seek to meet its needs in a world mediated by symbols. Through conscious coaching by others, and through simple trial and error, the infant comes to use significant symbols to denote objects relevant to satisfying its needs (e.g., food, mother, etc.). To consummate other impulses, the infant eventually must acquire greater capacities to use and understand language; once an infant can use language, it can begin to read the gestures of others and call out in itself the dispositions of others. When a young child can role-take, it can soon begin to consciously think, reflect, and rehearse responses. In other words, it reveals the rudimentary behavioral abilities that Mead termed *mind*.[12]

The causal arrows in Figure 15.1 actually represent a series of preconditions for the next stage of development. The model is "value added" in that certain conditions must be met before subsequent events can occur. Underlying these conditions is Mead's implicit vision of "social selection," which represents his reconciliation of learning-theory principles with pragmatism and Darwinism. The development of abilities for language, role-taking, and mind are selected as the infant seeks to consummate impulses in society. If the infant is to adjust and adapt to society, it must acquire the ability for minded behavior. Thus, as the infant lives in a social environment must successively develop those behavioral capacities—first significant symbols, then role-taking, and eventually mind—that facilitate, to ever-increasing degrees, its adjustment to the social environment.

---

[12]For other published statements by Mead on the nature and operation of mind, see "Image and Sensation," *Journal of Philosophy* 1 (1904), 604–607; "Social Consciousness and the Consciousness of Meaning," *Psychological Bulletin* 7 (1910), 397–405; "The Mechanisms of Social Consciousness," *Journal of Philosophy* 9 (1912), 401–406; "Scientific Method and Individual Thinker," in *Creative Intelligence* (New York: Holt, Rinehart & Winston, 1917), 176–227; and "A Behavioristic Account of the Significant Symbols," *Journal of Philosophy* 19 (1922), 157–163.

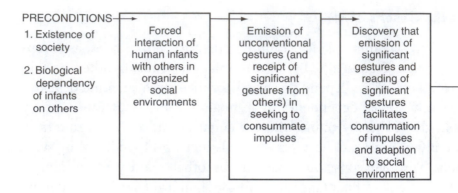

Figure 15.1   Mead's Model of the Genesis of Mind

The model presented in Figure 15.1 underscores Mead's view that there is nothing mysterious or mystical about the human mind. It is a behavior acquired like other behavioral tendencies as a human organism attempts to adapt to its surroundings. Mind is a behavioral capacity acquired in stages, with each stage setting the conditions for the next. As mind emerges, so does self-awareness. In many respects, the emergence of mind is a precondition for the genesis of self. Yet the rudiments of self begin with an organism's ability to role-take, for the organism can then derive self-images or see itself as an object.

Mead's Behavioristic View of Self

The Social Nature of Self

As a "social behaviorist," Mead emphasized that the capacity to view oneself as an object in the field of experience is a type of learned behavior. This behavior is learned through interaction with others:

> The self is something which has a development; it is not initially there, at birth, but arises in the process of social experience and activity, that is, develops in the given individual as a result of his relations to that process as a whole and to other individuals within that process.[13]

Self emerges from the capacity to use language and to take the role of the other. Borrowing the essentials of Charles Horton Cooley's

---

[13]Mead, *Mind, Self, and Society*, 135.

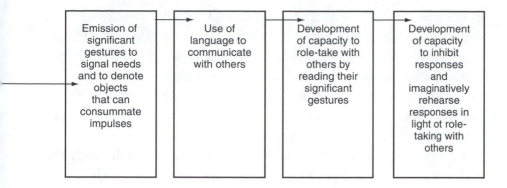

Emission of significant gestures to signal needs and to denote objects that can consummate impulses	Use of language to communicate with others	Development of capacity to role-take with others by reading their significant gestures	Development of capacity to inhibit responses and imaginatively rehearse responses in light ot role-taking with others

"looking-glass self,"[14] Mead viewed the social self as emerging from a process in which individuals read the gestures of others, or "take their attitudes," and derive an image, or picture, of themselves as a certain type of object in a situation. This image of oneself then acts as a behavioral stimulus, calling out certain responses in the individual. In turn, these responses of an individual cause further reactions by others, resulting in the emission of gestures that make possible role-taking by an individual, who then derives new self-images and new behavioral stimuli. Thus, like mind, self arises from the triadic matrix of people interacting and adjusting their responses to one another. The individual does not experience self directly but only through reading the gestures of others:

> The individual experiences himself, not directly, but only indirectly, from the particular standpoints of other individual members of the same social group, or from the generalized standpoint of the social group as a whole to which he belongs . . . and he becomes an object to himself only by taking the attitudes of other individuals toward himself within a social environment or context of experience and behavior in which both he and they are involved.[15]

The Structure of Self

Mead appeared to use the notion of "self" in two different ways. One usage involves viewing self as a "transitory image" of oneself as an object in a particular situation. Thus, as people interact, they role-take and derive self-images of themselves in that situation. Second,

---

[14]Mead did reject many of the specifics in Cooley's argument about "the looking-glass self." See, for example, *Mind, Self, and Society*, 173; "Cooley's Contribution to American Social Thought," *American Journal of Sociology* 35 (1929–1930), 385–407; and "Smashing the Looking Glass," *Survey* 35 (1915–1916), 349–361.

[15]Mead, *Mind, Self, and Society*, 138.

in contrast with this conceptualization, Mead also viewed self as a structure, or configuration of typical habitual meanings toward self, that people carry to all situations. For "after a self has arisen, it in a certain sense provides for itself its social experiences."[16]

These views are not, of course, contradictory. The process of deriving self-images in situations leads, over time, to the crystallization of a more permanent, transsituational set of attitudes toward oneself as a certain type of object. Humans begin to interpret selectively the gestures of others in light of their attitudes toward themselves, and thus, their behaviors take on a consistency. For if the view of oneself as a certain type of object is relatively stable, and if we use self like all other environmental objects as a stimulus for behavior, overt behavior will reveal a degree of consistency across social situations.

Mead sometimes termed this development of stable attitudes toward oneself as an object the *complete*, or *unified*, self. Yet he recognized that this complete self was not a rigid structure and that it was not imperviously and inflexibly imposed on diverse interactions. Rather, in different social contexts various aspects of the complete self are more evident. Depending on one's audience, then, different "elementary selves" will be salient:

> The unity and structure of the complete self reflects the unity and structure of the social process as a whole; and each of the elementary selves of which it is composed reflects the unity and structure of one of the various aspects of that process in which the individual is implicated. In other words, the various elementary selves that constitute, or are organized into, a complete self are the various aspects of the structure of that complete self answering to the various aspects of the structure of the social process as a whole; the structure of the complete self is thus a reflection of the complete social process.[17]

In this passage, a further insight into the structure of self is evident: Although elementary selves are unified by a complete self, people who experience a highly contradictory social environment with *dis*unity in the social process will also experience difficulty in developing a complete self, or a relatively stable and consistent set of attitudes toward themselves as a certain type of object. To some extent, then, people present different aspects of their more complete and unified selves

---

[16]Ibid., 140.
[17]Ibid., 144.

to different audiences, but when these audiences demand radically contradictory actions, the development of a unified self-conception becomes problematic.

In sum, then, Mead's conceptualization is behavioristic in that he viewed seeing oneself as an object as a behavior unique to humans. Moreover, like other objects in one's environment, the self is a stimulus to behavior. Thus, as people develop a consistent view of themselves as a type of object—that is, as their self reveals a structure—their responses to this stable stimulus take on a consistency. Mead's conceptualization of the structure of self involves the recognition that the stability of self is largely a consequence of the unity and stability in the social processes from which the self arises.

Phases of the Self

Mead wanted to avoid connoting that the structure of self limited a person's repertoire of potential responses. Although a unified self-conception lends considerable stability and predictability to overt behaviors, there is always an element of spontaneity and unpredictability to action. This is inherent in the "phases of self," which Mead conceptualized in terms of the *I* and *me*.

The image that a person derives from his or her behavior in a situation is what Mead termed the *me*. As such, the "me" represents the attitudes of others and the broader community as these influence an individual's retrospective interpretation of his or her behavior. For example, if we talk too loudly in a crowd of strangers, we see the startled looks of others and will become cognizant of general norms about voice levels and inflections when among strangers. These "me" images are received by reading the gestures of specific others in a situation and by role-taking, or assuming the attitude of the broader community. In contrast with the "me" is the "I," which is the actual emission of behavior. If a person speaks too loudly, this is "I," and when this person reacts to his or her loudness, the "me" phase of action is initiated. Mead emphasized that the "I" can only be known in experience because we must wait for "me" images to know just what the "I" did. People cannot know until after they have acted ("I") just how the expectations of others ("me") are actually carried out.

Mead's conceptualization of the "I" and "me" allowed him to conceptualize the self as a constant process of behavior and self-image. People act; they view themselves as objects; they assess the consequences of their actions; they interpret others' reactions to their actions; and they resolve how to act next. Then, they act again, calling forth new self-images of their actions. This conceptualization of the "I" and "me" phases of self enabled Mead to accomplish several conceptual tasks. First, he left room for spontaneity in human action; if the "I" can be known only in experience, or through the "me," one's actions are never completely circumscribed, nor are actions wholly predictable. Second, as we will explore in more detail later, it gave Mead a way of visualizing the process of self-control. Humans are, in his view, cybernetic organisms who respond, receive feedback and make adjustments, and then respond again. In this way, he emphasized that self like mind is a process of adaptation; it is a behavior in which an organism successively responds to itself as an object as it adjusts to its environment. Third, the "I" and "me" phases of self gave Mead a way to conceptualize variations in the extent to which the expectations of others and the broader community constrain action. The *relative values* of the "I" and "me," as he phrased the matter,[18] are a positive function of people's status in a particular situation. The more involved they are in a group, the greater the values of "me" images and the greater is the control of "I" impulses. Conversely, the less the involvement of a person in a situation, the less salient are "me" images, and hence, the greater is the variation in that person's overt behavior.

The Genesis of Self

Mead devoted considerable attention to the emergence of self and self-conceptions in humans. This attention allowed him to emphasize again that the self is a social product and emerges from the efforts of the human organism to adjust and adapt to its environment. Self arises from the same processes that lead to the development of "mind," while depending on the behavioral capacities of mind.

For self to develop, a human infant must acquire the capacity to use significant symbols. Without this ability, it is not possible to role-take with others and thereby develop an image of oneself by interpreting the gestures of others. Self also depends on mind because people must be able to designate themselves linguistically as an object in their field of experience and to organize responses toward themselves as an object. Thus, the use of significant symbols, the ability to role-take, and the behavioral capacities of mind are all preconditions for the development of self, particularly a more stable self-conception, or "unified" self.

Mead visualized self as developing in three stages, each marked by an increased capacity to role-take with a wider audience of others. The first

---

[18]Ibid., 199.

stage is *play*, which is marked by a very limited capacity to role-take. A child can assume the perspective of only one or two others at a time, and play frequently involves little more than discourse and interaction with "imaginary companions" to whom the child talks in enacting a particular role. Thus, a child who plays "mother" can also, at the same time, assume the role of "baby," and the child might move back and forth between the mother's and infant's roles. The play stage is thus typified by the ability to assume the perspective of only a few others at a time.

With biological maturation and with practice at assuming the perspectives of others, a child eventually acquires the capacity to take the role of multiple others engaged in ongoing and organized activity. The second stage is what Mead termed the *game* in which individuals can role-take with multiple others at the same time. Perhaps the most prototypical form of such role-taking is to be a participant in a game, such as baseball, where the child must assume the role of other players, anticipate how they will act, and coordinate responses with other people's likely courses of actions. Thus, children begin to see themselves as objects in an organized field, and they begin to control and regulate other people's responses to themselves and to others in order to facilitate the coordination of activity. During this stage in the development of self, the number and variety of such game situations expand:

> There are all sorts of social organizations, some of which are fairly lasting, some temporary, into which the child is entering, and he is playing a sort of social game in them. It is a period in which he likes "to belong," and he gets into organizations which come into existence and pass out of existence. He becomes something which can function in the organized whole, and thus tends to determine himself in his relationship with the group to which he belongs.[19]

In both the play and game situations, individuals view themselves in relation to specific others. By role-taking with specific others lodged in particular roles, individuals derive images of themselves from the viewpoint of these others. Yet the self, Mead contended, is incomplete until a third stage is realized: role-taking with *the generalized other*. He saw the generalized other as a "community of attitudes" among members of an ongoing social collective. When individuals can view themselves in relation to this community of attitudes and then adjust their conduct in accordance with the expectations of these attitudes,

---

[19]Ibid., 160.

they have reached the third stage in the development of self. They can now role-take with the generalized other. For Mead, the play and game represent the initial stages in the development of self, but in the final stage, individuals can generalize the varied attitudes of others and see themselves and regulate their actions from a broader perspective.

Without this capacity to view oneself as an object in relation to the generalized other, behavior could only be situation specific. Unless people can see themselves as objects implicated in a broader social process, their actions cannot reveal continuity across situations. Moreover, humans could not create larger societies, composed of multiple groupings, without the members of the society viewing themselves, and controlling their responses, in accordance with the expectations of the generalized other.[20]

Mead recognized that in complex social systems, there could be multiple generalized others. Individuals can view themselves and control their behaviors from a variety of broader perspectives. Moreover, a generalized other can represent the embodiment of collective attitudes of concrete and functioning groups, or it can be more abstract, pertaining to broad social classes and categories:

> In the most highly developed, organized, and complicated human social communities . . . , [the] various socially functional classes or subgroups of individuals to which any given individual belongs . . . are of two kinds. Some of them are concrete social classes or subgroups, such as political parties, clubs, corporations, which are all actually functional social units, in terms of which their individual members are directly related to one another. The others are abstract social classes or subgroups, such as the class of debtors and the class of creditors, in terms of which their individual members are related to one another only more or less indirectly, and which only more or less indirectly function as social units, but which afford or represent unlimited possibilities for the widening and ramifying and enriching of the social relations among all the individual members of the given society as an organized and unified whole.[21]

---

[20]The similarity between Durkheim's notion of the collective conscience and Mead's conception of generalized other should be immediately apparent. But in contrast with Durkheim, Mead provided the mechanism—role-taking and self-related behaviors—by which individuals become capable of viewing and controlling their actions in the perspective of the collectivity. For more details along this line, see Jonathan H. Turner, "A Note on G. H. Mead's Behavioristic Theory of Social Structure," *Journal for the Theory of Social Behavior* 12 (July 1982), 213–222; and *A Theory of Social Interaction* (Palo Alto, CA: Stanford University Press, 1988), Chapter 10.

[21]Mead, *Mind, Self, and Society*, 157.

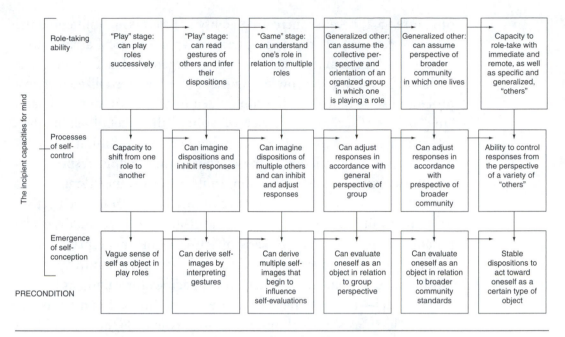

Figure 15.2   Mead's Model of the Genesis of Self

The capacity to take the role of multiple and diverse generalized others—from the perspective of a small group to that of an entire society—enables individuals to engage in the processes of self-evaluation, self-criticisms, and self-control from the perspective of what Mead termed *society*. Thus, by virtue of self-images derived from role-taking with specific others in concrete groups as well as from role-taking with generalized others personifying varying communities of attitudes, people come to see themselves as a particular type of object, with certain strengths, weaknesses, and other attributes.

Moreover, people become capable of regulating their responses to sustain this vision of themselves as a certain type of object. As people come to see themselves, and consistently respond to themselves, through their particular configuration of specific and generalized attitudes of others, they come to possess what Mead termed a *complete* and *unified* self.

Figure 15.2 attempts to summarize the dynamic processes involved in creating a self. It is more complex than Figure 15.1 because Mead used the concept of "self" in several interrelated ways. Thus, for purposes of interpreting the model portrayed in Figure 15.2, let us recapitulate his various notions about self. First, he saw the development of self as a process of role-taking with increasingly varied and generalized "others." This facet of self is represented across the top of Figure 15.2, because increasing acuity at role-taking influences the other aspects of self (this is emphasized by the vertical arrows connecting the boxes at each stage in the emergence of self). Second, as is shown in the middle row of Figure 15.2, Mead visualized self as a process of self-control. As he emphasized in his notion of the "I" and "me" phases of self and in his view of "mind," this facet of self involves the growing ability to read the gestures of others, to inhibit inappropriate responses in relation to these others, and to adjust responses in a way that will facilitate interaction. In its more advanced stages, self-control also includes the capacity to assume the "general" perspective, or "community of attitudes," of specific groups and, eventually, of the broader community. The process of self-control thus represents the extensions of the capacities for mind, and for this reason the precondition for self—that is, the "incipient capacities for mind" at the left of the model—is seen to tie almost directly into the self-control aspect of self. Third, as shown along the bottom row in Figure 15.2, Mead also saw self as involving the emergence of a self-conception, or stable disposition to act toward oneself as a certain type of object. Such a stable self-conception evolves out of the accumulation of self-images and self-evaluations with reference to specific, and then increasingly generalized, others.

Thus, in reading Mead's model, the arrows that move from left to right denote the development of each aspect of self. The arrows that move down the columns stress his emphasis on the role-taking process and on how developments in the ability to role-take influence the etiology of self-control processes and self-conceptions. Of course, we might also draw arrows back up the columns because to some extent, self-control processes and self-conceptions influence role-taking abilities. But we feel that the arrows, as currently drawn, best capture Mead's vision of causal processes in the initial emergence of those multiple behavioral capacities that he subsumed under the label *self*. These capacities are, in turn, vital to the production and reproduction of society.

Mead's Conception of Society

The Behavioral Basis of Society

Mead labeled as *mind* those behavioral capacities in organisms that allow the use of symbols to denote objects and to role-take, to use objects as stimuli for various behaviors, to inhibit responses, to imaginatively rehearse alternative responses, and to select a line of conduct. Thus, mind allows cooperation among individuals as they attempt to select behaviors that will facilitate cooperation. *Self* is the term Mead used to describe the behavioral capacity to see oneself as an object in the environment and to use a stable conception of oneself as a certain type of object as a major stimulus for organizing behavior. The capacity for mind and self arises from, and continues to depend on, the process of role-taking because one's view of oneself as an object and one's capacity to select among alternative behaviors are possible through reading the gestures of others and determining their attitudes and dispositions.

In many ways, mind is the capacity for denoting alternatives, whereas self involves the capacity for ordering choices in a consistent framework. An organism with only mind could visualize alternatives but could not readily select among them. The capacity for self allows the selection of behaviors among alternatives. In so doing, self provides a source of stability and consistency in a person's behavior, while integrating that behavior into the social fabric or society.

Mead saw several ways in which self provides for the integration of behavior into society. First, the capacity to see oneself as an object in a field of objects allows individuals to see themselves in relation to other individuals. They can see their place in the field of perception and, hence, adjust their responses (through the capacity for mind) to coordinate their activities.

Second, the emergence of a unified and complete self, or stable self-conception, means that individuals consistently place into their perceptual field a view of themselves as a certain *type* of object. This ability makes behaviors of individuals more consistent and predictable because people generally seek to affirm their conceptions of themselves. People's behavior across widely divergent situations thus reveals consistency because they interject, to some degree, a stable self-conception of themselves as a certain type of individual who is deserving of certain responses from others. This object, as much as any of the objects peculiar to a situation, serves as a stimulus in organizing behaviors. The more rigid the self-conception, the more the gestures of others are selectively interpreted and used to organize responses consistent with one's self-conception. The consequence for society of these self-related processes is that as people's actions take on consistency from situation to situation or from time to time in the same situation, their behaviors become predictable, thereby making it easier for individuals to adjust to, and cooperate with, one another.

Third, the process of role-taking allows individuals to see themselves not only in relation to specific others in particular situations but also in relation to varieties of generalized others. Thus, if a person's actions are assessed by reference to the same generalized others, behaviors will take on consistency from situation to situation and across time. Moreover, to the degree that all participants to an interaction role-take with the same generalized other, they will approach and perceive situations within "common meanings," and they will be prepared to act in terms of the same perspective. By viewing themselves as objects relative to the same set of expectations, people approach situations with common understandings that will facilitate their adjustment to one another.

A fourth—and related—point is that the capacity to role-take with varieties of generalized others allows individuals to elaborate patterns of social organization. Individuals are now liberated from the need for face-to-face interaction as the basis for coordinating their activities. Once they can role-take with varieties of generalized others, some of whom are abstract conceptions, they can guide their conduct from a common perspective without directly role-taking with one another. Thus, the capacity to view oneself as an object and to adjust responses in relation to the perspective of an abstract generalized other greatly extends the potential scope of patterns of social organization.

Fifth, in addition to providing behavioral consistency and individual integration into extended networks of interaction, self also serves as a vehicle of social change. The phases of self—the "*I*" and "*me*," as Mead termed them—ensure that individual behaviors will, to some degree, alter the flow of the social process. Even if "me" images reflect perfectly the expectations in a situation, and even if one's view of oneself as a certain type of object is totally congruent with these expectations, actual behavior—that is, the "I"—can deviate from what is anticipated in "me" images. This deviation, however small or great, forces others in the situation to adjust their behaviors, providing new "me" images to guide subsequent behaviors ("I")—and so on, in the course of interaction that moves in and out of "I" and "me" phases. Of course, when expectations are not clear and when one's self-conception is at odds with the expectations of others, "I" behaviors are likely to be less predictable, requiring greater adjustments by others. Or when the capacity to develop "me" images dictates changes in a situation for an individual—and this is often the case among individuals whose self-conception or generalized others are at odds—even greater behavioral variance and social change can be expected as the "I" phase of action occurs. Thus, the inherent phases of self—the "I" and "me"—make inevitable change in patterns of interaction. Sometimes these changes are small and imperceptible, and only after the long accumulation of small adjustments is the change noticeable.[22] At other times, the change is great, as when a person in political power initiates a new course of activity. In either case, as Mead went to great lengths to emphasize, self not only provides a source of continuity and integration for human behavior, but also is a source of change in society.[23]

What emerges from Mead's view of society is not a vision of social structure and the emergent properties of these structures. Rather, he reaffirmed that patterns of social organization, whatever their form and profile, are mediated by human behavioral capacities for language, role-taking, mind, and self. Apart from a general view stressed by all thinkers of his time, that societies are becoming more differentiated and complex, he offered only a few clues about the properties of social structures in human societies. Mead's analysis of society, therefore, is actually a series of statements on the underlying behavioral processes that make coordination among individuals possible.

The Process of Society

For Mead, the term *society* is simply a way of denoting that interactive processes can reveal stability and that humans act within a framework imposed by stabilized social relations. The key to understanding society lies in the use of language and the practice of role-taking by individuals with mind and self. By means of the capacity to use and read significant gestures, individuals can role-take and use their mind and self to articulate their actions to specific others in a situation and to a variety of generalized others. Because generalized others embody the broader groups—organizations, institutions, and communities— that mark the structure of society, they provide a common frame of reference for individuals to use in adjusting their conduct.

Society is thus maintained by virtue of humans' ability to role-take and to assume the perspective of generalized others. Mead implicitly argued that society as presented to any given individual represents

---

[22]Ibid.,180, 202, and 216 for the relevant statements.

[23]For Mead's explicitly published works on self, see "The Social Self," *Journal of Philosophy* 10 (1913), 374–380; "The Genesis of the Self and Social Control," *International Journal of Ethics* 35 (1924–1925), 251–277; and "Cooley's Contribution."

a series of perspectives, or "attitudes," which the individual assumes in regulating behavior. Some attitudes are those of others in one's immediate field; other perspectives are those of less immediate groups; still other attitudes come from more remote social collectives; additional perspectives come from the abstract categories used as a frame of reference; and ultimately, the entire population using a common set of symbols and meanings constitutes the most remote generalized other. Thus, at any given time an individual is role-taking with some combination of specific and generalized others. The attitudes embodied by these others are then used in the processes of mind and self to construct lines of conduct.

Mead believed, then, that the structure and dynamics of society concern those variables that influence the number, salience, scope, and proximity of generalized others. Thus, by implication, Mead argued that to the degree individuals could accurately take the role of one another and assume the perspective of common generalized other(s), patterns of interaction would be stable and cooperative. Conversely, to the degree that role-taking is inaccurate and occurs relative to divergent generalized other(s), interaction will be disrupted and perhaps conflictual.[24]

From this perspective, the theoretical key to explaining patterns of social organization involves isolating those variables that influence (1) the accuracy of role-taking and (2) the convergence of generalized others. What might some of these variables be? Mead did not discuss them in detail because he was not interested in building formal sociological theory. Rather, his concerns were more philosophical, and hence he stressed recognizing the general nature of the processes underlying the maintenance of the social order. In a number of places, however, he offered some clues about what variables influence the capacity of actors to role-take with the same generalized other.

One barrier to role-taking with the same generalized other is social differentiation.[25] In complex societies, people play different roles, and often, the immediate generalized others for these roles will vary. This is, of course, a somewhat different way of stating Comte's and Durkheim's concerns about the mal-integrative effects of differentiation. Mead recognized that when individuals' immediate generalized others vary, it is possible to have a more general or abstract generalized

---

[24]Mead, *Mind, Self, and Society*, 321–322.
[25]Ibid., 321–322.

other with which they can mutually role-take. As a result, despite their differences, people can role-take with a common perspective and use it to guide their conduct. Durkheim's similar conceptualization emphasized the "enfeeblement" or abstractness of the collective conscience (or culture) and the resulting anomie and egoism.

Mead's view, however, offers the recognition that although the community of attitudes of two individuals' immediate groups might diverge somewhat, they can at the same time assume the perspective of a more remote, or abstract, generalized other and use this community of attitudes as a common perspective for guiding their conduct. Unlike Durkheim, who saw structural units such as "occupational groups" as necessary mediators between the "collective conscience" and the individual, Mead's formulation of mind and self implicitly argues that through the capacity to role-take with multiple and remote others, diversely located individuals can become integrated into a common social fabric. Thus, structural differentiation will tend, Mead appears to have argued, to force role-taking with more remote and abstract generalized others. Thus, the dimensions of a society can be greatly extended because people's interactions are mediated and regulated by reference to a common community of attitudes rather than by face-to-face interaction.

Also related to differentiation—indeed, it is a type of differentiation—is stratification.[26] Class barriers increase the likelihood that individuals in different classes will not share the same community of attitudes. To the degree that a system of hierarchical differentiation is to be integrated, role-taking with a more distant generalized other will supplement the community of attitudes peculiar to a particular social class.

Another aspect of differentiation is population.[27] As populations increase in size, it becomes increasingly likely that any two individuals will role-take with somewhat different perspectives in their interaction with specific others in their immediate groups. If a large population is to remain integrated, Mead argued, individuals will supplement their immediate communities of attitudes by role-taking with more abstract generalized others. Hence, as the size of interaction networks increases, these networks will be integrated by role-taking with an increasingly abstract perspective or community of attitudes.

---

[26]Ibid., 327.
[27]Ibid., 326.

In sum, then, Mead's view of society is dominated by a concern with the social–psychological mechanisms by which social structures are integrated. For Mead, *society* is just a term for the processes of role-taking with varieties of specific and generalized others and the consequent coordination of action made possible by the behavioral capacities of mind and self. By emphasizing the processes underlying social structures, Mead presented a highly dynamic view of society. Not only is society created by role-taking dynamics, but it can be changed by these same processes. Thus, as diverse individuals come into contact, role-take, and adjust their responses, they create a community of attitudes, which they then use to regulate their subsequent actions. As more actors are implicated, or as their roles become more differentiated, they generate additional perspectives to guide their actions. Similarly, because actors possess unique self-conceptions and because they role-take with potentially diverse perspectives, they often must restructure existing patterns as they come to adjust to one another.

Thus, we get little feeling in Mead's work for the majesty of social structure. His conceptualization can perhaps be seen as a demystification of society, because society is nothing more than a process of role-taking by individuals who possess mind and self and who seek to make adjustments to one another. We should note, however, that Mead did offer some partial views of social morphology—that is, of the structural forms created by role-taking. We now briefly examine these more morphological or structural conceptualizations of society.

The Morphology of Society

Mead frequently used terms that carry structural connotations, with notions of *group*, *community*, *institution*, and *society* being the most common. To some degree, he used these terms interchangeably to denote regularity in patterns of interaction among individuals. Yet at times he appears to have had an image of basic structural units that compose a total society.

Mead used the term *society* in two senses: (1) society simply refers to ongoing, organized activity and (2) society pertains to geopolitical units, such as nation-states. The former usage is the most frequent, and thus, we will retain the view that *society* is the term for ongoing and organized activity among pluralities of actors, whether this activity is that of a small group or of a total society.

Mead's use of *community* was ambiguous, and he often appeared to equate it with society. His most general usage referred to a plurality of actors who share a common set of significant symbols, who perceive that they constitute a distinguishable entity, and who share a common generalized other, or community of attitudes. As such, a community can be quite small or large, depending on whether people perceive that they constitute an entity. Mead typically employed the concept of community to denote large pluralities of actors, and thus other structural units were seen to operate within communities.

Within every community, there are certain general ways in which people are supposed to act. These are what Mead defined as *institutions*:

> There are, then, whole series of such common responses in the community in which we live, and such responses are what we term "institutions." The institution represents a common response on the part of all members of the community to a particular situation.[28]

Institutions, Mead argued, are related, and thus, when people act in one institutional context, they implicitly invoke responses to others. As Mead emphasized,

> institutions . . . present in a certain sense the life-habits of the community as such; and when an individual acts toward others in, say, economic terms, he is calling out not simply a single response but a whole group of related responses.[29]

Institutions represent only general lines of response to varying life situations, whether economic, political, familial, religious, or educational. People take the role of the generalized other for each institution, and because institutions are interrelated, they tend to call out appropriate responses for other institutions. In this way, people can move readily from situation to situation within a broader community, calling out appropriate responses and inhibiting inappropriate ones. One moves smoothly, for example, from economic to familial situations because responses for both are evoked in the individual during role-taking with one or the other.

---

[28]Ibid., 261.
[29]Ibid., 264.

Mead recognized that institutions, and the attendant generalized other, provide only a broad framework guiding people's actions. People belong to a wide variety of smaller units that Mead tended to call *groups*. Economic activity, for example, is conducted by different individuals in varying economic groups. Familial actions occur within family groups, and so on for all institutional activity. Groups reveal their own generalized others, which are both unique and yet consistent within the community of attitudes of social institutions or of the broader community. Groups can vary enormously in size, differentiation, longevity, and restrictiveness, but Mead's general point is that activity of individuals involves simultaneous role-taking with the generalized other in groups, clusters of interrelated institutions, and broad community perspectives.

The Culture of Society

Mead never used the concept of *culture* in the modern sense of the term. Yet his view of social organization as mediated by generalized others is consistent with the view that culture is a system of symbols by which human thought, perception, and action are mobilized and regulated. As with social structure or morphology, however, Mead was not interested in analyzing in detail the varieties of symbol systems humans create and use to organize their affairs. Rather, he was primarily concerned with the more general insight that humans use significant symbols, or language, to create communities of attitudes. And by virtue of the capacity for role-taking, humans regulate their conduct not only in relation to the attitudes of specific others but also relative to generalized others who embody these communities of attitudes.

The concept of *generalized other* is Mead's term for what would now be seen as those symbol systems of a broader cultural system that regulate perception, thought, and action. His generalized other is thus composed of norms, values, beliefs, and other regulatory systems of symbols. He never made careful distinctions, for example, among values, beliefs, and norms, for he was interested only in isolating the basic processes of society: Individuals with mind and self role-take with varieties of generalized others to regulate their conduct and, thus, to coordinate their actions.

Mead's conception of society, therefore, emphasizes the basic nature of the processes underlying ongoing social activity. He was not concerned, to any great degree, with the details of social structure or the components of culture. His great insight was that regardless of the specific structure of society, the processes by which society is created, maintained, and changed are the same. Social organization is the result of behavioral capacities for mind and self as these allow actors to role-take with varieties of others and, thus, to regulate and coordinate their actions. This insight into the fundamental relationship between the individual and society marks Mead's great contribution in *Mind, Self, and Society.*[30]

The Philosophy of the Act

Mead left numerous unpublished papers, many of which were published posthumously in *The Philosophy of the Act.*[31] Much of this work is not of great interest to sociologists; in the first essay, however, one on which the editors imposed the unfortunate title "Stages of the Act," Mead offered new insights that cannot be found in his other essays or in his lectures. In this piece, he presented a theory of human motivation that should be viewed as supplemental to his conceptualization of mind, self, and society.

Mead did not present his argument as the concept of *motivation*, but his intent was to understand why and how human action is initiated and given direction. For Mead, the most basic unit of behavior is "the act," and much of *The Philosophy of the Act* concerns understanding the nature of this fundamental unit. The behavior of an individual is ultimately nothing more than a series of acts, sometimes enacted singularly but more often emitted simultaneously. Thus, if we are to gain insight into the nature of human behavior, we must comprehend the constituent components of behavior—that is, "acts."

In his analysis of the act, Mead retained his basic assumptions. Acts are part of a larger life process of organisms adjusting to the environmental conditions in which they find themselves. Moreover, human acts are unique because of people's capacities for mind and self. Thus, Mead's theory of motivation revolves around understanding how the behavior of organisms with mind and self and operating within society is initiated and directed. He visualized

---

[30]See, in particular, Weber's and Durkheim's analyses to appreciate how crudely the interactive basis of social structure had been conceptualized before Mead's synthesis.

[31]Mead, *Philosophy of the Act.*

the act as composed of four "stages," although he emphasized that humans could simultaneously be involved in different stages of different acts. He also recognized that acts vary in length, degree of overlap, consistency, intensity, and other variable states, but in his analysis of the stages of the act, he was more interested in isolating the basic nature of the act than in developing propositions about its variable properties.

Mead saw acts as consisting of four stages: (1) impulse, (2) perception, (3) manipulation, and (4) consummation.[32] These are not entirely discrete, for they often blend into one another, but they constitute distinctive phases involving somewhat different behavioral capacities. Our discussion will focus on each stage separately, but we must emphasize that Mead did not view the stages of a given act as separable or as isolated from the stages of other acts.

Impulse

For Mead, an *impulse* represents a state of disequilibrium, or tension, between an organism and its environment. Although he was not concerned with varying states of impulses—that is, their direction, type, and intensity—he did offer two implicit propositions: (1) The greater the degree of disequilibrium between an organism and its environment, the stronger is the impulse and the more likely is behavior to reflect this. (2) The longer an impulse persists, the more it will direct behavior until it is consummated.

The source of disequilibrium for an organism can vary. Some impulses come from organic needs that are unfulfilled, whereas others come from interpersonal maladjustments.[33] Still other impulses stem from self-inflicted reflections, and many are a combination of organic, interpersonal, and intrapsychic sources of tension. The key point is that impulses initiate efforts at their consummation, while giving the behavior of an organism a general direction. Mead was quick to point out, however, that a state of disequilibrium could be eliminated in

---

[32]For an excellent secondary discussion of Mead's stages of the act, see Tamotsu Shibutani, "A Cybernetic Approach to Motivation," in *Modern Systems Research for the Behavioral Scientist*, ed. Walter Buckley (Hawthorne, NY: Aldine, 1968); and *Society and Personality, An Interactionist Approach to Social Psychology* (Englewood Cliffs, NJ: Prentice Hall, 1961), 63–93.

[33]For Mead's conceptualization of biologic needs, see the supplementary essays in *Mind, Self, and Society*, particularly Essay 2.

many different ways and that the conditions of the environment determined the specific direction of behavior. For Mead, humans are not pushed and pulled around by impulses. On the contrary, an impulse is defined as the degree of harmony with the environment, and the manner in which an organism is prepared to adjust to its environment influences the precise ways an impulse is consummated.

For example, even seemingly organic drives such as hunger and thirst are seen as arising from behavioral adaptations to the environment. Hunger is often defined by cultural standards for when meals are to be eaten, and it arises when the organism has not secured food from the environment. The individual's social world greatly constrains the way in which this disequilibrium will be eliminated. As environmental forces impinge on actors with mind and self, they will shape the types of foods considered edible, the way they are eaten, and when they can be eaten. Thus, for Mead, an impulse initiates behavior and gives it only a general direction. The next stage of the act—perception—will determine what aspects of the environment are relevant for eliminating the impulse.

Perception

What humans see in their environment, Mead argued, is highly selective. One basis for selective perception is the impulse: People become attuned to those objects in their environment perceived relevant to the elimination of an impulse. Even here, past socialization, self-conceptions, and expectations from specific and generalized others all constrain what objects are seen as relevant to eliminating a given impulse. For example, a hungry person in India will not see a cow as a relevant object of food but rather will become sensitized to other potential food objects.

The process of *perception* thus sensitizes an individual to certain objects in the environment. These objects become stimuli for repertoires of behavioral responses. Thus, as individuals become sensitized to certain objects, they are prepared to behave in certain ways toward those objects. Mead believed, then, that perception is simply the arousal of potential responses to stimuli; that is, as the organism becomes aware of relevant objects, it is also prepared to act in certain ways. Humans thus approach objects with a series of hypotheses, or notions, about how certain responses toward objects can eliminate their state of disequilibrium.

Manipulation

The testing of these hypotheses—that is, the emission of behaviors toward objects—is termed *manipulation*. Because humans have mind and self, they can engage in covert as well as overt manipulation. A human can often covertly imagine the consequences of action toward objects for eliminating an impulse. Hence, humans frequently manipulate their world mentally, and only after imagining the consequences of various actions do they emit an overt line of behavior. At other times, humans manipulate their environment without deliberate or delayed thinking; they simply emit a behavior perceived as likely to eliminate an impulse.

What determines whether manipulation will be covert before it is overt? The key condition is what Mead saw as *blockage*, a condition where the consummation of an impulse is inhibited or delayed. Blockage produces imagery and initiates the process of thinking. For example, breaking a pencil while writing (creating impulse or disequilibrium with the environment) leads to efforts at manipulation: One actor may immediately perceive a pile of sharpened pencils next to the writing pad, pick up a new pencil, and continue writing without a moment's reflection. Another writer, who did not prepare a stack of pencils, might initially become attuned to the drawer of the desk, open it, search for a pencil, and generally start searching "blindly" for a pencil. At some point, frequently after a person has "wandered around unconsciously" for a while, the blockage of the impulse begins to generate conscious imagery, and a person's manipulations become covert. Images of where one last left a pencil are now consciously evoked, or the probable location of a pencil sharpener is anticipated. Thus, when the impulse, perception, and overt manipulation stages of the act do not lead to consummation, thinking occurs, and manipulation becomes covert, using the behavioral capacities of mind and self.

Thinking can also be initiated earlier in the act. For example, if perception does not yield a field of relevant objects, blockage occurs at this stage, with the result that by virtue of the capacities for mind, an actor immediately begins covert thinking. Thus, thinking is a behavioral adaptation of an organism experiencing disequilibrium with its environment and unable to perceive objects or manipulate behaviors in ways leading to consummation of an impulse.

In the process of thinking, then, an actor comes to perceive relevant objects; the actor might even role-take with the object if it is another individual or a group; a self-image may be derived, and one may see self as yet another object; and then various lines of conduct are imaginatively rehearsed until a proper line of conduct is selected and emitted. Of course, if the selected behavior does not eliminate the impulse, the process starts over and continues until the organism's behavior allows it to achieve a state of equilibrium with its environment.

The stage of manipulation is thus "cybernetic" in that it involves behavior, feedback, readjustment of behavior, more feedback, readjustment, and so on until an impulse is eliminated.[34] Mead's vision of thinking as "imaginative rehearsal" and his conceptualization of the "I" and "me" fit into this more general cybernetic view of the act. Thinking involves imagining a behavior and then giving oneself the feedback about the probable consequences of the behavior. The "I" and "me" phases of self involve deriving "me" images (feedback) from behaviors ("I") and then using these images to adjust subsequent behaviors. Unlike many theorists of motivation, Mead saw acts as constructed from a succession of manipulations that yield feedback, which, in turn, is used to make subsequent manipulations. Thus, motivation is a process of constant adjustment and readjustment of behaviors to restore equilibrium with the environment.

Although Mead did not develop any formal propositions on the manipulatory stage of the act, he implicitly assumed that the more often an impulse is blocked, the more it grows in intensity and the more it consumes the process of thinking and the phases of self. Thus, individuals who have not eliminated a strong impulse through successful manipulation will have a considerable amount of their thinking and self-reflection consumed by imagery pertaining to objects and behaviors that might eliminate the impulse. For example, people who cannot satiate their hunger or sexual appetites or who cannot achieve the recognition they feel they deserve are likely to devote a considerable, and ever-increasing, amount of their time in covert and overt manipulations in an effort to control their impulses.

---

[34]See Shibutani, "Cybernetic Approach," for a more detailed discussion.

Consummation

The *consummation* stage of the act simply denotes the act's completion through the elimination of the disequilibrium between an organism and its environment. As a behaviorist, Mead emphasized that successful consummation of acts by the emission of behaviors in relation to certain objects leads to the development of stable behavior patterns. Thus, general classes, or types, of impulses will tend to elicit particular responses from an individual if these responses have been successful in the past in restoring equilibrium. Individuals will tend to perceive the same or similar objects as relevant to the elimination of the impulse, and they will tend to use these objects as stimuli for eliciting certain behaviors. In this way, people develop stable behavioral tendencies to act on their environment.

Figure 15.3 represents Mead's conceptualization of these phases of the act. For any person, of course, multiple impulses are operating, each at various stages of consummation and at potential points of blockage. For humans, perception involves seeing not only physical objects but also oneself, others, and various generalized others as part of the environment. Manipulation for humans with the capacities for mind and self involves both overt behavior and covert deliberations where individuals weigh alternatives and assess their consequences with reference to their self-conception, the expectations of specific others, and various generalized others. Consummation for humans, who must live and survive in social groups, almost always revolves around adaptation to, and cooperation with, others in ongoing collective enterprises. As the feedback arrows denoting blockage emphasize, the point of blockage influences the salience of any phase in the flow of an act. Moreover, this process of blockage determines the strength of the causal arrows connecting stages in the act. Intense impulses are typically those that have been blocked, thereby causing heightened perception. In turn, heightened perception generates greater overt and covert manipulation; if blockage occurs, perception is further heightened, as are impulses. If manipulation is unsuccessful, escalated covert manipulation ensues, thereby heightening perception and the impulse (via the feedback arrows at the top of Figure 15.3).

This model of the act allows for an understanding of how individuals can be "driven" to seemingly irrational or excessively emotional behavior, and it can provide insight into the dynamics of compulsive

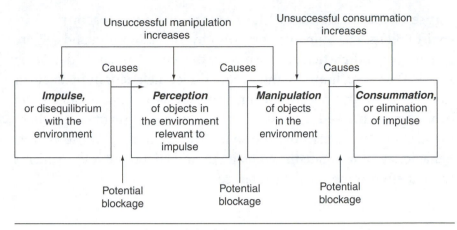

Figure 15.3   Mead's Model of the Act

behavior. These behaviors would result from the blockage of powerful impulses that persist and escalate in intensity, thereby distorting an individual's perceptions, covert thinking, and overt behavior. For example, individuals who were rejected by significant others in their early years might have a powerful series of unconsummated impulses that distort their perceptions and manipulations to abnormal extremes. Given that the unstable or abnormal self-conceptions of such individuals can distort the process of perception, as well as covert and overt manipulation, they might never be able to perceive that they have consummated their impulses in interpersonal relations.

Unlike Freud or other clinicians and psychologists of his time, Mead was not interested in types of abnormal behavior. He was more concerned with constructing a model that would denote the fundamental properties of human action, whether normal or abnormal. His critics often portray Mead's social behaviorism as overly rational, but this view does not consider his model of the act. This model contains the elements for emotional as well as rational action, and although he was not interested in assessing the consequences of various weights among the arrows in Figure 15.3, the model provides a valuable tool for those who are concerned with how various types of impulses, when coupled with different patterns of impulse blockage, will produce varying forms of covert and overt behavior.

Mead's view of motivation is distinctly sociological, emphasizing the relationship of individuals to one another and to the social as well as physical environments. What drives actors and shapes the course of their behaviors is the relationship of the organism to its environment. For human actors, who by virtue of mind and self are able to live and participate in society, this environment is decidedly social. Therefore, humans initiate and direct their actions in an effort to achieve integration into the ongoing social process. Mead's *social* behaviorism marked a synthesis of utilitarian, pragmatist, behaviorist, and even Darwinian notions. Mead's basic premise is this: Behaviors that facilitate the adjustment and adaptation of organisms to their environment will be retained.

Critical Conclusions

Before Mead, the process of interaction was not well understood. Various thinkers had captured a portion of the process, but Mead synthesized various lines of thinking into a coherent conceptual framework. The strength of Mead's analysis resides in his understanding of the relationship among ongoing patterns of social organization, or society, and the behavioral capacities that arise from human needs to adapt to these patterns and that, as a result, sustain society. Using conventional gestures, role-taking, mind, and self are, in Mead's eyes, behaviors rather than entities or things, and they are learned like all behaviors because they provide reinforcement to individuals or, alternatively in pragmatist terminology, because they allow for adaptation to society. Thus, for Mead, society always stands above the individual in the sense that it exists before a person is born and, consequently, is the environment to which individuals must adjust and adapt. Yet without learning conventional gestures and role-taking, and without acquiring the ability to engage in minded deliberations or self-reflection and appraisal from the perspective of society and its various generalized others, society would not be possible.

It is difficult to criticize the thinker who, in essence, unlocked the mysteries of micro social processes, but we can offer several criticisms. One is that Mead never developed a very clear conception of society or culture. He saw "institutions" as ongoing patterns of cooperative behavior, and he viewed culture in terms of various generalized others. Yet this is a rather minimal conception of macrostructures that are sustained by micro processes; so even though Mead saw society as standing above the individual, his theory is really about how people acquire the behavioral capacities to adjust to society and culture. We are not, however, given a theory of society or culture.

One result of this failure is that many contemporary theorists assume that a separate theory, or set of theories, about the dynamics of society and culture is not necessary. Instead, all that is needed is a theory of interpersonal behavior to explain institutional and cultural systems. Such theories become, however, little more than pronouncements that, for example, assert that "society is symbolic interaction,"[35] which says very little and explains virtually nothing about society beyond the interpersonal processes necessary to sustain it. Thus, Mead's sociology is decidedly micro, which is fine as long as we realize this limitation; many contemporary sociologists unfortunately forget this fact.

We can even criticize Mead on the more micro level of analysis. Probably his greatest failing is the lack of a theory of emotions. One of the most critical aspects of interaction is its emotional content, and when individuals role-take, engage in minded deliberations, or make self-appraisals, they are being emotional. Mead even had a Freudian-looking theory of "the act" that could easily have been used to address the emotions involved as impulses go unconsummated or as they are consummated. Moreover, Mead had used Darwinian metaphors in all his work, and he was certainly aware of Darwin's book[36] on expressions and emotions in animals, and yet, he did not pick up this lead. Thus, because Mead was considered the key figure in micro sociology for most of the century, his lapse became the discipline's gap in knowledge. For, not until the late 1970s did the sociology of emotions emerge as a field of inquiry in interactionist theorizing.[37] The only explanation for this late interest is the slavish conformity to Mead's lead, which, as profound as it was, did not tell a complete story of micro social processes.

---

[35]Herbert Blumer, *Symbolic Interactionism: Perspective and Method* (Englewood Cliff, NJ: Prentice Hall, 1969).

[36]Charles Darwin, *The Expressions of Emotions in Man and Animals* (London: Wats, 1982).

[37]For a review, see Jonathan H. Turner and Jan E. Stets, *The Sociology of Emotions* (Cambridge, UK: Cambridge University Press, 2005).

CHAPTER 16

The Emergence of Contemporary Theoretical Perspectives

Contemporary theorizing in sociology still derives much inspiration from the theorists examined in the pages of this book. Present-day theorizing has, like everything else in sociology, become more specialized since the writings of the early masters of sociology. Many current theories examine only a small range of phenomena, and thus, there are many more theories than we can briefly review here. But, even with high degrees of specialization, there are still more general theoretical approaches, almost all of which have been built on the insights of these early masters. Within each of these perspectives, there are a number of variants whose adherents argue with each other or, sometimes, even pretend that a rival camp simply does not exist. Intellectual life is always competitive, and scholars compete for limited attention space,[1] with the result that they work to differentiate their theories from the competition. But, even with these tendencies for grabbing attention space by specialization, at least 9 approaches can be isolated—which is a few too many for the current intellectual space in sociology. As a consequence, just some are dominant, while the rest must compete with each other to find a way into the sociological imagination.

---

[1]Randall Collins, *The Sociology of Philosophies: A Global Theory of Intellectual Change* (Cambridge, MA: Harvard University Press, 1998).

Nine Theoretical Traditions and Perspectives

Functional Theorizing

Functional theorizing was sociology's first theoretical perspective. Auguste Comte was followed by Herbert Spencer and, then, by Émile Durkheim who incorporated elements from both Comte and Spencer in his mode of functional analysis. The basic essence of functional analysis can be summarized as follows:

1. Social systems are composed of interrelated parts.

2. These systems confront both internal and external problems of adaptation to their environments that must be resolved if the system is to endure.

3. These problems of survival and adaptation can be visualized as system "needs" or "requisites" that must be met.

4. Understanding of social systems as a whole and their constituent parts is only possible by analyzing the need(s) or requisite(s) of the system that any given part meets.

Differences among functional theories revolve around the number of functional requisites that are posited. Some theorists like Émile Durkheim[2] posited only one master need: *social integration* or the need for coordination and control of system parts. Thus, societies should be examined with respect to how each of its parts—whether structural, cultural, or interactional—contributes to the integration of the social whole. Other early functionalists like Herbert Spencer[3] delineated several functional requisites: (1) *production* or the securing of resources and their conversion into usable commodities; (2) *reproduction* of societal members and social structures; (3) *distribution* of resources, information, and people around a society and its social structures; and (4) *regulation* or coordination and control through the consolidation and use of power.

With Spencer's death in the first decade of the twentieth century, and then Durkheim's in the second decade, functional theorizing disappeared from sociology. The approach was kept alive by anthro-

---

[2]For a review of Émile Durkheim's functionalism, see pp. 260–274.
[3]For a review of Herbert Spencer's functional theorizing, see pp. 58–66.

pologists such as A. R. Radcliffe-Brown[4] and Bronislaw Malinowski,[5] because functionalism allowed them and other anthropologists to theorize about why a particular cultural form—such as a belief, ritual, or social structure—existed in preliterate societies. They could ask the basic question of all functional theory: What does a part in any social system do to sustain the system in its environment? About the time that the problems[6] in this mode of analysis caused a sharp decline in anthropological functionalism, it came roaring back in sociology during the 1950s and continued to be the dominant theoretical approach of sociology until the mid-1970s, when it once again began to decline and, then, almost disappeared.

All hard-core functional theories from the middle decades of the twentieth century continue to emphasize the requisites of a social system. For Talcott Parsons,[7] there were four requisites, roughly paralleling those of Herbert Spencer and the anthropologist Bronislaw Malinowski. These include the needs for *adaptation* (production), *goal attainment* (regulation through power), *integration* (coordination), and *latency* (tension management and reproduction). In contrast, the German functionalist Niklas Luhmann[8] posited one master requisite—*complexity reduction*—along several dimensions of human existence—temporal, material, and symbolic. Thus, social structures and culture are viewed as arising to reduce the potential complexity of the *temporal* dimension (which can extend back in all of history or forward toward infinity), the

---

[4]A. R. Radcliffe-Brown, *Structure and Function in Primitive Society* (Glencoe, IL: Free Press, 1952).

[5]Bronislaw Malinowski, *A Scientific Theory of Culture* (Chapel Hill: University of North Carolina Press, 1944). For a review of the history of functional theorizing in sociology and anthropology, see Jonathan H. Turner and Alexandra Maryanski, *Functionalism* (Menlo Park, CA: Benjamin/Cummings, 1979).

[6]Many of the problems of functionalism concerned its apparent conservative assumptions that any part exists because it meets functional needs. Thus, functionalism justified the status quo even if it was oppressive and unjust. Another problem was the tautological nature, or circular reasoning, in functional explanations. For example, how do I know that a part has functions for a social system? *Answer:* Because the system is functioning and surviving.

[7]Talcott Parsons, *The Social System* (Glencoe, IL: Free Press, 1951); and Talcott Parsons, Robert F. Bales, and Edward A. Shils, *Working Papers in the Theory of Action* (Glencoe, IL: Free Press, 1953). For a more contemporary theorist, who carries forth Parsons' functionalism, see Richard Munch's *Theory of Action: Towards Going Beyond Parsons* (London: Routledge, 1988).

[8]Niklas Luhmann, *Systems Theory* (Palo Alto, CA: Stanford University Press, 1995); and *The Differentiation of Society*, trans. S. Holmes and C. Larmore (New York: Columbia University Press, 1982).

material dimension (which can include all possible social relations in infinite space), and the *symbolic* dimension (which includes all possible symbol systems). Social systems thus develop mechanisms—structural and cultural—to reduce this potential complexity, and so social systems are to be understood by how these mechanisms for reducing complexity have evolved and how they operate now.

Other sociologists sympathetic to functional analysis but suspicious of the notion of universal requisites and needs took somewhat different tacks. Jeffrey Alexander and Paul Colomy[9] have emphasized structural differentiation and integration by culture as key dynamics of societies without invoking the notion of requisites. Jonathan Turner[10] has converted requisites to a conception of fundamental *forces* that vary in intensity and that increase selection pressures on actors to create sociocultural formations to reduce the intensity of these pressures. Thus, even though they are now known by other names, functional theory still persists in contemporary sociology, and the reason that it persists is that it has always asked an interesting question: What adaptive problems must all societies, and systems within societies, resolve if they are to sustain themselves in their respective environments? An answer to this question gets at what is essential to human existence in societies, and therefore, it remains at the center of sociological theory, even as functional theory has declined in influence.

Evolutionary Theorizing

Stage Theories. Among the classical sociologists, theories about the stages of societal evolution from simple to more complex forms were common. Among functionalist theorists today, all theories still emphasize the increasing differentiation of social structures and culture in societies. Most of these early theories had some notion of stages in this movement toward higher levels of differentiation. Some

---

[9]Jeffrey C. Alexander, ed., *Neofunctionalism* (Beverly Hills, CA: Sage, 1985); Jeffrey C. Alexander and Paul Colomy, "Neofunctionalism Today: Restructuring a Theoretical Tradition," in *Frontiers of Social Theory*, ed. George Ritzer (New York: Columbia University Press, 1990); and Paul Colomy, ed., *Neofunctionalist Sociology: Contemporary Statements* (London: Edward Elgar, 1990).

[10]Jonathan H. Turner, *Macrodynamics: Toward a Theory on the Organization of Human Populations* (New Brunswick, NJ: Rutgers University Press, 1995); and *Theoretical Principles of Sociology, Vol. 1: Macrodynamics* (New York: Springer, 2010).

like Émile Durkheim[11] posited two basic stages from "mechanical" to "organic" solidarity; others like Herbert Spencer[12] outlined in rather great detail the different stages of society from a simple (nomadic hunting and gathering without a head), to a simple with head (settled hunting and gathering as well as horticultural societies), followed by a double compound (agrarian), and finally a triple compound (industrial) society, while at the same time trying to explain the dynamics that cause this movement from simple to highly compounded or differentiated societies. Other theorists like Max Weber[13] focused on the overarching evolutionary process of rationalization (although he would not have used the term evolutionary); Karl Marx[14] posited four stages of history from primitive communism (hunting and gathering) through slavery (roughly horticulture and early agrarianism), feudalism (agrarian), and industrial capitalism to the end of evolutionary history, communism; Georg Simmel[15] and George Herbert Mead,[16] like most functionalists, tended to view evolution as a master process of differentiation. Despite their many differences, all stage theories of evolution include the following assumptions:

1. Societies evolve from simple to ever-more complex forms.

2. This evolution always involves several discrete stages.

3. There are always forces or mechanisms driving this movement of societies from simple to complex formations.

4. These forces can be constant or varying, depending on the stage of development of a society.

5. Depending on the evolutionary theory, these mechanisms of change tend to revolve around (a) functional requisites pushing on actors to develop structures to meet these requisites, (b) technology and production, (c) power and inequality, (d) geopolitics, (e) market dynamics, (f) energy capture, (g) population growth, and (h) other forces or mechanisms that push societies along evolutionary stages.

---

[11]For Durkheim's simply two-stage model, see pp. 331–334.

[12]For Herbert Spencer's more elaborate stage model, one that is still contemporary, see pp. 82–102.

[13]For Max Weber's more implicit stage model, see pp. 225–228.

[14]For Karl Marx's stage-model and theory, see pp. 160–162.

[15]For Georg Simmel's models of stages of differentiation, see pp. 272–274.

[16]For George Herbert Mead's very implicit assumptions about differentiation as the master trend in societies, see pp. 269–272, 288.

Like functionalism, this line of theorizing disappeared by the third decade of the twentieth century, just as the classical period of sociological theorizing was coming to a close. In the 1960s, however, after a half century in hiding, stage modeling made a dramatic comeback and has ever since remained a part of the theoretical landscape in sociology. There is, however, no clear consensus about which mechanisms, or which combination of mechanisms, listed under (5) is the key to explaining evolution. But what is particularly important is that the comeback occurred not just in functional theories, where stage models had always been present throughout the nineteenth century, but also in other theoretical approaches.[17] For example, ecological, conflict, world-systems, cultural, postmodern, and even critical theories have all introduced elements of stage modeling back into contemporary theory. Like earlier theories, a series of stages of societal development are posited, and then the driving forces—listed under (5)—are posited. These new theories also introduce, as did Spencer in his analysis of power, the more cyclical dynamics of societal oscillations within each stage.

Biological Theories. Social scientists in general, but a relative few sociologists, have sought to bring biological ideas and some elements of the general theory of biological evolution into sociological theorizing. Charles Darwin's *On the Origin of Species* was not published until 1859, right in the middle of sociology's emergence, but evolutionary thinking

---

[17]Prominent stage-model theorists include Gerhard Lenski, *Power and Privilege* (New York: McGraw-Hill, 1964, reissued by the University of North Carolina Press); Talcott Parsons, *Societies: Evolutionary and Comparative Perspectives* (Englewood Cliffs, NJ: Prentice Hall, 1966); *The System of Modern Societies* (Englewood Cliffs, NJ: Prentice Hall, 1971); Patrick Nolan and Gerhard Lenski, *Human Societies* (Boulder, CO: Paradigm, 2009); and Jonathan H. Turner, *Human Institutions: A Theory of Societal Evolution* (Boulder, CO: Rowman & Littlefield, 2003). Theorists working in other traditions (denoted in parentheses) include Christopher Chase-Dunn and Thomas D. Hall (conflict theory), *Rise and Demise: Comparing World Systems* (Boulder, CO: Westview Press, 1997); Amos Hawley (ecological theorizing), *Human Ecology: A Theoretical Essay* (Chicago: University of Chicago Press, 1986); Stephen K. Sanderson (evolutionary biology/conflict theory), *Social Transformations: A General Theory of Historical Development* (Oxford, UK: Routledge, 1999); W. G. Runciman (ecology theory), *A Theory of Cultural and Social Selection* (Cambridge, UK: Cambridge University Press, 2009); Immanuel M. Wallerstein (conflict theory), *The Modern World System* (New York: Academic Press, 1974); and Jürgen Habermas (critical theory), *Communication and the Evolution of Society*, trans. T. McCarthy (London: Heinemann, 1979). Thus, as is evident, elements of stage modeling of evolution are still present in sociology, just as they were in the first 100 years of sociological theory.

had been in the air for some decades. Some of this early evolutionary thinking was stage modeling, as discussed earlier, but there were other ideas that were closer to Darwin's theory of evolution by natural selection that, later (in the early twentieth century), was expanded to include the mechanisms of variation on which selection works.

Auguste Comte had realized, long before Darwin, that biology would be the dominant science of the nineteenth century, and this is why he postulated his hierarchy of the sciences with sociology as the last great science emerging from biology and, surprisingly, becoming the "queen" of all the sciences. Herbert Spencer always had a vision of evolution as an outcome of competition, before Darwin published his great work, with the more fit organism or superorganism (society) prevailing and passing on its forms. George Herbert Mead, as a pragmatist philosopher and social behaviorist, had a similar view that behaviors or societal forms that facilitate adaptation are retained in the behavioral repertoire and structural forms of the social universe. Émile Durkheim explicitly borrowed Darwin's views on material and moral density increasing competition in his ecological analysis of societal evolution (see section Ecological Theorizing on page 442). Thus, evolutionary thinking in sociology was getting closer to that of biology, even before the modern synthesis in biological evolution was reached near the end of sociology's classical period in 1830. This connection between sociology and biology was lost in the middle decade of the twentieth century, but it returned in the later decades and now constitutes a controversial approach, but one that is not likely to disappear as it did by this time in the last century. All these theories share certain assumptions listed below:

1. Humans are animals and thus evolved like any other life-form under the basic forces (outlined in the modern synthesis) of evolutionary theory.

2. The traits that human possess, including biologically based propensities for certain types of behaviors, are the outcome of natural selection as it worked on variations in human phenotypes (and underlying genotypes) to promote fitness in particular environments.

3. Of particular importance are selection pressures that worked on the neuroanatomy of humans' ancestors because thinking, emotions, decisions, behavior, and social organization are the

outcome of processes operating in the brain as they direct and guide behaviors that build up the sociocultural formations that make up societies.

4. It is important to understand how selection worked on particular parts of humans and their ancestors' brains to produce generalized human propensities to behave and, hence, organize in particular ways.

5. Patterns of human social organization are not the direct causal outcomes of humans' biologically based behavioral propensities, but these propensities exert some pressure on humans to interact and organize in certain general ways, although these can be significantly modified by nonbiological forces.

6. There are numerous ways to gain information about how natural selection worked on hominin and then human anatomy and neuroanatomy, including (a) cross-species comparisons of different life forms that organize themselves into macro societies (e.g., insects and humans); (b) comparison of human anatomy, behaviors, and social structures with those of their closest primate relatives, the great apes; (c) analyzing the changing ecology of Africa to understand the selection pressures from the environment that were working on the anatomy of our ancestral line; and (d) extending biological ideas in evolutionary theory to see if biological concepts and theories can explain the evolution of superorganisms or sociocultural formations organizing humans into large-scale societies.

There are several related approaches in biological theories that share these assumptions and that have made inroads into present-day sociological theorizing. One is sociobiology,[18] where the argument

---

[18]Sociobiology was born in the study of insects, with Edward G. Wilson's large work *Sociobiology: The New Synthesis* (Cambridge, MA: Harvard University Press, 1978) taking dead aim at sociology, although the key ideas in this work were developed by a creative set of early thinkers in sociobiology. For sociologists who adhere to all or at least some of the assumptions of sociobiology, see Pierre van den Berghe, *Age and Sex in Human Societies: A Biosocial Perspective* (Belmont, CA: Wadsworth, 1973); *The Ethnic Phenomenon* (New York: Elsevier, 1981); Joseph Lopreato, *Human Nature and Biosocial Evolution* (London: Allen & Unwin, 1984); Joseph Lopreato and Timothy Crippen, *Crisis in Sociology: The Need for Darwin* (Piscataway, NJ: Transaction Publishers, 1999); and Sanderson, *Social Transformations: A General Theory of Historical Development*.

made is that natural selection has generated particular behavioral propensities, all addressing the issue of fitness or the capacity of organisms to keep their genes in the gene pool. The structure of organisms and superorganisms (societies) are viewed as "survivor machines" that enable genes of organisms to remain in the gene pool. And thus, by viewing how natural selection created these "survival machines," it becomes possible to understand the sociocultural world as evolving in response to blind natural selection that increased fitness of organisms and the superorganisms or societies in which they and their genes live.

Related to sociobiology is evolutionary psychology,[19] which argues much in the same way as sociobiology but adds the important caveat that natural selection worked mostly on the brain and wired in the brain certain behavioral capacities and propensities that make societies possible. By examining the ecology in which the human line evolved and the selection pressures from this environment on our ancestral line's neuroanatomy, it becomes possible today to discover the modules of the brain that give humans their unique behavioral characteristics that, in turn, can help explain the sociocultural universe studied by sociologists.

Another approach goes back to issues of human nature by performing a comparative analysis of humans with their closest primate relatives, chimpanzees and other great apes. In this approach, contemporary apes, the closest living relatives to humans, are considered to be a "distant mirror" in which to see human beings' remote ancestors reflected. By studying the behavioral and organizational propensities of primates, it will be possible to understand human nature and how this biological nature still exerts some influence on human behavior and societal evolution.[20]

---

[19]For foundational statements of evolutionary psychology, see Leda Cosmides and John Tooby "Evolutionary Psychology and the Generation of Culture," *Ethology and Sociobiology* 10 (1989), 51–97. For sociologists who employ this perspective, see Timothy Crippen, "Toward a neo-Darwinian Sociology," *Sociological Perspectives* 37 (1994), 309–335; Satoshi Kanazawa and Mary C. Still, "Why Men Commit Crimes," *Sociological Theory* 18 (2000), 434–448; and Richard Machalek and Michael Martin, "Sociology and the Second Darwinian Revolution," and Christine Horne, "Values and Evolutionary Psychology," both in *Sociological Theory* (2004), 434–493.

[20]For examples of this approach to "human nature," see Alexandra Maryanski and Jonathan H. Turner, *The Social Cage: Human Nature and the Evolution of Society* (Palo Alto, CA: Stanford University Press, 1992); and Jonathan H. Turner and Alexandra Maryanski, *On The Origin of Societies by Natural Selection* (Boulder, CO: Paradigm Press, 2008).

Still, many sociologists remain fearful about bringing biological ideas into sociology, especially since sociocultural evolution is not the same as biological evolution. Many of these fears are that societal complexity will be subordinated to simple and simplistic explanations that ignore the larger repertoire of theories that have been developed within sociology proper to explain the social world. These fears have some merit because, thus far, the theories introduced by sociobiology and evolutionary psychology tend to be too simple and almost always ignore the emergent properties of the social world that are built from human behaviors and, more significantly, from interpersonal behaviors. Yet at times the fears of sociologists are somewhat irrational and prejudicial against any effort to understand human societies by the biological characteristics of humans.

Ecological Theorizing

Almost hidden in the functional theories of Herbert Spencer and Émile Durkheim are two ecological theories that converge with the biological theory of evolution as it developed in the second half of the nineteenth century and early part of the twentieth century. These ecological theories might be seen as a subtype of evolutionary theory because they were a part of the stage theories of Spencer and Durkheim, while hinting at notions of selection contained in more biological theories. Yet as they developed during the 1920s and 1930s and, then, during the last third of the twentieth century, ecological theory became a highly distinctive theoretical perspective that had long shed its functional roots. These ecological theories still contain elements of biological theory—for example, resource niches, density, selection, and evolution—but these theoretical ideas are adapted to understanding distinctly sociological phenomena.

Herbert Spencer's most famous phrase—"survival of the fittest"—was probably his biggest mistake, but this phrase—hitting on the essence of natural selection—was uttered some 9 years before the publication of Charles Darwin's *On The Origin of Species* in 1859; and it was used by Spencer to explain the evolution of societal complexity in terms of intersocietal warfare. For Spencer, warfare among societies had been a powerful evolutionary force because the larger, more complex society would typically win a war; and as the victorious society would incorporate the conquered population, the level of differentiation and complexity of the consolidated society would increase, and over the long run, the size and complexity of societies in general would successively increase as a consequence of war. Unfortunately, however, Spencer also used this phrase to emphasize competition among individuals and collective units *within* a society, with the "more fit" selecting out the "less fit" as a natural part of the social order. This idea meant, literally, the death of individual and collective actors through the competition for resources (without societal intervention), and Spencer felt that this process was inevitable in the organization of human beings. But, at times in his more philosophical works, he went further: Selection operated to increase the fitness of those individuals who "won out" in the competition. Later, this idea was used to justify arguments in favor of what became known as *Social Darwinism* ("Social Spencerianism" would probably have been a more accurate description), where programs of eugenics were proposed in which the genetically unfit would be allowed to die or, worse, be killed, to sustain the fitness of humans. Spencer never went this far in advocating eugenics; however, his reputation never recovered from the association of his ideas with this discredited school of thought.

Émile Durkheim[21] had a more benign view of competition and selection. For him, as populations grow, their material density and, hence, their moral density increase, thus raising the level of competition and selection for resources among individuals and collective actors in a given resource niche. For Durkheim, however, people did not die; they simply went to a new niche or created a new type of niche in which to secure resources, thereby increasing the differentiation of human societies. The rather idealized view was probably as extreme as Spencer's overly harsh view of competition.

Human ecology, as it came to be known, first emerged from scholars at the University of Chicago in the early twentieth century and, later, also migrated to the human ecology program at the University of North Carolina at Chapel Hill. At Chicago, the ecologists downsized the ideas of Spencer and Durkheim about competition and selection to a more meso-level analysis of particular types of structures within communities. This Chicago School, as it became known, began to

---

[21]Durkheim's model of ecological processes is outlined in pp. 335–336.

develop models of *urban ecology,*[22] in which the zones and sectors of urban areas were seen as the outcome of competition among actors with different levels of resources to purchase or rent urban space. This competition was seen to be institutionalized by real estate markets, which sorted people and corporate actors by their ability to "pay" for space. The result was that urban areas become differentiated by functions—for example, business, industry, schools, government, and the like. Similarly, residential neighborhoods become differentiated by class, ethnicity, and immigration status as a consequence of individuals' ability to afford different types of housing, all sorted by cutthroat real estate markets. They also noted, of course, that other forces such as prejudice and discrimination intersected with the housing market and unfairly confined some individuals to less desirable neighborhoods.

In the last third of the twentieth century, a new form of ecological analysis emerged: *organizational ecology.*[23] Organizational ecology emphasizes that populations of organizations seek resources in niches; and as the density of organizations in a niche increases, so does the competition and selection among them. As density and competition increase, some organizations die out while others survive. Thus, there are patterns to organizational founding and rates of demise. When niche density is low, organizational foundings will increase; and as they prove successful, their structures and cultures are copied as other organizations enter the niche. But, as density increases, there comes a point when too many organizations now exist relative to the resources available in a niche, with the result that many begin to fail. As more organizations fail, the niche eventually becomes less dense, allowing existing organizations to sustain themselves; and often deaths overshoot the carrying capacity of the niche with the result that there is, once again, a more modest increase in organizational founding but never to the extent that was the case when the initial founders opened up the niche.

---

[22]The Chicago School was famous for using the city of Chicago as a laboratory for empirical work, but members of this school also tried to understand the dynamics of cities, per se, in terms of their ecology; for early urban ecological works, see Chauncey Harris and Edward Ullman, "The Nature of Cities," *The Annals of the American Academy of Political and Social Sciences* 242 (1945), 7–14; Richard M. Hurd, *Principles of City Growth* (New York: Record and Guide, 1903); and Amos Hawley, *Human Ecology* (New York: Ronald Press, 1950), *Urban Society: An Ecological Approach* (New York: Ronald Press, 1981).

[23]Michael T. Hannan and John L. Freeman, "The Population Ecology of Organizations," *American Sociological Review* 82 (1977), 929–964.

Organizational ecology more explicitly adopted ideas from evolutionary biology and ecology, but the mentor (Amos Hawley) of the original organizational ecology theorists was from the Chicago School, where the Spencerian and Durkheimian roots of ecological theorizing were still recognized. Interestingly, late in his career, Amos Hawley[24] began to take ecological ideas back to the macro level, producing a theory more like the original theories of Spencer and Durkheim. Not surprisingly, the theory emphasized the ecological dynamics generating increased differentiation within societies, but with many new conceptual twists. Other theorists have also retained the macro-level emphasis and, like Spencer and Durkheim, blended functional and ecological ideas to produce new kinds of evolutionary and ecological theories.

The key ideas of sociological ecological theorizing have spread to many other theoretical perspectives and research traditions. All these ecological theories emphasize a set of important points:

1. The social world, like the biotic world, can be viewed as composed of resource niches that are essential to the survival of social units in societies.

2. Different types of units seek resources from different niches.

3. The number of different types of social units making up a society is related to the number of diverse niches and the resources in these niches that can be used to sustain these units and their members.

4. The rate of founding of new types of organizational units is (a) positively related to the level of resources in a niche and (b) inversely related to the density of units in a resource niche.

5. The intensity of competition for resources in any given niche is a function of the density of corporate units seeking resources in a niche.

6. The death rate of corporate units in a niche and/or the rate of movement of corporate units out of a niche are both a function of (a) the density among social units and (b) the level of competition among social units in a niche.

---

[24]Amos Hawley, *Human Ecology: A Theoretical Essay* (Chicago: University of Chicago Press, 1986).

7. The level and patterns of social differentiation in a society are the outcome of processes of competition among social units in diverse resource niches.

These ideas can be applied to many different levels of social organization. Like Spencer and Durkheim, along with others in contemporary theory, these ideas can be employed to analyze societies or even intersocietal systems. They can be used to analyze urban dynamics within and between communities or organizational processes within and between societies. It is unlikely that ecological theories can explain all social dynamics, but like Spencer and Durkheim, contemporary theory in sociology now appreciates that there are always ecological dimensions to almost every property of the social universe because, in the end, social structures and their cultures can only survive by securing resources from their environments.

Conflict Theorizing

All conflict theories emphasize that inequalities in the distribution of resources create tensions in societies and, eventually, cause conflict among subpopulations. Those who control resources seek to continue to do so, while those who do not have resources attempt to increase their shares of resources. Thus, all conflict theories begin with a view of societies and even intersocietal systems as stratified, with some sectors and classes receiving more resources than other sectors and classes. Inherent in this inequality is one of the driving forces of all patterns of social organization. Karl Marx[25] and Max Weber[26] are given the most credit for emphasizing this fundamental property of social systems, but Herbert Spencer[27] also made significant contributions that have been lost and then rediscovered in the latter half of the twentieth century. Georg Simmel[28] also analyzed conflict but from a different perspective, emphasizing the integrative functions of conflict as much as their disintegrative consequences for societies.

---

[25]For Karl Marx's analysis of inequality, stratification, and conflict, see pp. 129–141.
[26]For Max Weber's analysis of conflict, see pp. 174–180.
[27]For Herbert Spencer's analysis of power and conflict, see pp. 60–84.
[28]For Georg Simmel's analysis of conflict, see pp. 220–226.

While sociologists have always studied stratification, conflict theorizing remained recessive in American sociology (unlike European sociology), especially its Marxist variants, until the 1960s. Because of Marx's association with communism, conflict theory became conflated with the politics of the Cold War and, hence, was discouraged in academia, even within sociology. Only with the discrediting of McCarthyism in the 1950s were European conflict theories embraced once again in the United States. Yet it was not the power of conflict theory, per se, that led to its renaissance in sociology but, rather, its use as a means of discrediting functional theorizing. Functionalism became the dominant theoretical perspective in American sociology in the 1950s and, to a lesser extent, in world sociology, but it never lacked critics. At mid-century, European critics had begun to portray functionalism as a conservative, if not utopian, theory that served to legitimate the status quo (see Note 6)—a reasonable point of discussion that became rather overblown in the turbulent 1960s. Functionalism was seen to have failed to analyze inequality, conflict, and change; and thus, conflict theory was a mode of theorizing that could challenge the intellectual hegemony of functionalism.

Conflict theory was successful in toppling functionalism and, indeed, virtually eliminating it from sociology, although functionalism has never died but simply reconstituted itself in a different form (see section on Functional Theorizing on page 434). With the spread of conflict dynamics all over the real world during the 1960s, the rise of conflict theory was perhaps inevitable, even without the added bonus of its attack on functionalism. And for a time, almost all theoretical approaches began emphasizing power, inequality, and conflict dynamics, while often ignoring the integrative processes that functional theory had perhaps overemphasized. Thus, a rather one-sided functionalism was replaced by an equally one-sided conflict theory, but only for a time. Just as functionalism disappeared only to rise again in a different guise, so conflict theory was simply reabsorbed across many perspectives and, in the present day, it is difficult to identify "conflict theory" as a distinctive theoretical approach. Just as few walk around calling themselves functionalists, not many proclaim themselves to be conflict theorists, as they did in the 1960s and 1970s. Indeed, both forms of theorizing persist but in more muted and less polarizing forms, which is probably a useful turn of events. Still, the result of the intellectual clash between functionalism and conflict theory produced a number of distinctive types of theorizing. All emphasize most of the following points:

1. All social systems reveal inequalities in the distribution of valued resources.

2. These inequalities generate conflicts of interests between those subpopulations with varying levels of resources.

3. These inequalities also generate negative emotions and grievances among those who receive the lowest levels of resources.

4. Mobilization for conflict is likely to occur when individuals perceive that the distribution of resources is unfair and unjust.

5. Mobilization for conflict among subordinates revolves around (a) the development of ideologies and beliefs about inequalities, (b) the emergence of leaders to articulate grievances, and (c) the mobilization of material or resources to forge organizations dedicated to conflict.

6. Conflicts will generally cause some reorganization of a social system, typically creating new patterns of inequality that will serve as the target for the next round of conflict and change.

There have been a number of prominent approaches to conflict dynamics that begin with the above assumptions. Each approach takes a somewhat different tack in conceptualizing the operation of the processes listed above.

Neo-Marxist Theories. The thrust of Marx's analysis persists until the present day,[29] with many theorists employing Marxist assumptions and vocabulary and, yet at the same time, trying to account for why Marx's prediction about the eminent revolution by the proletariat never occurred in a capitalist society. Moreover, these approaches have also tried to explain why polarization of classes into two camps—the bourgeoisie and proletariat—never materialized. Instead, more like Weber's[30] prediction, the number of classes has proliferated with capitalism, especially middle classes, with the

---

[29]For representative neo-Marxian theorists, see Michael Burawoy and Erik Olin Wright, "Sociological Marxism," in *Handbook of Sociological Theory*, ed. Jonathan H. Turner (New York: Springer 2001); Michael Burawoy, *The Politics of Production* (London: New Left Books, 1985); and Erik Olin Wright, *Classes* (London: Verso, 1985) and *Class Counts* (Cambridge, UK: Cambridge University Press, 1997).

[30]For Weber's conception of classes in emerging capitalist societies, see pp. 218–228.

boundaries among these middle classes being somewhat amorphous. They have also sought to account for the fact that ownership and management of capitalist organizations of production is often divided. Moreover, the creation of joint stock companies has diffused the ownership of companies to the point that it is hard to know just who the bourgeoisie are. Other issues that neo-Marxist theories have confronted included the rise of financial services industries and the employment of significant portions of labor by government, which is not profit making and, hence, not driven by capitalist needs for wealth and capital accumulation. Yet, even as they take account of changes in capitalism since Marx's time, neo-Marxist theories still want to sustain the emancipatory thrust of Marx's analysis, the value-theory of labor as the metric by which the rate and level of exploitation of workers is measure, and the belief that socialism still remains a viable alternative to capitalism.

Neo-Weberian Theories. These theories can be analytical, and they emphasize the degree of correlation among the dimensions of stratification as outlined by Weber[31]—material wealth (class), power (party), and prestige (status groups)—as these cause conflict. These theories often emphasize the culture of diverse classes, the organizations that sustain inequalities, while consolidating and using power to maintain the stratification system. They emphasize that conflict is often local, rather than society-wide, and they do not have the same political agenda of neo-Marxists theories, revolving around the emancipation of the lower classes.

Probably the most frequent adoption of Weber's ideas comes in the historical-comparative sociological analysis,[32] where considerable emphasis has been placed on revolutions and other transforming conflict processes—a subject more in line with Marx, but the mode of

---

[31]For Weber's analysis of class, party, and status groups, see pp. 218–224.

[32]For representative and widely available neo-Weberian analyses, see Randall Collins, *Conflict Sociology* (San Diego, CA: Academic Press, 1975); and *Weberian Sociological Theory* (Cambridge, UK: Cambridge University Press, 1986). And, for classic Weberian conflict analyses within comparative-historical sociology, see Barrington Moore, *Social Origins of Dictatorship and Democracy* (Boston: Beacon Press, 1966); Charles Tilly, *From Mobilization to Revolution* (Reading, MA: Addison-Wesley, 1978) and *European Revolutions, 1492–1992* (Oxford, UK: Blackwell, 1993); Theda Skocpol, *States and Social Revolutions* (New York: Cambridge University Press, 1979); and Jack Goldstone, *Revolution and Rebellion in the Early Modern World* (Berkeley: University of California Press, 1991).

analysis is entirely different and, in the end, more Weberian. A good deal of this historical-comparative analysis focuses on the powers of the state. Here, the processes that weaken state power, especially fiscal crises but also political delegitimization, are explored, emphasizing that conflict can be initiated by either elites or the masses, and sometimes both, and lead to state breakdown as the state's power is weakened.

These theories usually examine a series of internal dynamics of various historical societies. These dynamics can include some combination of population growth, price inflation, fiscal crises, demands for state patronage by elites, excessive elite consumption, downward mobility by the elites and upward mobility by the bourgeoisie, rural revolts, and migrations of younger age cohorts that are more likely to be restive to urban areas. These events are seen to erode the state's power by sapping its financial strength and causing fiscal crises that, in turn, lead to the state's delegitimization. At the same time, these internal events are often accelerated by other societal factors, such as market failures and inefficient tax collection, as well as by intersocietal pressures stemming from failure of chartered corporations in economic competition with other societies, wars that deplete even further the resources of the state and hasten fiscal crises, and most important, loss of a war. All these events increase the likelihood of state breakdown and cause the reorganization of a society.

These neo-Weberian theories remain true to the historical-comparative methods championed by Weber, the general variables that he saw as important in understanding conflict processes, and the emphasis on understanding how these variables play out under different historical conditions. At times, elements of Marxian analysis are combined with those of Weber's approach, especially since revolutions (in more agrarian societies, some of which reveal elements of capitalism) are a common theme in neo-Weberian theorizing.[33]

Analytical Conflict Theory. This group of conflict theories has taken the basic Marxian model of conflict and revised it in several ways.[34]

---

[33]See for a blend of Marxian and Weberian analysis Jeffrey Paige, *Agrarian Revolution: Social Movements and Export Agriculture in the Underdeveloped World* (New York: Free Press, 1975).

[34]For representative analytical conflict theories, see Ralf Dahrendorf, *Class and Class Conflict in Industrial Societies* (Palo Alto, CA: Stanford University Press, 1967) and "Toward a Theory of Social Conflict," *Journal of Conflict Resolution* 2 (1958), 170–183; and Jonathan H. Turner, "A Strategy for Reformulating Dialectical and Functional Conflict Theories," *Social Forces* 53 (1975), 433–444.

First, the theory is made more abstract, abandoning all of the Marxian terminology, which confines the theory to a particular historical time and place (i.e., industrial capitalism and mobilization by the proletariat against the bourgeoisie). For contemporary Marxist theories, however, such an exercise "takes the Marx out of Marx," but for analytical theorists, the goal is to make Marx's key ideas about the conditions of conflict mobilization relevant to contemporary societies, as well as to societies of the future or distant past. Instead, relations are simply conceptualized as those between superordinates and subordinates in a system of inequality within social systems. Second, in making the ideas of Marx's theory more abstract, it also becomes possible to extend Marx's ideas to any type of social system, such as a group, organization, or community, rather than just a society. Third, all of these more analytical theorists add the necessary correctives to Marx's theory, particularly those suggested by his fellow Germans, Max Weber and Georg Simmel.

The end result is a general theory of conflict mobilization in all social systems revealing inequality in the distribution of resources. The theory then outlines basic conditions (specified by Marx) that sharpen conflicts of interests, increase awareness of subordinates for their interest in changing the system of inequality, mobilize subordinates for conflict, and raise the intensity and violence of the conflict. The biggest correction in Marx's basic theory is that internal violence in a society does not come from highly organized conflict parties but, rather, from situations where the subordinates are just beginning to get organized around counterideologies, competing leaders, escalated negative emotions, and diverse structures channeling subordinates' anger. Under these conditions, conflict can become more violent. In contrast, when subordinates become well organized and instrumental (Marx's notion of a "class for itself"), they are more likely to negotiate and compromise because they are now clearly organized with explicit goals that can only be partially met through compromises.

Fourth, there is also a conscious effort to convert Marx's time bound (in the historical epoch of capitalism) into formally stated principles or abstract laws of conflict. The principles are presumed to be relevant to all times and places and to all social systems revealing inequalities. A group, organization, community, or whole society all can be seen as operating in terms of a common set of laws about conflict mobilization among subordinates in a system of inequality.

A related field of inquiry into the dynamics of social movements also borrows key ideas from Marx in trying to explain the origins and operation of social movements. These theories draw from many other theoretical traditions, such as the symbolic interactionism initiated by Mead, Weber's emphasis on charisma, and variants of economic theory emphasizing resource mobilization and calculations of risks and benefits to be gained from collective participation in social movement organizations.[35] The goal is to explain how shared grievances push individuals to become collectively organized to pursue conflict (of varying types and forms) against the system of authority within various institutional domains such as polity, economy, and religion.

World-Systems Theorizing. This approach shifts the unit of analysis from societies to intersocietal systems.[36] Relations among societies are conceptualized as being stratified in the sense that some societies have more resources than others and are, thereby, able to exploit weaker societies. They often do so by imposing unbalanced systems of trade in which raw resources are taken from dependent societies at low costs and used to generate wealth in the more dominant society, where extracted resources are converted to finished goods and products. Distinctions between geopolitical and geoeconomic systems are often made with the geopolitical system being built by patterns of warfare and conquest and with dominant societies winning wars and controlling the resources of conquered societies. Empire formation is typically the main topic of these geopolitical systems, and their analysis is often conducted under historical-comparative approaches drawing from Weber as much as Marx.

When analysis shifts to geoeconomic systems, however, Marxian ideas become more prominent. In many respects, these geoeconomic theories retain the emancipatory thrust of Marx by emphasizing that the "contradictions" of capitalism will work themselves

---

[35]For examples, see David A. Snow and Sarah A. Soule, *A Primer on Social Movements* (New York: W. W. Norton, 2010).

[36]For well-known and accessible world-system theories, see Christopher Chase-Dunn, *Global Formation: Structures of the World Economy*, 2nd ed. (Lanham, MD: Rowman & Littlefield, 1998); Andrew Gunner Frank, *Crisis in the World Economy* (New York: Holmes & Meier, 1980) and *Reorient: Global Economy in the Asian Age* (Berkeley: University of California Press, 1998); and Immanuel Wallerstein, *The Modern World System*, Vol. 1 (of 3 vols.) (New York: Academic Press, 1974).

out in global economic system. Here, the difficulties of ever forming a strong world-level government like those that operate within individual capitalist societies open the doors for economic actors to use their power and control of world markets to exploit less developed and less powerful societies in a manner predicted by Marx's analysis of capitalist societies. This world-level system of stratification of societies reveals many of the contradictions of capitalism emphasized by Marx and eventually pushes for the mobilization for conflict as workers resent their exploitation and as global markets speculation leads to market collapse. Under these conditions, sectors with exploited societies will mobilize for conflict and seek to form less exploitive intersocietal relations within and between societies. Thus, a good portion of world-system theorists recognize that the contradictions of capitalism have not produced conditions for intrasocietal revolutions, especially in capitalist societies, but the spread of capitalism across the globe has finally, it is believed, generated the conditions where these contradictions of capitalism will be exposed. The result will be conflict at many intra- and intersocietal levels that, in the end, will create world government dedicated to socialism—or so it is hoped by many world-system theorists.

Functional Conflict Theory. For a period in the second half of the twentieth century, especially while the intellectual battle between conflict and functional theories raged on, scholars such as Lewis Coser[37] put "a pox on both of these houses" of thought. The argument was derived primarily from Georg Simmel's emphasis that conflict can have integrative consequences for societies and the parties to the conflict. Conflict theory, it was argued, overemphasized the disintegrative effects of conflict, while functional theory overemphasized the integrative consequences of all social processes to the exclusion of conflict. What was needed, then, is a theoretical perspective—functional conflict theory—that reduces the overemphasis on either disintegrative or integrative processes.

---

[37]See, for example, Lewis A. Coser, *The Functions of Social Conflict* (Glencoe, IL: Free Press, 1956); "Some Social Functions of Violence," *Annals of the American Academy of Political and Social Science* 364 (1966), 8–18; "Some Functions of Deviant Behavior and Normative Flexibility," *American Journal of Sociology* 68 (1962), 172–181; and *Continuities in the Study of Social Conflict* (New York: Free Press, 1967).

With this kind of rhetorical ploy, functional conflict theory, derived from Simmel's thinking and, to a lesser extent, from Weber's sociology, produced a theory emphasizing the causes of conflict (inequality, deprivations, and emotional arousal), the violence of conflict, the duration of conflict, the effects of conflict on the respective parties of conflict, and the consequences of conflict for the more inclusive structure (society) in which conflict has occurred. Similar arguments were made about other social processes, such as deviance, that are typically seen as dysfunctional; instead, these processes can have positive consequences for both individuals and societies. This approach did not last long, but it represented an effort to bring the other two German conflict theories—those formulated by Max Weber and Georg Simmel—into the modern canon.

Interactionist Theorizing

George Herbert Mead's[38] synthesis of pragmatist theories into a general theory of interaction has continued to exert a strong influence on all of micro sociology, although other early masters such as Charles Horton Cooley,[39] Émile Durkheim,[40] and Alfred Schutz[41] are also part of interactionist theorizing as it has developed over the past century. There are now distinctive traditions of interactionist theorizing, some retaining all of Mead's and other approaches introducing new ideas into Mead's general approach. Yet all interactionist theories begin with at least these assumptions, derived from George Herbert Mead:

1. Individuals are born into ongoing social structures and will retain in their behavioral repertoire those behaviors that facilitate adjustment and adaptation to these ongoing patterns of cooperative interpersonal behaviors.

---

[38]For the basic outline of George Herbert Mead's synthesis, as outlined in *Mind, Self, and Society* (Chicago: University of Chicago Press, 1934), see pp. 313–340.

[39]Charles Horton Cooley had been a colleague of Mead at the University of Michigan, early in Mead's career; see pp. 306–310.

[40]Émile Durkheim's analysis of religion, especially emotionally arousing rituals, was never a part of Mead's approach but became important to interactionist theorizing in general in the later decades of the twentieth century.

[41]Alfred Schutz's career extends beyond the time frame adopted in this book (1830–1930), and his work has not been highly influential in mainstream interactionism today, nor in general sociology. Yet it is important in some of its variants, and thus, we are including a mention and, later, a more detailed summary of what we term *phenomenological interactionism*.

2. The behavioral capacities for cooperation with others emerge from a process of imitation, active coaching by caretakers, and biological maturation.

3. The first critical behavioral capacity is learning conventional or significant gestures that mean the same thing to the person emitting the gestures as to the person reading these gestures.

4. With the capacity to understand conventional gestures, individuals can role-take and place themselves in the role of others and thus anticipate their likely actions and, thereby, cooperate with them.

5. With role-taking comes the capacity for mind, or the ability to imaginatively rehearse (in the mind, as it were) consequences of various alternative behaviors, to inhibit those that would be inappropriate, and finally to emit those that would facilitate cooperation.

6. With role-taking, individuals can begin to see themselves as objects in all situations; and by reading the gestures of others, they can derive self-images about how others think of them and adjust their conduct so as to gain a positive evaluation from others.

7. These self-images will, over time, crystallize into more permanent conceptions of self along many dimensions, including how self is viewed in particular roles, in types of situations and social structures, or in all situations (in recent years, these types of selves have been denoted by the concept of the multiple *identities*).

8. Individuals can also role-take with generalized others—or communities of attitudes, or beliefs—and use these in minded deliberations over alternative lines of potential conduct that will verify self and facilitate cooperation.

9. Societies are built by individuals exhibiting these behavioral capacities outlined above, but more important, it is these capacities that enable societies and institutions within them to reproduce themselves.

10. At the same time, existing social structures and their cultures (Mead's generalized others) constrain the significant gestures

that people employ, their role-taking, their minded deliberations, and their sense of self or selves (identities) invoked in interaction, with the result that the behavioral capacities of individuals become aligned with the constraints and demands of social structure and culture.

Symbolic Interactionism. After his death, lecture notes from several years of George Herbert Mead's famous social psychology course at the University of Chicago were edited and bundled into the posthumously published book, *Mind, Self, and Society.* Later, Herbert Blumer, who had actually taken over Mead's course in the semester when he died, began to use the label "symbolic interactionism" to describe Mead-inspired theories.[42] These theories emphasized that humans create symbols to denote aspects of the social world, to role-take with various others including generalized others (culture), and to use what they learn in role-taking to select courses of action that will facilitate cooperation. Humans also see images of self in the gestures of others (Charles Horton Cooley's famous notion of the "looking-glass self"), and on the basis of these images, they experience emotions about how others evaluate them. All of these processes enable individuals to construct societies from the behavioral capacities for mind and self.

Almost immediately, as it evolved into a coherent theoretical perspective in the mid-twentieth century, symbolic interactionism split into two general camps. One emphasized that symbolic interactionism can develop scientific theory to explain even the seemingly fluid social processes of interaction, while the other argued that this fluidity is not amenable to the formulation of scientific laws but, instead, to only a general sensitizing conceptual scheme for describing empirical events. Most of those who held to this latter epistemology employed qualitative research methods involving thick descriptions of interaction processes, explained with the vocabulary in Mead's (and later symbolic interactionists') conceptualizations of how humans interact with each other. But those who advocated scientific use of symbolic interactionist ideas adopted more quantitative methods in experimental research designs and began to emphasize identities as the key dynamic in human interaction and, ultimately, in the building up of social structure and culture.

---

[42]See Herbert Blumer, *Symbolic Interactionism* (Englewood Cliffs, NJ: Prentice Hall, 1969).

Identity Theories. All symbolic interactionist theories emphasize self as the basic gyroscope of behavior and interaction, but the more scientifically oriented symbolic interactionists began to conceptualize self as a series of identities that individuals present in various situations and that they seek to have verified in the eyes of others.[43] Several levels of identity have been theorized:[44] (1) role identities (for roles that people play), (2) group identities (or social structures to which people belong or to which they identify if they do not actually belong), (3) social identities (about the social categories such as gender and/or ethnicity to which people belong), (4) moral identities (tied to values and beliefs about what is right and proper), and (5) core identities (about the person as an individual). These identities obviously vary by their scope. Role identities are tied to just one specific role, while group identities are built around distinct groups. In contrast, social, moral, and core identities can be invoked in virtually all situations and, thus, are very general and portable to any group or role that a person may play.

These identities also vary in their importance to individuals, and, to some extent, they can be arranged as a hierarchy of "salience" or "prominence."[45] Those identities high in the hierarchy are more likely to be presented to others, but if a person cannot have an identity verified, this identity is likely to fall down the hierarchy or the individual will seek out others who are willing to verify the identity. Identity theories also emphasize emotions—a topic that Mead virtually ignored—as will be examined in the section Theories of Emotions.

Role Theories. At one time, theories of role dynamics were quite common in the social sciences, especially sociology and psychology. Within sociology, they had a symbolic interactionist bias, emphasizing the process of role-taking (determining the behavior dispositions of others) and, in Ralph Turner's works,[46] role-making as the complement of

---

[43]For examples, see Peter J. Burke and Jan E. Stets, *Identity Theory* (Oxford, UK: Oxford University Press, 2009); George McCall and J. L. Simmons, *Identities and Interactions* (New York: Free Press, 1978); and Sheldon S. Stryker, *Symbolic Interactionism: A Social Structural Version* (Menlo Park, CA: Benjamin-Cummings, 2002).

[44]Jonathan H. Turner, *Theoretical Principles of Sociology*, Vol. 2 (New York: Springer, 2010).

[45]See McCall and Simmons, *Identities and Interactions*, and Stryker, *Symbolic Interactionism*.

[46]Ralph H. Turner, "Role Taking: Process vs. Conformity," in *Human Behavior and Social Processes*, ed. A. Rose (Boston: Houghton Mifflin, 1962) and "Role Theory" in *Handbook of Sociological Theory*, ed. Jonathan H. Turner (New York: Kluwer Academic/Plenum, 2006).

Mead's concept of role-taking (emitting gestures to signal the role that self is trying to play). There has also been a more phenomenological element (see discussion in the next section) to role theory, emphasizing that individuals assume in any interaction that others are trying to play an identifiable role; and so they are generally willing to postpone judgments about another's behavior until they discern the role that is being made or presented by this person. Individuals have in their stocks of knowledge inventories of various types and variants of roles, and thus role-taking involves reading the role-making gestures of others and then scanning these cognitive inventories of roles to determine the role that a person is seeking to make.

Like any symbolic interactionist approach, there is always an emphasis on self in the role-taking and role-making processes. Individuals always try to present self to others, and one of the principle vehicles for doing so is through role-making. Individuals are thus very motivated to have their roles verified by others because a sense of self or, in more contemporary terms, an identity or a set of identities is almost always at stake in making roles. As will be evident below, role theories blend into dramaturgical theories because they emphasize that culture provides a script for how to play a role, but this role must be played on a stage in front of an audience that also has expectations for how roles should be played. Individuals are given a certain amount of dramatic license in playing roles because they also must verify an identity in each of their performances on stage.

Roles are also a point of connection between individuals, on the one hand, and social structure, on the other. Individuals seek to play roles that meet the cultural expectations and normative requirements attached to status positions in social structures. Roles are not, however, mere behaviors that meet the expectations attached to status locations in social structures; they are also used strategically to receive valued resources and to verify self. As a result, role enactments can change social structure and culture, especially if many individuals seek to do so.

The most recent work on roles has emphasized that roles can be used as resources that can be deployed to gain access to other valued resources, and thus the strategic dimension of roles has gained more emphasis in recent years.[47] And thus, from Mead's early work and

---

[47]Peter Callero "From Role-Playing to Role-Using: Understanding Role as Resource," *Social Psychology Quarterly* 57 (1994), 228–243.

then from efforts of theorists in the early and late twentieth century to develop a theory of roles, there exists a rather sophisticated set of theoretical generalizations about role dynamics. Yet, over the past 30 years, theorizing has emphasized status processes over role dynamics, as will be examined later in Structuralist Theorizing.

Dramaturgical Theorizing. Like role theories, dramaturgical approaches often make an analogy to the theater. There is a cultural script of norms and beliefs (ideologies); there is a cast or team of actors playing roles outlined by the cultural script; there is a stage that makes available various props to be used in dramatic presentations of self and that determines the ecology of performances; and there is an audience who evaluate actors' performances. Unlike most symbolic interactionist perspectives, however, the importance of self and identities is given less emphasis as the central dynamic around which interaction revolves. Instead, self is less enduring and transitory, becoming part of the performance on a stage. And like any part of a dramatic performance, it can be altered and discarded for another self if required by the cultural script. In fact, self is presented strategically to carry off a performance.

Apart from the metaphor to the theater, dramaturgical theories emphasize that interactions occur in encounters that, in turn, are typically lodged inside more inclusive social units.[48] Encounters can be focused, whereby individuals face each other and mutually respond to each other's talk and body language. Encounters are often unfocused, typically occurring in public spaces where persons monitor each other's movements but avoid face-to-face engagement and talk. Because encounters are embedded in larger social structures, the script is often written by the culture of this structure, with each encounter representing an opportunity and obligation to present an appropriate self to others and to play roles, talk, and emote in accordance with the cultural script.

It is through encounters that social structures and their cultures are built and reproduced over time, and once in place, these sociocultural formations constrain the dynamics of encounters

---

[48]Erving Goffman, *The Presentation in Everyday Life* (Garden City, NY: Anchor Books, 1959); *Encounters: Two Studies in the Sociology of Interaction* (Indianapolis, IN: Bobbs-Merrill, 1961); *Interaction Ritual* (Garden City, NY: Anchor Books, 1967); *Behavior in Public Places* (New York: Free Press, 1963); and *Relations in Public* (New York: Harper & Row, 2009).

by providing the stage and the script for dramatic performances. Interaction in focused encounters then proceeds by successfully categorizing the type of interactions along several dimensions, such as (a) the relative amounts of work—practical, social, or ceremonial content in the interaction; (b) the level of appropriate intimacy or formality; (c) the social categories (gender, ethnicity, age) of self and others; (d) the forms of appropriate talk; (e) the rituals that are to be used to open, structure, and close the encounter; (f) the feelings that should be felt and displayed; (g) the particular roles that should be taken up; (h) the situational props that can be used; (i) the appropriate spacing among participants; and (j) the type of self that can or should be presented. In unfocused encounters, the emphasis is more on (a) the appropriate spacing of individuals in an ecological setting, (b) the proper movements through space and use of available props, (c) the avoidance of face-to-face engagement and talk, and (d) the use of proper rituals when face-to-face engagement inadvertently occurs or when unintended violations of spacing occur.[49]

Theories of Emotions. Because George Herbert Mead did not analyze emotions, they were not part of most interactionist theories for two thirds of the twentieth century. If Charles Horton Cooley[50] had been the dominant theorist in the symbolic interactionist tradition, the study of emotions such as shame and pride would have become part of theorizing, and the sociology of emotions would have emerged in the early decades of the twentieth century. Interactionist theories are not the only theories that include emotions, but it is within this theoretical tradition that theorizing on the dynamics of emotions emerged in the 1970s.

Dramaturgical theories were an early perspective in which emotions were analyzed. Scholars like Erving Goffman, the founder of this approach, emphasized that emotions such as embarrassment emerge when individuals breach the smooth flow of the encounter, forcing them to offer repair rituals to restore the micro order. Others like Arlie Hochschild[51] combined dramaturgical and Marxist

---

[49]Jonathan H. Turner, *Human Emotions: A Sociological Theory* (London: Routledge, 2007).

[50]Charles Horton Cooley, *Human Nature and Social Order* (New York: Charles Scribner's, 1902).

[51]Arlie Hochschild, *The Managed Heart: The Commercialization of Human Feeling* (Berkeley: University of California Press, 1983).

theorizing by emphasizing that there is an *emotion culture* in a society, composed of emotion ideologies (about the emotions that should be felt and expressed in various types of situations), feeling rules about the specific emotions that should be experienced by individuals in different types of situations, and display rules about the specific emotions that should be displayed in various roles. Moreover, because modern, market-driven societies often require that individuals display emotions that they do not feel, a great many encounters—particularly those associated with work—involve a considerable amount of "emotion work" in which individuals try, at a minimum, to display the appropriate emotions and, if they can, to feel these emotions. Such emotion work is inherently alienating because individuals often feel the opposite of the emotions that must be displayed, thereby forcing them to engage in alienated labor, which only increases their emotional burden.

Symbolic interactionists also began to emphasize emotions in the 1970s, along several lines of inquiry.[52] One was the view that individuals seek to sustain consistency among their cognitions and emotions about self, situations, others, and behaviors; and when there is inconsistency among these elements of all interaction situations, individuals will experience negative emotions and be motivated to bring conceptions of self, behaviors, situation, and others back into line. Another way was to emphasize that all individuals seek to have their identities verified by others in situations. When an identity is accepted by others, persons will experience positive emotions, whereas when an identity is not verified by others in a situation, individuals will adopt various strategies to bring their identities, behavioral outputs, and perceptions of others' responses to these outputs back in line; if they cannot, they may have to change identities, change behaviors, or leave the situation where their identities cannot be verified. A third line of inquiry involved blending more psychoanalytic ideas with interactionist theories. The goal of the more psychoanalytic variants of symbolic interactionisms is to emphasize that negative emotions in general, and negative emotions about self in particular, are highly painful and are often pushed below the level of consciousness. These repressed emo-

---

[52]See for detailed summaries of these approaches, Jonathan H. Turner and Jan E. Stets, *The Sociology of Emotions* (Cambridge, UK: Cambridge University Press, 2005); and Jan E. Stets and Jonathan H. Turner, *Handbook of the Sociology of Emotions* (New York: Springer, 2006).

tions, however, can be transmuted (e.g., repressed shame may show up as anger) and almost always intensified; and the result is that the flow of interaction is always influenced by the emotions that break through the mechanisms of repression. And moreover, if sufficiently large numbers of individuals experience similar emotions and repress them, these emotions can have large effects on social structures and cultures when they emerge collectively.

Phenomenological Theories. The term phenomenology generally denotes the study of consciousness. In Germany, a philosophical school with this name emerged under the influence of Edmund Husserl.[53] Alfred Schutz,[54] converted Husserl's ideas into a more sociological approach that continues to inspire sociology because it converges with Mead's sociology. Husserl's philosophical project emphasized that the external world "out there" is mediated through the senses as these register on people's consciousness. Prior to any question about the nature of this external world, then, is the question of how consciousness works since the world "out there" is filtered through consciousness. He began using the terms "world of the natural attitude," later shortened to lifeworld, to emphasize that humans take for granted much of the world around them. Moreover, this lifeworld is reality for humans; and the critical points for the more sociological application of his ideas are that (a) the lifeworld is taken for granted and yet it structures people's thoughts and perceptions of what is real and (b) that the lifeworld promotes the presumption among humans that they share the same experiences of the world "out there." This lifeworld is the essence of consciousness, but the

---

[53]Edmund Husserl, *Phenomenology and the Crisis of Western Philosophy* (New York: Harper & Row, 1965 [1936]) is the best statement of his philosophy, but the philosophy itself developed many years earlier.

[54]Alfred Schutz, *The Phenomenology of the Social World* (Evanston, IL: Northwestern University Press, 1967 [1932]). Schutz was a young scholar when he wrote this work, but it came out 2 years before Mead's collated lectures in *Mind, Self, and Society*. One can see immediately the differences between Mead's pragmatist philosophical background and Schutz's phenomenological approach, but they are, in reality, addressing similar processes of interaction and society. Schutz was not included in the classical canon because he was never part of sociology until the mid- to late twentieth-century sociology, when interactionist approaches drawing from phenomenology began to appear. See also Alfred Schutz and Thomas Luckmann, *The Structure of the Lifeworld* (Evanston, IL: Northwestern University Press, 1973); and Thomas Luckmann, ed. *Phenomenology and Sociology* (New York: Penguin Books, 1978). Schutz's collected papers are found in Alfred Schutz, *Collected Papers I, II, III* (The Hague, Netherlands: Marinus Nijhoff, 1962, 1963, and 1966).

substance of this consciousness is less important than the process of consciousness, per se. Husserl then set about a philosophical project of trying to discover "pure mind" or the fundamental nature of consciousness by divorcing the substance of consciousness from the processes of consciousness. The project inevitably stalled, but it was taken up by Alfred Schutz to build a more sociologically informed phenomenological theory.

Phenomenological Interactionism. Schutz took the basic problematic portions of Husserl's phenomenology and first blended it with Max Weber's concerns with action and verstehen and later with elements of symbolic interactionism. Schutz's critique of Weber was the latter's failure to explain how individuals come to experience the world subjectively and how intersubjectivity emerges—that is, how do people come to feel that they are experiencing the same world. His theory parallels Mead's analysis of role-taking and perhaps even the notion of a "generalized other," but early pragmatists philosophers like Mead did not have a great influence on Schutz's early formulation of phenomenological sociology. His basic argument is that humans operate under the presumption of "reciprocity of perspectives" and the presumption of sharing a common world, despite unique biographical experiences. This presumption allows individuals to engage in the process of "typification," where others and situations are portrayed as having certain basic qualities.

In this manner, people come to act *as if* they see the world in similar ways and to believe that they can treat others and the situation *as if* it had common properties understood by all. By making these presumptions, individuals can interact and engage in cooperative behaviors. Thus, it is not so critical that individuals actually achieve true intersubjectivity; it is only necessary that they *think that they have* achieved intersubjectivity.

Ethnomethodology. It is this line of thinking that provided one of the key ideas for contemporary ethnomethodology. Founded by Harold Garfinkel[55] and carried forth by his students, this approach empha-

---

[55]Harold Garfinkel, *Studies in Ethnomethodology* (Englewood Cliffs, NJ: Prentice Hall, 1967). For more readable summaries of this approach, see Warren Handel, *Ethnomethodology: How People Make Sense* (Englewood Cliffs, NJ: Prentice Hall, 1982); George Psathas, ed. *Everyday Language Studies: Studies in Ethnomethodology* (New York: Irvington, 1979); and Roy Turner, ed. *Ethnomethodology* (Baltimore: Penguin Books, 1974).

sizes that individuals use a series of "folk methods"—hence, the name ethnomethodology—to sustain the illusion that they experience a common world. Unlike Mead's work, where emphasis was on reading gestures to place oneself in the other's role so as to anticipate the latter's behaviors, individuals employ a series of interpersonal techniques or methods that allow them to perceive and believe that they share a common world, without actually questioning this presumption. The goal of ethnomethodology is to isolate these ethnomethods.

One of the common research strategies became the "breaching experiment" in which the experimenter would deliberately break the presumption of intersubjectivity to see how others tried to use ethnomethods to reconstruct the presumption of intersubjectivity. Early research looked promising as a number of such methods were uncovered by carefully reviewing transcripts of conversation of people in interaction, and while this approach still continues, it now has less theoretical impact than it did in the last third of the twentieth century.

Exchange Theorizing

Exchange theorizing does not have its roots in the classical tradition of sociology, except perhaps indirectly via Adam Smith in economics and behaviorism in psychology. Adam Smith's[56] work had its greatest effect on the early masters of sociological theorizing in the question he posed in his *The Theory of Moral Sentiments:* If the social world is differentiating and becoming more complex, individuals are living out their lives and daily routines in somewhat different niches in society and, thus, are experiencing different social worlds. If such is the case, what "force" can integrate social relations among these individuals? The force emphasized in *The Theory of Moral Sentiments* is, as the title suggests, a common morality of beliefs and values, but Smith's other answer in *The Wealth of Nations* is that the pursuit of self-interest in markets miraculously reveals an "invisible hand of order" promoting social equilibrium, just as it does for prices in markets. Sociologists of the nineteenth century were highly skeptical of this second argument, as are many contemporary sociologists. The first argument in *Moral Sentiments*, however, was in essence functional theorizing, especially in the French tradition of Comte

---

[56]For a discussion of Adam Smith in this book, see pp. 101–102.

and Durkheim. But the notion of life as a kind of marketplace where social relations are, in essence, exchanges of resources can certainly be found in Smith, even if most classical theorists did not pursue this lead. Only Karl Marx, who sought to improve on Smith's analysis of market dynamics in capitalism, appears to have paid much attention to Smith. But the notion of individuals seeking utility, or reward value, was not pursued as a general model of social life until well into the twentieth century.[57]

The other indirect route to exchange theory comes from behaviorism, which owes its initial inspiration to Ivanovich Pavlov in Russia and Edward Thorndike in America. Here, organisms are seen as retaining those behavioral responses to stimuli that have brought rewards and abandoning those that fail to bring gratification or imposed punishment. Only George Herbert Mead,[58] who considered himself to be a *social* behaviorist, pursued this idea among the pantheon of classical sociological theorists. Mead reacted against what became known as behaviorism in the early twentieth century because of its extreme assumptions: Speculation about behaviors and psychological processes that cannot be directly observed is *not* subject matter of behaviorist theorizing; thus, the "black box "of nonobservables— human thought, emotions, and cognition—must be ignored in favor of theories that explain the effects of only *observable* stimuli on *observable* behaviors. For Mead, however, many of the key behavioral capacities of humans—use of significant gestures, role-taking, minded deliberations, and conceptions of self—are not directly observable but are nonetheless critical to understanding human behavior and society. Hence, he added the adjective "social" to his form of behaviorism—hence, social behaviorism—in order to distinguish it from the extreme assumptions of behaviorism in American psychology.

Yet, despite Mead's sympathy for a more social behaviorism, sociologists stayed away from extreme behaviorism in psychology, and coupled with sociologists' antipathy for overly economic and utilitarian views of rational and maximizing actors as the best model

---

[57]Vilfredo Pareto, an early economist who by the turn of the twentieth century became a general sociological theorist and whose ideas are still prominent in neoclassical economics, certainly understood the arguments of the utilitarians like Adam Smith, but in many ways, his sociology is a repudiation of the limitations of classical and, hence, neoclassical economics today.

[58]See pp. 298–300 for a review of the behaviorism that influenced Mead.

for understanding social action, it is not surprising that exchange theorizing was a late arrival to contemporary sociological theory. In the 1950s, however, exchange theories began to appear in sociology, and as this theoretical perspective developed, each theory tended to begin with either the assumptions of utilitarianism or behaviorism. These two perspectives converge on a number of assumptions, the most important of which are as follows:

1. The actions of individuals and collective actors are driven by needs for rewards or utilities.

2. The more rewarding or the more utilities to be gained from social relationships, the more likely are individuals and collective actors to pursue lines of conduct and action that secure these rewards.

3. Individuals assess the reward value of alternative lines of behavior and choose that which offers the most, if not maximum, reward.

4. The more valuable the rewards received are to the individuals, the more likely are these individuals to pursue conduct allowing them to receive these valuable rewards.

5. Individuals will implicitly or explicitly calculate the costs (alternative sources of rewards forgone or resources that must be given up) and the investments (accumulated costs) in pursuing a line of conduct, and they will always seek to make a "profit" in the resources received. A profit is the value of the resources received less the costs and investments to get them, and those lines of conduct that yield the most profit are the most likely to be pursued.

6. The more of a reward of a given type has been received in the recent past, the more will an individual's preferences for this reward decline, and the less valuable to an actor will this reward become. In psychology this is the principle of "satiation," whereas in economics it is described as "marginal utility"; still, the dynamic is the same for both perspectives: The more of a reward that a person gets, the less valuable it becomes, or the less utility is has for actors.

7. Individuals and collective actors thus exchange resources, giving up some as costs to receive resources from others; and

most resources in human interaction are intrinsic (e.g., affection, approval, prestige and honor, liking, self-verification), although some are also extrinsic (e.g., money, power).

8. Individuals and collective actors assess the "fairness" and "justice" of the resources that they received relative to their costs and investments, and they can invoke a number of different comparison points or standards for making this justice calculation. (For instance, they may invoke general cultural norms specifying what is fair; they may compare their rewards with those actors incurring equivalent costs and investments; they may use a sense of the rewards that they could have received in an alternative exchange; or they may invoke as a comparison point the rewards that they expected to receive relative to the rewards that they actually received.)

9. When payoffs to a person or collective actor fall below any of the several comparison points that can be invoked to assess the fairness, individuals (and individuals making decisions for collective actors) will experience negative emotions and seek to renegotiate the exchange; they may pursue any number of strategies in these renegotiations, including punishing (and thus incurring costs on) those who have failed to provide a fair and just reward or, alternatively, seeking new exchange partners who will provide a fairer level of reward.

For sociological exchange theories, all social relations are driven by these basic assumptions listed above. And all social structures and cultures are ultimately built from the actions of individual and collective actors behaving in ways outlined by these assumptions. Yet, within exchange theories, despite the common set of assumptions, theories emphasize different aspects of the exchange process.

One exchange approach termed *rational choice theory* follows the utilitarian model, emphasizing that individuals seek to maximize their utilities and minimize their costs.[59] There are many different versions of rational choice theorizing, but they all emphasize that social relations and social structures are created when actors

---

[59]For prominent examples, see James Coleman, *Foundations of Social Theory* (Cambridge, MA: Harvard University Press, 1990); and Michael Hechter, *Principles of Group Solidarity* (Berkeley: University of California Press, 1988).

perceive that they can lower "negative externalities" (or costs) and thereby increase their profits in exchanges. For example, if individuals are engaged in concerted and coordinated action, one negative externality is that some do not contribute their fair share effort to the outcome but still receive the same utilities as those who have; and as a result of this type of negative externality, actors will develop norms, monitoring, and sanctioning procedures to ensure that individuals do not "free ride." Thus, social structures and cultures are built to decrease negative externalities and, thereby, to ensure that each actor is contributing his or her (or its) fair share of effort to coordinated tasks.

Other approaches emphasize *power dynamics*.[60] Actors who have highly valued resources that are scarce and in high demand always enjoy an advantage over those who have needs for these resources. The result is that those who hold valued resources will begin to impose higher costs on those who seek these highly valued resources by demanding more resources from these dependent actors. In many ways, this is the power dynamic emphasized by Karl Marx. In Marx's theory, capitalists are in a position to exploit labor because they have a resource that is difficult to attain (money), while workers have a resource that is in oversupply (labor or willingness to work). The capitalist can thus offer less money than the work is actually worth (by Marx's "labor theory of value") and, thereby, make a profit when the capitalist sells the goods that are produced by exploited workers. All exchange theories that examine power dynamics follow Marx in recognizing that when exploitation by powerful actors occurs, those at a disadvantage seek to reduce their exploitation by a variety of strategies, including leaving the exchange relationship, seeking alternative sources for a highly valued resource, learning to do without a resource, collectively mobilizing to make their resources more valuable to exploiters or by agreeing to hold resources back from exploiters, or mobilizing to pursue conflict that will impose high costs on exploiters. Thus, exchange theories that emphasize the power dynamic in exchanges converge with conflict theories examined earlier.

Exchange dynamics have been added to other theoretical traditions. For instance, some symbolic interactionist[61] theories recog-

---

[60]Peter M. Blau, *Exchange and Power in Social Life* (New York: Wiley, 1964); Richard Emerson, "Power-Dependence Relations," *American Sociological Review* 27 (1962), 31–41.

[61]For example, McCall and Simmons, *Identities and Interactions.*

nize that approval and verification of self are highly valued rewards, and individuals always calculate implicitly whether or not others in situations are providing enough of this valued reward relative to the resources that must be given up to receive approval. Another example is the piggybacking of exchange ideas to network theories (summarized later in the chapter), where relations among points in a network (actors) are viewed as resource flows governed by exchange assumptions.[62] If actors must give up too many resources to secure resources in a given network, they will engage in balancing actions that increase the sense of fairness in the network and, in the process, change the structure of the network itself and the flow of resources among actors. As noted earlier, conflict theory has always had an implicit exchange dynamic, and some more contemporary theories have made this exchange process more explicit. Theories in the sociology of emotions have adopted exchange ideas, especially the notion that when exchanges are seen as unfair, deprived parties will experience a variety of negative emotions and engage in behaviors to ensure that they receive some profit in their exchanges with others.[63] Thus, although exchange theory was not prominent in the early sociological canon, it can now be found virtually everywhere in current theorizing, either as an explicit exchange theory or as a new element in an older theoretical tradition.

Structuralist Theorizing

Since the study of social structures is one of the defining features of sociology, it should not be surprising that there are numerous theories on this topic. Indeed, almost all sociological theories emphasize social structure, to some degree, and thus it becomes a somewhat arbitrary exercise to isolate a few general types of theories that can be labeled "structuralist theories." Among the early masters, several distinctive modes of structural inquiry emerged and have been carried forward.

---

[62]See, for examples, Emerson, "Power-Dependence Relations"; Karen S. Cook, Richard M. Emerson, Mary R. Gillmore, and Toshio Yamagishi, "The Distribution of Power in Exchange Networks: Theory and Experimental Results," *American Journal of Sociology* 89 (1983), 275–305; David Willer and Pamela Emanuelson, "Elementary Theory," in *Contemporary Social Psychological Theories*, ed. Peter J. Burke (Palo Alto, CA: Stanford University Press, 2006).

[63]Edward J. Lawler, Shane Thye, and Jeongkoo Yoon, *Social Commitments in a Depersonalized World* (New York: Russell Sage, 2009).

One of the most enduring structural approaches comes from functionalist theories such as those developed by Comte,[64] Spencer,[65] and Durkheim,[66] where structure is conceptualized in terms of patterns of differentiation among institutional domains, and among social units in these domains. Another related approach was initiated by Weber[67] who emphasized that structure is built from patterns of action among actors that generate inequalities and stratification, systems of power and domination, social orders that link organizations together, and legitimization through cultural beliefs. When stated at this level of abstraction, Weber's ideas converge with those of Marx who emphasized that social structure is built from inequalities in the distribution of resources. The dynamics of societies are thus played out as the contradictions within the system of inequality, legitimatized by culture, and as enforced by polity emerge and set off the process of conflict. This vision of structure emphasizes that relations to the means of production are the core of social structures, with other structures such as the state and cultural forces such as ideologies being superstructures arising from the economic base of societies.

Émile Durkheim's sociology inspired several views of structure.[68] One emphasized the number, nature, and relations among the parts making up a society, a line of thinking that converges with Simmel's[69] and, as we will see, modern-day network analysis. Another view of structure is the emphasis on how patterns of social structure shape individuals' mental categories about fundamental dimensions of the world such as time, causality, classifications, and space. People's cognitive categories will, therefore, reflect the patterns of social structure as they organize routines over time and in space.[70]

This argument influenced the emergence of various versions of structuralism. One version flipped Durkheim's approach on its head,

---

[64]See pp. 35–40 for Comte's conception of social structure.

[65]See pp. 66–79 for Spencer's evolutionary conception of social structure.

[66]See pp. 260–267 for Durkheim's conception of social structure, which, while looking similar to Spencer's, was to be used in many different ways in structural analysis inside and outside of sociology.

[67]Weber's conception of social structure is best captured in Figures 9.2, 9.3, and 9.7.

[68]See Note 66.

[69]See pp. 209–218, 230–234 for Simmel's conception of social structure.

[70]The outline for this view of structure appeared in Émile Durkheim and Marcel Mauss, *Primitive Classification* (London: Cohen & West, 1963[1903]).

viewing patterns of structure as reflections of "deeper structures" lodged in human neurology.[71] Another, less dramatic version, is an emphasis on viewing existing structures and their cultures as deeper structural principles inhering in social relations. This approach converges with Marx's view of superstructures reflecting the operation of economic structures.

Georg Simmel's[72] view of structure as forms of social relationships in which the properties of relationships are more significant than the nature of the units in these relationships represented a radical break from early sociological views of structure. This kind of thinking would inspire contemporary network theory, where the patterns of relations among nodes units are more important than the nature of the units or nodes in these relationships.

George Herbert Mead's more micro view of structure as institutionalized patterns of relationships that are produced and reproduced by the behavioral capacities of individuals represents a final view of social structure.[73] Here, the capacity to role-take with others and with generalized others, to evaluate self from the perspective of generalized others (or cultural beliefs), and to make minded deliberation in order to select lines of conduct facilitating cooperation all signal that micro-level processes must be a part of structural analysis. Other, more micro traditions, such as psychoanalytical theories and dramaturgical theories, have also been incorporated into this form of analysis initiated by Mead.

---

[71]*Primitive Classification* is a work that had little direct influence in sociology but it set off structuralisms as a broad intellectual movement in the twentieth century. Even Ferdinand de Saussure, *Course in General Linguistics* (New York: McGraw-Hill, 1966[1915]) and Roman Jakobson [see his collected works in *Philosophical Studies*, multiple volumes (The Hague, Netherlands: 1971) but written decades before]; these founders of structural linguistics and grandfathers of structuralism considered themselves to be more Durkheimian. Yet Claude Lévi-Strauss hinted in *The Elementary Structures of Kinship* (Paris: University of France, 1969) what was to come. Still, as he pursued a linguistic analysis borrowing from Durkheim, de Saussure, and Jakobson, he turned Durkheim and all earlier structural analysis "on their heads" in works such as *Myth and Meaning* (New York: Schocken, 1979) and *A World on the Wane* (London: Hutchinson, 1961), arguing that structures come from mental categories and principles of the brain rather than the reverse.

[72]Simmel's methodology arguing for a formal sociology, summarized on pp. 262–269, offers the best glimpse of this conception of social structure that was later adopted by network analysis.

[73]See Note 39 on Mead's views.

Structural analysis, however, has moved in many different directions. Still, they all share a small number of assumptions:

1. Structure represents a set of relations among social units that persists over time.

2. These relations among units can take many different forms, and it is the nature of connections among units that is essential to understanding the dynamics of social structure.

3. Sometimes the nature of the units is critical in understanding the relationships that make up social structures, but at other times, the only critical information is knowledge about the dynamics of relations, per se, regardless of the units standing in these relationships.

4. Relations among units evolve from varying sources, including (a) relations of power, (b) neurology of the human brain, (c) human behavioral propensities as they affect social interaction, (d) systems of cultural symbols, and (e) means of economic production.

This obvious lack of shared assumptions would indicate that structural theories are a rather eclectic mix of approaches, none of which has ever gained dominance. In many ways, the lack of consensus over how to analyze the central topic of sociology—social structure—indicates how much more theoretical work must be done in the discipline. Indeed, sociologists often talk as if the notion of structure is so obvious that it requires no conceptualization, but, in fact, it is probably sociology's most used and, yet, least defined concept. And even when "structure" is the focus of theorizing, it will be evident that these specific theories remain, for the most part, rather vague.

Structuralism. This approach has a number of variants, but the general goal is to discover the underlying structures that generate surface empirical regularities that can be observed and measured. It is assumed that social regularities in patterns of social relationships are generated by less visible, underlying structures and that, until the principles of these underlying structures are discovered, empirical social structures cannot be fully explained. Much of the imagery of this approach was adopted from structural linguistics in which languages are compared and analyzed for their underlying forms in an effort to discover which languages are related to each other and from which older root languages related languages have evolved.[74] Structuralism became a broader intellectual movement outside of sociology, penetrating fields such as cultural anthropology, English, linguistics and languages, and sociology.[75] There emerged three variants: (1) those theories that searched for the underlying principles of social structures, (2) those that sought for the underlying cultural principles directing both culture and empirical social structures, and (3) those that argued that social structures and their cultures are generated by the underlying neurology of the human brain.

Network Theory. This approach to theorizing social structure has its origins outside of sociology, but it was adopted by sociologists by the mid-twentieth century. By employing matrices that indicated who forms relations with whom in variously sized groups, the network patterns among those forming relationships could be drawn. Most of the early work was done in social psychological theory, derived from Gestalt psychology, but adopting mathematical conventions of digraph theory where actors were points in a network connected by lines indicating direction of positive or negative relations. With the use of computers, much more complicated matrices could be developed revealing relations among large numbers of individual or collective actors. Key properties of networks such as their size (number of nodes and relations), density (extent to which all possible relations among nodes are present in the network), cliques (subdensities of actors in the overall network), centrality (the extent to which resources flow through particular nodes in the network), bridges (nodes that connect to cliques or subnetworks), and brokerage nodes (that distribute resources across gaps between networks or subnetworks) were viewed to drive the dynamics of networks, and, hence, all social structures.[76] While

---

[74]See references to Jakobson and de Saussure in Note 71.

[75]None of this theorizing took a firm hold and was dying out by the end of the 1970s, although much of the imagery remained. See, for an overview from various authors, Ino Rossi, ed., *Structural Sociology* (New York: Columbia University Press, 1984). For a more general review, see Mirian Glucksmann, *Structural Analysis in Contemporary Social Thought* (London: Routledge, 1974).

[76]For early network worlds in sociology and anthropology, see S. F. Nadel, *The Study of Social Structures* (London: Cohen and West, 1957); and J. Clyde Mitchell, "The Concept and Use of Social Networks," in *Network Analysis: Studies of Human Interaction* (The Hague, Netherlands: Mouton, 1973); for more recent network theoretical works, see Ronald Burt, "Models of Network Structure," *Annual Review of Sociology* 6 (1980), 79–141; and Stanley Wasserman and Katherine Faust, *Network Analysis: Models and Methods* (Cambridge, UK: Cambridge University Press, 1994).

network analysis holds great potential, most work has been on the methodology for describing networks through computer programs; comparatively little theorizing within network analysis proper has been developed, although a number of other theoretical perspectives in sociology, such as exchange theorizing, has incorporated network principles and provided some explanatory power to network sociology.

Structuration Theory. Some structuralist theories emphasize that structure is a mix of discursive practices and actions that generates structural principles that are used to organize social actions and to regulate talk and thinking at the micro level of social organization. The actions of individuals guided by these structural principles are, on the one hand, constrained and thus more likely to reproduce structures. On the other hand, actors always have some capacity for agency to change, if only slightly, structural principles that guide their actions. Some of these approaches blend into cultural theories summarized below, or structuralist theories outlined earlier. In both cases, theorizing emphasizes that individuals create systems of cultural codes, often as the result of underlying cognitive structures of the human brain, that drive the formations of social structures. Others are more purely Durkheimian and emphasize that the cultural codes of social groups have large effects on the basic cognitive capacities of humans and on how they think and act. These approaches are not, however, fully in the camp of structuralism examined earlier. They typically add more elements.

For example, Anthony Giddens's structuration theory[77] emphasizes that there are structural principles or general cultural conceptions of social organization that constrain the formation of structural sets, which are bundles of rules and resources that are used by individuals to form social relations. As these principles and sets are used by agents and reproduced over time, they create the structural properties or the institutional systems of a society. There are, of course, structural contradictions in these structural properties because structural principles and sets are rarely without inconsistencies and conflicts of meaning and intent. And so, as institutional systems evolve, they almost always carry contradictions that, over time, become the focus for conflict and mobilization for change, as Marx would have emphasized.

---

[77]Anthony Giddens, *The Constitution of Society* (Berkeley: University of California Press, 1984).

There is always a certain vagueness in these kinds of structuralist theories, but the goal is to recognize that social structures have a cultural basis, emphasizing that structural principles that undergird everything are sets of ideas that channel the actions of agents as they mobilize resources to form structural properties of a society. They are much like a blueprint, but a blueprint in the categories of the mind that have combined key ideas into structural principles and sets and that outline how elements of culture and social structure are to be put together. Yet they are not as explicit as a blueprint; they operate more covertly by constraining both perceptions and behaviors as actors build social structures or act within structures that have already been built.

Cultural Theorizing

As these structuralist theories were emerging, so was a movement toward a more explicit analysis of culture. Conflict theories had tended to see culture as a "superstructure," to use Marx's terms, when it reemerged in American sociology in the 1960s. Yet Max Weber had clearly argued that culture operates as an independent force in societies, as did Émile Durkheim. Weber's analysis of religion in general and Protestantism in particular underscores the causal power of culture, while Durkheim's early emphasis on the collective conscience is, in essence, an analysis of the power of culture. Indeed, even within conflict theory, some of the newer theories are quite conscious of cultural forces. But the intellectual movement toward reintroducing cultural theorizing wanted more: the recognition that culture is a force *in its own right*. As an autonomous force, it must be analyzed in terms of its own distinctive properties and dynamics. Only after this kind of analysis should it be connected to other, more structural forces.

Cultural theorizing can be found in all of contemporary theory. For example, functional theories almost always emphasize the importance of cultural values and beliefs; and conflict theories stressed the creation of ideologies in mobilizing individuals to pursue and legitimate conflict. Even early cultural theorists such as Robert Wuthnow[78] combined elements of structuralism, ideology from conflict theory, and even exchange theory in emphasizing how the moral order is created, sustained, changed, and institutionalized in social structures.

---

[78]Robert Wuthnow, *Meaning and Moral Order: Explorations in Cultural Analysis* (Berkeley: University of California Press, 1987).

Similarly, Pierre Bourdieu[79] began to conceptualize social relations as organized by the distribution of material, social, cultural, and symbolic capital, thereby blending elements of traditional sociology into a new view of structures. Social structures are built by the distribution of various forms of capital that circulate in a society and generate common worldview among individuals with varying shares and configurations of these four forms of capital. Cultural capital is composed of habits, manners, linguistic styles, credentials, tastes, lifestyles, while symbolic capital is the set of symbols (ideologies, beliefs, and values) used to legitimate the holding of other types of capital—social, material, and cultural. Social capital is having access to networks of social relations, and material capital includes money and other forms of material resources that can be spent to buy other forms of capital. Thus, actors with different shares and mixes of capital can operate within particular structural domains, and not others; and the dynamics of the social universe revolve around how actors use their capital to form social structures or to navigate through existing structures, either changing or reproducing these structures.

As the movement to bring culture back into sociology as a distinctive topic of inquiry increased, much analysis was empirical and examined the symbol systems that individuals and groups developed. Yet there was a more explicit push for a "strong program" in cultural sociology spearheaded by Jeffrey Alexander and colleagues.[80] Their argument is that cultural sociology as it reemerged in modern theory was more of a "weak program" that was always subordinate to the analysis of social structure, whereas what is needed is a strong program that engages in thick descriptions of symbolic meanings and the mechanisms by which these are constructed. Such an analysis views culture as a text with themes, plotlines, moral evaluations, and other properties that give it some autonomy from social structures. Only after the analysis of culture, per se, can this strong program begin to examine the relationships of culture to other forces, such as rituals, interactions, and social structures.

---

[79]Pierre Bourdieu, *Language and Symbolic Power* (Cambridge, MA: Harvard University Press, 1989); and *Distinction: A Social Critique of the Judgment of Taste* (Cambridge, MA: Harvard University Press, 1984).

[80]See for a review, Jeffrey C. Alexander and Philip Smith, "The Strong Program in Cultural Theory," in *Handbook of Sociological Theory*, ed. Jonathan H. Turner (New York: Springer, 2001), 135–150.

Thus far, there are only a few coherent theoretical approaches in this strong program, but there is now an expanding set of descriptive works analyzing the textual qualities of culture. As these are used to develop more general theoretical ideas or to assess the plausibility of existing theoretical ideas, the analysis of culture will achieve the same status as the analysis of social structure and interaction, and indeed, it will contribute significantly to these analyses—or so it is presumed. For example, Jeffrey Alexander[81] has launched a program of "cultural pragmatics" that blends Durkheim and Erving Goffman's dramaturgy[82] with one strand of new cultural theorizing that emphasizes rituals and performances. In Alexander's scheme, actors are seen as motivated by moral concerns, seeking to bring background collective representations and scripts to the forefront of action and interaction with audiences. The background representations and scripts are decoded into texts that are, thereby, made available for performances; and the behaviors in a performance revolve around achieving emotional attachment of both performer and audience to these decoded texts. In their performances, actors have access to the "symbolic means of production" and thus stages and props, but their performances are constrained by the available texts, by their power to gain access to stages and props, and by the audiences that are available. In simple societies, much like Durkheim's conceptualization of "mechanical solidarity,"[83] the elements of performances—collective representations, texts, stages, audiences, power, and the means of symbolic production—are fused together and taken for granted, thereby creating an easy basis for social solidarity. With differentiation and complexity of society, however, these elements of performances are not fused, nor are they so easily lined up or *re*-fused to give a successful performance. Differentiation of societies thus "de-fuses" the key elements of performances, with the result that it becomes necessary to reassemble the elements through considerable dramatic effort. A performance thus revolves around "re-fusing" what has been "de-fused" by differentiation. There are various mechanisms, although Alexander does not use this term, that re-fuse background collective

---

[81]Jeffrey C. Alexander, "Cultural Pragmatics: Social Performances Between Ritual and Strategy," *Sociological Theory* 22 (2004), 527–573. See also his *Meaning and Social Life: A Cultural Sociology* (New York: Oxford University Press, 2003).

[82]See Note 48.

[83]See Table 13.1 for Durkheim's distinction between mechanical and organic solidarity.

representations with the performance and that make texts salient to the performance: cognitive simplification, moral antagonisms, and twistings and turnings in the plot and story line. Re-fusing script, action, and performance spaces are achieved by walking and talking in space, with some discretion for how actors (and directors) should do so. Re-fusing of social power involves efforts to find the appropriate means of symbolic reproduction, the best means of symbolic distribution, and the appropriate forms of debate, discourse, and criticism. The re-fusing of the actor and the role must seem to be natural as part of an ongoing interpersonal flow. And, re-fusing audience with performance texts, actors must pull them in and make them part of the performance and its text, script, and background representations.

Thus, Alexander's cultural pragmatics brings Durkheim's analysis of collective conscience, ritual, and emotions into a new form of cultural theorizing. His efforts represent only one of many new lines of theorizing about culture, which in the past decade have been reinvigorated by emphasis of having a "strong program" of cultural analysis. Time will tell how far this new cultural thrust in sociology will go.

Critical Theorizing

Sociology emerged, as we pointed out in Chapter 1, to explain the transformations associated with modernity. There has always been a critical bent to this analysis of modernity and, later, to postmodernism. The early masters all addressed the issue of what modernity was doing to humans as new cultural and structural formations were emerging. Marx, of course, was the most critical, but there were more implicit critiques in Weber's analysis of rationalization, in Durkheim's concerns about anomie and egoism, and in Spencer's concern with concentrated power and its use to wage unnecessary warfare. There was also a quiet dialogue and disagreement about the effects of modernity. For example, Simmel acknowledged both Durkheim's concerns about egoism and Marx's about alienation, but in the end, he argued that modern, highly differentiated, market-driven societies were more emancipatory than pathological. They give individuals freedom and options, and hence provide rewards and value. Durkheim was implicitly critical of Marx in arguing that the "forced division of labor" was only a passing pathology that would eventually go away as organic solidarity became fully established; Weber saw Marx's inevitable march to revolution and communism as most unlikely, given the power of rationalization in the modern world.

Since most of the major founders of sociology were European, one of the forms of critical theory that emerged in the twentieth century carries forward this European legacy and concern about the modern condition. The other critical theoretical lineage is distinctly American and focuses on domestic social problems, mostly injustices to particular subpopulations in societies (e.g., women, minorities, poor, lower classes). Both lines of thought remain critical of modern societies, especially of capitalism, but the European critical approach is more detached, abstract, and intellectual, whereas the American approach retains its roots in twentieth-century social movements that were carried into academia and institutionalized as intellectual disciplines, and whose members are often still engaged activists.

European Critical Theory. Unlike the United States, which repressed Marxist theorizing during the peak of the Cold War (especially during McCarthyism), European scholars considered the implications of Marxist theory for the whole of the twentieth century. With the installation of communism in the emerging Soviet Union (and later in China), theorizing began to ask the following questions: Why had not these "revolutions" been more emancipatory? Why did they lead to concentrations of oppressive power? During the 1930s as fascism spread across Europe, a group of thinkers at the University of Frankfurt in Germany formed what became known as the Frankfurt School, even though not everyone identified with the school was German. And, as Hitler's hold over Germany increased, some of these scholars, many of whom were Jews, escaped to the United States and continued the work of the Frankfurt School in several elite American universities. The basic problematic, which persists in all forms of most critical theories today, was as follows: How to retain the emancipatory thrust of Marx's argument against the backdrop of Weberian rationalization, where the state, legal system, and most institutional domains continue to oppress and dominate sectors of the population through rational–legal authority and its institutionalization in bureaucracies? Their answer was that the conditions had not yet emerged for emancipation, and so, in the meantime, the members of the Frankfurt School and their sympathizers should stress the importance of continuing to expose patterns of oppression in a wide variety of contexts until conditions would be in place for social movements, leading to the elimination of such oppression.[84] And, to very great extent, this kind of theorizing persists today in sociology, not only in Europe and the United States but also in many other parts of the world. It is a highly intellectualized critique, confined primarily to academics who theorize and conduct research that exposes abuses of power and law without leaving the safety of the ivory tower.

American-Style Critical Theory. The two great social movements in the second half of the twentieth century—the civil rights movement for minorities and the feminist movement for women—are the sources of a critical approach that emphasizes the continued existence of racism and sexism and, more broadly, that criticizes the failure of a more "civil rights approach" to eliminate both subtle and obvious forms of discrimination. These approaches were institutionalized in academia not only in many sociology departments but also in various types of ethnic and women studies departments/ programs within academia.

Much as critical theory in Europe seeks to expose persisting patterns of oppression, critical theories in the United States document continued discrimination and oppression at many levels of social organization. Micro-interactions, cultural beliefs, inadequacy of laws or failure to enforce them, subtle forms of discrimination in a wide variety of contexts, continued stereotyping of minorities and women, the failures in seeking to eliminate "difference," the need to create new forms of consciousness among those oppressed in both subtle and obvious ways, and many other points of argumentation have been developed in *feminist theorizing*[85] and in *critical race theory.*[86]

---

[84]The most visible modern-day European critical theorist in the Frankfurt tradition is Jürgen Habermas. See his *Knowledge and Human Interest*, trans. J. Shapiro (London: Heinemann, 1970[1968]); and *Theory of Communicative Action*, 2 vols. (Boston: Beacon Press, 1981, 1984).

[85]For overviews, see Pamela Abbott and Clare Wallace, *An Introduction to Sociology: Feminist Perspectives* (London: Routledge, 1990); Elizabeth Hackett and Sally Anne Haslanger, *Theorizing Feminism: A Reader* (New York: Oxford University Press, 2006); bell hooks, *Feminist Theory From Margin to Center* (Boston: South End Press, 1984); Patricia Madoo Lengermann and Jill Niebrugge, "Contemporary Feminism," in *Sociological Theory*, ed. George Ritzer (New York: McGraw-Hill, 1996); and Paula England, ed. *Theory on Gender/Feminism on Theory* (Chicago: Aldine, 1985).

[86]Kimberlie Crenshaw, Neil Gotanda, Garry Peller, and Kendall Thomas, eds. *Critical Race Theory* (New York: New Press, 1996); Richard Delgado, *Critical Race Theory: An Introduction* (New York: New York University Press, 2001); and *Critical Race Theory* (Philadelphia: Temple University Press, 1999).

These approaches are explicitly activist, although many of the theorists within this tradition can be highly philosophical in their theorizing.

Critical race theory is an extension of early American sociologists' concerns with amelioration, but there is a major difference: Critical theorists are, first and foremost, critical of such ameliorative efforts to extend civil rights because they have led to continued discrimination in new, more subtle forms. While there can be Marxist ideals as well as elements of all who have theorized about stratification in these critical approaches, they have adopted many other methodological and theoretical (and philosophical) approaches to understanding the wide spectrum of ways and contexts in which racism continues to operate. Indeed, much analysis is highly micro, examining how racism and sexism operate at the interpersonal level; and so, early phenomenology and symbolic interactions might be relevant, although critical theorists rarely explicitly rely on these early theoretical approaches of the classical period.

Thus, while feminist and critical race theories have their European counterparts, this kind of theorizing in the United States remains distinctive. The main reason for this distinctiveness, we believe, is that this critical tradition is based on bringing the ideologies of social movements into academia. Such approaches are caught between converting ideological goals into topics of more detached academic inquiry, while sustaining the emancipatory zeal of the early days of feminism and the peak of the civil rights protest.

Postmodern Theorizing. Yet another critical approach that has both European and American sources postulates a new "postmodern condition" in which the fundamental way that individuals, social structures, and culture are linked has changed under the effects of information media and the globalization of the economy by transportation/communications technologies and global markets. There are two clear branches of postmodern theory: one concerned with economic forces[87] and globalization and another a more purely

---

[87]For more economically oriented postmodern theories, see Fredric Jameson, *The Postmodern Condition* (Minneapolis: University of Minnesota Press, 1984); David Harvey, *The Conditions of Postmodernity* (Oxford, UK: Blackwell, 1989); and Scott Lash and John Urry, *The End of Organized Capitalism* (Madison: University of Wisconsin Press, 1987).

cultural approach[88] that emphasizes the increasing importance of culture, detached from its structural roots. The economic approach owes some of its inspiration to Marx, while the cultural approach reveals glimpses of Weber, Durkheim, Simmel, and Mead. Still, despite the concerns with the classical theorists with the "pathologies" of modernity, it is argued that the transformation of societies into a postmodern condition makes the analyses of the first masters less relevant. So what are these fundamental changes? They include (a) the compression of time and space by communication and transportation technologies; (b) the spread of markets that can commodify virtually everything, including the elements of culture; (c) the growing importance of culture, often detached from its structural sources by commodification in global markets; (d) the rapid circulation in markets of standardized goods with little intrinsic meaning embedded in culture; and (e) the overreflexive self that is constantly redefined by purchases of cultural and material commodities in markets, and so on.

What is evident is that the same themes of early classical theorists reappear in postmodernism, despite postmodernists' claims that modernity and postmodernity represent distinct stages of societal evolution. Still, the question remains as to whether or not postmodernists have moved very far beyond the classical theorists.[89] But they have made far more explicit the critique that modernity—markets, media, compression of space/time, overreflexivity, the detachment of culture from its structural roots, and the circulation of culture as a commodity in global markets—has weakened the power of social structure and culture to provide anchorage for individuals who now have shallow, unstable, and reflexive selves that are no longer attached and embedded in communities. These concerns hearken back to Marx's concern with alienation, Durkheim's concern with anomie and egoism, Simmel's marginality, and Weber's emphasis

---

[88]For more cultural postmodern theories, see Steven Seidman, ed. *The Postmodern Turn: New Perspectives on Social Theory* (Cambridge, UK: Cambridge University Press, 1994); Jean Baudrillard, *Simulacra and Simulation* (Ann Arbor: University of Michigan Press, 1994); and Jean-Francois Lyotard, *The Postmodern Condition: A Report on Knowledge* (Minneapolis: University of Minnesota Press, 1978).

[89]See Kenneth Allan and Jonathan H. Turner, "A Formalization of Postmodern Theory," *Sociological Perspectives* 43 (2000), 363–385, for a critical review of the theoretical and empirical claims of postmodern theory.

on rationality and rational–legal domination but with a somewhat different vocabulary. Still, is there anything dramatically new about an updated critique of presumed pathologies of the postmodern condition?

Conclusion

As is evident, the early masters continue to inspire sociological theorizing in obvious and more subtle ways. Over the past 80 years, theoretical sociology has gone in many directions and has proliferated into many specialized approaches. Yet each of these specialized theories reveals the influence of the first masters, as we have tried to emphasize in footnotes pointing to relevant portions of the text that can be consulted. The classical theorists from 1830 to 1930 thought "big" and broadly. It should not be surprising, therefore, that their works would have relevance for a wide range of more specialized theories, and since many of the masters addressed modernity critically, it is also not surprising that their ideas are woven through the various branches of critical theorizing that now pervade sociology. Thus, the classical tradition is alive and well, not just *as an academic pursuit in itself* but also as a source of continued inspiration to theorists writing today almost a century after the early masters had all died.

Author Index

Subject Index